CICERO
XII

LCL 309

CICERO

PRO SESTIO
IN VATINIUM

WITH AN ENGLISH TRANSLATION BY

R. GARDNER

HARVARD UNIVERSITY PRESS
CAMBRIDGE, MASSACHUSETTS
LONDON, ENGLAND

ISBN 0-674-99341-1

Printed in Great Britain by St Edmundsbury Press Ltd,
Bury St Edmunds, Suffolk, on acid-free paper.
Bound by Hunter & Foulis Ltd, Edinburgh, Scotland.

CONTENTS

PREFACE

MANY years ago I accepted an invitation from the Editors of the Loeb Classical Library to revise and complete the five speeches of Cicero now comprised in two volumes, a work which had been left unfinished by their contributor, the late J. H. Freese, M.A., formerly Fellow of St. John's College, Cambridge, and Assistant Master at Repton School and at St. Paul's School. His earlier contribution to the Loeb Library was a volume published in 1930 which contained Cicero's speeches *Pro P. Quinctio, Pro Sex. Roscio Amerino, Pro Q. Roscio Comoedo,* and *De lege agraria, i-iii.*

I regret that the completion of this task has been gravely interrupted and delayed by the claims of administrative work and other duties. It is, however, possible that some advantage may have been gained by this delay. Within the last generation scholars have assiduously investigated the wealth of literary evidence that has made political and prosopographical studies of the late Roman Republic so profitable a field of inquiry. Their labours have thrown new light upon some aspects of the setting and the subject-matter of Cicero's speeches. To these recent re-

searches and, no less, to those of earlier date, I have
been under a constant obligation. The Bibliography
which will be found on pp. 353-360 is, naturally, far
from exhaustive ; it is no more than a list of such
books and articles as have been found useful in the
preparation of these volumes, and may indicate the
amount of work which has been done in this field.
My chief debt is to those annotated editions without
whose aid I could have done nothing. Over seventy
years have passed since two of them were published :
J. S. Reid's edition of the *Pro Balbo* appeared in
1878, H. A. Holden's edition of the *Pro Sestio* in
1883. Two are more recent. In 1924 H. E. Butler
and M. Cary published their edition of the *De provinciis consularibus*, and L. G. Pocock's edition of the
In Vatinium is dated to 1926. The most recent
commentary on the *Pro Caelio* is Professor R. G.
Austin's revision (1952) of his earlier work (1933).
For the guidance and help which I have received
from this indispensable work I am obviously indebted
and I am deeply grateful.

I have departed but rarely from the text used by
the original translator, the Teubner edition (1904) by
C. F. W. Müller, and then only to adopt suggestions
by editors of the annotated editions. Müller's text
has now been superseded by the Teubner edition of
1919 by A. Klotz and F. Schöll.

In any assessment of the qualities of the Ciceronian
corpus these five speeches, taken as a whole, must
be judged worthy of a high place. They not only
vividly illustrate some of those literary qualities which

viii

PREFACE

link Cicero with Virgil as the most influential of the Romans, but they also illuminate many aspects of Cicero's amazing versatility as an orator. The *Pro Sestio* and the *In Vatinium*, with the *Pro Caelio* presenting some tantalizing glimpses of late Republican society, are a contemporary source of great value for the history of the short but crowded interlude between the bloodless revolution of 59 B.C. and the Conference of Luca. The *De provinciis consularibus* and the *Pro Balbo*, expressions of Cicero's loss of political independence, show how effectively the opposition to the coalition of Pompey, Caesar and Crassus had been paralysed, and almost point the way to the great laws of 55 B.C., the *lex Pompeia Licinia* and the *lex Trebonia*, which set up armed *principes* in control of the State.

The matter supplementary to the text and translation has been provided, possibly at the cost of treading paths already well worn, in an attempt to expound the historical setting of these speeches, to discuss some topics arising from their subject-matter, and to comment on those abundant references to earlier periods of Roman History which enhance the value of Cicero's work.

R. GARDNER

EMMANUEL COLLEGE
CAMBRIDGE
6 *January* 1958

TABLE OF EVENTS
IN ROMAN POLITICS
FROM 60 B.C. TO 56 B.C.[a]

[a] Where chronology is precise, we are indebted, first and foremost, to Cicero's *Letters*, and, to a lesser degree, to the speeches delivered by him in 57 and 56 B.C. In general, the sequence of events in the years from 60 to 56 B.C. can be determined with fair accuracy, except where the sources are either silent or conflicting or variously interpreted. For a most helpful table of dates see R. G. Nisbet's edition of Cicero, *De domo sua*, pp. xxxv-xxxvii.

60 B.C.

Consuls : Q. Caecilius Metellus Celer and L. Afranius

Early
months.

Political deadlock arising from the Senate's refusal to ratify Pompey's settlement of the Near East and to allot lands to his veterans, and from Cato's opposition to a proposal to revise a tax-contract for the province of Asia.

P. Clodius, desirous of becoming tribune, plans to have himself declared a plebeian, a move successfully opposed by the consul Q. Metellus.

June.

Caesar returns from his propraetorship in Further Spain. He abandons his claim to a triumph and appears as a candidate for the consulship. The Senate assign the province of *silvae callesque* (forests and stock-routes) for the prospective consuls of 59.

July.

Caesar enters into negotiations with Pompey leading to the coalition known as " The First Triumvirate." Caesar and M. Calpurnius Bibulus elected consuls for 59.

December.

Cicero, approached by Caesar's agent L. Cornelius Balbus, refuses to support Caesar's agrarian bill and so to enter into political partnership with him. Crassus enlisted by Caesar as a third partner in the Triumvirate.

TABLE OF EVENTS IN ROMAN POLITICS

59 B.C.

Consuls : C. Iulius Caesar and M. Calpurnius Bibulus

Caesar's first agrarian bill is passed by uncon- From January to the end of April. stitutional and violent methods, the Senate having refused to discuss it. Caesar reveals his coalition with Pompey and Crassus, disregards tribunes' vetoes and drives from the Forum his colleague Bibulus and other opponents. Bibulus, having withdrawn to his house, gives notice that he is " watching the heavens " and publishes edicts against Caesar.

Cicero criticizes the illegalities of Caesar and his partners in his unsuccessful defence of C. Antonius (consul 63 and proconsul of Macedonia 62–60) when prosecuted by M. Caelius Rufus, probably for *maiestas*. On the same day P. Clodius is transferred to plebeian status by the *comitia curiata*, under the presidency of Caesar as consul and Pontifex Maximus, and with the approval of Pompey as an augur.

Death of Q. Metellus Celer, proconsul-designate of Transalpine Gaul, and husband of Clodia, sister of P. Clodius.

Confirmation, probably by a *lex Vatinia*, of Pompey's settlement of the Near East.

Revision, probably by a *lex Vatinia*, of the tax-contract for the province of Asia.

Recognition, by a decree of the Senate and a law, of Ptolemy Auletes as King of Egypt.

Promulgation of the *lex Iulia de agro Campano*.

Marriage of Pompey and Julia, daughter of Caesar. Before 10 May.

Passing of the *lex Iulia de agro Campano*. May.

A *lex Vatinia* gives Caesar the provinces of Cis- May (or June). alpine Gaul and Illyricum.

June (or July).	A decree of the Senate gives Caesar the province of Transalpine Gaul.
June and July.	Unpopularity of the Triumvirate : demonstrations at public festivals, *e.g.* at the Ludi Apollinares (6-13 July) ; the *affaire* Vettius.
July.	L. Antistius, P. Clodius, Sex. Aelius Ligus, L. Ninnius Quadratus, among others, elected tribunes for 58. Clodius begins openly to threaten Cicero.
25 July.	Pompey publicly protests against the edicts of Bibulus.
18 October.	L. Calpurnius Piso and A. Gabinius elected consuls for 58. Among the praetors elected are L. Domitius Ahenobarbus, L. Flavius, C. Memmius.
November.	Acquittal of L. Flaccus (praetor 63 and propraetor of Asia 62) on a charge of *repetundae*, defended by Hortensius and Cicero.
10 December.	P. Clodius enters tribunate.

58 B.C.

Consuls : L. Calpurnius Piso and A. Gabinius

Early in the year.	Attacks on Caesar by L. Domitius Ahenobarbus and C. Memmius, praetors, and by L. Antistius, tribune.
3 January.	P. Clodius promulgates and soon passes laws *de censoria notione, de legibus Aelia et Fufia, frumentaria, de collegiis*.
February.	P. Clodius promulgates laws *de capite civis Romani, de provinciis, de Cypro*.

TABLE OF EVENTS IN ROMAN POLITICS

Cicero leaves Rome. Laws *de capite civis* and *de provinciis* passed. — About 20 March.

Cicero's house on the Palatine destroyed.

Law *de Cypro* passed. Caesar leaves for Gaul. — March.

Clodius promulgates law *de exsilio Ciceronis*. — About 25 March.

Clodius promulgates law *de Catone*. — April.

Clodius promulgates law *de exsilio Ciceronis* in revised form. — 3 April.

Laws *de exsilio Ciceronis* and *de Catone* passed. — 24 April.

Cato leaves for Cyprus. — Soon afterwards.

Outbreak of feud between Pompey and Clodius, who contrives the release, from custody as a hostage, of an Armenian prince, Tigranes the younger. — April or May.

Pompey begins to urge the recall of Cicero. Clodius at feud with the consul Gabinius. — May.

Proposal for Cicero's recall made in the Senate by L. Ninnius Quadratus vetoed by Sex. Aelius Ligus. — 1 June.

The College of Augurs having declared illegal Clodius' election as tribune, Clodius attacks Caesar's *acta* as consul. — ? July (or later in the year).

P. Lentulus Spinther and Q. Metellus Nepos elected consuls for 57. — ? late July.

Attempt by Clodius to intimidate, or to assassinate, Pompey, who withdraws from public life till the end of Clodius' tribunate. — 11 August.

Sex. Aelius Ligus vetoes a bill for Cicero's recall promulgated by eight tribunes. — 29 October.

The consuls leave for their provinces : Piso for Macedonia, Gabinius for Syria. — Before the end of the year.

CICERO

TABLE OF EVENTS IN ROMAN POLITICS

Later.	Arrival in Rome of a large deputation from Alexandria, led by Dio, to protest against the restoration of Ptolemy Auletes.
Before end of the year.	The Senate decree that P. Lentulus Spinther, proconsul-elect of Cilicia, shall restore Ptolemy.

56 B.C.

Consuls : Cn. Cornelius Lentulus Marcellinus and L. Marcius Philippus

Before 13 January.	The statue of Juppiter on the Alban Mount struck by lightning. The keepers of the Sibylline Books, consulted as to expiation, announce an oracle forbidding the restoration of an Egyptian king " with a multitude." The Senate reconsider their decree commissioning P. Lentulus Spinther to restore Ptolemy and decide that Roman intervention in Egypt shall not be military.
13 and 15 January.	Indecisive debates in the Senate on the proposed restoration of Ptolemy.
20 January.	Clodius elected aedile.
Early in the year.	L. Domitius Ahenobarbus, a candidate for the consulship of 55, announces that if elected he will as consul take steps to deprive Caesar of his provinces.
2 February.	Clodius begins prosecution of Milo *de vi*, before the Assembly.
6 February.	Adjournment of Milo's trial. Pompey speaks in support of him amid uproar from Clodius' *operae*. Clodius attacks Pompey as corn-controller and presses Crassus' claims to restore Ptolemy.
8 February.	Pompey, attacked in the Senate by a tribune C. Cato, accuses Crassus of plotting his murder.

xviii

TABLE OF EVENTS IN ROMAN POLITICS

Trial of P. Sestius, defended by Cicero and others, when prosecuted by Cn. Nerius *de ambitu* and by P. Tullius Albinovanus *de vi.*   10 February to 11 March.

Cicero successfully defends L. Calpurnius Bestia when prosecuted *de ambitu* by M. Caelius Rufus.   11 February.

Unanimous acquittal of Sestius.   11 March.

Acquittal of Sextus Clodius, prosecuted by Milo at Pompey's instance.   End of March.

Cicero successfully defends P. Asicius, accused of murdering Dio, leader of the deputation of Alexandrians sent to protest against the restoration of Ptolemy Auletes.   Before beginning of April.

Cicero successfully defends M. Caelius Rufus when prosecuted (3-4 April) by L. Sempronius Atratinus.   4 April.

The Senate vote a grant of 40,000,000 sesterces to Pompey as corn-controller, and approve Cicero's proposal for a debate *de agro Campano* at a full meeting on 15 May.   5 April.
Crassus at once leaves Rome and meets Caesar at Ravenna.

Cicero leaves Rome for a tour of his country houses, intending to return on 6 May.   8 April.

Pompey leaves Rome for a port of embarkation (Pisae or Labro) for corn-control business in Sardinia and Africa.   11 April.

Pompey reaches Pisae where he is joined by Caesar and Crassus.   ? 16 April.

Conference of Pompey, Caesar, and Crassus at Luca, after which Caesar returns to Gaul and Pompey sails to Sardinia where he plans, through Q. Cicero and   ? 17 April.

	L. Vibullius Rufus, to dissuade Cicero from making his motion *de agro Campano* before his own return.
6 May.	Date of Cicero's proposed return to Rome from a tour of his country houses.
Soon afterwards.	Cicero, informed of Pompey's representations, sends him the letter described as παλινῳδία in *Epp. ad Att.* iv. 5. 1.
15 and 16 May.	Meetings of the Senate. No debate *de agro Campano*. The Senate refuse a *supplicatio* for Gabinius' victories in Syria.
? May (or September).	Cicero delivers in the Senate his speech *De haruspicum responsis*.
Late May or early June.	On Cicero's proposal, the Senate pass decrees authorizing pay for Caesar's four new legions and assigning him *decem legati*.
Late June or early July.	Cicero's speech in the Senate *De provinciis consularibus*.
July.	Cn. Lentulus Marcellinus, consul, refuses to accept the candidatures of Pompey and Crassus for the consulship of 55.
July to December.	C. Cato, tribune, in the employment of Pompey and Crassus, maintains his veto on the election of curule magistrates.
Late summer or autumn.	Cicero successfully defends L. Cornelius Balbus when prosecuted by an unknown Gaditane in respect of the citizenship conferred on him by Pompey under the *lex Gellia Cornelia* (72 B.C.).
Autumn.	M. Cato returns from Cyprus.

ROMAN POLITICS
FROM 63 B.C. TO 57 B.C.

Roman Politics from the breaking of the Second Catilinarian Conspiracy (63 b.c.) to Cicero's Return from Exile (September 57 b.c.).

Since the setting and much of the subject-matter of the speeches of Cicero comprised in these volumes are very closely interwoven with the political history of the previous seven years, some account of events in Rome from the breaking of the Second Catilinarian Conspiracy to Cicero's return from exile may be attempted as a preliminary.

In Cicero's consulship (63 b.c.) the Second Catilinarian Conspiracy, organized by an impoverished and ambitious patrician noble for the overthrow of the constitution, was broken by a combination of good fortune and good management. While its repercussions were to be felt in Roman public life for many years, it had immediate results for several leading men in the State. The antagonism which it induced between Caesar and Cato was to become an important determinant of Roman politics. Pompey was disappointed at being denied an opportunity of rounding-off his feats overseas by a commission to end the Catilinarian movement at home. Cicero, whose execution of the conspirators left in the city had received the moral, but not the legal, support of the Senate, was quick to see the significance of

2

his enlistment against Catiline of those elements in Roman society that had nothing to gain from anarchy. Internal stability, in his view, could be secured by making permanent the temporary alliance of all loyal citizens (*boni*), senators, *equites* and commons, who had supported him as consul, and the commonwealth could be saved from the menace of military adventurers by setting up Pompey, then at the height of his prestige, as its defender. Having championed Pompey's interests during his long absence in the Near East, Cicero, shortly before Pompey's return, sedulously devoted himself to the task of winning the general to the cause of his *concordia ordinum*, an alliance of senators and *equites*. In one of the most important of his early letters (*Epp. ad Fam.* v. 7, of 62 B.C.) Cicero cast for Pompey the part of Scipio Aemilianus, the great conqueror of the mid-second century B.C. who practised a conservative policy, and for himself that of a joint-leader with Pompey of a coalition of all loyal citizens.

By the summer of 60 B.C. Cicero's *concordia* lay in ruins, the victim of political misfortunes and private animosities.[a] Two episodes of the year 61 B.C. opened up a rift between senators and *equites* which had grave consequences.

In December 62 B.C. a young patrician, P. Clodius, disguised as a female slave, broke into the house of Julius Caesar, Pontifex Maximus and a praetor of the year, where the worship of an archaic deity, Bona Dea, whose rites were forbidden to men, was being celebrated. Clodius was suspected of an intrigue with Pompeia, Caesar's wife. As even Cicero

---

[a] Cicero, *Epp. ad Att.* i. 18. 3.

could admit, this was an escapade which need not
have serious consequences. But, invested by Cato
and others of his kind with special significance and
mismanaged by the Senate, the trial of Clodius for
sacrilege became a *cause célèbre* which began the
dissolution of Cicero's *concordia*. By abandoning
their original plan of commissioning a praetor to try
Clodius by a specially empanelled jury, the Senate
permitted the jurors to be chosen in the ordinary
way. This was playing into the hands of Crassus,
who bribed the jury to acquit Clodius. No doubt
Crassus and Caesar saw that Clodius might be useful
to them. The trial had two important results. First,
it marked for Cicero the beginning of a long and
bitter feud with Clodius. Not only had Cicero given
evidence at Clodius' trial which disproved a plea of
alibi submitted by the defendant, but the orator's
gibes [a] humiliated one who claimed a family connexion with the bluest blood in Rome. Clodius swore
to be revenged. Secondly, a grave menace to
Cicero's *concordia* was that before the end of the year,
the Senate, indignant at the venality of the jury
which had acquitted Clodius, and following the lead
of Cato, attempted to deprive non-senatorial jurymen
of a strange immunity from prosecution for corruption which they had enjoyed since the passing of
C. Gracchus' jury-law, the *lex Acilia* (122 B.C.).[b]

The second episode which produced strained relations between *equites* and senators was the Senate's
refusal, at the instigation of Cato and Q. Metellus
Celer, consul-elect for 60 B.C., to sanction a rebate

---

[a] For example, in the Senate on 15 May 61 B.C. Cicero,
Epp. ad Att. i. 16. 9-10.
[b] Cicero, *Epp. ad Att.* i. 17. 8.

for a company of *publicani* which was finding onerous
the terms of its contract for the collection of the
tithes payable by the province of Asia.[a] Crassus was
behind the *publicani* ; Cato denounced their rapacity ;
Cicero, fearful for his *concordia*, urged concessions
both in this matter and in that of the non-senatorial
jurors' privilege, but strove in vain. But it was on
the rock of prejudice and animosity that Cicero's
concordia foundered. Would there be a reconciliation between Pompey and the Senate ? The conqueror of the Near East was widely distrusted for
his part in overthrowing the Sullan constitution and
for his elevation to an unrepublican position by the
Gabinian and Manilian laws. His behaviour towards
contemporaries who had commanded in the Near
East, such as Marcius Rex, Metellus Creticus, and
L. Lucullus, had been less than creditable, and
through his agent Metellus Nepos he had schemed
for dominance in Italy. But Pompey's dismissal of
his army on his return at the end of 62 B.C. dispelled
fears of a second *Sullanum regnum*. The studied yet
clumsy courtesy which he showed in public was a
friendly gesture which the Senate would have been
wise to welcome. This was a situation from which
neither party emerged with credit : Pompey's de-
fects of personality, acutely observed by Cicero,[b]
gave an impression of a lack of sincerity and states-
manlike qualities ; many senators, too mindful of
the past, allowed reason to be overruled by prejudice.
The Senate therefore threw away a golden opportunity of a friendly understanding with Pompey by its
reaction to two reasonable requests submitted to it

[a] Cicero, *Epp. ad Att.* i. 17. 9.
[b] Cicero, *Epp. ad Att.* i. 13. 4.

by him : the ratification of his settlement of the Near
East, and the pensioning-off of his veterans by grants
of land. By obstructive tactics in the Senate Pompey's opponents, instead of giving general approval
to his eastern dispositions, insisted on their examination in detail, and dallied obstinately over the problem of settling his veterans on the land.

Pompey attempted to outflank the Senate by
employing a tribune, L. Flavius, to present to the
concilium plebis an agrarian bill for the benefit of
the urban populace as well as of Pompey's veterans.
Under it certain public lands in Italy were to be
resumed and distributed ; use was to be made of
the new revenue from the Near East for the purchase
of other land. Not only did Cicero, who strangely
claimed to be rendering Pompey a service, severely
criticize some provisions of the bill, but the Senate,
led by the consul Q. Metellus Celer who was even
imprisoned by Flavius for his obstruction, opposed
the bill so vigorously that Pompey abruptly dropped
it.[a]

Having thus rendered Pompey helpless, the Senate
fondly imagined that Caesar could be similarly
treated. About June 60 B.C. Caesar returned to
Rome after a year in which as propraetor of Further
Spain he had governed so successfully that Cicero
could say that " the wind was now blowing full into
his sails." [b] He hoped to win a triumph for his
victories, a consulship, and, above all, a proconsular
command for the further exercise of his abilities as a
general. Refused permission by the Senate to submit by proxy his nomination as a candidate for the

---

[a] Cicero, *Epp. ad Att.* i. 19. 4 ; Dio Cassius, xxxvii. 50. 1-3.
[b] Cicero, *Epp. ad Att.* ii. 1. 6.

consulship of 59 B.C., Caesar entered the city and so forfeited his right to a triumph. Anticipating his election as consul and bent on ruining his subsequent career, the Senate made an unorthodox disposition of provinces for the prospective consuls of 59 B.C. by assigning to them the superintendency of forests and stock-routes,[a] almost a civilian function.

Pompey and Caesar, therefore, smarting over these set-backs, entered into secret negotiations which led ultimately to the coalition commonly but irregularly called " The First Triumvirate." [b] At the consular elections Caesar, backed by Crassus' wealth, won his own election, but found that his colleague was a rigid Optimate, M. Calpurnius Bibulus, whose return Caesar's enemies secured by lavish bribery, condoned even by Cato as being " in the interest of the State."

The original agreement between Pompey and Caesar provided that Caesar, with help if need be from his partner, would force the two concessions refused to Pompey by the Senate. The pact between the two men was sealed and a strong link was forged between them by Pompey's marriage early in 59 B.C. with Julia, Caesar's only child. To sound other political leaders whose relations with the Senate were strained was Caesar's next undertaking. These were Cicero and Crassus. Cicero, whose oratory in Rome and influence in Italy were highly assessed by Caesar, was lamenting the intransigence of Cato and other extremists and the ruin of the *concordia* from which

---

[a] Suetonius, *Div. Iul.* 19. 1 : " silvae callesque." *Calles* were " routes " or " tracks " connecting winter and summer grazing-grounds. See p. 51, note *c*.

[b] See p. 8, note *c*.

he had hoped so much. He refused, however, Caesar's invitation to an alliance. Although he had toyed with the idea of winning Caesar over to the Senate,[a] he was obsessed by a suspicion, if not a growing belief, that Caesar was guilty of complicity in the Catilinarian Conspiracies. He remained, therefore, true to his instincts : an unwavering loyalty to the established constitution and a reluctance to ally himself with Caesar against the Senate.[b] Crassus, however, accepted Caesar's overtures. Financial necessity had played some part in Caesar's earlier partnership with Crassus during Pompey's absence from Italy (67–62 B.C.), and Caesar's invitation to Crassus to join his coalition was partly prompted by the large sums which Crassus had advanced to him before he left for his propraetorship in Spain. On his side, Crassus saw two positive gains in an alliance with Caesar : for himself, protection against Pompey, and, for his friends the *publicani*, a rebate from their unfavourable tax-contract.

Caesar's coalition with Pompey and Crassus has come to be known as " The First Triumvirate." [c] It sprang from the ruins of Cicero's *concordia*, dominated Roman politics for ten years and made possible warfare between armed dynasts. Asinius Pollio [d] rightly dated the origins of the Civil War to " the consulship of Metellus (60 B.C.)."

" Weak as he then was, he was stronger than the

[a] *Epp. ad Att.* ii. 1. 6.
[b] *Epp. ad Att.* ii. 3. 3 ; iv. 6. 2 ; *De prov. cons.* 41.
[c] It had neither legal nor constitutional basis, unlike the Second Triumvirate which was established by the *lex Titia* of 27 November 43 B.C.
[d] Horace, *Odes*, ii. 1. 1-7 : " Motum ex Metello consule civicum bellique causas . . . tractas."

whole State," [a] is an apt commentary on the character of Caesar's first consulship. Not only were the main objects of his compact with Pompey and Crassus secured by a determination which reduced the Senate to helplessness, but steps also were taken towards the maintenance of the legislation of the year and the perpetuation of the rule of the Triumvirate.

Caesar began by a proposal to provide land for Pompey's veterans and some of the superfluous population of Rome. The Senate having refused to discuss his first bill for the use of money provided by Pompey's conquests to buy land from private owners, Caesar submitted his measure to the Assembly and passed it into law by ruthless treatment of the opposition, both physical and constitutional, vainly offered by his colleague Bibulus, and by Cato and several tribunes. He then remained contemptuous of Bibulus' claim that, under the *lex Aelia Fufia*,[b] Caesar's land law and whatever other proposals might be passed into law during the remainder of the year were invalidated by his announcements (*obnuntiationes*) that he was " watching for something coming down from the sky " (*servare de caelo*). Shortly afterwards, a supplementary bill having been found necessary, Caesar passed with less difficulty the *lex Iulia de agro Campano* which settled Pompey's veterans and some civilians also on valuable public land around and near Capua,[c] from which sitting tenants had presumably been evicted.

Further legislation to satisfy the Triumvirate was then carried by P. Vatinius, a tribune in Caesar's employment : *leges Vatiniae* not only ratified Pom-

[a] Cicero, *Epp. ad Att.* vii. 9. 3.
[b] See pp. 315-316.   [c] Suetonius, *Div. Iul.* 20. 3.

pey's settlement of the Near East but also met
Caesar's obligation to Crassus by relieving the *publicani* of one-third of the price of their Asiatic tax-
contract. For himself, again through the agency of
Vatinius, Caesar secured no ordinary proconsulate :
the governorship of Cisalpine Gaul and of Illyricum
for five years from 1 March 59 B.C. Further, a vacancy
having been created in the governorship of Gallia
Narbonensis by the death of Q. Metellus Celer, the
Senate by its own decree assigned to Caesar that
province also.[a] Magnificent as was the opportunity
thus presented to Caesar for enterprise north of the
Alps, it should not be overlooked that as governor
of Cisalpine Gaul, called by Appian [b] the "Acropolis
of Italy," Caesar was well placed also for observation
and control, as in 56 B.C., of affairs in Rome. Further
steps were taken to safeguard the ascendancy of the
Triumvirate. At home there were designated consuls
for the next year an aristocrat, L. Calpurnius Piso,
whose daughter Caesar took in marriage, and A. Gabinius, who had served as a legate under Pompey.
In 57 and 56 B.C. consulships were held by adherents
of the three partners. Moreover, it had become
clear to Caesar, that, once he had left Rome for
his provinces, his legislation would be exposed to
determined attack, especially by Cicero and Cato.
After refusing to enter into partnership with Caesar,
Cicero temporarily quitted politics and played no
part in the opposition to Caesar's earliest proceedings as consul. But his indignation soon got the
better of him, for in March (or early April) 59 B.C.,

---

[a] Cicero, *Epp. ad Att.* viii. 3. 3; Suetonius, *Div. Iul.* 22. 1.
[b] *Bell. Civ.* iii. 27. 103. See also Cicero, *Epp. ad Att.* ii.
16. 2.

while defending C. Antonius, his former colleague as praetor (66 B.C.) and as consul (63 B.C.), on a charge of *maiestas*, probably covering treasonable conduct in Macedonia and collusion with Catiline,[a] he frankly criticized the methods of Caesar and his partners. Caesar at once saw that decisive action was required. Ever since his acquittal in 61 B.C. Clodius had been nursing a passion to revenge himself on Cicero for the incriminating evidence which he had given at the trial and for his sarcasms in the Senate. To this end he sought a tribunate, but so far had been unsuccessful in attempts to remove the disqualification of his patrician blood by adoption into a plebeian family. Cicero's indiscretion in his defence of Antonius made it clear to Caesar that Clodius, invested with plebeian status, would as a tribune be conveniently available to avert any danger which Cicero (or Cato) might threaten to the legislation of 59 B.C. Three hours, therefore, after Cicero's speech Caesar, consul and Pontifex Maximus, convened the *comitia curiata* and, with the approval of Pompey as an augur, carried a *lex curiata* which sanctioned the adoption of Clodius into a plebeian family.[b]

At first the connexion between Caesar and Clodius was not revealed ; Clodius, by parading a pretended quarrel with Caesar, seems to have misled Cicero about his intentions. But after July, when he was elected a tribune, Clodius cast off the mask and

---

[a] Antonius was condemned and went into exile. For the case against Antonius see Cicero, *Pro Caelio*, R. G. Austin (Second Edition, 1952), Appendix vii, pp. 156-157.

[b] Suetonius, *Div. Iul.* 20. 4 ; Cicero, *De domo*, 41, *De prov. cons.* 42.

11

began to threaten Cicero openly. Cicero, however, disregarded, or claimed to disregard, danger from Clodius ; he trusted in the unpopularity of the Triumvirs and in frequent assurances from Pompey. Caesar at first tried to conjure the danger anticipated from Cicero by tempting offers of honourable employment : membership of the Land Commission, a *legatio libera*, appointment to his proconsular staff in Gaul.[a] Cicero declined all these offers and, as the year was ending, enumerated to his brother Quintus [b] the resources of friendship and support by which he hoped to defy whatever attack on him might be launched by Clodius.

On 3 January 58 B.C. Clodius brought forward four bills, to win popular support and to prepare the way for action which he proposed to take later against Cicero and Cato, the two most dangerous senatorial leaders. The first, which was perhaps intended in a general way to discourage a revival of the censorial power and, in particular, to safeguard the status as senators of himself and others, limited the censors' power of expelling members of the Senate to action only after an agreed condemnation on a specific charge. The remaining three were intended to invest his tribunate with autocratic power for the discomfiture of enemies of the Triumvirate. One of these angled for the favour of the *plebs urbana* by substituting a free distribution of public corn for the previous sales at less than half the normal market price. The second withdrew the ban which in 64 B.C. the Senate had placed upon all *collegia* or clubs, save upon a few genuine artisans' unions. In effect, Clodius' bill so

---

[a] Cicero, *De prov. cons.* 41.
[b] *Epp. ad Quintum fratrem*, i. 2. 16.

encouraged the growth of new *collegia* that he had
ready to hand the material for that trained force of
operae, or armed rioters, that was to make him the
virtual ruler of the city for a year and a half. The
scope of the fourth bill has been much disputed.
Statements in Cicero's speeches delivered during the
years 57–55 B.C. declare that Clodius repealed the
lex Aelia Fufia (or *leges Aelia et Fufia*), passed about
the middle of the second century B.C., which regulated the powers of curule magistrates and tribunes
to obstruct the holding of legislative and elective
assemblies by watching for omens (*spectio*, or *servare
de caelo*) and by reporting unfavourable ones to a
presiding magistrate (*obnuntiatio*). An advance was
made in the interpretation of Clodius' measure by
the conclusion [a] that Clodius repealed part only of the
lex Aelia Fufia : tribunes and augurs were to retain the
right of *obnuntiatio*, curule magistrates were to retain
this right for elective, but to lose it for legislative,
assemblies. Later a more drastic solution was proposed : that Clodius wholly repealed the *lex Aelia
Fufia* in order to facilitate his legislation and, in
particular, his proceedings against Cicero, but that
the Senate proclaimed the nullity of his legislation on
the ground that his adoption and therefore his tribunate were illegal.[b]

Clodius then launched his attack against Cicero.
In February 58 B.C. he promulgated a bill (*de capite
civis Romani*) which " interdicted from fire and water
(*i.e.* outlawed) anyone who had put to death, or

[a] W. F. McDonald, " Clodius and the *Lex Aelia Fufia*,"
in *J.R.S.* xix, pp. 164 ff.
[b] S. Weinstock, " Clodius and the *Lex Aelia Fufia*," in
J.R.S. xxvii, pp. 215 ff. See p. 22, note *b*, p. 318.

should thereafter put to death, a Roman citizen uncondemned.'' Although expressed in general terms, this bill was clearly aimed at Cicero, in allusion to his summary execution of Catiline's accomplices in Rome. Cicero had been uneasy in 59 B.C., but seemed somewhat reassured as the year ended. He at once struggled desperately to avert the blow. Genuine sympathy and support came in from many sides. But the Triumvirs showed no disposition to help him, Pompey callously rebuffing his appeals, Caesar openly supporting Clodius' action. The consuls, Piso and Gabinius, were actively hostile. By a bill which was promulgated on the same day as his proposal *de capite civis Romani* Clodius defied the *lex Sempronia* by which consular provinces were assigned before the election of the consuls who were to hold them : Piso and Gabinius were to be allowed to select their own provinces and ultimately did so, the former taking Macedonia and the latter Syria. In the end, although Lucullus advised resistance, Cato and Hortensius urged surrender. So about 20 March Cicero left Rome for voluntary exile, and on the same day Clodius' two bills, *de capite civis Romani* and *de provinciis*, were passed. A few days later, about 25 March, Clodius published another bill which formally declared Cicero an outlaw (*de exsilio Ciceronis*), thereby making his life unsafe probably anywhere within the Roman world. But on 3 April this bill was promulgated in a revised form which limited the area of outlawry to one within five hundred miles from Italy, and was passed into law by the *concilium plebis* on 24 April. This law appears to have enacted also that Cicero's property should be confiscated and that no resolution for his recall should be submitted to the

14

Senate or the Assembly. Cicero's house on the Palatine was looted and demolished, but, if the orator is to be believed, Clodius was not empowered by his *lex de exsilio Ciceronis* to consecrate the house or its site. Cicero's villas at Tusculum and Formiae were destroyed. Clodius' procedure in driving Cicero from Rome may have been of doubtful legality, but it was unquestionably effective.[a]

For Caesar's purposes the removal from Rome of the inflexible Cato was no less urgent than that of Cicero. Since no ground for a prosecution of Cato could be discovered, he was not humiliated, but was entrusted with what was ostensibly an honourable commission. Since 88 B.C. the island of Cyprus had been ruled by a Ptolemy, brother of Ptolemy XI Auletes of Egypt who in 59 B.C. had purchased from Caesar and Pompey for six thousand talents the recognition of his precarious royal title. But the ruler of Cyprus showed no disposition to secure his crown by a similar insurance. Clodius therefore proposed and carried a bill under which Cyprus was declared a Roman province, the official pretext being that Ptolemy had aided piracy in the Levant. Politically, the annexation of Cyprus would round-off the bequest of Cyrene and the conquests of Syria, Cilicia and Crete. A second bill was passed into law commis-

---

[a] Cicero argued that Clodius' *lex de exsilio* was null and void, for two reasons : it was a capital sentence passed, not by the *comitia centuriata*, but by the *concilium plebis* ; it was a *privilegium* which, since there had been no trial, could not be a formal bill of outlawry. Modern writers are divided in their views. Rice Holmes, *The Roman Republic*, i, p. 334, accepts Cicero's version of the matter ; Greenidge, *Legal Procedure of Cicero's Time*, p. 363, thinks that Clodius' actions may have been legal.

sioning Cato to confiscate the royal treasures, annex the island, and restore certain exiles to Byzantium. It is said that Cato went only because the Stoic doctrines made him consider first the interest of the State. Ptolemy, on hearing that he was to lose his treasures, made away with himself. Cyprus was annexed to the province of Cilicia. Cato was thus virtually banished till his return to Rome late in 56 B.C.[a]

With the departure of Cicero and Cato the Triumvirate was freed from the danger of attack by its two most redoubtable critics. But its internal weakness was soon demonstrated by the disorderly proceedings of Clodius during the remainder of his tribunate. He was soon at feud with his nominal allies, Pompey and Gabinius. A movement which Pompey had initiated almost at once for Cicero's restoration evoked in April a hostile response from Clodius. Bribed by Tigranes, the client-king of Armenia, Clodius had contrived the escape from custody in Rome of his son, Tigranes, who had appeared as a captive at Pompey's triumph, and was detained as a hostage. Not only Pompey but Gabinius also took umbrage at this, and in the resultant street-fighting the consul had his *fasces* broken and his goods consecrated to Ceres, by act of Clodius.[b] That the incident of Tigranes' escape might lead to a rupture between Pompey and Caesar (as Clodius' employer) was a hope which by the end of May Cicero regretfully abandoned.[c] Early in August Clodius' feud with Pompey became even

[a] Cicero, *De domo*, 22 and 65 ; *Pro Sestio*, 60.
[b] Cicero, *De domo*, 125.
[c] Cicero, *Epp. ad Att.* iii. 8. 3 of 29 May.

more sensational : on the 11th of that month he
introduced an armed slave into the Senate either to
alarm or even to assassinate Pompey, and succeeded
in driving him into seclusion for the rest of the year.
Moreover, if we may believe Cicero, Clodius in the
later months of his tribunate even turned upon
Caesar and denounced as illegal his legislation of
59 B.C. ; the College of Augurs, after hearing the
evidence of Bibulus at a *contio* convened by Clodius,
expressed their opinion that the tribunate of Clodius,
based on his adoption, and the acts of Caesar were
alike illegal.[a]

Meantime Pompey's movement for the restoration of Cicero gathered strength. As early as 1 June
a tribune L. Ninnius Quadratus made in the Senate
a proposal for Cicero's recall which was accepted
by a full house, but vetoed by a hostile tribune,
Aelius Ligus.[b] In July Cicero received from Atticus

---

[a] Cicero, *De domo*, 40 ; *De prov. cons.* 43 ; *De haruspicum
responsis*, 48. These three passages are difficult. Interpreted literally, they suggest that in the later months of his
tribunate Clodius behaved with wanton recklessness. For
example, Strachan-Davidson, *Cicero*, p. 242, compares his
proceedings with " the tricks of a mischievous monkey."
R. G. Nisbet (Cicero, *De domo*, p. 105) thinks it very possible
that Cicero's evidence is substantially true, that Caesar had
ordered Clodius to halt, and that there had been some rupture
between them. On the other hand, L. G. Pocock (*In Vatinium*, pp. 152 ff.) holds that this was no more than a
sham attack made by Clodius upon Caesar at a time when
his own position was threatened ; for an offer, possibly inspired by Pompey, was made by the Optimates to Caesar
that his measures should be re-enacted with due observance
of the auspices (*De prov. cons.* 46), that Caesar should sever
his connexion with the *populares*, and that Clodius and his
offensive legislation should be sacrificed.

[b] Cicero, *Pro Sestio*, 68.

17

an assurance that Pompey was well disposed towards him and that as soon as Caesar had expressed his approval of Cicero's proposed recall, he would instruct some magistrate to act. Moreover, the elections for 57 B.C. turned out favourably for Cicero. Of the consuls designate, P. Lentulus Spinther was an intimate friend both of Pompey and of Cicero; his colleague, Q. Metellus Nepos, a cousin of Clodius, had as tribune been hostile to Cicero, but was to prove a placable enemy.[a] Eight of the incoming tribunes were well disposed; but Cicero's cause was to be opposed by two tribunes, Serranus and Numerius Quintius Rufus, and by a praetor, Appius Claudius, brother of Clodius. It was with Pompey's approval, or perhaps at his initiative, that P. Sestius, one of the tribunes-elect, undertook before he entered upon his tribunate a journey to Cisalpine Gaul with a view to winning Caesar's consent. What Sestius accomplished was not at first revealed,[b] but Caesar must later have expressed his approval of the measures which Pompey wished to take for Cicero's recall, the pact being sealed by Quintus Cicero, who gave certain pledges on his brother's account to the Triumvirs.[c] On 29 October eight of the tribunes in office promulgated a bill for Cicero's recall, with the warm support of P. Lentulus Spinther, consul-elect; this, however, was not only opposed by the consuls and vetoed by the tribune Aelius Ligus, but was also criticized by Cicero for flaws in its drafting.[d] It was withdrawn. So these uncertain prospects of recall

[a] Cicero, *De prov. cons.* 22; *Pro Sestio*, 130.
[b] Cicero, *Pro Sestio*, 71.
[c] Cicero, *Epp. ad Fam.* i. 9. 9; *De prov. cons.* 43.
[d] Cicero, *Epp. ad Att.* iii. 23.

are reflected in the despairing tone of Cicero's letters written from Dyrrhachium towards the end of the year.[a]

The year 57 B.C. opened with a determined attempt by Cicero's supporters to secure his recall. In the Senate on 1 January the consul, P. Lentulus Spinther, proposed that Cicero should be recalled; his colleague, Q. Metellus Nepos, did not demur; Appius Claudius, Cicero's only enemy among the praetors, was silent. In a discussion about procedure, an eminent jurist, L. Aurelius Cotta (consul 65 B.C.), thought that legislation was unnecessary, but Pompey advised that a resolution of the Senate should be confirmed by a vote of the Assembly. But the passing of a resolution was obstructed by Atilius Serranus, one of the two tribunes hostile to Cicero; and although discussion in the Senate was resumed whenever possible, continued obstruction prevented a resolution from being passed. Nevertheless a tribune, Q. Fabricius, made preparations to bring a bill before the Assembly on 23 January. But Clodius' *operae* were already found in occupation of " the Forum, the Comitium, and the Senate House," [b] and with the help of gladiators borrowed from his brother, the praetor Appius Claudius, Clodius frustrated this attempt to hold an Assembly. In this murderous riot, the like of which, Cicero said, had not been seen in Rome since the civil war between Cinna and Octavius (87 B.C.),[c] Q. Cicero barely escaped with his life. In a later affray Sestius, after announcing an evil omen (*obnuntiatio*) to the consul

---

[a] *e.g. Epp. ad Att.* iii. 23; *Epp. ad Fam.* xiv. 3.
[b] Cicero, *Pro Sestio*, 75.
[c] The " Bellum Octavianum." Cicero, *Pro Sestio*, 77.

CICERO

Metellus Nepos against some proposal or measure to Cicero's detriment, was attacked in the Temple of Castor and left for dead.[a] His assailants, having admitted their guilt before the Senate, were imprisoned by Milo but released by Atilius Serranus. Certainty as to what followed cannot be reached, and the following narrative is tentative.[b] Probably in February Milo attempted to prosecute Clodius for a breach of the peace committed on 23 January under the *lex Plautia de vi,*[c] not as a tribune before the *concilium plebis* but before a *quaestio perpetua* presided over by a praetor. But the consul Metellus Nepos, supported by the praetor Appius Claudius and by the tribune Serranus, and appealing to a general suspension of public business announced by the Senate, refused to accept Milo's charge and thus brought at least criminal jurisdiction to a standstill. Our sources say that in 57 B.C. Milo twice attempted to prosecute Clodius, but was twice baulked by Metellus Nepos. The above was the first occasion, the second occurring in November (see p. 30).

Clodius then announced his candidature for an aedileship as a precaution against a renewal of Milo's intended prosecution *de vi,* since, once elected, he

[a] Cicero, *Epp. ad Quintum fratrem,* ii. 3. 6 ; *Pro Sestio,* 79.
[b] The main sources are : Cicero, *Post reditum in senatu,* 6 and 19 ; *Pro Sestio,* 85, 89, 95 ; *Pro Milone,* 35, 38, 40 ; *Epp. ad Att.* iv. 3. 2 ; *Epp. ad Fam.* i. 9. 5 ; v. 3 ; Plutarch, *Cicero,* 33 ; Dio Cassius, xxxix. 7. 4. The above version is based on E. Meyer, *Caesars Monarchie,* 1922, pp. 109-112. See also Rice Holmes, *The Roman Republic,* ii, p. 59, and Holden, *Pro Sestio,* p. 195, both of whom stress the point that as the quaestors, who appointed the jurors, had not been elected, Metellus forbade the praetor to hear any prosecution before the jurors had been duly chosen.
[c] Or *Plotia.*

could not be tried for any offence save for one arising
from his election. Milo retaliated by raising a troop
of gladiators [a] and, with the help of his colleague
Sestius and others, proceeded slowly to wear down
Clodius' resistance so that constitutional steps could
be taken to recall Cicero. Pompey also did much to
forward this movement. By inducing Capua to pass
a vote in Cicero's favour, he created a sympathy for
him which he later fostered by going from town to
town to speak on his behalf.[b]

During the early summer the Senate passed a
number of decrees favourable to Cicero at three
sittings which may be distinguished. In the Temple
of Honos and Virtus early in July, the Senate on the
motion of Lentulus commended Cicero to the protection of provincial governors and peoples and summoned citizens from all parts of Italy to vote for his
recall. This was followed by a great demonstration
in honour of Cicero in the theatre at the Ludi Apollinares (6–13 July).[c] Later, the Senate, meeting in
the Temple of Iuppiter Capitolinus, accepted by 416
votes to Clodius' solitary dissent,[d] a written statement read by Pompey that Cicero had saved the
State, and instructed the consuls to bring in a bill
for his recall. At that meeting the consul Metellus
Nepos declared himself reconciled to Cicero.[e] On
the following day, assembled in the *curia*, the Senate
resolved that whoever should attempt to block by

---

[a] Dio Cassius, xxxix. 8. 1.
[b] Cicero, *Post reditum in senatu*, 29 ; *In Pisonem*, 25
and 80 ; *Pro Milone*, 39.
[c] Cicero, *Pro Sestio*, 115 ff.
[d] Cicero, *Post reditum in senatu*, 26.
[e] Cicero, *Pro Sestio*, 130 ; *De prov. cons.* 22.

CICERO

obnuntiatio or otherwise to obstruct the holding of an Assembly to order Cicero's recall, should be declared a public enemy ; also that, if such obstruction should take place on five *dies comitiales*, Cicero should be free to return with full citizen rights.[a]   In fact, Cicero owed his recall to a *senatus consultum* which, it is thought, like the *lex Clodia* of 58 B.C., repealed the *lex Aelia Fufia* for a special purpose.[b] On 4 August, voters from all Italy being present, the *comitia centuriata* sanctioned Cicero's return, probably by declaring ineffective the previous acts against him on the ground that no banishment could be legal unless it followed a formal trial and condemnation.   On 4 September Cicero was welcomed back to Rome.

[a] Cicero, *Pro Sestio*, 129. See p. 319.
[b] S. Weinstock, *J.R.S.* xxvii, p. 220 ; Rice Holmes, *The Roman Republic*, ii, p. 60, note 5.
An important note on Clodius' " repeal " of the *lex Aelia Fufia* was published just as these volumes had reached their penultimate stage of preparation. In *J.R.S.* xlvii (1957), pp. 15-20, " Roman History, 58–56 B.C.: Three Ciceronian Problems," J. P. V. D. Balsdon discusses (pp. 15-16) Clodius' " repeal " of the *lex Aelia Fufia*. Having pointed out objections to previous hypotheses, he cannot detect in Cicero's many attacks against Clodius after his return from exile any evidence which might support Weinstock's view (*op. cit.* p. 220) that the Senate decided against the legality of Clodius' tribunate and legislation. He makes the cogent suggestion that Clodius' bill was framed to counter any repetition of such obstructive tactics as those of Bibulus in 59 B.C., by empowering the *comitia* and the *concilium plebis* to order that *obnuntiatio*, if attempted, should be disallowed. On this interpretation, the *lex Clodia* was the model for the decree (*Pro Sestio*, 129) passed by the Senate before the *comita centuriata* sanctioned Cicero's recall.

PRO SESTIO
AND
IN VATINIUM

I. Introduction to the *Pro Sestio* and the *In Vatinium*

The period of rather more than five months between Cicero's return from exile and his delivery of the *Pro Sestio* and the *In Vatinium* was marked by events which, though isolated in context and seemingly unrelated, yet collectively contributed to the setting and the purpose of these speeches. These events require some consideration also in the light of their bearing on two leading questions of the time : whether the Triumvirate could maintain itself against the Senate as the *de facto* government of Rome ; and how far stability within the Triumvirate, always potentially uncertain, was likely to be affected by an internal pull of forces or by an attack from outside.

On 5 September 57 B.C., the day after his return to Rome, Cicero in the speech *Post reditum in senatu* thanked the Senate for his recall, and on the same day or two or three days later addressed a similar speech to the People (*Post reditum ad Quirites*). He then took the lead in a senatorial debate on a crisis caused by an unforeseen shortage of food, supply difficulties having no doubt been intensified by a temporary increase in the city population due to Cicero's return and the Ludi Romani (4-12 September). On the proposal of the consuls, supported by Cicero, Pompey was given a *cura annonae* throughout the Roman world for five years with proconsular power and fifteen legates. This commission not only helped to express Cicero's gratitude to Pompey for assisting in his restoration but also provided Pompey with a congenial piece of administrative work. A proposal by a tribune C. Messius to invest Pompey with specially wide powers has been interpreted as " an unauthorized speculation by a free-lance tribune," [a] rather than as a move by Pompey for a military command.

About this time, the Senate, on the proposal of Cicero, approved a special distinction to Caesar by the ordering of a public thanksgiving (*supplicatio*) of the unprecedented length of fifteen days in honour of his Gallic victories in 58 and 57 B.C.[b]

On 29 September Cicero delivered before the *pontifices* his speech *De domo sua*, since Clodius, after demolishing his house on the Palatine, had built a portico which encroached on its site, with a small shrine of Libertas adjoining, so as to exclude Cicero, on religious grounds, permanently from it. The Senate having endorsed the verdict of the *pontifices* in favour of Cicero, compensation was paid to him for his house and his villas. In November the rebuilding of Cicero's house was violently interrupted by Clodius, whose *operae* were employed also in setting fire to Q. Cicero's house and in attacking Milo's. An encounter with Cicero's escort on 11 November might have been the end of Clodius, but Cicero allowed him to escape.

---

[a] *C.A.H.* ix, p. 530. See also *J.R.S.* xlvii (1957), pp. 16-18.
[b] Cicero, *De prov. cons.* 27 ; *Pro Balbo*, 61 ; *Epp. ad Fam.* i. 9. 7, 14. Caesar, *Bell. Gall.* ii. 35.

So for some time after his return Cicero remained in cautious mood and disinclined to any move which might give offence.

A matter which was the subject of much discussion and intrigue in the Senate late in 57 and early in 56 B.C. was the question of a proposal to restore Ptolemy Auletes to the throne of Egypt. This had an important bearing on the stability of the Triumvirate, for it awoke the latent repulsion between Pompey and Crassus and revealed Crassus as a rival to Pompey for a commission to restore the exiled king ; and it was one of the factors which encouraged Cicero to the line which he was to take in his defence of Sestius.

The reigning king of Egypt Ptolemy XI Auletes (80–51 B.C.) had an uncertain title to his throne. His predecessor Ptolemy X Alexander II was put on the throne by Sulla in 80 B.C. after the death of Ptolemy Lathyrus, and was said to have made a will at Sulla's dictation, under which Egypt was bequeathed to Rome.[a] On the death of Ptolemy X in 80 B.C. after a reign of a few days the throne was seized by an illegitimate son of Ptolemy Lathyrus, who reigned as Ptolemy XI Auletes but had no qualification for the throne either by birth or by merit. His usurpation was tolerated but not formally accepted by Rome. He therefore anxiously desired recognition and, although Rome took no action, annexation of Egypt under the will of Ptolemy X might be expected at any time. In 59 B.C. Caesar had Ptolemy recognized at a price of 6000 talents, in the name of Pompey as well as of himself. But in 58 B.C. the king was forced to quit Alexandria before subjects

[a] Cicero, *De lege agraria*, ii. 41.

infuriated by the new taxes which he had imposed to pay his debt to Caesar and Pompey. In 57 B.C. the fugitive arrived in Rome to press a claim for restoration and expressly named Pompey as commander of the necessary force. The Senate at first commissioned the consul P. Lentulus Spinther, who was due to proceed to Cilicia as proconsul in 56 B.C., to restore Ptolemy. But early in 56 B.C. the Senate seized on a pretext afforded by a passage in the Sibylline Books and vetoed the use of an army. Although feuds between Lentulus Spinther and other nobles may, to some extent, have influenced the senatorial decision, it is more probable that, since it was widely assumed that Pompey desired the commission, the Senate's veto of military action was largely due to a desire to baulk Pompey's real or supposed ambitions. On 6 February, however, as will be mentioned in a later context, the pressing by Clodius of Crassus' claims as superior to those of Pompey for a commission to restore Ptolemy, was a strong suggestion to Cicero that a rift existed within the Triumvirate which determined action might widen into a fatal breach.

As Cicero's action was to take the form of a proposal to re-open in the Senate the question of Caesar's Campanian land law, reference may now be made to the circumstances under which that matter had already been raised in a preliminary way. In the Senate, shortly after 10 December 57 B.C., one of the new tribunes, P. Rutilius Lupus, brought up for discussion Caesar's legislation on the *ager Campanus*, the *lex Iulia de agro Campano*.[a] Rutilius Lupus was a consistent partisan of Pompey, and early in 56 B.C.

---

[a] Cicero, *Epp. ad Quintum fratrem*, ii. 1. 1.

exerted himself in the Senate for Pompey to be commissioned to restore Ptolemy Auletes.[a] The terms of Lupus' motion are not known, but he mentioned Cicero's speeches on the subject, made some sharp thrusts at Caesar, and addressed appeals to Pompey, who was not present. It was clearly an attempt to sound the feeling of the Senate on the matter. As the Senate received Lupus' speech in silence and as Marcellinus, one of the consuls-elect for 56 B.C., was unwilling for any resolution about the *ager Campanus* to be made in the absence of Pompey, the matter was dropped. It has been plausibly conjectured [b] that the attempt of Lupus to test the feeling of the Senate was inspired by Pompey himself. On such an interpretation, Pompey would appear as the author of the attack on the *lex Iulia de agro Campano*, which Cicero proposed to launch in the Senate on 15 May 56 B.C.,[c] in his confident belief that Pompey had so far compromised himself by his support of Lupus in December 57 B.C. that he would not openly oppose Cicero's proposed action.

Though Clodius was something of a spent force, the hostilities between Milo and himself, which reopened about two months after Cicero's restoration and which were continued into the year 56 B.C., were to provide a setting for the revelation of serious differences between two members of the Triumvirate, Pompey and Crassus.

It has been stated (p. 20) that after the riot on 23

[a] Cicero, *Epp. ad Fam.* i. 1. 3 ; i. 2. 2.
[b] M. Cary, " Asinus Germanus," *Classical Quarterly*, xvii, pp. 103-107.
[c] Cicero, *Epp. ad Fam.* i. 9. 8.

January 57 B.C. Milo made an unsuccessful attempt
to prosecute Clodius *de vi* and that, with a view to
evading prosecution, Clodius became a candidate for
election as aedile. Some seven months later, Clodius'
outbursts of violence on 3, 11 and 12 November against
M. and Q. Cicero and against Milo were brought up
for discussion in the Senate on 14 November with
a view to passing a bill for a prosecution. But such
a proposal was talked out by the consul, Q. Metellus
Nepos, who once again came to Clodius' rescue as he
did earlier in the year (February). But Marcellinus,
consul-elect for 56 B.C., prepared a comprehensive
indictment of Clodius for his recent violence, with a
view to bringing him to trial before he could be saved
from prosecution by election as aedile. Milo co-
operated by announcing that on every day when the
Assembly might meet for an election he would
obstruct proceedings by *obnuntiatio*, and on 20 November [a] he succeeded in so doing. On 10 December
Milo ceased to be tribune. The question of the
priority of Clodius' trial or the election of aediles was
discussed by the Senate at a meeting about the
middle of December.[b] The consuls-elect for 56,
Marcellinus and Marcius Philippus, having moved
that Clodius be put on trial at once, the senators
proceeded to a division. But no vote was taken :
Clodius prepared to talk out the sitting ; his *operae*
outside were in uproar ; the House dispersed in
alarm. Clodius was not brought to trial and on 20
January 56 B.C. was elected aedile.[c]

---

[a] Cicero, *Epp. ad Att.* iv. 3. 4.
[b] Cicero, *Epp. ad Quintum fratrem*, ii. 1. 2-3.
[c] Cicero, *Epp. ad Quintum fratrem*, ii. 2. 2 ; *Epp. ad
Fam.* i. 9. 14-15.

PRO SESTIO and IN VATINIUM

Clodius, thus a magistrate, at once retaliated on Milo, out of office, by preparing to impeach him before the *comitia*, on the charge " *de vi*," " *quod gladiatores adhibuisset ut rogationem posset de Cicerone perferre.*" [a] Under this procedure a magistrate first summoned the defendant to appear before him on a certain day, and then examined him publicly before three *contiones*. The charge was then embodied in a *rogatio* which was promulgated and voted on by the *comitia* (*centuriata* for a capital penalty, *tributa* for a fine). We hear of proceedings against Milo on 2 and 6 February, and of an adjournment to 7 February, with a view to a formal trial on 17 February, which was later postponed to 7 May. Eventually Clodius dropped the charge. The proceedings, however, at a notorious *contio* in the Forum on 6 February [b] are of great political interest as revealing a rift between Pompey and Crassus : Clodius, in Crassus' employment, heaped abuse on Pompey and advertised his patron's superior claims to restore Ptolemy Auletes. Further, in the Senate on 8 February, Pompey, exasperated by these affronts, responded to an attack from a hostile tribune, C. Cato, by bluntly accusing Crassus of plotting his murder. [c] Pompey frankly confessed his troubles to Cicero : plots against his life ; and Clodius and a tribune C. Cato, encouraged and subsidized by Crassus and his enemies among the extreme Optimates. This revelation of grave differences within the Triumvirate was an immediate encouragement to Cicero and to a deter-

[a] Cicero, *Pro Sestio*, 95 ; *Pro Milone*, 40. *Schol. Bob.* p. 125 (Stangl).
[b] Cicero, *Epp. ad Quintum fratrem*, ii. 3. 2.
[c] Cicero, *Epp. ad Quintum fratrem*, ii. 3. 3.

31

mined enemy of Caesar, L. Domitius Ahenobarbus,[a] who were planning an attack from outside.

On 10 February,[b] four days after Pompey's outburst, legal proceedings were begun against P. Sestius, who when tribune in 57 B.C. had worked with Milo for Cicero's restoration, by the lodging of two charges against him. The former charge, *de ambitu*, in the name of an informer Cn. Nerius but probably, in effect, prepared by Vatinius, may have concerned Sestius' candidature for his tribunate. We know nothing more of it. The latter charge, probably under the *lex Plautia de vi*,[c] was identical with that under which Milo was then being arraigned, and was based on Sestius' enrolment and use of an armed bodyguard during his tribunate. Although Clodius was the real prosecutor, the charge itself stood in the names of P. Tullius Albinovanus and T. Claudius. Albinovanus, whose name does not appear in the *Pro Sestio*, receives incidental mention twice only in the *In Vatinium*[d]; of Claudius, his junior (*subscriptor*), mentioned only once,[e] nothing is known.

[a] Suetonius, *Div. Iul.* 23.

[b] Cicero, *Epp. ad Quintum fratrem*, ii. 3. 5.

[c] The evidence for the *lex Plautia de vi* has recently been examined by J. N. Hough, " The *Lex Lutatia* and the *Lex Plautia de Vi* " (*American Journal of Philology*, li (1930), pp. 135-147), and by J. Cousin, " *Lex Lutatia de Vi* " (*Revue historique de Droit français et étranger*, 1943, pp. 88-94). Hough concludes that the *lex Plautia de vi* was passed about 65–64 B.C., and was a re-enactment of the *lex Lutatia de vi*, which is to be dated to the revolt of Lepidus in 78–77 B.C., and which lapsed on the suppression of those disturbances. Cousin, however, holds that both laws were in operation in 56 B.C. and served different purposes, the *lex Plautia* dealing with cases of *vis contra privatos*, the *lex Lutatia* with *vis contra rem publicam*. See Austin, *Pro Caelio* (1952), pp. 42-43.

[d] *In Vatinium*, 3 and 41.   [e] *In Vatinium*, 3.

PRO SESTIO and IN VATINIUM

Cicero says that, as Sestius was indisposed, he at once went in person to his house and offered him his services,[a] to show consideration and gratitude to a courageous helper, but a difficult individual who perhaps was thought to bear Cicero a grudge for scanty recognition of his services as tribune. On the next day, 11 February,[b] Cicero defended L. Calpurnius Bestia, tribune in 62 B.C. and aedile in 59 B.C., who had failed in 57 B.C. to win election to a praetorship and was being prosecuted for bribery. In his speech (now lost) delivered in the Forum before a praetor, Cn. Domitius Calvinus, Cicero took an opportunity to predispose a large audience favourably towards Sestius with a view to his subsequent defence of him.

Thus the proceedings against Sestius began on 10 February. To counter the plea of the defence that Sestius had been driven to use force, the prosecution claimed that Sestius had had recourse to arms before he was threatened.[c] Evidence for the prosecution was given by P. Vatinius, L. Gellius Poplicola,[d] half-brother of L. Marcius Philippus, a consul of 56 B.C., and L. Aemilius Paullus,[e] apparently a friend of Cicero. The president of the *quaestio* was M. Aemilius Scaurus,[f] son of M. Aemilius Scaurus, consul 115 B.C., who was *princeps senatus* from his consulship till his death soon after his prosecution in 90 B.C., and of Caecilia Metella, later the wife of Sulla. Sestius was defended by the leading advocates of the

[a] Cicero, *Epp. ad Quintum fratrem*, ii. 3. 5.
[b] Cicero, *Epp. ad Quintum fratrem*, ii. 3. 6.
[c] Cicero, *Pro Sestio*, 84.
[d] Cicero, *Pro Sestio*, 110.
[e] Cicero, *Epp. ad Quintum fratrem*, ii. 4. 1.
[f] Cicero, *Pro Sestio*, 101, 116.

day : Hortensius, Crassus, C. Licinius Calvus Macer
(82–47 B.C., orator and poet), and Cicero. Evidence
of character (*laudatio*) was given by Pompey [a] and
by a deputation from Capua.[b] Cicero directed the
case so as to assign to each counsel his special function : to Hortensius [c] a treatment of the case as a
whole, and to himself the winding-up of the defence
by a political manifesto examining the motives of
the prosecution in the light of the events leading to
his own exile and restoration. The trial ended in
Sestius' unanimous acquittal on 11 March.[d] In the
course of the trial of Sestius, Cicero made Vatinius,
who had given evidence against the defendant, the
subject of a cross-examination which has been preserved under the title of *In P. Vatinium testem inter-
rogatio.*[e] The ostensible purpose of this, which was
an answer to a speech which Vatinius had already
made and in which he had vehemently attacked
Cicero, was to impugn the value of Vatinius' evidence.
But as five paragraphs only of the *In Vatinium* (1-3 ;
40-41) refer to the case itself or to the evidence of
Vatinius, the real aim of the speech was to abuse
a political enemy. Two interpretations have been
put upon the form of the *In Vatinium*. One is that
Cicero's cross-examination of Vatinius took the shape
of alternate question and answer, so that the *In
Vatinium*, as we have it, may represent only in a
general way what was said, and was composed later
as a political pamphlet.[f] The other, which on general

[a] Cicero, *Epp. ad Fam.* i. 9. 7.
[b] Cicero, *Pro Sestio*, 9.   [c] Cicero, *Pro Sestio*, 3.
[d] Cicero, *Epp. ad Quintum fratrem*, ii. 4. 1.
[e] See *A Commentary on Cicero in Vatinium* (1926), by
L. G. Pocock.
[f] Meyer, *Caesars Monarchie*, p. 135.

grounds seems more probable, and which has specific support in a passage of Quintilian,[a] is that the *In Vatinium* is the record of a continuous speech delivered by Cicero in the form of a reply to a speech already made by Vatinius, and of a series of questions to which Vatinius was expected to reply at the close of Cicero's questioning.[b]

[a] Quintilian, v. 7. 6.   [b] *In Vat.* 10 and 40.

II. M. TULLI CICERONIS
PRO PUBLIO SESTIO ORATIO

1 I. Si quis antea, iudices, mirabatur, quid esset,
quod pro tantis opibus rei publicae tantaque dignitate
imperii nequaquam satis multi cives forti et magno
animo invenirentur, qui auderent se et salutem suam
in discrimen offerre pro statu civitatis et pro communi libertate, is hoc tempore miretur potius, si
quem bonum et fortem civem viderit, quam si quem
aut timidum aut sibi potius quam rei publicae con-
sulentem. Nam ut omittatis de unius cuiusque casu
cogitando recordari, uno aspectu intueri potestis eos,
qui cum senatu, cum bonis omnibus rem publicam
adflictam excitarint et latrocinio domestico liberarint,
maestos sordidatos reos, de capite, de fama, de civitate, de fortunis, de liberis dimicantes ; eos autem,
qui omnia divina et humana violarint, vexarint,
perturbarint, everterint, non solum alacres laetosque
volitare, sed etiam fortissimis atque optimis civibus
periculum moliri, de se nihil timere.

2 In quo cum multa sunt indigna, tum nihil minus est

ᵃ From the disorder caused by the hired bands of Clodius.
ᵇ The *caput* of a Roman citizen comprised his rights and
privileges as such.   ᶜ A criminal trial. See § 9.
36

II. A SPEECH OF M. TULLIUS CICERO IN DEFENCE OF PUBLIUS SESTIUS

I. If before this, gentlemen of the jury, anyone 1 wondered what was the reason why, great as are the resources of our State and the prestige of our Empire, no sufficient number of brave and great-hearted men could be found who would dare to expose themselves and their very lives to danger for our constitution and for the general liberty, at this present time he should rather wonder if he finds any patriotic and courageous citizen, than if he finds anyone who is either faint-hearted or studies his own interest more than that of the State. There is no need to recall to your thoughts the fate of this or that individual ; one comprehensive look will show you the plight of those who joined with the Senate and all good citizens in lifting up our afflicted State and freeing it from brigandage at home.[a] You can see them in sorrow, in mourning, before judges, fighting for their rights,[b] their good name, their citizenship, their fortunes, their children ; whereas those who have violated, injured, confounded and overturned everything human and divine, not only bustle about brisk and joyful, but also devise danger [c] for the bravest and best of our citizens, while they have no fear for themselves.

And in this, although there is much to call forth 2 indignation, the most intolerable thing is that they

37

ferendum, quam quod iam non per latrones suos, non per homines egestate et scelere perditos, sed per vos nobis, per optimos viros optimis civibus periculum inferre conantur et, quos lapidibus, quos ferro, quos facibus, quos vi, manu, copiis delere non potuerunt, hos vestra auctoritate, vestra religione, vestris sententiis se oppressuros arbitrantur. Ego autem, iudices, quoniam,[1] qua voce mihi in agendis gratiis commemorandoque eorum, qui de me optime meriti sunt, beneficio esse utendum putabam, ea nunc uti cogor in eorum periculis depellendis, iis potissimum vox haec serviat, quorum opera et mihi et vobis et populo Romano restituta est.

3 II. Et quamquam a Q. Hortensio, clarissimo viro atque eloquentissimo, causa est P. Sesti perorata nihilque ab eo praetermissum est, quod aut pro re publica conquerendum fuit aut pro reo disputandum, tamen adgrediar ad dicendum, ne mea propugnatio ei potissimum defuisse videatur, per quem est perfectum, ne ceteris civibus deesset. Atque ego sic statuo, iudices, a me in hac causa atque hoc extremo dicendi loco pietatis potius quam defensionis, querellae quam eloquentiae, doloris quam ingenii partes 4 esse susceptas. Itaque si aut acrius egero aut liberius, quam qui ante me dixerunt, peto a vobis, ut tantum orationi meae concedatis, quantum et pio do-

---

[1] *Added by Halm* : quamquam *Reid.*

[a] By securing my return from exile.

no longer use their hired brigands, no longer men ruined by want and wickedness, but it is you, gentlemen, they employ to bring danger upon us—the best men to ruin the best citizens. And they flatter themselves that, by the aid of your authority, your conscience, your votes, they will be able to crush those whom they have been unable to annihilate by stones, by steel, by fire, by force, violence, and bands of brigands. But for myself, gentlemen, I thought that I should have found employment for my voice in returning thanks and commemorating the service done me by those who have earned my deepest gratitude [a]; since, however, I am compelled to use it in repelling the dangers that threaten them, may that voice then be of service to those above all others by whose exertions it has been restored to myself, and to you, and to the Roman People !

II. And although that distinguished and eloquent 3 man, Quintus Hortensius, has fully dealt with the case of Publius Sestius and has omitted nothing which was rightly put forward as a complaint in the interest of the State or argued in defence of the accused, nevertheless I shall venture to address you, for fear that my advocacy may seem to have failed that man above all others, thanks to whose efforts it has not failed the rest of our fellow-citizens. And, indeed, I am convinced, gentlemen, since I speak last and in such a cause, that I have undertaken a duty of gratitude rather than of defence, of complaint rather than of eloquence, of sorrow rather than of ability. If, therefore, I express myself more passionately and 4 with greater freedom than those who have spoken before me, I beg you will excuse everything in my speech that you think can be rendered excusable by

lori et iustae iracundiae concedendum putetis. Nam neque officio coniunctior dolor ullus esse potest quam hic meus susceptus ex hominis de me optime meriti periculo, neque iracundia magis ulla laudanda est quam mea inflammata eorum scelere, qui cum omnibus meae salutis defensoribus bellum esse sibi gerendum iudicaverunt. Sed quoniam singulis criminibus ceteri responderunt, dicam ego de omni statu P. Sesti, de genere vitae, de natura, de moribus, de incredibili amore in bonos, de studio conservandae salutis communis atque otii contendamque, si modo id consequi potero, ut in hac confusa atque universa defensione nihil a me, quod ad vestram quaestionem, nihil, quod ad reum, nihil, quod ad rem publicam pertineat, praetermissum esse videatur. Et quoniam in gravissimis temporibus civitatis atque in ruinis eversae atque adflictae rei publicae P. Sesti tribunatus est a Fortuna ipsa collocatus, non adgrediar ad illa maxima atque amplissima, priusquam docuero, quibus initiis ac fundamentis haec tantae summis in rebus laudes excitatae sint.

6   III. Parente P. Sestius natus est, iudices, homine, ut plerique meministis, et sapiente et sancto et severo ; qui cum tribunus pl. primus inter homines nobilissimos temporibus optimis factus esset, reliquis honoribus non tam uti voluit quam dignus videri. Eo auctore duxit honestissimi et spectatissimi viri,

---

    [a] *i.e.* not taking the case point by point.
    [b] Referring to the military tribunate and quaestorship of Sestius.
    [c] As long as a son was subject to the *patria potestas* his father's consent was necessary for his marriage.

dutiful sorrow and just indignation. For no sorrow can be more closely united to duty than this of mine, which has been caused by the peril of a man who has done me the greatest service ; nor does any indignation deserve greater praise than this of mine, which has been fired by the villainy of those who have decided to wage war against all the champions of my welfare. But since other speakers have replied 5 separately to the several charges, I propose to speak of the general position of Publius Sestius as a citizen, of his manner of life, of his character, of his habits, of his extraordinary affection for the loyal, of his zeal for the preservation of the general welfare and security ; and I shall do my utmost—if only I can succeed —to see, that, while making this comprehensive [a] and general defence, I may seem to have overlooked nothing which is relevant to your investigation, to the accused, or to the public interest. And since it is due to Providence itself that Publius Sestius was tribune at a time of public crisis, when the State, afflicted and prostrate, was threatened with destruction, I will not approach those supremely important matters, until I have shown you the beginnings and the foundations on which he has built up so great a reputation in high office.[b]

III. Publius Sestius, gentlemen, was the son of 6 a man, as most of you remember, who was wise, scrupulous, and strict ; who also, after being elected tribune of the commons, as the first in a most distinguished list at a very happy period, showed himself less desirous of enjoying other offices of state than of appearing worthy of them. With his father's consent,[c] he married a daughter of Gaius Albinus, a most honourable and esteemed citizen, by whom he

C. Albini, filiam, ex qua hic est puer et nupta iam
filia. Duobus his gravissimae antiquitatis viris[1] sic
probatus fuit, ut utrique eorum et carus maxime
et iucundus esset. Ademit Albino soceri nomen
mors filiae, sed caritatem illius necessitudinis et
benevolentiam non ademit. Hodie sic hunc diligit,
ut vos facillime potestis ex hac vel adsiduitate eius
7 vel sollicitudine et molestia iudicare. Alteram duxit[2]
patre vivo optimi et calamitosissimi viri filiam, L.
Scipionis. Clara in hoc P. Sesti pietas exstitit et
omnibus grata, quod et Massiliam statim profectus
est, ut socerum videre consolarique posset fluctibus
rei publicae expulsum in alienis terris iacentem,
quem in maiorum suorum vestigiis stare oportebat,
et ad eum filiam eius adduxit, ut ille insperato
aspectu complexuque si non omnem, at aliquam
partem maeroris sui deponeret, et maximis praeterea
adsiduisque officiis[3] et illius aerumnam, quoad vixit,
et filiae solitudinem sustentavit. Possum multa
dicere de liberalitate, de domesticis officiis, de tribunatu militari, de provinciali in eo magistratu

---

[1] duobus gravissimis ac plenissimis antiquitatis viris
Busche : gravissimis summae antiquitatis viris *Mommsen* :
gravissimis antiquae severitatis *Eberhard.*

[2] *MSS.* duxit uxorem : alteram duxit *Schütz.*

[3] maximis pro illa necessitudine studiis et officiis *Peterson*:
praeterea adsiduisque officiis *Mommsen.*

---

[a] Sestius had brought his son with him to the court, to
arouse the sympathy of the jury. He was a boy who had not
yet taken the *toga virilis*, assumed, generally, at seventeen
or earlier when military service began. See Warde Fowler,
The Roman Festivals, p. 56. *Cf.* § 144. Young Sestius
became *consul suffectus* in 23 B.C. See pp. 326-327.

[b] Which he only held as long as the marriage lasted.
Death or divorce dissolved the ties of *affinitas.*

[c] L. Cornelius Scipio Asiaticus who, when consul in 83 B.C.,

had a son whom you see here,[a] and a daughter now married. He so won the approval of these two men of most dignified and old-fashioned manners, that he was especially dear and agreeable to both. By the death of his daughter Albinus lost the name of father-in-law,[b] but did not lose the affection and goodwill arising from that close connexion. Even to-day you can easily judge of his fondness for Sestius either from his constant attendance in court, or his anxiety and distress. While his father was still alive, Sestius 7 married a second wife, a daughter of Lucius Scipio,[c] an excellent and yet most unfortunate man. Publius Sestius showed remarkable affection for him, as all willingly acknowledged, by leaving at once for Massilia, that he might be able to see and comfort his father-in-law, a man who deserved to stand where his fathers had stood, but who languished an outcast in a foreign land, a victim of the storms of trouble at home.[d] And he brought his daughter to him, in the hope that her unexpected appearance and embrace might cause him to forget some portion at least, if not all of his sorrow ; and by his marked and unceasing devotion he comforted him in his affliction till his death and his daughter in her bereavement. I can say much of his noble spirit, of his kindly services at home, of his military tribunate,[e] of his incorruptibility in the discharge [f]

unsuccessfully opposed Sulla in Italy ; at Teanum, on the Via Latina, N.W. of Casilinum, his army deserted. He died in exile at Massilia. [d] The Civil War of 83–82 B.C.

[e] Twenty-four military tribunes were elected annually at the *comitia tributa* ; hence the office was a magistracy.

[f] *Provincialis* means as observed by a man in his "*provincia*," here referring to a sphere of action, not to a territorial province.

abstinentia; sed mihi ante oculos obversatur rei
publicae dignitas, quae me ad sese rapit, haec minora
8 relinquere hortatur. Quaestor hic C. Antoni, collegae mei, iudices, fuit sorte, sed societate consiliorum meus. Impedior non nullius officii, ut ego
interpretor, religione, quo minus exponam, quam
multa P. Sestius, cum esset cum collega meo, sen-
serit, ad me detulerit, quanto ante providerit. Atque
ego de Antonio nihil dico praeter unum, numquam
illum illo summo timore ac periculo civitatis neque
communem metum omnium nec propriam non nullorum de ipso suspicionem aut infitiando tollere aut
dissimulando sedare voluisse. In quo collega susti-
nendo atque moderando si meam in illum indulgen-
tiam coniunctam cum summa custodia rei publicae
laudare vere solebatis, par prope laus P. Sesti esse
debet, qui ita suum consulem observavit, ut et illi
quaestor bonus et bonis[1] omnibus optimus civis videretur.
9   IV. Idem, cum illa coniuratio ex latebris atque ex
tenebris erupisset palamque armata volitaret, venit
cum exercitu Capuam, quam urbem propter plurimas
belli opportunitates ab illa impia et scelerata manu
temptari suspicabamur; C. Mevulanum, tribunum
militum Antoni, Capua praecipitem eiecit, hominem
perditum et non obscure Pisauri et in aliis agri

---

[1] nobis *Peterson-Klotz* : bonis *omitted by Köchly.*

---

[a] Gaius Antonius Hybrida, Cicero's colleague as consul in
63 B.C.   Each consul had a quaestor assigned to him by lot.
[b] Partly about Antonius' connexion with the Catilinarians.
[c] In the double sense of " kept an eye upon him," and
" treated him with respect."   [d] In 63 B.C.
[e] In Umbria.   It received a colony of Roman citizens in
184 B.C. Livy, xxxix. 44. 10.

of that office. But it is the high claims of the State which confront me, which seize my attention, and urge me to pass over these less important matters. My client, gentlemen, was by lot the quaestor of 8 Gaius Antonius, my colleague,[a] but by his participation in my counsels he was mine. A certain regard for what is due to a colleague, as I interpret the matter, makes me scruple to set out how many matters Publius Sestius discovered,[b] when he was with my colleague, how much he communicated to me, and what great foresight he displayed. And of Antonius himself I will say one word only : that never, in those days of exceeding fear and public peril, did he show any desire either to remove by disavowal or to allay by pretended ignorance either the general fear of all men or the particular suspicion entertained by some about himself. And if you did often praise me, very properly, for my efforts in checking and managing my colleague and my indulgent treatment of him, together with my utmost watchfulness over the public interest, equal praise almost is due to Publius Sestius, who was so careful of his consul[c] that Antonius found in him a good quaestor, and all loyalists a most patriotic citizen.

IV. Also, after that conspiracy[d] had burst out from 9 its hiding-place in the dark, and was openly winging its way in arms, Sestius was sent with an army to Capua, since we suspected that that city might be made the object of a sudden attack by that villainous band of rascals owing to the many advantages of its military situation. He drove headlong out of Capua Gaius Mevulanus, Antonius' military tribune, a desperate man, who had openly taken part in that conspiracy at Pisaurum[e] and in other parts of the Gallic terri-

CICERO

Gallici partibus in illa coniuratione versatum. Idemque C. Marcellum, cum is non Capuam solum venisset,
verum etiam se quasi armorum studio in maximam
familiam coniecisset, exterminandum ex illa urbe
curavit. Qua de causa et tum conventus ille Capuae,
qui propter salutem illius urbis consulatu conservatam
meo me unum patronum adoptavit, huic apud me
P. Sestio maximas gratias egit, et hoc tempore eidem
homines nomine commutato coloni decurionesque,
fortissimi atque optimi viri, beneficium P. Sesti
testimonio declarant, periculum decreto suo depre-
10 cantur. Recita, quaeso, L. Sesti, quid decrerint
Capuae decuriones, ut iam puerilis tua vox possit
aliquid significare inimicis vestris, quidnam, cum se
conroborarit, effectura esse videatur.

DECURIONUM DECRETA

Non recito decretum officio aliquo expressum
vicinitatis aut clientelae aut hospitii publici aut
ambitionis aut commendationis gratia, sed recito
memoriam perfuncti periculi, praedicationem amplissimi beneficii, vocem[1] officii praesentis, testimonium
11 praeteriti temporis. Atque illis temporibus eisdem,

---

[1] vicem *MSS.*: indicem *Kayser-Köchly.*

---

[a] North of Picenum, formerly occupied by Senones who
were driven out in 284 B.C.
[b] For joining Hannibal Capua lost its *civitas sine suffragio*
(received in 338 B.C.), but regained it in 189. Its territory
became *ager publicus.* By the Social War most of its inhabitants had, no doubt, acquired full Roman citizenship in
various ways. But Capua had no municipal constitution till
(59 B.C.) the *Lex Iulia de agro Campano* made it a colony.
In 63, therefore, its inhabitants were a *conventus,* an informal
community of Roman citizens. Reid, *Municipalities of the
Roman Empire,* pp. 88-89 ; 199.

tory.[a] He also saw to it that Gaius Marcellus was expelled from Capua,[b] since he had not only come there, but had joined a large band of gladiators under the pretext of exercising himself in the use of arms.[c] For this reason not only did the community at Capua, who chose me as their only patron because their city's safety had been secured in my consulship, return most sincere thanks to this Publius Sestius at my house, but to-day also these same people, under their new name of colonists and decurions, these most gallant and excellent men, I say, publicly attest the services rendered them by Publius Sestius and by their decree plead against his being exposed to danger.[d] Read out, I beg you, Lucius Sestius,[e] the 10 resolutions of the decurions of Capua, that your boyish voice may now give a hint to the enemies of your family what it seems likely to accomplish when it shall have grown stronger.

[The Resolutions of the Decurions are read out.]

This decree which I read out is not one that has been extorted from them by some bond of proximity, or clientship, or public guest-friendship, nor to promote their own interests, nor with the object of commending Sestius to his judges. I am reading out a record of danger undergone, a declaration of a most signal favour rendered, an expression of present gratitude, a testimony from a time that is past. And more still; at that very same period, after 11

[c] Capua was one of the chief centres of schools of gladiators. Sallust, *Cat.* 30 ; Cicero, *Epp. ad Att.* vii. 14. 2.

[d] *Periculum* is used with special reference to a criminal trial. See § 1, and *Pro Balbo*, 41 and 64.

[e] P. Sestius' son. See pp. 326-327.

cum iam Capuam metu Sestius liberasset, urbem
senatus atque omnes boni deprehensis atque op-
pressis domesticis hostibus me duce ex periculis
maximis extraxissent, ego litteris P. Sestium Capua
arcessivi cum illo exercitu, quem tum secum habebat.
Quibus hic litteris lectis ad urbem confestim incredibili celeritate advolavit. Atque ut illius temporis atrocitatem recordari possitis, audite litteras
et vestram memoriam ad timoris praeteriti cogitatio-
nem excitate.

Litterae Ciceronis consulis

V. Hoc adventu P. Sesti tribunorum pl. novorum,
qui tum extremis diebus consulatus mei res eas, quas
gesseram, vexare cupiebant, reliquaeque coniura-
12 tionis impetus et conatus sunt retardati. Ac posteaquam est intellectum M. Catone tribuno pl., fortissimo atque optimo civi, rem publicam defendente
per se ipsum senatum populumque Romanum sine
militum praesidio tueri facile maiestate sua dignitatem eorum, qui salutem communem periculo suo
defendissent, Sestius cum illo exercitu summa celeritate C. Antonium consecutus est. Hic ego quid
praedicem, quibus hic rebus consulem quaestor ad
rem gerendam excitarit, quos stimulos admoverit
homini studioso fortasse victoriae, sed tamen nimium
communem Martem belli casumque metuenti ?

---

^a Q. Metellus Nepos and L. Calpurnius Bestia in particular.
^b The tribunes entered office on 10 Dec. 63 b.c.
^c Cato of Utica. When on his way to Lucania, hearing

Sestius had delivered Capua from fear, and the Senate and all loyal citizens, after surprising and crushing foes within their gates, had under my leadership saved the city from extreme peril, I recalled Publius Sestius from Capua by letter together with that army which he had with him at the time. As soon as he had read my letter he hastened to Rome with amazing speed. And, in order that you may be able to recall the horror of that time, hear my letter, awake your memory and imagine the terror that is past.

[*The Letter of Cicero the Consul is read out.*]

V. Thanks to the arrival of Publius Sestius, the new tribunes of the commons,[a] who at the time, during the last days of my consulship,[b] were eager to attack what I had accomplished, found their assaults and endeavours thwarted, as did the rest of the conspirators. And when it could be seen 12 that, while Marcus Cato,[c] tribune of the commons, a very courageous and patriotic citizen, was defending the State, the Senate and the Roman People, unaided and unprotected by soldiers, could easily by their sovereign sway uphold the position of those who had guarded the safety of the State at peril to themselves, Sestius hastened with his army in quest of Gaius Antonius. What need for me to set out here by what means a quaestor roused a consul to action, what incentives he brought to bear upon a man, who was eager perhaps to achieve a victory, but was much too afraid of the common fortune and

that Metellus was a candidate for the tribunate and thinking that his election would be disastrous to the State, he returned to Rome and was himself elected tribune for 62 B.C.

CICERO

Longum est ea dicere, sed hoc breve dicam : Si M. Petrei non excellens animus et amor rei publicae, non praestans in re publica virtus, non summa auctoritas apud milites, non mirificus usus in re militari exstitisset, neque adiutor ei P. Sestius ad excitandum Antonium, cohortandum, accusandum, impellendum fuisset, datus illo in bello esset hiemi locus, neque umquam Catilina, cum e pruina Appennini atque e nivibus illis emersisset atque aestatem integram nanctus Italiae calles et pastorum stabula prae- occupare[1] coepisset, sine multo sanguine ac sine 13 totius Italiae vastitate miserrima concidisset. Hunc igitur animum adtulit ad tribunatum P. Sestius, ut quaesturam Macedoniae relinquam et aliquando ad haec propiora veniam. Quamquam non est omit- tenda singularis illa integritas provincialis, cuius ego nuper in Macedonia vidi vestigia non pressa leviter ad exigui praedicationem temporis, sed fixa ad memoriam illius provinciae sempiternam ; verum haec ita praetereamus, ut tamen intuentes et re-

---

[1] praedari *Kayser* : peragrare *Madvig* : praeclara cepisset best *MSS.*

---

[a] Because war favoured sometimes one side, sometimes the other; *cf.* Cicero, *Epp. ad Fam.* vi. 4. 1 : "nam cum omnis belli Mars communis et cum semper incerti exitus proeliorum sint," and *Iliad*, xviii. 309 : ξυνὸς Ἐνυάλιος.

[b] Winter would have prevented the pursuit of Catiline. Early in 62 B.C., Catiline, trapped near Pistoria between the armies of Q. Metellus Celer, propraetor, and C. Antonius, was defeated and slain. Antonius' command was taken

chances of war ? *a* To tell all this would be a long story ; but I will say just this much. Had not Marcus Petreius shown pre-eminent spirit and devotion to the State, admirable courage in the public interest, great influence with the soldiers, and wonderful experience in military matters ; yes, and had not Publius Sestius been there to help him in rousing, exhorting, reproving, and urging Antonius on, winter would have played its part in that war *b* ; and, had Catiline once made his escape from those frost- and snow-bound Apennines, and, with a whole summer before him, had he begun to seize in advance the Italian sheep-walks and herdsmen's huts,*c* he would never have been overthrown without much bloodshed and most terrible devastation throughout Italy. Such then was the spirit that Publius Sestius 13 brought to his tribunate, that I may pass over his quaestorship in Macedonia,*d* and come at length to events that are more recent. Yet I ought not to remain silent about that remarkable honesty which he displayed in his province—of which I lately saw traces in Macedonia,*e* not faintly impressed as the record of a brief space of time, but so fixed that that province might ever remember it. But let us pass over all this, still holding it, however, in view, still

over by his experienced legate, M. Petreius (Sallust, *Cat.* 59), afterwards a leading Pompeian commander.

c The Italian *tratturi*, tracks for the movement of cattle and sheep between lowland and mountain pastures, seem to be largely ancient in origin and to correspond with the *calles* of Roman times. See H. F. Pelham, *Essays on Roman History*, pp. 305-306 (" Pascua "). The *pastorum stabula* were perhaps the *ergastula*, slave-prisons.

d Whither he had accompanied C. Antonius.

e When Cicero was in exile at Thessalonica.

spectantes relinquamus ; ad tribunatum, qui ipse ad
sese iam dudum vocat et quodam modo absorbet
orationem meam, contento studio cursuque veniamus.

14 VI. De quo quidem tribunatu ita dictum est a
Q. Hortensio, ut eius oratio non defensionem modo
videretur criminum continere, sed etiam memoria
dignam iuventuti rei publicae capessendae auctoritatem disciplinamque praescribere. Sed tamen,
quoniam tribunatus totus P. Sesti nihil aliud nisi
meum nomen causamque sustinuit, necessario mihi
de isdem rebus esse arbitror si non subtilius disputandum, at certe dolentius deplorandum. Qua in
oratione si asperius in quosdam homines invehi
vellem, quis non concederet, ut eos, quorum sceleris
furore violatus essem, vocis libertate perstringerem ?
Sed agam moderate et huius potius tempori serviam
quam dolori meo ; si qui occulte a salute nostra
dissentiunt, lateant ; si qui fecerunt aliquid aliquando
atque eidem nunc tacent et quiescunt, nos quoque
simus obliti ; si qui se offerunt, insectantur, quoad
ferri poterunt, perferemus, neque quemquam offendet
oratio mea, nisi qui se ita obtulerit, ut in eum non
invasisse, sed incucurrisse videamur.

15 Sed necesse est, antequam de tribunatu P. Sesti
dicere incipiam, me totum superioris anni rei publicae

---

a Here not the military tribunate, but his office as tribune
of the commons (57 B.C.).

b *Absorbeo* is used of a strong tide which carries everything along with it ; *cf.* Cicero, *Brutus*, 282 and *De leg.*
ii. 4. 9.

regardful as we abandon it ; let us come with might and main and all speed to that tribunate *a* which itself has this long while been calling to us and almost sweeps my speech away *b* with it.

VI. About this tribunate, indeed, Quintus Hor- 14 tensius has spoken already in such a manner that his words appeared not only to contain a defence against the charges made, but also to prescribe for the young a pattern and a lesson on political life well worth remembering. But since Publius Sestius, throughout his tribunate, did nothing but support my reputation and cause, I feel obliged to deal with the same subject, if not arguing with any minuteness, at least showing some indignation in my regrets. And if, as I speak, I should wish to attack certain persons with some asperity, who would not leave me free to scarify *c* with my tongue those who have assaulted me with criminal madness ? But I will plead with moderation, and will let my client's need influence me rather than my indignation. If any are secretly hostile to my welfare, let them not show themselves ; if any have at any time done anything, but now keep quiet and say nothing, we also, I hope, have forgotten ; if any place themselves in my way or follow on my heels, I will tolerate them as far as possible, and my speech will hurt no one, unless he puts himself straight before me—and then it will be clear that I did not deliberately assail him, but stumbled upon him.

But before I begin to speak of the tribunate of 15 Publius Sestius, I must tell you all about the complete shipwreck of the State in the year before : it was to

---

c *Perstringere* is a mild word = " graze," " inflict a super-ficial wound," and is in marked contrast to *violatus*.

naufragium exponere, in quo colligendo ac reficienda salute communi omnia reperientur P. Sesti facta, dicta, consilia versata.

VII. Fuerat ille annus iam[1] in re publica, iudices, cum in magno motu et multorum timore intentus est arcus in me unum, sicut vulgo ignari rerum loque- bantur, re quidem vera in universam rem publicam traductione ad plebem furibundi hominis ac perditi, mihi irati, sed multo acrius otii et communis salutis inimici. Hunc vir clarissimus mihique multis repug- nantibus amicissimus, Cn. Pompeius, omni cautione, foedere, exsecratione devinxerat nihil in tribunatu contra me esse facturum. Quod ille nefarius ex omnium scelerum colluvione natus parum se foedus violaturum arbitratus est, nisi ipsum cautorem alieni

16 periculi suis propriis periculis terruisset. Hanc tae- tram immanemque beluam vinctam auspiciis, alli- gatam more maiorum, constrictam legum sacratarum catenis solvit subito lege curiata consul vel, ut ego arbitror, exoratus vel, ut non nemo putabat, mihi

---

[1] furere coeperat ille annus iam *Halm* : iam *for* tam *Madvig. Peterson thinks something has fallen out after* iudices: <calamitosus quem fore suspicabamur tum> cum . . .

_a 59 B.C.

_b P. Clodius, who was adopted by a plebeian P. Fonteius, from whom he was immediately emancipated.

_c Clodius was angry with Cicero for giving evidence that destroyed his professed alibi in the Bona Dea scandal.

_d For a patrician to become plebeian was against usage.

_e For *leges sacratae* there is no concise English equivalent. According to Festus (p. 423 Lindsay) they placed a trans-

collecting the wreckage and to restoring the public safety that you will find my client's every deed, word, and thought to have been directed.

VII. That[a] year had already passed over our country, gentlemen, in which, amidst great disturbance and general panic, a bow was bent against me alone, as people said who knew nothing about politics, but in reality against the whole State, by the adoption into a plebeian family of a mad revolutionary,[b] a rogue who was angered with me,[c] but a far more savage enemy of security and the public safety. Gnaeus Pompeius, a most illustrious man and a great friend of mine (whereas many persons set themselves against me), had bound him by every kind of guarantee, agreement, and solemn oath that he would do nothing against me during his tribunate. But that abominable wretch, sprung from the offscourings of every sort of crime, thought that his bond would not be properly violated unless the very man who guaranteed another from danger should be threatened with dangers of his own. This foul and monstrous beast, although the 16 auspices had bound him, although ancient custom[d] had tied him down, although the fetters of the *leges sacratae*[e] held him fast, a consul suddenly released by a resolution of the *curiae*[f] either (as I suppose) because he had been over-persuaded, or (as some

gressor under the ban of some divinity, so that he could be slain with impunity. The *leges sacratae* of the early Republic were (Cary, *op. cit.* p. 84) " resolutions which the plebeians made binding upon themselves by oath." Under them the tribunate was made sacrosanct and was closed to patricians. See F. Altheim, *Lex Sacrata* (Amsterdam, 1939).

[f] In 59 B.C. Caesar as Pontifex Maximus convened the *comitia curiata* and passed a *lex curiata* for the adoption of Clodius into a plebeian family.

iratus, ignarus quidem certe et imprudens impendentium tantorum scelerum et malorum. Qui tribunus pl. felix in evertenda re publica fuit nullis suis nervis (qui enim in eius modi vita nervi esse potuerunt hominis fraternis flagitiis, sororiis stupris, omni inaudita libidine exsanguis ?) ; sed fuit profecto quaedam illa rei publicae fortuna fatalis, ut ille caecus atque amens tribunus pl. nancisceretur—quid dicam ? consules ? Hocine ut ego nomine appellem eversores huius imperii, proditores vestrae dignitatis, hostes bonorum omnium, qui ad delendum senatum, adfligendum equestrem ordinem, exstinguenda omnia iura atque instituta maiorum se illis fascibus ceterisque insignibus summi honoris atque imperii ornatos esse arbitrabantur ? Quorum, per deos immortales ! si nondum scelera vulneraque inusta rei publicae vultis recordari, vultum atque incessum animis intuemini ; facilius eorum facta occurrent mentibus vestris, si ora ipsa oculis proposueritis.

18 VIII. Alter unguentis affluens, calamistrata coma, despiciens conscios stuprorum ac veteres vexatores aetatulae suae, puteali et faeneratorum gregibus inflatus, a quibus compulsus olim, ne in Scyllaeo illo

---

a For some criticisms of the Triumvirate which Cicero had made at the trial of C. Antonius in March or April 59 B.C.

b A. Gabinius and L. Calpurnius Piso, consuls 58 B.C.

c *e.g.* the *sella curulis* and the *toga praetexta*.

d Gabinius.

e The *Puteal Libonis* or *Scribonianum*, a resort of moneylenders, was a stone enclosure built by a certain Scribonius Libo around a spot in the Forum that had been struck by lightning. *Puteal* means a curb-stone. See Platner and Ashby, *A Topographical Dictionary of Ancient Rome*, p. 434.

thought) because he was angry with me,*a* but certainly not knowing and not expecting the great crimes and troubles that were hanging over our heads. And this tribune of the commons was fortunate in attempts at overthrowing the State, by no vigour of his own—for what vigour could a man have who had lived such a life, exhausted by shameful intercourse with his brothers and sisters and by every kind of unexampled licentiousness ? But it must 17 have been some fatality ordained for the State, that this blind and senseless tribune of the commons managed to find two—what am I to say ? consuls ? *b* am I to call by this name those who overthrew this Empire, betrayed your high estate, were the enemies of all loyalists, and who thought that to confound the Senate, to humiliate the Equestrian Order, to abolish all the laws and institutions of our ancestors, was the purpose for which they had been decorated with those fasces and the other insignia *c* of their high office and command ? If you do not yet care to recall their crimes and the wounds they branded upon the State then, in the name of heaven, look in imagination upon their faces and their bearing ; their deeds will more readily suggest themselves to your minds, if you put their very looks before your eyes.

VIII. Here is one of them.*d* Dripping with un- 18 guents, with waved hair, looking down on the partners of his debaucheries and the greybeard abusers of his dainty youth, puffed up with rage against the Exchange *e* and the herds of usurers, who had once driven him to take refuge in the harbour of a tribunate *f*

---

f By holding a tribunate Gabinius won protection against his creditors, who could not proceed against him during his year of office.

aeris alieni tamquam in fretu ad columnam adhaere-
sceret, in tribunatus portum perfugerat, contemnebat
equites Romanos, minitabatur senatui, venditabat se
operis atque ab iis se ereptum, ne de ambitu causam
diceret, praedicabat ab isdemque se etiam invito
senatu provinciam sperare dicebat ; eamque nisi
adeptus esset, se incolumem nullo modo fore arbitra-
19 batur.   Alter, o di boni !   quam taeter incedebat,
quam truculentus, quam terribilis aspectu !   Unum
aliquem te ex barbatis illis, exemplum imperii veteris,
imaginem antiquitatis, columen rei publicae diceres
intueri.   Vestitus aspere nostra hac purpura plebeia
ac paene fusca, capillo ita horrido, ut Capua, in qua
ipse tum imaginis ornandae causa duumviratum
gerebat, Seplasiam sublaturus videretur.   Nam quid
ego de supercilio dicam, quod tum hominibus non
supercilium, sed pignus rei publicae videbatur ?   Tanta
erat gravitas in oculo, tanta contractio frontis, ut illo
supercilio annus ille niti tamquam vade¹ videretur.
20 Erat hic omnium sermo : " Est tamen rei publicae

---

¹ vade *supplied by Madvig from Valerius Probus.*

ᵃ Scylla, a sea-monster, was located opposite Charybdis,
a whirlpool in a narrow channel later identified with the
Sicilian Straits.   North of Rhegium on the Straits stood a
column to Poseidon.   Cases of debt were tried in the Forum
near the *columna Maenia*, probably a column in honour of
the victory over Antium of C. Maenius (cos. 338).   Platner
and Ashby, *op. cit.* p. 131, but see *Oxford Class. Dict.*
p. 528.   Hence the double meaning : " shipwreck in the
Sicilian Straits " ; " posting-up as a debtor."

ᵇ In 59 B.C. a vain attempt was made to bring Gabinius
to trial for *ambitus*.   See Cicero, *Epp. ad Quintum fratrem*,
i. 2. 15.

ᶜ By reversing the Senate's assignment of consular provinces made under the *lex Sempronia* of C. Gracchus.

ᵈ He would be obliged to become bankrupt.

from the danger of being stuck up on the Column in a
sea of debt as in those Straits of Scylla,[a] he spoke
with contempt of the Roman Knights, he threatened
the Senate, he ingratiated himself with hired ruffians,
and boasted that they had saved him from standing
his trial on a charge of bribery,[b] he said that he hoped
they would also help him to a province, Senate or no
Senate,[c] and if he failed to get it he thought nothing
could save him.[d] The other [e]—good heavens ! see 19
him marching along—how repulsive, how fierce, how
terrible he was to look at ! You would have thought
you saw one of our bearded forefathers, a perfect
specimen of the old regime, a mirror of antiquity, a
pillar of the State. Coarsely clad in our common
purple, almost in black, with hair in such a tangle
that at Capua, where he was then in office as duumvir [f]
in order to add another honour to his list, he looked
as if he meant to carry off the Seplasia with him.[g]
And what am I to say of his eyebrow,[h] which then
did not seem to men to be a high brow, but a guarantee for the State ? There was such a solemnity in his
eye, there were such wrinkles in his forehead, that
this eyebrow seemed to be sponsor for the year's
security. The common talk was—" After all, he is a 20

[e] Piso.
[f] Piso and Gnaeus Pompeius were *duoviri*, the two chief
magistrates, in the colony of Capua (see p. 46, note *b*). After
Piso's death this local magistracy would be recorded on the
inscription (*titulus*) beneath his wax portrait-mark (*imago*),
in the family *atrium*. Cicero thus taunts him with excessive
vanity.
[g] A fashionable street in Capua occupied by perfumers
and hairdressers. R. G. Nisbet's interpretation of *sublaturus*
is followed. See his edition of Cicero, *De domo sua*, p. 127.
[h] *Supercilium* here suggests, not " haughtiness," but
" sternness " or " authority," *cf.* Horace, *Odes*, iii. 1. 8.

magnum firmumque subsidium ; habeo, quem op-
ponam labi illi atque caeno ; vultu me dius fidius
collegae sui libidinem levitatemque franget ; habebit
senatus in hunc annum, quem sequatur ; non deerit
auctor et dux bonis.'' Mihi denique homines praecipue gratulabantur, quod habiturus essem contra
tribunum pl. furiosum et audacem cum amicum et
adfinem, tum etiam fortem et gravem consulem.

IX. Atque eorum alter fefellit neminem. Quis
enim clavum tanti imperii tenere et gubernacula rei
publicae tractare in maximo cursu ac fluctibus posse
arbitraretur hominem emersum subito ex diuturnis
tenebris lustrorum ac stuprorum, vino, ganeis, lenociniis adulteriisque confectum, cum is praeter spem
in altissimo gradu alienis opibus positus esset, qui
non modo tempestatem impendentem intueri temu-
lentus, sed ne lucem quidem insolitam aspicere
21 posset ? Alter multos plane in omnes partes fefellit.
Erat enim hominum opinioni nobilitate ipsa, blanda
conciliatricula, commendatus. Omnes boni semper
nobilitati favemus, et quia utile est rei publicae
nobiles homines esse dignos maioribus suis, et quia
valet apud nos clarorum hominum et bene de re
publica meritorum memoria etiam mortuorum. Quia
tristem semper, quia taciturnum, quia subhorridum
atque incultum videbant, et quod erat eo nomine,

ᵃ C. Calpurnius Piso Frugi, who died shortly before Cicero's
return from exile, was a relative of the consul and the first
husband of Cicero's daughter Tullia.   ᵇ P. Clodius.
ᶜ Gabinius.   ᵈ Pompey, Caesar, and Crassus.

great and strong pillar of the State ; I have some one
to set against that pest, that muckheap ; upon my
honour, he will break down his colleague's caprices
and levity by a look ; the Senate will have someone
to follow for this year ; loyal citizens will not lack a
leader and a chief." Lastly, people were congratu-
lating me in particular, because I was going to have
one who was not only a friend and kinsman,[a] but also
a courageous and dignified consul, to help me against
a raving and audacious tribune of the commons.[b]

IX. The first [c] of these men deceived no one. For
who could imagine that to hold the helm of so great
an empire, and guide the rudder of the ship of state,
as it sped along amid tempestuous waves, was in the
power of a man who had suddenly emerged from a
long sojourn in the dark, from haunts of debau-
chery, a man worn out with drunkenness, gluttony,
lewdness, and adultery : when, beyond his hopes, he
had been raised to the highest rank by the help of
others,[d] he who in his drunken bouts was not only
unable to see a threatening storm, but could not
even endure to look at the light, so long a stranger
to him ? The other [e] utterly deceived many of us in 21
every way. For his noble birth alone, that alluring
procurette, commended him to public opinion. All
we who are good citizens always favour noble birth,
both because it is good for the State that there
should be noblemen, worthy of their ancestors, and
because the memory of distinguished men and of
those who have deserved well of the State lives in
our hearts even after they are dead. Because they
saw him always grim, taciturn, somewhat rough and
unpolished, and because he bore a name which [f]

ut ingenerata familiae frugalitas videretur, favebant,
gaudebant et ad integritatem maiorum spe sua
22 hominem vocabant materni generis obliti. Ego
autem (vere dicam, iudices) tantum esse in homine
sceleris, audaciae, crudelitatis, quantum ipse cum
re publica sensi, numquam putavi ; nequam esse
hominem et levem et falsa opinione hominum ab
adulescentia commendatum sciebam. Etenim animus
eius voltu, flagitia parietibus tegebantur ; sed haec
obstructio nec diuturna est neque obducta ita, ut
curiosis oculis perspici non possit.

X. Videbamus genus vitae, desidiam, inertiam ;
inclusas eius libidines, qui paulo propius accesserant,
intuebantur ; denique etiam sermo nobis ansas da-
bat, quibus reconditos eius sensus tenere possemus.
23 Laudabat homo doctus philosophos nescio quos neque
eorum tamen nomina poterat dicere, sed tamen eos
laudabat maxime, qui dicuntur praeter ceteros esse
auctores et laudatores voluptatis ; cuius et quo tempore et quo modo, non quaerebat, verbum ipsum
omnibus animi et corporis partibus[1] devorarat ; eos-
demque praeclare dicere aiebat sapientes omnia sua
causa facere, rem publicam capessere hominem bene
sanum non oportere, nihil esse praestabilius otiosa
vita plena et conferta voluptatibus ; eos autem, qui
dicerent dignitati esse serviendum, rei publicae con-

---

[1] partibus *added by Orelli*: omni vi animi *Madvig. After*
omnibus *Wesenberg supplies* viribus.

---

[a] She was a daughter of Calventius of Placentia in Cisalpine Gaul. See note on *De prov. cons.* 7.
[b] He had apparently spent a moral youth and thus misled
people.
[c] The Epicureans. Piso had living with him Philodemus,
a member of that school.

seemed to have made frugality the hereditary virtue
of his family, they favoured him, they rejoiced, they
encouraged him to prove to be as honest a man as
his ancestors, forgetting his mother's blood.[a] But I 22
too—to tell the truth, gentlemen—never believed
that there was so much villainy, audacity, and cruelty
in the man, as I together with the whole State found
by experience. I certainly knew that he was a bad
man, unsteady, that public opinion was wrong in
allowing him to be recommended by his youth,[b] for
his heart was concealed by his face, his scandalous
acts by the walls of his house. But the screen is not
lasting, nor is it so thick that it cannot be seen through
by inquisitive eyes.

X. We observed his mode of life, his idleness and
inactivity ; his sequestered vices were on view for
those who came a little closer ; finally the man's
talk also would give us a handle by which we could
grasp his hidden feelings. The accomplished creature 23
used to praise some philosophers [c] or other, but
could not give their names ; still he praised those
most who are said to be above all others the teachers
and eulogists of pleasure [d] ; what pleasure, and when
and how he did not inquire ; he just swallowed the
single word with all his heart and with all his might ;
he added that these same men were quite right in
saying that the wise do everything for their own
interests ; that no sane man should engage in public
affairs ; that nothing was preferable to a life of tranquillity crammed full of pleasures ; but those who
said that men should aim at an honourable position,

[d] Epicurus did not consider the *summum bonum* to be
sensual pleasure, but calmness of mind and freedom from
disturbing emotions (ἀταραξία).

sulendum, officii rationem in omni vita, non commodi
esse ducendam, adeunda pro patria pericula, volnera
excipienda, mortem oppetendam, vaticinari atque
24 insanire dicebat. Ex his assiduis eius cotidianisque
sermonibus, et quod videbam, quibuscum hominibus
in interiore parte aedium viveret, et quod ita domus
ipsa fumabat, ut multa eius sordium[1] indicia re-
dolerent, statuebam sic, boni nihil ab illis nugis
esse exspectandum, mali quidem certe nihil pertime-
scendum. Sed ita est, iudices : ut, si gladium parvo
puero aut si imbecillo seni aut debili dederis, ipse
impetu suo nemini noceat, sin ad nudum vel fortissimi viri corpus accesserit, possit acie ipsa et ferri
viribus vulnerare, sic,[2] cum hominibus enervatis
atque exsanguibus consulatus tamquam gladius esset
datus, qui per se pungere neminem umquam potuissent, ii summi imperii nomine armati nudatam rem
publicam contrucidaverunt. Foedus fecerunt cum
tribuno pl. palam, ut ab eo provincias acciperent,
quas ipsi vellent, exercitum et pecuniam, quantam
vellent, ea lege, si ipsi prius tribuno pl. adflictam
et constrictam rem publicam tradidissent. Id autem
foedus meo sanguine ictum sanciri posse dicebant.
25 Qua re patefacta (neque enim dissimulari tantum
scelus poterat nec latere) promulgantur uno eodem-

---

[1] *MSS.* sermonis: *Halm suggests* sordium: *Eberhard*
nidoris: *C. F. W. Müller* faetoris: consortionis *Peterson.*
[2] sic *added by Halm.*

---

[a] The text is uncertain. Halm's *sordium* is the simplest
correction.

should consult the public interest, should think of
duty throughout life not of self-interest, should face
danger for their country, receive wounds, welcome
death; these he called visionaries and madmen. With 24
his talk of this kind going on all day and every day,
and because I saw what kind of men he lived with
in his inner chambers, and because the house itself so
reeked that there was many a stinking sign of his dirty
habits,[a] I made up my mind to expect no good from
such rubbish, although certainly I need fear no harm.
But it is like this, gentlemen. If you were to give a
sword to a little boy or a weak, feeble old man, he
would hurt no one by his own effort, but if he ap-
proaches a defenceless man, even though one of the
bravest, he may be able to wound him by the sharp-
ness and force of the weapon alone : so, when you had
put the consulship like a sword into the hands of men un-
nerved and exhausted, who of themselves would never
have been able to scratch anyone's skin, they, armed
with the name of supreme power, put the defenceless
State to the sword. They openly made an alliance
with a tribune of the commons,[b] to receive from him
what provinces they wanted, troops and money as
much as they wanted, on condition that they themselves should first hand over to him the State prostrate
and fettered. This alliance, they said, when struck
could be ratified by the shedding of my blood.[c] When 25
the plot was disclosed—for such a crime could neither
be disguised nor hidden—at one and the same time
two bills were brought forward by the same tribune [d]

---

[b] P. Clodius.
[c] Cicero is metaphorically the victim "struck" or "slain"
at early treaty-makings.
[d] By P. Clodius, in February 58 B.C. See p. 14.

que tempore rogationes ab eodem tribuno de mea
pernicie et de provinciis consulum nominatim.[a]

XI. Hic tum senatus sollicitus, vos, equites Romani, excitati, Italia cuncta permota, omnes denique
omnium generum atque ordinum cives summae rei
publicae a consulibus atque a summo imperio peten-
dum esse auxilium arbitrabantur, cum illi soli essent
praeter furiosum illum tribunum duo rei publicae
turbines, qui non modo praecipitanti patriae non sub-
venirent, sed eam nimium tarde concidere maererent.
Flagitabatur ab iis cotidie cum querellis bonorum
omnium, tum etiam precibus senatus, ut meam
causam susciperent, agerent aliquid, denique ad
senatum referrent; non modo negando, sed etiam
inridendo amplissimum quemque illius ordinis in-
26 sequebantur. Hic subito cum incredibilis in Capitolium multitudo ex tota urbe cunctaque Italia con-
venisset, vestem mutandam omnes meque iam omni
ratione privato consilio, quoniam publicis ducibus res
publica careret, defendendum putarunt. Erat eodem
tempore senatus in aede Concordiae,[c] quod ipsum
templum repraesentabat memoriam consulatus mei,
cum flens universus ordo cincinnatum consulem ora-
bat; nam alter ille horridus et severus consulto se
domi continebat. Qua tum superbia caenum illud
ac labes amplissimi ordinis preces et clarissimorum
civium lacrimas repudiavit, me ipsum ut contempsit

---

[a] *Nominatim* refers to the consular provinces only; the
first bill did not mention Cicero by name. The consuls
ought to have drawn lots for the provinces assigned by the
Senate before their election.

[b] Where the Senate had pronounced sentence of death
upon the Catilinarian conspirators.

[c] Because of Cicero's emergency coalition of senators and
equites, the genesis of his idea of a *concordia ordinum.*

to compass my ruin and to allot a province to each consul expressly.[a]

XI. At this point the Senate became anxious; you, Knights of Rome, were aroused; the whole of Italy was deeply moved; in fact, men of every rank and class were of opinion that help must be sought for the supreme interests of the State from the consuls and from their supreme authority—although they were the only persons except that raving tribune, those two whirlwinds that swept over the State, who not only failed to come to the support of their country when it was falling headlong, but lamented because it was collapsing too slowly. They were daily importuned by the complaints of all patriotic men, even by the entreaties of the Senate, to take up my cause, to do something, in fact, to bring the matter before the House; but not only with denials but also with mockery did they continue to assail every man of mark in that body. And then, straightway, when an amaz- 26 ing throng had assembled on the Capitol from the whole city and from the whole of Italy, all deemed it their duty to put on mourning, and to defend me also in every possible way by measures of their own, since the State had lost its public leaders. At the same time the Senate had assembled in the Temple of Concord,[b] the very temple that recalled the memory of my consulship,[c] and the whole Order with tears entreated the consul with curly hair [d]—for the other one, shock-headed and grave, carefully kept at home. With what haughtiness did that filthy pest then reject the entreaties of that illustrious Order and the tears of most eminent citizens! How contemptuously did

[d] Gabinius.

helluo patriae ! nam quid ego " patrimonii " dicam,
quod ille totum, quamvis[1] quaestum faceret, amisit ?
Venistis ad senatum vos, inquam, equites Romani et
omnes boni veste mutata vosque pro meo capite ad
pedes lenonis impurissimi proiecistis, cum vestris
precibus ab latrone illo repudiatis vir incredibili
fide, magnitudine animi, constantia, L. Ninnius, ad
senatum de re publica rettulit, senatusque frequens
vestem pro mea salute mutandam censuit.

27   XII. O diem illum, iudices, funestum senatui
bonisque omnibus, rei publicae luctuosum, mihi ad
domesticum maerorem gravem, ad posteritatis memoriam gloriosum ! Quid enim quisquam potest ex
omni memoria sumere inlustrius quam pro uno cive
et bonos omnes privato consensu et universum senatum publico consilio mutasse vestem ? quae quidem
tum mutatio non deprecationis causa est facta, sed
luctus. Quem enim deprecarere, cum omnes essent
sordidati, cumque hoc satis esset signi esse improbum,
qui mutata veste non esset ? Hac mutatione vestis
facta tanto in luctu civitatis omitto quid ille tribunus
omnium rerum divinarum humanarumque praedo
fecerit, qui adesse nobilissimos adulescentes, honestis-
simos equites Romanos, deprecatores salutis meae
iusserit eosque operarum suarum gladiis et lapidibus
obiecerit ; de consulibus loquor, quorum fide res
28 publica niti debuit. Exanimatus evolat ex senatu

---

[1] tum, qua *mss.* ; totum, quamvis *Halm* : tum cum quaestum faceret *Peterson.*

---

[a] *Quaestum facere* or *quaestum corpore facere* is used of
prostitutes.
[b] A supporter of Cicero who as tribune on 1 June 58 b.c.
made a proposal for his recall. See p. 17 and § 68.
[c] The consul Gabinius.

he treat me—this devourer of his country! for why should I say of his " patrimony," all of which he lost, in spite of the plying of his trade ?[a] You came to the Senate in mourning, you, I say, Roman Knights and all loyal citizens, and to save my life threw yourselves at the feet of that foul pimp. Then, after that brigand had rejected your prayers, a man of amazing loyalty, greatness of spirit, and firmness of purpose, L. Ninnius,[b] submitted to the Senate a motion to discuss the general state of public affairs, and a full House passed a resolution that my welfare demanded the wearing of mourning.

XII. Gentlemen, what a fatal day for the Senate 27 and all good citizens, deplorable for the State, a day made grievous to me for distress within my household, but glorious for remembrance in times to come ! For what greater distinction can anyone choose out of all the history of the past than that, to save one citizen, all good men personally by common consent, and the whole Senate by public resolution, put on mourning ? This change of dress, indeed, was not made then for the sake of intercession but only to show sorrow. For with whom could one intercede when all were in mourning, and when it was sufficient mark of a scoundrel, if a man had not changed his dress ? After this change of dress had been made, while the city was overwhelmed with sorrow, I say nothing of what that tribune did, that despoiler of all things divine and human ; how he summoned young men of the highest birth, most honourable Roman Knights, who interceded for my welfare, and exposed them to the swords and stones of his hirelings. Here I speak only of the consuls, on whose loyalty the State had a right to rely. Frightened out of his wits,[c] he flies from the 28

non minus perturbato animo atque voltu, quam si
annis ante paucis in creditorum conventum incidisset ;
advocat contionem, habet orationem talem consul,
qualem numquam Catilina victor habuisset : errare
homines, si etiam tum senatum aliquid in re publica
posse arbitrarentur ; equites vero Romanos daturos
illius diei poenas, quo me consule cum gladiis in clivo
Capitolino fuissent ; venisse tempus iis, qui in timore
fuissent (coniuratos videlicet decebat), ulciscendi sui.[1]
Si dixisset haec solum, omni supplicio esset dignus ;
nam oratio ipsa consulis perniciosa potest rem pub-
29 licam labefactare ; quid fecerit, videte. L. Lamiam,
qui cum me ipsum pro summa familiaritate, quae
mihi cum patre eius erat, unice diligebat, tum pro re
publica vel mortem oppetere cupiebat, in contione
relegavit edixitque, ut ab urbe abesset milia passuum
ducenta, quod esset ausus pro civi, pro bene merito
civi, pro amico, pro re publica deprecari.

XIII. Quid hoc homine facias aut quo civem im-
portunum aut quo potius hostem tam sceleratum
reserves ? qui, ut omittam cetera, quae sunt ei cum
collega immani impuroque coniuncta atque com-
munia, hoc unum habet proprium, ut ex urbe ex-
pulerit, relegarit non dico equitem Romanum, non

---

[1] *There is an erasure of three letters in the* MS.: sui *Halm* :
se *Peterson.*

[a] On 5 December 63 B.C. a body of *equites* under Atticus
(*signifer ac princeps*, Cic. *Epp. ad Att.* ii. 1. 7) occupied the
clivus Capitolinus to protect the senators in the Temple of
Concord, assembled to discuss the fate of Catiline's accomplices in Rome.

Senate, as disturbed in mind and countenance as if a few years before he had come upon his creditors in conclave. He calls a meeting ; consul as he was, he delivers a speech such as a victorious Catiline would never have uttered. People were mistaken, he said, if they thought that the Senate still possessed some power in the State ; but as for the Roman Knights, they would pay for the day on which, during my consulship, they had been on the slope of the Capitol in arms *a* ; that the hour of vengeance had arrived for those (he meant of course the conspirators) who had hitherto been in fear. If he had only so spoken, he would deserve every kind of punishment, for the mere speech of a consul, if mischievous, can shake the commonwealth. But mark what he did ! at 29 that meeting he banished *b* Lucius Lamia, who was specially devoted to me owing to my intimacy with his father, and was ready at that time to sacrifice even his life for the State ; and he issued an edict that he keep two hundred miles away from the city, on the ground that he had dared to intercede for a citizen—for a citizen who had served his country well, for a friend, for the public good.

XIII. What can you do with a man like this ? what punishment can you reserve for so abominable a citizen, or rather so vicious an enemy ? who, to pass over all else that he shares in common with his monstrous and infamous colleague, has one thing peculiar to himself—the fact that he expelled from the city, that he banished—I do not say a Roman Knight, a

b *Relegatio* was milder than *exsilium*. The offender was sent out of Rome for a limited space of time to a certain distance from the city, and did not suffer any loss of political rights.

ornatissimum atque optimum virum, non amicissimum rei publicae civem, non illo ipso tempore una cum senatu et cum bonis omnibus casum amici reique publicae lugentem, sed civem Romanum sine ullo
30 iudicio ut edicto ex patria consul eiecerit. Nihil acerbius socii et Latini ferre soliti sunt quam se, id quod perraro accidit, ex urbe exire a consulibus iuberi. Atqui[1] illis tum erat reditus in suas civitates ad suos Lares familiares, et in illo communi incommodo nulla in quemquam propria ignominia nominatim cadebat. Hoc vero quid est? exterminabit cives Romanos edicto consul a suis dis penatibus, expellet ex patria, deliget, quem volet, damnabit atque eiciet nominatim? Hic si umquam vos eos, qui nunc estis, in re publica fore putasset, si denique imaginem iudiciorum aut simulacrum aliquod futurum in civitate reliquum credidisset, umquam ausus esset senatum de re publica tollere, equitum Romanorum preces aspernari, civium denique omnium novis et inauditis edictis ius libertatemque pervertere?
31 Etsi me attentissimis animis summa cum benignitate auditis, iudices, tamen vereor, ne quis forte vestrum miretur, quid haec mea oratio tam longa aut tam alte repetita velit, aut quid ad P. Sesti causam

---

[1] atque MSS.: atqui *Fleckeisen*.

---

[a] The non-Roman members of the confederacy in Italy were known, before the *lex Iulia* of 90 B.C., as *socii* (non-Latins) *et Latini*.
[b] In 187 B.C. and 177 B.C. Latins unlawfully registered as

most distinguished and excellent man, a citizen most devoted to the State, not one who at that very moment was lamenting in company with the Senate and all loyal citizens the plight of his friend and the ruin of the State; but I do say that without any trial, he, as consul, expelled by edict a Roman citizen from his country. Our allies *a* and the Latins never 30 felt more bitterly aggrieved than when—as very rarely happened—they were ordered by the consuls to leave the city *b*; and yet they were then able to return to their own cities, to the gods of their homes, and amidst that general annoyance no personal disgrace fell upon any one expressly. But what is this present pass ? Shall a consul drive out by an edict Roman citizens from their very homes ? expel them from their country ? choose anyone he pleases, to condemn and cast him out expressly ? If he had thought that you would ever occupy the position in the State that you do to-day,—yes, if he had believed that any shadow or ghost of the Courts of Justice would be left in the State, would he ever have dared to wipe out the Senate from the constitution, to treat the prayers of Roman Knights with contempt, and, finally, to overthrow the rights and liberty of all citizens by new and unheard-of edicts ?

Although you are listening to me most attentively 31 and with the greatest indulgence, gentlemen, I am nevertheless afraid that some one of you may perhaps wonder what can be the meaning of this speech of mine, so long or going so far back, or what the

Roman citizens were ordered to return to their towns ; in 125 B.C. and 122 B.C. Latins and Italians were forbidden access to the city, and in 95 B.C. they were removed from the city by the *lex Licinia Mucia.*

eorum, qui ante huius tribunatum rem publicam
vexarunt, delicta pertineant. Mihi autem hoc propositum est ostendere, omnia consilia P. Sesti
mentemque totius tribunatus hanc fuisse, ut adflictae
et perditae rei publicae, quantum posset, mederetur.
Ac si in exponendis vulneribus illis de me ipso plura
dicere videbor, ignoscitote. Nam et illam meam
cladem vos et omnes boni maximum esse rei publicae
vulnus iudicastis, et P. Sestius est reus non suo, sed
meo nomine ; qui cum omnem vim sui tribunatus in
mea salute consumpserit, necesse est meam causam
praeteriti temporis cum huius praesenti defensione
esse coniunctam.

32 XIV. Erat igitur in luctu senatus ; squalebat
civitas publico consilio veste mutata ; nullum erat
Italiae municipium, nulla colonia, nulla praefectura,
nulla Romae societas vectigalium, nullum collegium
aut concilium aut omnino aliquod commune consilium,
quod tum non honorificentissime de mea salute
decrevisset : cum subito edicunt duo consules, ut ad
suum vestitum senatores redirent. Quis umquam
consul senatum ipsius decretis parere prohibuit, quis
tyrannus miseros lugere vetuit ? Parumne est, Piso,
ut omittam Gabinium, quod tantum homines fe-
fellisti, ut neglegeres auctoritatem senatus, optimi

---

^a By this list of three words, which recurs in Cicero,
In Pisonem, 51 and *Phil.* ii. 58, Cicero is summing-up the
towns of Italy, apart from Rome. The words are used merely
with reference to the historical origin of different communities
which, at the end of the Republic, had no difference of
legal status, for they were all communities of full Roman
citizens. See A. N. Sherwin-White, *The Roman Citizenship*,

case of Publius Sestius has to do with the crimes of
those who troubled the State before he was tribune.
But my intention is to show that the whole policy and
purpose of his tribunate was to heal, as far as it
could, the wounds of an afflicted and ruined State.
And if, in laying open these wounds, I seem to say
rather much about myself, you must pardon me. For
both you and all loyal citizens held that the disaster
that befell me was the greatest possible wound to the
State, and that Publius Sestius is a defendant not on
his own account, but on mine ; and since he devoted
all the strength his tribunate gave him to promoting
my welfare, my cause in past time must needs be
linked with the defence of Sestius in the present.

XIV. The Senate then was in grief. All citizens, 32
by public resolution, were drab in the garb of mourning ; there was in Italy no borough, no colony, no pre-
fecture,[a] no company of tax-farmers [b] in Rome, no
club nor association, nor, in short, any deliberative
body, which had not at that time passed a decree in
the most complimentary terms concerning my welfare,
when suddenly the two consuls published an edict
that senators should resume their usual dress. What
consul ever prohibited the Senate from obeying its
own decrees ? what tyrant ever forbade the unhappy
to mourn ? Are you not content, Piso (to say nothing
of Gabinius), with having so deceived public expectation as to ignore a resolution of the Senate, to despise

pp. 143-144, and H. M. D. Parker's note in J. D. Denniston's
edition of the *Second Philippic*, pp. 133-134.

[b] The usual expression was *societas publicanorum* instead
of *societas vectigalium*. These *societates publicanorum* con-
tracted for the collection of provincial revenues, notably in
Asia.

cuiusque consilia contemneres, rem publicam pro-
deres, consulare nomen adfligeres ? etiamne edicere
audeas, ne maererent homines meam, suam, rei
publicae calamitatem, ne hunc suum dolorem veste
significarent ? Sive illa vestis mutatio ad luctum
ipsorum sive ad deprecandum valebat, quis umquam
tam crudelis fuit, qui prohiberet quemquam aut sibi
33 maerere aut ceteris supplicare ? Quid ? sua sponte
homines in amicorum periculis vestitum mutare non
solent ? pro te ipso, Piso, nemone mutabit ? ne isti
quidem, quos legatos non modo nullo senatus consulto, sed etiam repugnante senatu tibi tute legasti ?
Ergo hominis desperati et proditoris rei publicae
casum lugebunt fortasse, qui volent ; civis florentis-
simi benevolentia bonorum et optime de salute
patriae meriti periculum coniunctum cum periculo
civitatis lugere senatui non licebit ? Eidemque
consules, si appellandi sunt consules, quos nemo est
quin non modo ex memoria, sed etiam ex fastis
evellendos putet, pacto iam foedere provinciarum
producti in circo Flaminio in contionem ab illa furia ac
peste patriae maximo cum gemitu vestro illa omnia,
quae tum contra me contraque rem publicam agebantur,[1] voce ac sententia sua comprobaverunt.

[1] *This word, inserted by Halm, is not in the* MSS. *Among
other suggestions are* parabantur, fiebant, committebantur,
ferebantur.

---

[a] A hint that Piso may be brought to trial on some charge
when he returns from his province of Macedonia.
[b] *Legati* were properly nominated by the Senate. See *In
Vatinium*, 35.
[c] Gabinius was to be invested with Cilicia, and Piso with
Macedonia, despite any other arrangement by the Senate.
[d] The Circus Flaminius was in the southern part of the

the advice of every loyal citizen, to betray the State,
to degrade the name of consul ? were you even bold
enough to issue an edict that the people should not
lament my, their own, the public calamity, that they
should not show their sorrow by their dress ? Whether
that change of dress was intended to show their own
grief, or as a sign of entreaty, who ever was so
cruel as to prevent anyone either from mourning for
himself or from intercession on behalf of others ?
Again, are not men in the habit of changing their 33
dress by their own wish when their friends are in
danger ? Will no one go into mourning for you,
Piso ? [a] not even those whom you nominated to
your staff on your own authority,[b] not only without
a decree of the Senate, but even against its wish ?
The misfortune, then, of a desperate man and a
traitor to the State shall perhaps be lamented by
those who choose ; but when a citizen fully enjoys the
goodwill of loyal men and has done his utmost for
the welfare of his country, shall it not be lawful for
the Senate to lament his peril—a peril that involves
peril to the State ? And yet those very same consuls—if they are to be called consuls, whose names
all think ought to be torn out not only from human
memory but also from public records—after a bargain
had been struck about the provinces,[c] were brought
before a meeting in the Circus Flaminius [d] by that
madman, that curse of his country, and to your profound grief gave their approval, by both word and
vote, to all that was then being done against myself
and the State.

Campus Martius. *Contiones*, that is, meetings summoned
by magistrates or tribunes to witness public acts or to hear
speeches, were frequently held there.

XV. Isdemque consulibus sedentibus atque in-spectantibus lata lex est, NE AUSPICIA VALERENT, NE QUIS OBNUNTIARET, NE QUIS LEGI INTERCEDERET, UT OMNIBUS FASTIS DIEBUS LEGEM FERRI LICERET, UT LEX AELIA, LEX FUFIA NE VALERET; qua una rogatione quis est qui non intellegat universam rem publicam 34 esse deletam? Isdemque consulibus inspectantibus[1] servorum dilectus habebatur pro tribunali Aurelio nomine collegiorum, cum vicatim homines con-scriberentur, decuriarentur, ad vim, ad manus, ad caedem, ad direptionem incitarentur. Isdemque consulibus arma in templum Castoris palam com-portabantur, gradus eiusdem templi tollebantur, armati homines forum et contiones tenebant, caedes lapidationesque fiebant, nullus erat senatus, nihil reliqui magistratus, unus omnem omnium potestatem armis et latrociniis possidebat non aliqua vi sua, sed, cum duo consules a re publica provinciarum foedere retraxisset, insultabat, dominabatur, aliis pollice-batur, terrore ac metu multos, plures etiam spe et promissis tenebat.

35 Quae cum essent eius modi, iudices, cum senatus duces nullos ac pro ducibus proditores aut potius apertos hostes haberet, equester ordo reus a consuli-bus citaretur, Italiae totius auctoritas repudiaretur,

---

[1] *This word, inserted by Hotman, is not in the* MSS.: *Pluygers inserts* coniventibus.

---

[a] See pp. 309-322 (vi. The *Lex Aelia Fufia* in the Late Republic).
[b] Days on which business in the Courts of Law and As-semblies was allowed.
[c] A platform in the Forum, of unknown site, possibly constructed by M. Aurelius Cotta (consul 74 B.C.).

XV. And, while the same consuls sat there and looked on, a law was passed [a] that the auspices should have no validity, that no one should announce unfavourable omens, that no one should veto a law, that it should be permissible for laws to be passed on all *dies fasti*,[b] that the Aelian Law and the Fufian Law should be invalid. Who cannot see that by this single bill the constitution was utterly destroyed ? And with the same consuls looking on, a levy of slaves 34 was held on the front of the Tribunal of Aurelius [c] on the pretext of forming clubs [d] ; men were enlisted street by street, formed into squads, and incited to force, deeds of violence, murder and robbery. And with these same consuls in office, arms were openly carried into the Temple of Castor, the steps of the Temple itself were taken away,[e] the Forum and public meeting-places were packed with armed men, stoning and murders took place ; the Senate was nobody, the other magistrates were nothing ; one man alone held all power with the help of arms and brigandage, not by any force of his own, but after he had diverted the two consuls from the interests of the State by the bargain over the provinces, he behaved insolently, played the tyrant, made promises to some, kept his hold on many by fear and terror, on still more by hopes and promises.

Although things had come to this pass, gentlemen, 35 although the Senate had no leaders, and instead of leaders, traitors, or rather open enemies ; although the Equestrian Order was put on its trial by the consuls, the authority of the whole of Italy defied,

[d] Recruited from the roughs of the city and trained for political rioting. They had been banned by the Senate in 64 B.C.   [e] In order to convert it into a fortress.

alii nominatim relegarentur, alii metu et periculo
terrerentur, arma essent in templis, armati in foro,
eaque non silentio consulum dissimularentur, sed et
voce et sententia comprobarentur, cum omnes urbem
nondum excisam et eversam, sed iam captam atque
oppressam videremus : tamen his tantis malis tanto
bonorum studio, iudices, restitissemus ; sed me alii
metus atque aliae curae suspicionesque moverunt.

36 XVI. Exponam enim hodierno die, iudices, omnem
rationem facti et consilii mei neque huic vestro tanto
studio audiendi nec vero huic tantae multitudini,
quanta mea memoria numquam ullo in iudicio fuit,
deero. Nam si ego in causa tam bona tanto studio
senatus, consensu tam incredibili bonorum omnium,
tam parato equestri ordine,[1] tota denique Italia ad omnem contentionem expedita cessi tribuni pl., despica-
tissimi hominis, furori, contemptissimorum consulum
levitatem audaciamque pertimui, nimium me timidum, nullius animi, nullius consilii fuisse confiteor.

37 Quid enim simile fuit in Q. Metello ? cuius causam
etsi omnes boni probabant, tamen neque senatus
publice neque ullus ordo proprie neque suis decretis
Italia cuncta susceperat. Ad suam enim quandam

---

[1] *The words* equestri ordine, *inserted by Halm and
Kayser, are not in the text:* Mommsen *inserts* populo.

---

[a] Halm's *equestri ordine* is adopted.
[b] L. Appuleius Saturninus, in his second tribunate (100
B.C.), introduced measures for the allotment of lands, possibly
in Transalpine Gaul, and for the foundation of colonies in
various parts of the Empire and, with less probability, in
Italy. He inserted a penal clause (*sanctio*) in his colonial
bill, under which every senator was to take an oath within
five days of its enactment that he would observe its pro-

certain persons expressly banished, others terrified
by fear and danger ; although there were arms in the
temples, armed men in the Forum, and although all
this was not ignored in silence by the consuls, but
approved both by their word and their vote ; although
we all saw the city, not yet annihilated and overthrown, but already captured and subdued ; nevertheless, gentlemen, such was the enthusiasm of loyal
citizens that we should have resisted all these great
evils, had there not been other fears, other anxieties,
and other suspicions which influenced my conduct.

XVI. For I will set before you to-day, gentlemen, 36
a complete account of what I did, and the motives
which influenced me ; nor will I disappoint your
earnest desire of hearing me any more than I will
fail this great crowd, one greater than I ever remember attending a trial. For if I, in so good a
cause, with the enthusiastic support of the Senate,
with the extraordinary unanimity of all loyal citizens,
with the Equestrian Order ready,[a] and in short all
Italy prepared to fight to the utmost,—if I yielded
to the madness of that despicable tribune of the commons, if I showed myself afraid of the worthless-
ness and audacity of those contemptible consuls,
I confess myself to have been all too timid, a man
of no courage and of no judgment. For how can 37
the case of Quintus Metellus [b] be compared with
mine ? Although all loyalists favoured his cause, yet
neither the Senate by a public vote, nor any Order
by a private vote, nor the whole of Italy by its
decrees had taken it up. For the truth was that

visions under penalty of a fine and exile. Q. Metellus
Numidicus (consul 109 B.C.) alone refused to take the oath
and went into exile.

magis ille gloriam quam ad perspicuam salutem rei
publicae respexerat,[1] cum unus in legem per vim
latam iurare noluerat ; denique videbatur ea condicione tam fortis fuisse, ut cum patriae caritate constantiae gloriam commutaret. Erat autem res ei
cum exercitu C. Mari invicto, habebat inimicum C.
Marium, conservatorem patriae, sextum iam illum
consulatum gerentem ; res erat cum L. Saturnino,
iterum tribuno pl., vigilante homine et in causa populari si non moderate, at certe populariter abstinen-
terque versato. Cessit, ne aut victus a fortibus viris
cum dedecore caderet aut victor multis et fortibus
38 civibus rem publicam orbaret. Meam causam senatus palam, equester ordo acerrime, cuncta Italia
publice, omnes boni proprie[2] enixeque susceperant.
Eas res gesseram, quarum non unus auctor, sed dux
omnium voluntatis fuissem, quaeque non modo ad
singularem meam gloriam, sed ad communem salutem omnium civium et prope gentium pertinerent ;
ea condicione gesseram, ut meum factum semper
omnes praestare tuerique deberent.

XVII. Erat autem mihi contentio non cum victore
exercitu, sed cum operis conductis et ad diripiendam
urbem concitatis ; habebam inimicum non C. Marium,

---

[1] sumpserat *MSS.* ; spectarat *Orelli and the older editions* :
respexerat *Halm* : spiritus sumpserat *is the reading of H. A.
Koch* : " *he had plucked up his courage.*" *Peterson reads* re-
spiciens rem gesserat.
[2] proprie *MSS.* : propere *Kraffert.*

---

[a] Since the refusal of a single man to take the oath could
do no good to the State.
[b] Or, possibly, " as in their own cause."
[c] The execution of the Catilinarian conspirators.

he had shown greater regard for some sort of glory of his own than for the manifest welfare of the State,[a] when he alone had refused to take an oath to observe a law that had been passed by violence ; in short, there seemed to be a catch in that display of courage—he bartered away affection for his country in exchange for the credit of stedfastness. But he had to deal with the unconquered army of Gaius Marius ; he had as an enemy Gaius Marius, the saviour of his country, who was then for the sixth time consul ; he had to deal with Lucius Saturninus, tribune of the commons for the second time, a man fully alert and one who in supporting the popular cause behaved, if not with moderation, at least in the interest of the People and without self-seeking. He yielded, either for fear that if defeated by brave men he might fall with disgrace, or, if victorious, he might bereave the State of many brave citizens. But my cause was taken up 38 by the Senate openly, by the Equestrian Order with the greatest energy, by the whole of Italy through public resolutions, by all loyal citizens individually [b] and with the greatest enthusiasm. My measures were not grounded on my sole authority, but carried out the general will ; they not only concerned my personal reputation, but the general welfare of all citizens, I might say of all peoples ; in carrying them out I fully expected that all men would make it a duty always to uphold and defend what I had done.[c]

XVII. But I had to contend not with a victorious army, but with gangs of hirelings, made eager to plunder the city; I had as an enemy not Gaius Marius, the terror of his enemies, the hope and

terrorem hostium, spem subsidiumque patriae, sed
duo importuna prodigia, quos egestas, quos aeris
alieni magnitudo, quos levitas, quos improbitas tribuno
39 pl. constrictos addixerat ; nec mihi erat res cum Saturnino, qui quod a se quaestore Ostiensi per ignominiam
ad principem et senatus et civitatis, M. Scaurum, rem
frumentariam tralatam sciebat, dolorem suum magna
contentione animi persequebatur, sed cum scurrarum
locupletium scorto, cum sororis adultero, cum stuprorum sacerdote, cum venefico, cum testamentario, cum
sicario, cum latrone ; quos homines si, id quod facile
factu fuit, et quod fieri debuit, quodque a me optimi
et fortissimi cives flagitabant, vi armisque superassem,
non verebar, ne quis aut vim vi depulsam reprehen-
deret aut perditorum civium vel potius domesticorum
hostium mortem maereret. Sed me illa moverunt :
Omnibus in contionibus illa furia clamabat se, quae
faceret contra salutem meam, facere auctore Cn.
Pompeio, clarissimo viro mihique et nunc et, quoad
licuit, amicissimo. M. Crassus, quocum mihi omnes
erant amicitiae necessitudines, vir fortissimus, ab
eadem illa peste infestissimus esse meis fortunis
praedicabatur ; C. Caesar, qui a me nullo meo merito

---

^a He superintended the passage of imported corn-supplies
from Ostia to Rome.

^b M. Aemilius Scaurus (consul 115 B.C., censor 109 B.C.)
was made *princeps senatus* before his consulship was over.
The *princeps senatus* was the senator placed at the head of
the senatorial roll compiled by the censors. The title was
almost obsolete after the death by 60 B.C. of Q. Lutatius
Catulus.

support of his country, but two dangerous monsters, whom want, and enormous debts, and shifty character, and depravity, had assigned like slaves in bondage to a tribune of the commons ; nor had I 39 to deal with Saturninus, who because he knew that the import of corn had been, as an intentional insult, transferred from him when he was quaestor at Ostia *a* to Marcus Scaurus, Father of the Senate *b* and a leading man in the State, was with all energy seeking an outlet for his indignation *c* ; but I had to deal with a debauched favourite of wealthy rakes, a lover of his own sister, a priest of profligacy,*d* a poisoner, a forger of wills, an assassin, a brigand ; and if I had overcome these men by force of arms, as was easy to be done, as it would have been right to do, and as the best and bravest citizens demanded that I should do, I had no fear that anyone would blame me for repelling force with force, or that anyone would lament the death of abandoned citizens or rather enemies in our midst. But the reasons that decided me were these. In all his speeches that madman continued to shout that what he did to ruin me he did with the approval of that illustrious man, Gnaeus Pompeius, who both is now and was then, as far as was permitted him,*e* most friendly to myself. Marcus Crassus, to whom I was attached by all the ties of friendship, a man of the greatest courage, was declared by that same pest to be most hostile to my interests. Gaius Caesar, who

---

c This insult is said by Cicero (*De haruspicum responsis*, 43) to have driven him into the party of opposition to the Optimates : he became a *popularis*.

d An allusion to the scandal of the Bona Dea, Dec. 62 B.C.

e *i.e.* until he became a member of the Triumvirate.

alienus esse debebat,[1] inimicissimus esse meae saluti
40 ab eodem cotidianis contionibus dicebatur. His se
tribus auctoribus in consiliis capiendis, adiutoribus
in re gerenda esse usurum dicebat ; ex quibus unum
habere exercitum in Italia maximum, duo, qui privati
tum essent, et praeesse[2] et parare, si vellent, exercitum posse idque facturos esse dicebat. Nec mihi
ille iudicium populi nec legitimam aliquam contentionem nec disceptationem aut causae dictionem, sed
vim, arma, exercitus, imperatores, castra denuntiabat.

XVIII. Quid ergo ? inimici oratio, vana praesertim,
tam improbe in clarissimos viros coniecta me movit ?
Me vero non illius oratio, sed eorum taciturnitas, in
quos illa oratio tam improba conferebatur ; qui tum
quamquam ob alias causas tacebant, tamen hominibus
omnia timentibus tacendo loqui, non infitiando confiteri videbantur. Illi autem aliquo tum timore per-
territi, quod acta illa atque omnes res anni superioris
labefactari a praetoribus, infirmari a senatu atque a
principibus civitatis putabant, tribunum popularem a
se alienare nolebant suaque sibi propiora esse peri-

---

[1] debebat *MSS.* : credebatur *Halm* : videbatur *Urlichs*.
[2] praeesse *MSS.* : reipublicae praeesse *Orelli* : populo
Romano praeesse *Peterson* : praesto esse *F. C. Wolff*.

---

[a] Caesar, who had an army in Italy, mobilized for his
Gallic command.
[b] *Iudicium populi*, a trial before an Assembly of the
People ; *legitima contentio*, a law-suit based upon some
law, a legal proceeding such as took place in a *quaestio
perpetua*. *Disceptatio* is a judicial investigation with argu-
ments and counter-arguments. *Causae dictio* is a defence
against any charges raised.
[c] Or, " to whom such slanderous language was ascribed."

had no right to be estranged from me through any demerit of mine, was also said by Clodius at his daily meetings to be strongly opposed to my welfare. These three men, he said, he would use as his ad- 40 visers in framing his policy, and as his assistants in carrying it out. One of them, he said, had a very large army in Italy *a*; the two others, who were at the time in a private position, could if they wished both command and raise an army, and this he said they would do. Nor did he threaten me with a trial by the people, nor with any legal proceeding, nor with any disputed point or pleading of a cause,*b* but with violence, arms, armies, commanders, camps.

XVIII. Well then? did the language of an enemy, especially as it was false, so shamelessly directed against men of the highest distinction, shake my resolution? It was not his language, but the obstinate silence of those to whom that shameless language was made to refer,*c* who at that time remained silent for other reasons, yet to men who were afraid of everything they seemed by silence to speak, and by not denying, to confess. But they were just then under some great terror, because they thought that all those acts and all the measures of the previous year were being undermined by the praetors *d* and weakened by the Senate and the leading men in the State,*e* and being unwilling to estrange a popular tribune, they used to say that their own

---

d Early in 58 B.C. two praetors, C. Memmius and L. Domitius Ahenobarbus, invited the Senate to declare Caesar's laws of 59 B.C. null and void. Suetonius, *Div. Iul.* 23.

e Leading Optimates such as M. Bibulus, M. Cato, L. Lucullus and others, enemies of the Triumvirate.

41 cula quam mea loquebantur. Sed tamen et Crassus
a consulibus meam causam suscipiendam esse dicebat,
et eorum fidem Pompeius implorabat neque se privatum publice susceptae causae defuturum esse dicebat;
quem virum studiosum mei, cupidissimum rei publicae
conservandae domi meae certi homines ad eam rem
positi monuerunt, ut esset cautior, eiusque vitae a
me insidias apud me domi positas esse dixerunt,
atque hanc eius suspicionem alii litteris mittendis,
alii nuntiis, alii coram ipsi excitaverunt, ut ille, cum
a me certe nihil timeret, ab illis, ne quid meo nomine molirentur, sibi cavendum putaret. Ipse autem
Caesar, quem maxime homines ignari veritatis mihi
esse iratum putabant, erat ad portas, erat cum
imperio ; erat in Italia eius exercitus, inque eo
exercitu ipsius tribuni pl. inimici mei fratrem prae-
fecerat.

42 XIX. Haec ergo cum viderem (neque enim erant
occulta), senatum, sine quo civitas stare non posset,
omnino de civitate esse sublatum, consules, qui duces
publici consilii esse deberent, perfecisse, ut per ipsos
publicum consilium funditus tolleretur, eos, qui plurimum possent, opponi omnibus contionibus falso, sed

---

ᵃ *Pericula*, often used in reference to criminal trials ; see
§ 9 above.
ᵇ Cicero is complaining that his enemies put some of their
friends in his house to spy upon him.
ᶜ C. Claudius Pulcher, praetor 56 B.C.
ᵈ *Publicum consilium* here means " the policy of the

dangers [a] touched them more nearly than mine. Cras- 41
sus, however, said that my cause ought to be taken up
by the consuls, and Pompey also appealed to them,
declaring that he, though a private individual, would
not desert a cause officially taken up by them ; but
devoted as he was to me and most eager for the
salvation of the State, he was warned to be more
careful by certain persons, placed in my house for
that purpose,[b] who declared that a plot against his
life was being planned by me at my house. And they
kept this suspicion awake in him, some by sending
letters, some by messengers, others in person, so that
at last, although he certainly had nothing to fear from
me, he thought that he ought to be on his guard
against these people, for fear they might attempt
something in my name. Moreover, Caesar himself,
who by certain persons ignorant of the truth was
thought to be especially offended with me, was at
the gates of the city, with military authority ; his
army was in Italy, and in that army he had given a
command to a brother [c] of that very tribune of the
commons who was my enemy.

XIX. When I saw these things—for there was no 42
secret about them—that the Senate, without which
the State could not stand firm, had been uprooted
from the State ; that the consuls, who ought to
have been leaders of the policy of the State, had
by their own acts brought such policy to an utter
end [d] ; that those persons who had the greatest influence [e] were put up against me at all public meetings—not in real earnest, but still in a way to create

State " ; but, in other passages, it means " Council of State "
(*i.e.* the Senate). See p. 167, note *c*.
   [e] Pompey, Caesar, and Crassus.

formidolose tamen auctores ad perniciem meam, contiones haberi cotidie contra me, vocem pro me ac pro
re publica neminem mittere, intenta signa legionum
existimari cervicibus ac bonis vestris falso, sed putari
tamen, coniuratorum copias veteres et effusam illam
ac dissipatam Catilinae importunam manum novo duce
et insperata commutatione rerum esse renovatam :
haec cum viderem, quid agerem, iudices ? Scio enim
tum non mihi vestrum studium, sed meum[1] prope
43 vestro defuisse. Contenderem contra tribunum pl.
privatus armis ? Vicissent improbos boni, fortes in-
ertes ; interfectus esset is, qui hac una medicina sola
potuit a rei publicae peste depelli ; quid deinde ?
quis reliqua praestaret ? cui denique erat dubium,
quin ille sanguis tribunicius, nullo praesertim publico
consilio profusus, consules ultores et defensores esset
habiturus ? cum quidam in contione dixisset aut mihi
semel pereundum aut bis esse vincendum. Quid erat
bis vincere ? Id profecto, ut, cum amentissimo tribuno pl. si[2] decertassem, cum consulibus ceterisque
44 eius ultoribus dimicarem. Ego vero, vel si pereundum fuisset ac non accipienda plaga mihi sanabilis
illi mortifera, qui imposuisset, semel perire tamen
iudices, maluissem quam bis vincere. Erat enim illa
altera eius modi contentio, ut neque victi neque

---

[1] me prope *Fleckeisen.*
[2] si *added by Wesenburg.*

---

[a] To kill a tribune, whose person was sacrosanct, was an
offence against the *leges sacratae.* See p. 54, note *e.*

alarm—as men who planned my ruin; that such meetings were held every day in which I was attacked; that no one lifted up his voice on my behalf nor in defence of the State; that the standards of the legions were thought to be threatening your lives and property—wrongly, it is true, but it was still believed; that the veteran forces of the conspirators and that dangerous army of Catiline, once dispersed and daunted, had rallied under a new leader and an unexpected turn of events—when I saw all this, what was I to do, gentlemen? for I knew that at that time it was not your zeal that failed me, but perhaps my own that failed yours. Was I, a private individual, 43 to take up arms and make war upon a tribune of the commons? The loyal would have defeated the disloyal, the brave the slothful; he would have been slain who by this sole remedy could have been kept from ruining the country. Again, who would take the responsibility for what happened afterwards? In short, who could doubt that the blood of a tribune,[a] especially if shed without official authority, would find avengers and defenders in the consuls, when a certain person had declared in a meeting that I must either die once or conquer twice? What did he mean by conquering twice? No doubt, if I had fought it out with that frenzied tribune of the commons, I should have to fight with the consuls and the rest of his avengers. But even if I had been doomed to perish, 44 instead of receiving a wound which for me was curable but fatal to the man who had inflicted it, I would still have preferred, gentlemen, to perish once rather than to conquer twice. For the nature of that second struggle [b] was such that, whether vanquished or

[b] With the consuls.

victores rem publicam tenere possemus. Quid, si
in prima contentione vi tribunicia victus in foro cum
multis bonis viris concidissem ? Senatum consules,
credo, vocassent, quem totum de civitate delerant ;
ad arma vocassent,[1] qui ne vestitu quidem defendi
rem publicam sissent ; a tribuno pl. post interitum
meum dissedissent, qui eandem horam meae pestis et
suorum praemiorum esse voluissent.

45   XX. Unum enim[2] mihi restabat illud, quod forsitan
non nemo vir fortis et acris animi magnique dixerit :
" Restitisses, repugnasses, mortem pugnans op-
petisses." De quo te, te, inquam, patria, testor et vos,
penates patriique dei, me vestrarum sedum tem-
plorumque causa, me propter salutem meorum civium,
quae mihi semper fuit mea carior vita, dimicationem
caedemque fugisse. Etenim, si mihi in aliqua nave
cum meis amicis naviganti hoc, iudices, accidisset, ut
multi ex multis locis praedones classibus eam navem
se oppressuros minitarentur, nisi me unum sibi dedi-
dissent, si id vectores negarent ac mecum simul
interire quam me tradere hostibus mallent, iecissem
ipse me potius in profundum, ut ceteros conservarem,
quam illos mei tam cupidos non modo ad certam mor-
46 tem, sed in magnum vitae discrimen adducerem. Cum
vero in hanc rei publicae navem ereptis senatui guber-

---

[1] vocarent *MSS.* : concitassent *Halm.*
[2] enim *MSS.* : etiam *Halm* : autem *Peterson* : tamen *Keil.*

---

[a] For *rem publicam tenere* see Cicero, *De oratore*, i. 38.
[b] See R. G. Nisbet's note, *op. cit.* pp. 193-194.

victors, we should not have been able to preserve the constitution.[a] What would have happened if in the first struggle I had been defeated by a victorious tribune, and had fallen in the Forum with many a loyalist ? No doubt the consuls would have summoned the Senate, which they had uprooted from the constitution ; they would have called the people to arms although they had not allowed the State to be defended even by civil dress ; they would have quarrelled with a tribune of the commons after my death, although they had desired that the moment of my destruction should be that of their reward.

XX. One thing, indeed, was left for me, as perhaps 45 some persons of courage, energy, and high spirit may say : " You should have resisted, you should have fought back, you should have met death fighting." As to this, I call thee to witness, thee, thee, I say, my country, and you, ancestral Gods of our State,[b] that it was for the sake of your abodes and temples, for the salvation of my fellow-citizens, which has ever been dearer to me than life, that I avoided fighting and bloodshed. For if it had happened to me, gentlemen, when sailing in a ship with my friends, that pirates coming in numbers from many quarters threatened to sink that ship with their fleets, unless my friends surrendered me alone to them, if the passengers refused to do so, and preferred death with me to handing me over to the enemy, I would rather have cast myself into the deep to save the others, than I would bring those loving friends, I will not say to certain death, but into great danger of losing their lives. But when this ship of state, after the helm had 46 been torn from the grip of the Senate, tossing about

naculis fluitantem in alto tempestatibus seditionum
ac discordiarum armatae tot classes, nisi ego essem
unus deditus, incursurae viderentur, cum proscriptio,
caedes, direptio denuntiaretur, cum alii me suspicione
periculi sui non defenderent, alii vetere odio bonorum
incitarentur, alii inviderent, alii obstare sibi me arbitrarentur, alii ulcisci dolorem aliquem suum vellent,
alii rem ipsam publicam atque hunc bonorum statum
otiumque odissent et ob hasce causas tot tamque
varias me unum deposcerent, depugnarem potius cum
summo non dicam exitio, sed periculo certe vestro
liberorumque vestrorum quam id, quod omnibus im-
pendebat, unus pro omnibus susciperem ac subirem?

47   XXI. "Victi essent improbi." At cives, at
armis,[1] at ab eo privato, qui sine armis etiam consul
rem publicam conservarat. Sin victi essent boni,
qui superessent? nonne ad servos videtis rem publicam venturam fuisse? An mihi ipsi, ut quidam
putant, fuit mors aequo animo oppetenda? Quid
tum? mortemne fugiebam? An erat res ulla, quam
mihi magis optandam putarem? aut ego illas res
tantas in tanta improborum multitudine cum gere-
bam, non mihi mors, non exsilium[2] ob oculos versabatur? non haec denique a me tum tamquam fata in
ipsa re gerenda canebantur? An erat mihi in tanto

---

[1] at armis *inserted by Heraeus*: at ab eo privato armato
Lambinus.
[2] exsilium *MSS.*: exitium *Kayser, Eberhard, with others,*
after Hotman.

---

[a] According to Halm, this refers to the sentence of *aquae
et ignis interdictio* pronounced against Cicero after he had
voluntarily left Rome. Reid, however, takes it to mean a
regular Sullan proscription.

on the deep and buffeted by the blasts of sedition and discord, seemed likely to be attacked by many an armed fleet, unless I alone were given up ; when pro-scription,[a] bloodshed, and plunder were threatened; when some were prevented from defending me because they suspected it would be dangerous to themselves, others were roused by their inveterate hatred of loyal citizens ; while some envied me, others thought that I was an obstacle to their plans, others wanted to avenge some grievance of their own, others hated the State itself and the security now enjoyed by loyal citizens, and for these many and various reasons demanded that I alone should be sacrificed,—was it my duty to fight it out, I will not say to your utter ruin, but certainly with danger to you and to your children, rather than alone take upon myself and en-dure, on behalf of all, that which was threatening all ?

XXI. " The disloyal would have been conquered."[b] 47 But they were citizens, but it would have been by arms, but it would have been by a private citizen, who even as consul had saved the State without arms ! And if the loyalists had been conquered, who would be left now ? Do you not see that the State would have fallen into a condition of slavery ? Ought I myself, as some think, to have been resigned to death ? Why, was I avoiding death at such a time ? was there anything which I thought more desirable ? Or when I was doing all I did amidst so great a multitude of traitors, was not death, was not exile always before my eyes ? Nay, was it not, in fact, that which, even while I was carrying out that great task, I myself then predicted as my doom ? Was life worth

[b] §§ 47-48 seem based on a stock theme of the rhetorical schools. *Auct. ad Herennium* (L.C.L.), iv. 54 f.

luctu meorum, tanta diiunctione, tanta acerbitate,
tanta spoliatione omnium rerum, quas mihi aut natura
aut fortuna dederat, vita retinenda ? tam eram
rudis, tam ignarus rerum, tam expers consilii aut
ingenii ? nihil audieram, nihil videram, nihil ipse
legendo quaerendoque cognoveram, nesciebam vitae
brevem esse cursum, gloriae sempiternum ; cum esset
omnibus definita mors, optandum esse, ut vita, quae
necessitati deberetur, patriae potius donata quam re-
servata naturae videretur ? nesciebam inter sapien-
tissimos homines hanc contentionem fuisse, ut alii
dicerent animos hominum sensusque morte restingui,
alii autem tum maxime mentes sapientium ac fortium
virorum, cum ex corpore excessissent, sentire ac
vigere ? quorum alterum fugiendum non esse, carere
sensu, alterum etiam optandum, meliore esse sensu.
48 Denique, cum omnia semper ad dignitatem rettulis-
sem nec sine ea quicquam expetendum esse homini in
vita putassem, mortem, quam etiam virgines Athenis
regis, opinor, Erechthei filiae pro patria contemp-
sisse dicuntur, ego vir consularis tantis rebus gestis
timerem ? praesertim cum eius essem civitatis, ex
qua C. Mucius solus in castra Porsennae venisset
eumque interficere proposita sibi morte conatus esset;

---

a Erechtheus had been promised victory in war by an oracle,
if he sacrificed one of his daughters. He offered up Agraulos,
the youngest ; her two sisters also sacrificed themselves, the
three having taken an oath to share each other's fate.

b The story is in Livy, ii. 12.

keeping when my family and friends were plunged
in mourning, when the closest ties were broken,
when my heart was full of bitterness, when I had
been robbed of all the gifts which nature or fortune
had bestowed upon me ? Was I so ill-informed, so
ignorant of the world, was I so destitute of judgment
or ability ? Had I heard nothing, seen nothing,
had I learnt nothing myself by reading and inquiry ?
Did I not know that the duration of life is short,
that of glory everlasting ? that since death is the
appointed lot of all, it were to be wished that the
life, which was forfeit to necessity, should be seen
rather to have been offered as a tribute to my
country than to have been reserved as a debt due
to nature ? did I not know that among the wisest
philosophers this had been a subject of dispute,
some asserting that men's spirits and consciousness
were destroyed by death, others holding that it is
after they have left the body that the minds of wise
men and heroes possess most consciousness and
vigour ? that one of these cannot be avoided — the
loss of consciousness ; that the other was even to be
desired—the enjoyment of a higher consciousness !
Lastly, as I had always made honour my rule of life, 48
and thought that nothing in life was to be sought
for by a man without it, should I, a man of consular
rank, after I had accomplished such great deeds,
be afraid of death, which even young Athenian
maidens, the daughters, I fancy, of King Erechtheus,
are said to have despised for the sake of their
country ? [a] especially as I was a citizen of that
same city from which Gaius Mucius [b] came when
he entered the camp of Porsenna by himself, and,
with death staring him in the face, attempted to

ex qua P. Decius primum pater, post aliquot annos
patria virtute praeditus filius se ac vitam suam in-
structa acie pro salute populi Romani victoriaque
devovisset ; ex qua innumerabiles alii partim adi-
piscendae laudis, partim vitandae turpitudinis causa
mortem in variis bellis aequissimis animis oppetissent ;
in qua civitate ipse meminissem patrem huius M.
Crassi, fortissimum virum, ne videret victorem vivus
inimicum, eadem sibi manu vitam exhausisse, qua
mortem saepe hostibus obtulisset.

49   XXII. Haec ego et multa alia cogitans hoc videbam,
si causam publicam mea mors peremisset, neminem
umquam fore, qui auderet suscipere contra improbos
cives salutem rei publicae.   Itaque, non solum si vi
interissem, sed etiam si morbo exstinctus essem, fore
putabam ut exemplum rei publicae conservandae
mecum simul interiret.   Quis enim umquam me a
senatu populoque Romano tanto omnium bonorum
studio non restituto, quod certe, si essem interfectus,
accidere non potuisset, ullam rei publicae partem cum
sua minima invidia auderet attingere ?   Servavi igitur
rem publicam discessu meo, iudices ; caedem a vobis
liberisque vestris, vastitatem, incendia, rapinas meo
dolore luctuque depuli et unus bis rem publicam
servavi, semel gloria, iterum aerumna mea.   Neque

ᵃ In the Latin War (340-338 B.C.) P. Decius Mus (consul
340 B.C.) was said to have sought Rome's victory by vowing
himself and the enemy to Tellus and the Manes (Livy, viii. 9).
This is probably an anticipation of the *devotio* of his son P.
Decius Mus (consul 295 B.C.) at the battle of Sentinum (Livy,
x. 28), or even of his grandson (consul 279 B.C.), when defeated
by Pyrrhus at Ausculum.   See *Oxford Classical Dictionary*,
pp. 257 (E. T. Salmon), 270 (H. J. Rose).
ᵇ P. Licinius Crassus Lusitanicus (consul 97 B.C.) triumphed

kill him ; from which the elder Publius Decius first, and some years afterwards his son, endowed with the valour of his father, had devoted themselves and their lives, with their armies in battle array, for the safety and victory of the Roman People [a] ; from which countless others, partly to gain glory, partly to avoid disgrace, had met death in various wars with the greatest calmness ; from that city in which I myself remembered how that bravest of men, the father [b] of Marcus Crassus, here present in court, that he might not live to see his enemy victorious, ended his life with the same hand with which he had often dealt death unto his foes.

XXII. Thinking over these and many other matters, I saw that if my death should prove the final destruction of the State, there would never be anyone who would dare to undertake to save it against disloyal citizens. And so, not only if I perished by violence, but even if I died by disease, I thought that an example of how the State might be preserved would perish along with me. For if I had not been recalled by the Senate and People of Rome, amid remarkable enthusiasm of all patriots—and that surely my death would have rendered impossible— who would ever dare to take any part in public affairs when there was the least risk of personal unpopularity ? So then I saved the State by quitting Rome, gentlemen ; by my own grief and sorrow I kept off from you and your children devastation, fire, and rapine ; alone I twice saved the State, once with glory, the second time with misery to myself. For on

in 93 B.C. for victories over Lusitanians and in 90 B.C. served as a *legatus* in the Social War. Proscribed by Marius and Cinna, he committed suicide in 87 B.C.

enim in hoc me hominem esse infitiabor umquam, ut
me optimo fratre, carissimis liberis, fidissima coniuge,
vestro conspectu, patria, hoc honoris gradu sine dolore
caruisse glorier. Quod si fecissem, quod a me beneficium haberetis, cum pro vobis ea, quae mihi essent
vilia, reliquissem ? Hoc meo quidem animo summi
in patriam amoris mei signum esse debet certissimum,
quod, cum abesse ab ea sine summo dolore non pos-
sem, hunc me perpeti quam illam labefactari ab im-
50 probis malui. Memineram, iudices, divinum illum
virum atque ex isdem quibus nos radicibus natum ad
salutem huius imperii, C. Marium, summa senectute,
cum vim[1] prope iustorum armorum profugisset, primo
senile corpus paludibus occultasse demersum, deinde
ad infimorum ac tenuissimorum hominum Mintur-
nensium misericordiam confugisse, inde navigio per-
parvo, cum omnes portus terrasque fugeret, in oras
Africae desertissimas pervenisse. Atque ille vitam
suam, ne inultus esset, ad incertissimam spem et ad
rei publicae fatum[2] reservavit ; ego, qui, quem ad
modum multi in senatu me absente dixerunt, periculo
rei publicae vivebam, quique ob eam causam consularibus litteris de senatus sententia exteris nationibus
commendabar, nonne, si meam vitam deseruissem,
rem publicam prodidissem ? in qua quidem nunc me

---

[1] vim *MSS.*: vi *Halm.*
[2] ratum *MSS.*: fatum *Pantagathus* : et alium reipublicae
statum *Garatoni* : interitum *Peterson.*

---

[a] Or, possibly, "sprang from the same origins as myself."
Cicero may refer to their common birthplace Arpinum, their
origin as *novi homines*, and their equestrian rank.
[b] For the flight of Marius (88 B.C.), see Plutarch, *Marius*,
35-40.
[c] *fatum* is a conjecture ; the meaning may be that if he
returned he would put all the best citizens to death.

this point I will never deny that I am but human ; I will never boast that I felt no grief, when I found myself deprived of the best of brothers, of my dearest children, of my most faithful wife, of the sight of you, of my country, of this my honoured position. If I had felt none, what sacrifice should I have made for you, when for your sakes I had surrendered only what I held cheap ? This, to my mind, ought to be the surest proof of my love for my country, that although I could not live away from it without the most bitter sorrow, I preferred to endure that sorrow rather than to see it overthrown by scoundrels. I remember, 50 gentlemen, how that man, that more than man, Gaius Marius, born in my native place *a* for the salvation of this Empire, in extreme old age, when he had escaped from a violent struggle which was almost a pitched battle, first hid his aged body beneath the waters of a marsh, and afterwards took shelter under the pity of the humblest and poorest of the inhabitants of Minturnae, whence he reached the most desolate coast of Africa in a very small vessel, avoiding all harbours and inhabited lands.*b* Now he, in order that he might not die unavenged, reserved his life for a most uncertain hope and for the ruin of the State *c* ; but I, whose life, as was very often said in the Senate during my absence, was lived at the risk of the State *d* ; I, who for that reason was commended to foreign peoples in consular despatches in accordance with a vote of the Senate, if I had abandoned my life, should I not have betrayed the State ? in which, now that I have been recalled, there lives

d The safety of the State depended on his life, so that it may be said that he lived at the risk of the State ; risk to his life would have brought risk to the State.

restituto vivit mecum simul exemplum fidei publicae.
Quod si immortale retinetur, quis non intellegit immortalem hanc civitatem futuram ?

51 XXIII. Nam externa bella regum, gentium, na-
tionum iam pridem ita exstincta sunt, ut praeclare
cum iis agamus, quos pacatos esse patiamur ; denique
ex bellica victoria non fere quemquam est invidia
civium consecuta ; domesticis malis et audacium
civium consiliis saepe est resistendum, eorumque
periculorum est in re publica retinenda medicina ;
quam omnem, iudices, perdidissetis, si meo interitu
senatui populoque Romano doloris sui de me de-
clarandi potestas esset erepta. Quare moneo vos,
adulescentes, atque hoc meo iure praecipio, qui dignitatem, qui rem publicam, qui gloriam spectatis, ne,
si quae vos aliquando necessitas ad rem publicam
contra improbos cives defendendam vocabit, segniores
sitis et recordatione mei casus a consiliis fortibus
52 refugiatis. Primum non est periculum, ne quis
umquam incidat in eius modi consules, praesertim
si erit iis id, quod debetur, persolutum. Deinde
numquam iam, ut spero, quisquam improbus consilio
et auxilio bonorum se oppugnare rem publicam dicet
illis tacentibus nec armati exercitus terrorem opponet
togatis ; neque erit iusta causa ad portas sedenti
imperatori, quare suum terrorem falso iactari op-

---

a This suggests a belief that Caesar's campaigns of 58
and 57 B.C. had completed the conquest of Gaul. But see
De prov. cons. 34.

b The thought is that, although foreign wars have ceased,
and successful generals rarely cause animosity, men like
102

in my person an example of public good faith. And
if this example be preserved for ever, who can doubt
that this State will be immortal ?

XXIII. For wars abroad with kings, peoples, and 51
tribes have long ago so completely ceased,[a] that we
get on brilliantly with such as we treat as pacified
dependants. Moreover, from victory in war, hardly
anyone has incurred the hatred of his fellow-citizens.[b]
Internal troubles, on the other hand, and the designs
of aggressive citizens must often be opposed, and a
remedy for such dangers must be preserved in the
State ; and that, gentlemen, you would have lost
entirely, if my death had deprived the Senate and
the People of Rome of the power of declaring their
sorrow for my misfortune. Wherefore I warn you,
young Romans—and I have the right to give you this
advice—you who look for an honourable position, for
the welfare of the State, and for glory, do not hesitate or, from the recollection of my misfortune,
shrink from adopting a resolute policy, should
necessity ever call upon you to defend the State
against disloyal citizens. In the first place, there is 52
no fear of anyone ever again meeting with such consuls [c]—especially if that which is their due shall be
paid to them in full. In the next place, never again,
as I hope, will any scoundrel boast that he is attacking the State by the advice and with the help of
loyal citizens,[d] while they remain silent, nor confront
peaceable citizens with the terror of an armed force ;
nor will a commander [e] encamped at the gates of Rome
have any just reason for allowing the terror of his

Cicero who have saved the State from internal disorder will
always be needed.   [c] As Gabinius and Piso.
    [d] Pompey, Caesar, and Crassus.   [e] Caesar.

ponique patiatur. Numquam denique[1] erit tam
oppressus senatus, ut ei ne supplicandi quidem ac
lugendi sit potestas, tam captus equester ordo, ut
equites Romani a consule relegentur. Quae cum
omnia atque etiam multo alia maiora, quae consulto
praetereo, accidissent, videtis me tamen in meam
pristinam dignitatem brevi tempore doloris interiecto
rei publicae voce esse revocatum.

53   XXIV. Sed ut revertar ad illud, quod mihi in hac
omni est oratione propositum, omnibus malis illo anno
scelere consulum rem publicam esse confectam, primum illo ipso die, qui mihi funestus fuit, omnibus
bonis luctuosus, cum ego me e complexu patriae con-
spectuque vestro eripuissem et metu vestri periculi,
non mei, furori hominis, sceleri, perfidiae, telis minis-
que cessissem patriamque, quae mihi erat carissima,
propter ipsius patriae caritatem reliquissem, cum
meum illum casum tam horribilem, tam gravem, tam
repentinum non solum homines, sed tecta urbis ac
templa lugerent, nemo vestrum forum, nemo curiam,
nemo lucem aspicere vellet : illo, inquam, ipso die—
die dico, immo hora atque etiam puncto temporis
eodem mihi reique publicae pernicies, Gabinio et
Pisoni provincia rogata est. Pro dei immortales

---

[1] enim *MSS.* : denique *Garatoni* : autem *Peterson*.

[a] Cicero was in exile from about 20 March 58 to 4 September 57 B.C.
[b] Clodius' bill, *de capite civis Romani*, interdicted from
fire and water anyone who had put to death, or should
thereafter put to death, a Roman citizen uncondemned.
[c] This was contrary to the *lex Sempronia de provinciis
consularibus* of C. Gracchus (tribune Dec. 124–Dec. 122 B.C.),
which enacted that before the consuls were elected the Senate

name to be falsely flung in our faces. Finally, never shall the Senate be so crushed as not to have the right of entreating and showing its grief, never shall the Equestrian Order be so degraded that Roman Knights can be banished by a consul. Although these things and others of much greater importance, which I purposely pass over, did happen, you see me, after a brief period of sorrow,[a] recalled by the voice of the State to my former honourable position.

XXIV. But to turn to the object which I have set 53 before me throughout the whole of my speech,—to show, I mean, that in that year the State was ruined by all manner of evils through the wickedness of the consuls : first of all, on that very day, fatal to me and full of sorrow for all loyal citizens, when I had torn myself away from the arms of my country and from the sight of you ; when, through fear of danger to you, not to myself, I had yielded to a man's madness, to his crime, perfidy, arms and threats, and had left my country, which was dearer than anything else to me, for the very reason that it was so dear ; when not only men, but the houses and temples of the city were lamenting my disgrace, so horrible, so overwhelming, and so unexpected ; when none of you had any wish to look upon the Forum or the Senate House, or to face the light of day ; on that very day—do I say day ? nay rather, at the same hour, and at the same moment, laws were put to the vote to ruin myself[b] and the State, and to assign provinces to Piso and Gabinius.[c] Immortal Gods,

should assign the provinces they were to govern at the end of their year of office. Under Clodius' *lex de provinciis* Piso acquired Macedonia, Gabinius Syria, after first choosing Cilicia.

custodes et conservatores huius urbis atque imperii,
quaenam illa in re publica monstra, quae scelera vidistis ! Civis erat expulsus is, qui rem publicam ex
senatus auctoritate cum omnibus bonis defenderat, et
expulsus non alio aliquo, sed eo ipso crimine. Erat
autem expulsus sine iudicio, vi, lapidibus, ferro,
servitio denique concitato ; lex erat lata vastato ac
relicto foro et sicariis servisque tradito, et ea lex,
quae ut ne ferretur, senatus fuerat veste mutata.
54 Hac tanta perturbatione civitatis ne noctem quidem
consules inter meum interitum[1] et suam praedam
interesse passi sunt ; statim me perculso ad meum
sanguinem hauriendum et spirante etiam re publica
ad eius spolia detrahenda advolaverunt. Omitto
gratulationes, epulas, partitionem aerarii, beneficia,
spem, promissa, praedam, laetitiam paucorum in
luctu omnium ; vexabatur uxor mea, liberi ad necem
quaerebantur, gener, et Piso gener, a Pisonis consulis pedibus supplex reiciebatur, bona diripieban-
tur eaque ad consules deferebantur, domus ardebat
in Palatio ; consules epulabantur. Quodsi meis in-
commodis laetabantur, urbis tamen periculo com-
moverentur.
55   XXV. Sed ut a mea causa iam recedam, reliquas

---

[1] *Supplied by M. Seyffert.*

---

[a] To provide Piso and Gabinius with grants for expenses
in their provinces.

[b] After Clodius had pulled down Cicero's house on the
Palatine, Terentia took refuge with her sister Fabia, a Vestal,
but was seized and compelled to give security for handing
over any of her husband's ready money which she had in her
possession.

[c] C. Calpurnius Piso Frugi, who tried to conciliate his
kinsman the consul Piso, preferred watching over Cicero's

guardians and saviours of this city and Empire, what abominable atrocities, what crimes did ye then behold in the State ! A citizen had been driven out,—a citizen who had defended the State under a resolution of the Senate and in concert with all loyal citizens, driven out on that charge alone, and on no other. He had, also, been driven out without a trial, by violence, by stones, by the sword, yes, even by inciting slaves to join the tumult. A law had been passed, after the Forum had been ravaged and abandoned, and surrendered to assassins and slaves ; and to prevent that law being passed the Senate had put on mourning. While the State was in such con- 54 fusion, the consuls did not allow even a single night to intervene between my overthrow and the seizure of their booty. The moment I was struck down they flew to drink my blood, and while the State was still breathing, to strip it of their spoil. I say nothing about the giving of thanks, the banquets, the sharing out of public money,[a] favours, hopes and promises, plunder, the joy of a few amidst marks of universal sorrow. My wife was persecuted [b] ; my children's lives were threatened ; my son-in-law,[c] and that son-in-law a Piso, was driven away from the feet of Piso the consul, where he lay a suppliant ; my property was seized, and that also was carried off to the consuls ; my house on the Palatine was in flames—and the consuls were feasting. Yet even if they rejoiced at my disasters, they ought to have been affected by the peril of the State.

XXV. But to pass now from my own case, call to 55

interests in Rome to going to a province as quaestor. He married (63 B.C.) Tullia, Cicero's daughter, and died in 57 B.C. See p. 60, note a.

illius anni pestes recordamini (sic enim facillime per-
spicietis, quantam vim omnium remediorum a magistratibus proximis res publica desiderarit), legum
multitudinem cum earum, quae latae sunt, tum vero
quae promulgatae fuerunt. Nam latae quidem sunt
consulibus illis—tacentibus dicam ? immo vero etiam
adprobantibus, ut censoria notio et gravissimum iudicium sanctissimi magistratus de re publica tolleretur,
ut collegia non modo illa vetera contra senatus consultum restituerentur, sed ab uno gladiatore in-
numerabilia alia nova conscriberentur, ut remissis senis
et trientibus quinta prope pars vectigalium tolleretur,
ut Gabinio pro illa sua Cilicia, quam sibi, si rem
publicam prodidisset, pactus erat, Syria daretur et
uni helluoni bis de eadem re deliberandi et rogata
lege potestas per[1] novam legem fieret provinciae commutandae.

56   XXVI. Mitto eam legem, quae omnia iura re-
ligionum, auspiciorum, potestatum, omnes leges, quae
sunt de iure et de tempore legum rogandarum, una

———

[1] *Halm fills a gap in the* MS. *by inserting* lege potestas per
nov . . . *See p. 109, note d.*

———

[a] According to Asconius (*In Pisonianam*, p. 8 Clark), the
law of Clodius prohibited censors from expelling senators
except after a joint inquiry and condemnation. Cicero,
therefore, exaggerates, because the law did not abolish, but
restricted, the *censoria notio*. According to Dio Cassius
(xl. 57), the law was repealed in 52 B.C. by Q. Caecilius
Metellus Scipio (consul), Pompey's father-in-law.

[b] See § 34 ; p. 79, note *d*.

[c] By his *lex frumentaria* C. Gracchus issued a monthly
ration of corn, of unknown amount, at 6⅓ asses a *modius*
(peck). This concession was abolished by Sulla, but restored
to some extent by the *lex Terentia Cassia* (73 B.C.). M. Cato
(tribune 62 B.C.) issued a monthly ration of five *modii* to some
320,000 applicants at less than half the normal price, the

mind the other iniquities of that year; for by so doing you will most readily perceive what a world of remedies of all kinds the State craved from the magistrates of the next year—a multitude of laws, both those that were passed, and those that were only put forward. For laws were passed while those consuls were—shall I say silent? nay rather openly manifested their approval—to the effect that the censors' investigation of character, that is to say, the verdict, so authoritative, of a most hallowed magistracy, should be removed from the constitution [a]; that not only should those former clubs be restored in defiance of a decree of the Senate,[b] but that one single swordster should be able to enrol as many other new clubs as he pleased; that by remission of the six and one-third asses the revenues should be diminished by nearly a fifth [c]; that Syria should be given to Gabinius instead of his proper province Cilicia, which he had bargained for as the price of betraying the State, and that a single bloodsucker should be given the power of deliberating twice about the same thing, and after the passing of one law he should by a new law have the power of changing his province.[d]

XXVI. I pass over that law,[e] which by a single 56 proposal abolished all the rules of law about ritual observances, the auspices, and the powers of the magistrates, and all the laws which have reference to the legal forms of proposing laws and the time for

remission of which by Clodius cost about 70,000,000 sesterces a year.

[d] In the mss. there is a gap after *rogata* with room for twenty letters, after which came *am legem fieret provinciae commutandae*. The insertion is due to Halm. The first law is that which assigned Cilicia to Gabinius.

[e] See pp. 13, 22, 78, 79 and 317 ff.

rogatione delevit, mitto omnem domesticam labem ;
etiam exteras nationes illius anni furore conquassatas
videbamus. Lege tribunicia Matris Magnae Pessinun-
tius ille sacerdos expulsus et spoliatus sacerdotio est
fanumque sanctissimarum atque antiquissimarum re-
ligionum venditum pecunia grandi Brogitaro, impuro
homini atque indigno illa religione, praesertim cum
eam sibi ille non colendi, sed violandi causa ad-
petisset ; appellati reges a populo, qui id numquam ne
a senatu quidem postulassent, reducti exsules Byzantium condemnati tum, cum indemnati cives e civitate
57 eiciebantur. Rex Ptolemaeus, qui si nondum erat
ipse a senatu socius appellatus, erat tamen frater
eius regis, qui cum esset in eadem causa, iam erat
a senatu honorem istum consecutus, erat eodem
genere eisdemque maioribus, eadem vetustate
societatis, denique erat rex si nondum socius, at
non hostis ; pacatus, quietus, fretus imperio populi
Romani regno paterno atque avito regali otio per-
fruebatur— : de hoc nihil cogitante, nihil suspicante
eisdem operis suffragium ferentibus est rogatum, ut
sedens cum purpura et sceptro et illis insignibus regiis

---

^a In Galatia where Cybele was worshipped, under the
name of Agdistis.
^b Son-in-law of King Deiotarus of Galatia. See F. E.
Adcock, " Lesser Armenia and Galatia after Pompey's
Settlement of the East," *J.R.S.* xxvii, pp. 14-17.
^c Cicero and Cato.
^d The independent ruler of Cyprus, the younger of the two
illegitimate sons of Ptolemy Lathyrus, king of Egypt, who
died in 80 B.C. Since he refused to purchase recognition
from the Triumvirs, M. Cato was sent in 58 B.C. to dethrone
him. See pp. 15-16.
^e Ptolemy Auletes, the elder of the two illegitimate sons of
Ptolemy Lathyrus, referred to in the previous note. Since

doing so. I pass over all that we suffered at home : we saw even foreign peoples shaken by the frenzy of that year. By a tribunician law, the priest of the Great Mother at Pessinus [a] was expelled from his temple and deprived of his priesthood, and a sanctuary of most holy and most ancient religious cults was sold for a large sum to Brogitarus,[b] a most immoral man, and unworthy of that sacred office, especially as he had desired it, not for the purpose of worship, but of profanation. Persons who had never asked even the Senate to give them such titles, were called kings by the People. Condemned exiles were brought back to Byzantium, at a time when citizens who had not been condemned were being driven from Rome.[c] King Ptolemy,[d] who if he himself had not yet 57 been declared our ally by the Senate, was yet the brother of that king [e] who, though his circumstances were the same, had already obtained that honour from the Senate, who belonged to the same race, had the same ancestors, and was united to us by the same long-standing ties. In short, he was a king, and if not yet an ally, was at least not an enemy. Living in peace and quietness under the protection of the rule of the Roman People, he was enjoying to the full his paternal and ancestral realm in kingly ease. While he was ignorant of what was afoot and suspected nothing, a proposal was brought forward and voted for by these same hirelings, that Ptolemy, seated on his throne, arrayed in purple, with sceptre in hand and wearing his royal diadem, should be

80 B.C. his title to the throne of Egypt had been uncertain, but won official recognition from Rome in 59 B.C., when, in return for a promise of 6000 talents, his status as king was confirmed by Caesar and his partners. See p. 27.

111

CICERO

praeconi publico subiceretur et imperante populo
Romano, qui etiam bello victis regibus regna reddere
consuevit, rex amicus nulla iniuria commemorata,
nullis rebus repetitis cum bonis omnibus publicaretur.

58   XXVII. Multa acerba, multa turpia, multa turbulenta habuit ille annus ; tamen illi sceleri, quod in me
illorum immanitas edidit, haud scio an recte hoc
proximum esse dicamus.   Antiochum Magnum illum
maiores nostri magna belli contentione terra marique
superatum intra montem Taurum regnare iusserunt,
Asiam, qua illum multarunt, Attalo, ut is regnaret in
ea, condonaverunt ; cum Armeniorum rege Tigrane
grave bellum nuper ipsi diuturnumque gessimus, cum
ille iniuriis in socios nostros inferendis bello prope
nos lacessisset.   Hic et ipse per se vehemens fuit et
acerrimum hostem huius imperii Mithridatem pulsum
Ponto opibus suis regnoque defendit et a L. Lucullo,
summo viro atque imperatore, pulsus animo tamen
hostili cum reliquis suis copiis in pristina mente
mansit.   Hunc Cn. Pompeius cum in suis castris
supplicem abiectum vidisset, erexit atque insigne
regium, quod ille de suo capite abiecerat, reposuit et
certis rebus imperatis regnare iussit nec minus et

ª His fleets were defeated off Corycus (191 B.C.) and at
Side and Myonnesus (190 B.C.).   He himself was defeated
at   Thermopylae   (191 B.C.) and at Magnesia (probably
January 189 B.C.).
    ᵇ i.e., to retire from all Asia Minor north and west of
Mount Taurus.
    ᶜ A mistake for Eumenes II of Pergamum (197–160 B.C.).
    ᵈ Tigranes I (c. 94–66 B.C.) was defeated by L. Lucullus
near his capital Tigranocerta on 6 October 69 B.C.

112

delivered over to a public auctioneer ; and that by the sovereign will of the Roman People, which has often restored their kingdoms even to kings who have been defeated in war, a friendly king, against whom no charge of wrong-doing had been brought, nor demand for satisfaction made, should, together with all his goods, be put up for public auction.

XXVII. That year was marked by many cruel, 58 many disgraceful, many revolutionary acts. Yet I am inclined to think we may fairly say that the crime which follows comes nearest to that crime, which their barbarism perpetrated against myself. Antiochus the Great, when after an obstinate resistance he had been defeated both by land and sea,[a] was directed by our ancestors to be king " within Mount Taurus " [b] ; Asia, which they took from him as a punishment, was presented to Attalus [c] to form part of his kingdom. We ourselves lately carried on a long and serious war against Tigranes, king of Armenia,[d] since, by inflicting injuries on our allies, he had virtually provoked us with war. He was both a vigorous enemy himself and he used all the resources of his kingdom to defend Mithridates, a most bitter foe of this Empire, after Mithridates had been driven from Pontus. And Tigranes, although he had been repulsed by that illustrious man and commander, Lucius Lucullus, nevertheless, together with the remains of his forces, still showed the same spirit of hostility and his old resolution. Gnaeus Pompeius, however, when he saw him in his camp a suppliant at his feet, raised him up, and replaced the royal diadem which Tigranes had cast from his head ; and, having imposed certain conditions, bade him continue to be king, thinking that it would be no less glorious both for himself and

113

sibi et huic imperio gloriosum putavit constitutum
59 a se regem quam constrictum videri. Rex igitur
Armenius,[1] qui et ipse hostis fuit populi Romani et
acerrimum hostem in regnum recepit, qui conflixit,
qui signa contulit, qui de imperio paene certavit,
regnat hodie et amicitiae nomen ac societatis, quod
armis violarat, id precibus est consecutus ; ille Cy-
prius miser, qui semper amicus, semper socius fuit,
de quo nulla umquam suspicio durior aut ad senatum
aut ad imperatores allata nostros est, vivus, ut aiunt,
est et videns cum victu ac vestitu suo publicatus. En,
cur ceteri reges stabilem esse suam fortunam arbi-
trentur, cum hoc illius funesti anni prodito exemplo
videant per tribunum aliquem et sescentas operas se
fortunis spoliari et regno omni posse nudari !
60 XXVIII. At etiam eo negotio M. Catonis splendorem maculare voluerunt ignari, quid gravitas,
quid integritas, quid magnitudo animi, quid
denique virtus valeret, quae in tempestate saeva
quieta est et lucet in tenebris et pulsa loco manet
tamen atque haeret in patria splendetque per sese
semper neque alienis umquam sordibus obsolescit.
Non illi ornandum M. Catonem, sed relegandum,
nec illi committendum illud negotium, sed imponen-

---

[1] *After* videri *the Paris ms. has a gap of about fifteen letters,
followed by the unintelligible* tulit, gessit. *Various inser-
tions are suggested, among them* rex igitur Armenius *Halm* :
is igitur qui bellum intulit, qui lacessivit *Koch* : qui bellum
sociis intulit, gessit *Maehly.*

---

[a] Tigranes, who surrendered to Pompey in 66 B.C., was
left as a dependent king with reduced dominions.
[b] Halm's conjecture is translated.
[c] Literally, " with all he had to live on or to wear." The
phrase depends for its effects on alliteration, like the pro-

this Empire that men should see that he had been
set up on his throne by him rather than thrown into
fetters.[a] So then this king of Armenia,[b] who was not 59
only himself an enemy of the Roman People, but had
received into his kingdom our bitterest foe, who had
fought against us, engaged in close combat with us,
who had all but struggled with us for power, reigns
at the present day, and obtained by entreaty that
title of Friend and Ally which he had forfeited by
war. But that unfortunate king of Cyprus, who had
always been our Friend and Ally, concerning whom
no serious suspicion had ever reached the Senate or
our commanders, saw himself, with his own living
eyes, as they say, put up to auction together with
every single thing he had in the world.[c] Other kings,
of course, should have good reason to regard their
position as secure, when, with the precedent of that
disastrous year before their eyes, they see some tribune or other and countless hirelings able to deprive
them of their thrones and all they possess !

XXVIII. Moreover their intention in this business 60
was to tarnish the illustrious name of Marcus Cato,
ignorant as they were what strength there is in
character, in integrity, in greatness of soul, and in
that virtue which remains unshaken by violent
storms ; which shines in darkness ; which though dis-
lodged still abides and remains unmoved from its true
home ; is radiant always by its own light and is never
sullied by the baseness of others. They did not propose to honour Cato, but to banish him ; not to entrust him with a mission, but to impose a task upon

verbial *vivus et videns*, used of a person who meets with some
calamity, which, though in full vigour and clearly seeing
what is coming, he cannot avert.

dum putaverunt, qui in contione palam dixerint linguam se evellisse M. Catoni, quae semper contra extraordinarias potestates libera fuisset. Sentient, ut spero, brevi tempore manere libertatem illam atque hoc etiam, si fieri potuerit, esse maiorem, quod cum consulibus illis M. Cato, etiam cum iam desperasset aliquid auctoritate sua profici posse, tamen voce ipsa ac dolore pugnavit et post meum discessum iis Pisonem verbis flens meum et rei publicae casum vexavit, ut illum hominem perditissimum atque im-
61 pudentissimum paene iam provinciae paeniteret. Cur igitur rogationi paruit ? Quasi vero ille non in alias quoque leges, quas iniuste rogatas putaret, iam ante iurarit ! Non offert se ille istis temeritatibus, ut, cum rei publicae nihil prosit, se civi rem publicam privet. Consule me cum esset designatus tribunus pl., obtulit in discrimen vitam suam ; dixit eam sententiam, cuius invidiam capitis periculo sibi praestandam videbat ; dixit vehementer, egit acriter, ea, quae sensit, prae se tulit, dux, auctor, actor rerum illarum fuit, non quo periculum suum non videret, sed in tanta rei publicae tempestate nihil sibi nisi de patriae periculis cogitandum putabat.
62   XXIX. Consecutus est ipsius tribunatus. Quid ego de singulari magnitudine animi eius ac de incredibili virtute dicam ? Meministis illum diem, cum templo

---

a In April 58 B.C. Cato was sent (*quaestor cum iure praetorio*, Vell. Pat. ii. 45) to take over Cyprus from the dispossessed Ptolemy and to restore Byzantine exiles, an unusual but legitimate method of appointment to a foreign command. See p. 16.

b In 59 B.C. he was persuaded by Cicero to take an oath of obedience to Caesar's first agrarian law.

c His speech on 5 Dec. 63 B.C. (Sallust, *Cat.* 52) was virtually responsible for the execution of Catiline's associates.

him ; since they openly boasted in public that they
had plucked out Cato's tongue, which had always
freely denounced extraordinary commissions.[a] They
will feel, and I hope shortly, that our freedom of
speech still remains ; and even that it is all the
greater, if possible, because Cato, even when he no
longer had any hope that anything could be accomplished by his personal influence, nevertheless fought
against those consuls even with his outspoken indignation, and after my departure, deploring my misfortune and that of the State, he harassed Piso with
such language that that most abandoned and shameless villain almost regretted that he had been given
a province. Why then did he obey this resolution ? 61
As if he had not already taken an oath to obey other
laws, which he considered had been unjustly brought
forward ! [b] He is not prepared, by sacrificing himself
to their reckless designs, to rob the State of a citizen
like himself, when his loss is of no advantage to the
State. During my consulship, when he was tribune-
elect of the commons, he exposed his life to danger ;
he expressed that opinion, for the unpopularity of
which he saw that he would have to hold himself responsible at the risk of his life ; he put vehemence
into his words, energy into his actions ; he openly
expressed what he felt ; he was the leader, the insti-
gator, the authority for those measures [c] ; not that
he did not see the danger which threatened him, but
he thought, that when such a storm was raging in the
State, nothing should occupy his mind except the
dangers of his country.

XXIX. His tribunate followed. What shall I say 62
of his remarkable greatness of soul and amazing
courage ? You remember that day, when a temple

117

a collega occupato, nobis omnibus de vita eius viri
et civis timentibus ipse animo firmissimo venit in
templum et clamorem hominum auctoritate, impetum
improborum virtute sedavit. Adiit tum periculum,
sed adiit ob eam causam, quae quanta fuerit, iam
mihi dicere non est necesse. At si isti Cypriae
rogationi sceleratissimae non paruisset, haereret illa
nihilo minus rei publicae turpitudo ; regno enim iam
publicato de ipso Catone erat nominatim rogatum.
Quod ille si repudiasset, dubitatis, quin ei vis esset
allata, cum omnia acta illius anni per unum illum
63 labefactari viderentur ? Atque etiam hoc videbat,
quoniam illa in re publica macula regni publicati
maneret, quam nemo iam posset eluere, quod ex malis
boni posset in rem publicam pervenire, id utilius esse
per se conservari quam per alios.[1] Atque ille etiamsi
alia quapiam vi expelleretur illis temporibus ex hac
urbe, facile pateretur. Etenim, qui superiore anno
senatu caruisset, quo si tum veniret me tamen

---

[1] *It is suggested that a verb has been lost, opposed to* conservari. *Among those suggested are* dissipari, alienari, amitti,
diripi. *The* MS. *reading is translated.*

---

[a] Early in January 62 B.C. Q. Metellus Nepos (tribune),
in collusion with Caesar (praetor), attempted to propose that
Pompey be recalled and be given the command against
Catiline. Cato made his way to the Temple of Castor and
Pollux where Metellus and Caesar had established themselves, and vetoed the bill. The scene is described by Plutarch, *Cato Minor*, 27-29.

[b] Cicero says this for fear of offending Pompey.

[c] Clodius' law annexing Cyprus was passed in March ;

had been occupied by a colleague, and we were all afraid for the life of that great man and great citizen, how he himself proceeded to the temple [a] with the most steadfast spirit, and calmed the shouts of the people by his authority, the vehemence of the disloyal by his courage. At that time he braved danger, and he braved it for a most important reason which I need not now state.[b] But if he had not obeyed that infamous bill concerning Cyprus, that disgrace would none the less cling to the State ; for it was not until the kingdom had been confiscated [c] that a motion was brought forward in which Cato himself was expressly mentioned. But, if he had refused the commission, have you any doubt that violence would have been done to him, since it would have looked as if, by the action of that one man, all the measures of that year were being rendered ineffective ? Be- 63 sides, he felt, that since the confiscation of this kingdom would leave a lasting stain upon the State which no one could now wash out, it would be better that the advantage which the State might obtain from this evil should be secured by himself rather than by others.[d] And even if at that time he had been driven out of this city by any other form of violence, he would easily have resigned himself to it. For could a man who, in the preceding year,[e] had not attended the meetings of the Senate, although, if he had done so then, he might at least have

his law commissioning Cato was promulgated early in April and passed on 24 April 58 B.C.

[d] The Treasury was enriched by 7000 talents. The shrewd business-man in Cato saw that it would be more satisfactory for an honest man to carry out the appropriation of Ptolemy's kingdom.

[e] 59 B.C., the year of Caesar's consulship.

socium suorum in re publica consiliorum videre posset,
is aequo animo tum me expulso et meo nomine cum
universo senatu, tum sententia sua condemnata in
hac urbe esse posset ? Ille vero eidem tempori cui
nos, eiusdem furori, eisdem consulibus, eisdem mi-
nis, insidiis, periculis cessit. Luctum nos hausimus
maiorem, dolorem ille animi non minorem.

64   XXX. His de tot tantisque iniuriis in socios, in reges,
in civitates liberas consulum querella esse debuit ; in
eius magistratus tutela reges atque exterae nationes
semper fuerunt. Ecquae vox umquam est audita
consulum ? Quamquam quis audiret, si maxime queri
vellent ? De Cyprio rege quererentur, qui me civem
nullo meo crimine patriae nomine laborantem non
modo stantem non defenderunt, sed ne iacentem
quidem protexerunt ? Cesseram, si alienam a me
plebem fuisse voltis, quae non fuit, invidiae ; si com-
moveri omnia videbantur, tempori ; si vis suberat,
armis ; si societas magistratuum, pactioni ; si peri-
65 culum civium, rei publicae. Cur, cum de capite civis
(non disputo, cuius modi civis) et de bonis proscriptio
ferretur, cum et sacratis legibus et xii tabulis sanctum
esset, ut ne cui privilegium inrogari liceret neve de

---

^a His vote in the Senate in favour of the execution of the
Catilinarian conspirators, which, according to Cicero, was
condemned by the exile of Cicero himself because of that
execution.

^b The inhabitants of Pessinus, Ptolemy king of Cyprus,
and Byzantium.

^c Because the Senate was powerless and the populace over-
awed by Clodius.

^d The bargain between Clodius and the consuls Piso and
Gabinius.

^e See § 16 (*leges sacratae*). The Twelve Tables, mostly a
codification of existing practice, were drawn up by two special commissions in 451–450 B.C.

found in me a supporter of his political views,—
could he then have remained calmly in Rome, after
I had been banished from it, and in my person both
the entire Senate and his own vote [a] had been condemned ? But he certainly yielded to the same
circumstances as I did—to the madness of the same
tribune, to the same consuls, to the same threats, to
the same intrigues, to the same dangers. I drank
more deeply of sorrow, but his heart was as sore as
mine.

XXX. It was the consuls' duty to have complained 64
of these many and great wrongs inflicted upon allies,
upon kings, upon free states [b] ; for they are the magistrates under whose protection kings and foreign
peoples have always been placed. Did the consuls
ever utter a word on the subject ? And yet who
would have listened to them, [c] if they had chosen to
complain ever so much ! Were they to make a complaint about the king of Cyprus, the very men who,
far from defending me, a citizen with no accusation
against me, suffering in the name of my country, while
I still held my ground, did not even protect me when
I was prostrate ? If you maintain that the commons
were hostile to me, which they were not, then I yielded
to unpopularity ; to circumstances, if a general disturbance seemed imminent ; to force of arms, if
violence was impending ; to a bargain, if there was
a partnership between magistrates [d] ; to love for
my country, if danger threatened its people. Why, 65
then, when a motion was brought in concerning a
man's rights as a citizen—I do not discuss what sort
of citizen—and the forfeiture of his property, in spite
of the *leges sacratae* and the Twelve Tables, [e] which
expressly forbid a resolution being passed concerning

121

capite nisi comitiis centuriatis rogari, nulla vox est
audita consulum, constitutumque est illo anno, quantum in illis duabus huius imperii pestibus fuit, iure
posse per operas concitatas quemvis civem nominatim tribuni pl. concilio ex civitate exturbari?

66 Quae vero promulgata illo anno fuerint, quae promissa multis, quae conscripta, quae sperata, quae
cogitata, quid dicam? Qui locus orbi terrae iam non
erat alicui destinatus? Cuius negoti publici cogitari,
optari, fingi curatio potuit, quae non esset attributa
atque discripta? quod genus imperii aut quae provincia, quae ratio aut flandae aut conflandae pecuniae
non reperiebatur? quae regio orave terrarum erat
latior, in qua non regnum aliquod statueretur? quis
autem rex erat, qui illo anno non aut emendum sibi,
quod non habebat, aut redimendum, quod habebat,
arbitraretur? quis provinciam, quis pecuniam, quis
legationem a senatu petebat? Damnatis de vi re-

---

[a] Such a law was called a *privilegium*. See Cicero, *De
domo sua*, 43: " vetant leges sacratae, vetant XII tabulae,
leges privatis hominibus inrogari ; id est privilegium " (an
enactment in favour of or against an individual).

[b] Cicero here refers to the *concilium plebis tributum* and
claims that no citizen could legally forfeit his *caput* except by
order of the *comitia centuriata*. The distinction between
comitia (Assembly of the whole People) and *concilium*
(Meeting of a section) is precisely expressed by Laelius Felix,
a jurist of Hadrian's reign, in Aulus Gellius, xv. 27. 4. See
also Livy, xxxix. 15.

[c] *Flare* is to coin money officially. *Conflare* is often used
by Cicero of any irregular or underhand procedure directed
to the detriment of others, *e.g.*, in *Pro Cluentio*, 18 *conflare
malum* = " to plot mischief." See Reid's note on Cicero,
Pro Sulla, 13.

an individual [a] or any decision being made regarding
a man's rights as a citizen except in the *comitia centuriata*—why, I ask, did the consuls never utter a
word, and why was a rule established during this
year, so far as it was possible under those two curses
of this Empire, that any citizen could be expressly
named and legally driven out of the State by gangs
of hirelings at a Meeting [b] summoned by a tribune
of the commons ?

But why need I speak of all the proposals that 66
were put forward during that year, of the promises
made to many, of the written engagements, of the
hopes and plans that were entertained ? What spot
in the world was not already allotted to some one ?
What public business could be thought of, desired or
dreamed of, where the management had not been
already assigned and parcelled out ? what sort of
command, what sphere of activity, what method of
coining or forging money [c] was not discovered?
what district or country in the world of any size [d]
was not made the seat of some kingdom ? and what
king was there who in that year did not feel himself
obliged to buy for himself what he had not, or to buy
back what he had ? Who ever asked the Senate
for a province, or money,[e] or a staff-appointment ? [f]
There had been convictions for violence [g] : restitu-

[d] Kock suggests *latentior* (" more out of the way ") for
the MSS. *latior*.

[e] A grant towards the expenses of a governorship.

[f] Or, possibly, a *legatio libera*, a privilege enabling
senators to visit provinces as state ambassadors. Cicero in
63 B.C. limited this privilege to one year and Caesar imposed
further restrictions.

[g] Catilinarians exiled in 62 B.C. under the *lex Plautia de vi.*
See Sallust, *Cat.* 31 ; Cicero, *Pro Flacco,* 96 ; and p. 32, note *c.*

stitutio, consulatus petitio ipsi illi populari sacerdoti
comparabatur. Haec gemebant boni, sperabant improbi, agebat tribunus pl., consules adiuvabant.

67 XXXI. Hic aliquando, serius, quam ipse vellet,
Cn. Pompeius invitissimis iis, qui mentem optimi ac
fortissimi viri suis[1] consiliis fictisque terroribus a
defensione meae salutis averterant, excitavit illam
suam non sopitam, sed suspicione aliqua retardatam
consuetudinem rei publicae bene gerendae. Non est
passus ille vir, qui sceleratissimos cives, qui acerrimos
hostes, qui maximas nationes, qui reges, qui gentes
feras atque inauditas, qui praedonum infinitam manum, qui etiam servitia virtute victoriaque domuisset,
qui omnibus bellis terra marique compressis imperium populi Romani orbis terrarum terminis de-
finisset, rem publicam everti scelere paucorum, quam
ipse non solum consiliis, sed etiam sanguine suo saepe
servasset ; accessit ad causam publicam, restitit
auctoritate sua reliquis rebus, questus est de praeter-
itis. Fieri quaedam ad meliorem spem inclinatio visa
68 est. Decrevit senatus frequens de meo reditu Kalen-
dis Iuniis dissentiente nullo referente L. Ninnio, cuius

---

[1] suis *MSS.* : saevis *Reid* : stultis *Holden* : insanis *Clark.*

[a] Clodius ; a reference to the affair of the Bona Dea.
[b] The Marian remnants under Cn. Papirius Carbo, Cn.
Domitius Ahenobarbus, and Q. Sertorius, were defeated by
Pompey in Sicily, Africa, and Spain respectively. More-
over, the Senate had to invoke the aid of Pompey to crush
M. Aemilius Lepidus, the disloyal consul of 78 B.C.

tion was devised; for that priest [a] so devoted to the people a candidature for the consulship was arranged. This was what loyalists deplored, what traitors hoped for, what a tribune of the commons schemed, what consuls aided and abetted.

XXI. Here at length, later than he himself might 67 have wished, utterly against the will of those who, by their advice and false alarms, had turned the mind of the best and bravest of men from undertaking my defence—here at length Gnaeus Pompeius revived that old practice of his of service for the welfare of the State, which had indeed never slept, but had been rendered inactive by some sort of suspicion. That hero, who by the valour of his victorious arms had conquered our most impious citizens, [b] our bitterest enemies, mighty tribes, kings, savage and hitherto unknown peoples, countless hordes of pirates and a band of slaves as well, [c] who, after he had put an end to all wars both on land and sea, had set the boundary of the Empire of the Roman People at the limits of the world, could not suffer the crimes of a few to overthrow that State which he had often saved not only by his policy, but even by his own blood. [d] He took up the cause of the State; he resisted by his influence any further proceedings; he lodged complaints of what had been done. There seemed to be a sort of tendency towards better hopes. On the first of June [e] a full Senate 68 unanimously passed a decree for my return, moved

[c] After the defeat, by M. Crassus, and death of Spartacus in 71 B.C., Pompey rounded up the fugitive slaves.

[d] Pompey was wounded when fighting against Sertorius on the Sucro (75 B.C.) in Spain. *Pro Balbo*, 5.

[e] In 58 B.C. For L. Ninnius see § 26.

in mea causa numquam fides virtusque contremuit.
Intercessit Ligus iste nescio qui, additamentum inimicorum meorum. Res erat et causa nostra eo iam
loci, ut erigere oculos et vivere videretur.[1] Quisquis
erat qui aliquam partem in meo luctu sceleris Clodiani
attigisset, quocumque venerat, quod iudicium cumque subierat, damnabatur ; inveniebatur nemo, qui
se suffragium de me tulisse confiteretur. Decesserat
ex Asia frater meus magno squalore, sed multo etiam
maiore maerore. Huic ad urbem venienti tota ob-
viam civitas cum lacrimis gemituque processerat ;
loquebatur liberius senatus ; concurrebant equites
Romani ; Piso ille, gener meus, cui fructum pietatis
suae neque ex me neque a populo Romano ferre licuit,
a propinquo suo socerum suum flagitabat ; omnia
senatus reiciebat, nisi de me primum consules ret-
tulissent.

69   XXXII. Quae cum res iam manibus teneretur, et
cum consules provinciarum pactione libertatem omnem perdidissent, qui, cum in senatu privati, ut de
me sententias dicerent, flagitabant, legem illi se
Clodiam timere dicebant, cum hoc non possent iam
diutius sustinere, initur consilium de interitu Cn.
Pompei. Quo patefacto ferroque deprehenso ille in-

---

[1] videretur *MSS.* : videremur *Reid*.

---

[a] Sextus Aelius Ligus, a tribune of 58 B.C.
[b] Q. Cicero, propraetor of Asia 61–58 B.C.
[c] He died before Cicero's return from exile. See §§ 20
and 54.   [d] In the shape of a public appointment.
[e] L. Calpurnius Piso, consul 58 B.C.
[f] Which declared that no one should make a motion to
recall Cicero.

by Lucius Ninnius, whose loyalty and courage in my cause have never wavered. Some one named Ligus [a] interposed his veto, some nobody, some addition to the ranks of my enemies. The situation and my cause were now such that they seemed to lift up their eyes and live. All those who at the time of my sorrow had taken any part in the crime of Clodius, wherever they showed themselves, whatever court of justice they entered, were condemned ; no one was found to acknowledge that he had voted about me. My brother [b] had left Asia in deep mourning, with far deeper sorrow in his heart. When he approached the city, all the people went forward to meet him with tears and lamentation. The Senate was speaking more frankly ; the Roman Knights held frequent meetings. Piso, my son-in-law, who was not permitted to reap the fruits of his affection either from me [c] or from the Roman People,[d] urgently demanded from his kinsman [e] the restoration of his father-in-law ; the Senate refused to consider anything until the consuls had first brought in a motion about me.

XXXII. Success seemed already within our grasp. 69 The consuls, however, had lost all freedom of action by their bargain about the provinces and, in answer to some private members in the Senate who asked leave to speak on my case, declared that they were afraid of the Clodian Law.[f] When they could no longer offer resistance [g] a conspiracy was formed against the life of Gnaeus Pompeius. The plot was discovered, a weapon was seized,[h] and Pompeius remained

---

[g] *i.e.*, withstand the pressure put upon them to recall Cicero. Alternatively : " When they could not keep up the excuse about the Clodian Law any longer."

[h] On 11 August 58 B.C.

clusus domi tamdiu fuit, quamdiu inimicus meus in tribunatu. De meo reditu octo tribuni promulgave-runt. Ex quo intellectum est non mihi absenti crevisse[1] amicos, in ea praesertim fortuna, in qua non nulli etiam, quos esse putaveram, non erant, sed eos voluntatem semper eandem, libertatem non eandem semper habuisse. Nam ex novem tribunis, quos tunc habueram, unus me absente defluxit, qui cognomen sibi ex Aeliorum imaginibus arripuit, quo magis nationis eius esse quam generis videretur. 70 Hoc igitur anno magistratibus novis designatis cum omnes boni omnem spem melioris status in eorum fidem convertissent, princeps P. Lentulus auctoritate ac sententia sua Pisone et Gabinio repugnantibus causam suscepit tribunisque pl. octo referentibus praestantissimam de me sententiam dixit. Qui cum ad gloriam suam atque ad amplissimi beneficii gratiam magis pertinere videret causam illam in-tegram ad suum consulatum reservari, tamen rem talem per alios citius quam per se tardius confici malebat.

71 XXXIII. Hoc interim tempore P. Sestius, iudices, designatus iter ad C. Caesarem pro mea salute sus-

---

[1] crevisse MSS. : decrevisse *Kayser* : defuisse *Mommsen*.

---

[a] On 29 October 58 B.C.
[b] When he went into exile.
[c] This was Aelius Ligus, who, according to Cicero, had sneaked into the Aelian family. The cognomen also means a Ligurian, a people, perhaps a prehistoric remnant, regarded by the Romans as barbarians.
[d] Piso and Gabinius were still consuls ; P. Lentulus Spinther and Q. Metellus Nepas were consuls-elect for 57 B.C., T. Annius Milo and P. Sestius, tribunes-elect.

shut up in his house as long as my enemy remained
tribune. Eight tribunes announced a proposal for my
recall.[a] And thus it was made clear not that the
number of my friends had increased during my
absence, especially as I found myself in a situation
in which even some whom I had thought to be my
friends turned out not to be so ; but that their disposition had always been the same, although they
had not always had the same freedom of action. For
of the nine tribunes, whom I had on my side at
that time,[b] one fell away from me in my absence.
By stealing a cognomen from the ancestral effigies
of the Aelii, he got the reputation of belonging to the
Ligurian people instead of to the Aelian family.[c] So
then, in this same year, when the new magistrates
were elected,[d] and all loyal citizens had put all their
hopes of a better order of things upon their good
faith, Publius Lentulus first supported my cause by
his influence and opinion, in spite of the opposition
of Piso and Gabinius, and when the eight tribunes
of the commons moved their proposition, delivered an
excellent opinion about me. Although he was aware
that it would redound more to his glory and would
bring him greater gratitude for so signal a service if
the whole case were reserved for his consulship, he
preferred that a matter of such importance should be
settled by others without delay rather than more
slowly by himself.

XXXIII.[e] It was then[f] that Publius Sestius,
gentlemen, tribune-elect, undertook a journey to
Gaius Caesar to interest him in my welfare. What he

[e] Cicero here takes up his account of Sestius' career, interrupted by a long digression (§§ 15-70).
[f] *i.e.*, after the tribunician elections in 58 B.C.

cepit. Quid egerit, quantum profecerit, nihil ad causam (equidem existimo, si ille, ut arbitror, aequus nobis fuerit, nihil ab hoc profectum ; sin iratior, non multum) ; sed tamen sedulitatem atque integritatem hominis videtis. Ingredior iam in Sesti tribunatum ; nam hoc primum iter designatus rei publicae causa suscepit ; pertinere et ad concordiam civium putavit et ad perficiundi facultatem animum Caesaris a causa non abhorrere.[1] Abiit ille annus ; respirasse homines videbantur nondum re, sed spe rei publicae recuperandae. Exierunt malis ominibus atque exsecrationibus duo vulturii paludati. Quibus utinam ipsis evenissent ea, quae tum homines precabantur ! neque nos provinciam Macedoniam cum exercitu neque equitatum in Syria et cohortes optimas perdidissemus.

72 Ineunt magistratum tribuni pl., qui omnes se de me promulgaturos confirmarant ; ex iis princeps emitur ab inimicis meis is, quem homines in luctu inridentes Gracchum vocabant, quoniam id etiam fatum civi-

---

[1] *Peterson transposes the words* pertinere . . . abhorrere *to a position immediately following* pro mea salute suscepit *in l. 3 of this paragraph.*

---

[a] Caesar seems to have given a qualified assent to Cicero's recall, stipulating, probably, that a law should be passed.

[b] Piso and Gabinius, who left Rome before the new tribunes entered office on 10 December, *i.e.* before the end of their own magistracy on 29 December. The wearing of the *paludamentum* marked the beginning of their provincial commands. J. P. V. D. Balsdon ("Consular Provinces under the later Republic," i, *J.R.S.* xxix, p. 67) thinks that if the consuls had spent the year in Rome they were free of routine duties after the Ides of November, and could then leave for their provinces.

[c] The Roman arms met with disaster and the province was overrun by Thracians (*De prov. cons.* 4-5).

[d] Losses sustained by Gabinius at the outset of the rebel-

130

did, how far he succeeded, has nothing to do with the case. For my own part I think, if Caesar was (as I believe) well-disposed towards me, that Sestius did no good; and if he was offended with me, not much[a]; but still you see the devotion, the sincerity of the man. I now come to the actual tribunate of Sestius; for this first journey he undertook in the public interest when he was only tribune-elect, since he thought that to establish civic harmony and to carry out his purpose it was important that Caesar should not be unfavourable to my cause. That year came to its end: men seemed to breathe again, not yet in reality, but in hope that the constitution would be restored. Away from the city, under evil omens and amid general maledictions, went a pair of vultures,[b] in the garb of generals; and would that the curses which men uttered at that time had brought disaster upon them alone! We should have lost neither the province of Macedonia and an army,[c] nor some cavalry and excellent infantry in Syria.[d] The tribunes of the commons enter into office; [72] they had all assured me that they would announce a motion for my recall. Of these, the first[e] to be bought over by my enemies was a man whom people, laughing in their sorrow, called Gracchus,[f] for it was even the fate of our country for that little

lion in Judaea of Alexander, son of Aristobulus II, crushed by him (Josephus, xiv. 5. 2–4; 6. 1). See vol. ii, p. 554, note d.

[e] Numerius Quintius Rufus.

[f] The text is suspect and the meaning conjectural. Reid regards *Gracchum* as a corruption of some word connected with gnawing or eating. G. M. Tucker (*Classical Review*, lvi, 1942, p. 68) suggests *Dentatum*; O. Skutsch (*ibid.* p. 117) conjectures *Brocchum*, but later (*ibid.* lvii, 1943, p. 67) supports the manuscript reading (*Gracchum*).

CICERO

tatis fuit, ut illa ex vepreculis extracta nitedula rem publicam conaretur adrodere. Alter vero, non ille Serranus ab aratro, sed ex deserto †gaviolaeliore[1] a calatis[2] Gaviis in Calatinos Atilios insitus, subito nominibus in tabulas relatis nomen suum de tabula sustulit. Veniunt Kalendae Ianuariae. Vos haec melius scire potestis, equidem audita dico, quae tum frequentia senatus, quae exspectatio populi, qui concursus legatorum ex Italia cuncta, quae virtus, actio, gravitas P. Lentuli consulis fuerit, quae etiam collegae eius moderatio de me. Qui cum inimicitias sibi mecum ex rei publicae dissensione susceptas esse dixisset, eas se patribus conscriptis dixit et temporibus rei publicae permissurum.

---

[1] Gavi(i) Oleli rure *Madvig*: deserta Gaviorum oliveti area *Koch*: Gavii Ofilii horto *Bake*.
[2] Galatis *Mommsen*.

---

[a] An allusion to his cognomen Rufus.
[b] Sextus Atilius Serranus, trib. 57 B.C.
[c] Gaius Atilius Serranus, consul 257 B.C., who left his fields, where he was found sowing, when summoned to be consul. He defeated the Carthaginians off the Liparaean islands (*Pro Roscio Amerino*, 50, and Virgil, *Aen.* vi. 844).
[d] Madvig's suggestion is translated. This Atilius had secured his transfer (perhaps fraudulently) from the *gens Gavia* to the *gens Atilia*. *Insitus* continues the reference to *serere* in the name Serranus. *Desertum rus* is an allusion to the obscure and decadent condition of the family.
[e] If *calatis* be correct, there is a play on *comitia calata* (see Greenidge, *Roman Public Life*, pp. 26, 27, 251), where adoption by *adrogatio* was performed, and the name Calatius. The Gavii had to agree to his changing over

132

red ^{a} field-mouse, pulled out of a bramble-bush, to try to nibble a piece out of the State. But another,^{b} not the great Serranus of the plough,^{c} but he who came from the deserted farm of Gavius Olelus ^{d} and had been ingrafted by the Gavii in council into the Calatini Atilii,^{e} suddenly, after he had posted up in his account-books the money he had received, removed his name from the posted list.^{f} The Kalends of January arrive.^{g} You are better informed than I am about what took place ; I speak only from hearsay. You know how full the Senate was, the people on the tiptoe of expectation, what a gathering of delegates from all Italy, the courage, the delivery, the weighty words of Publius Lentulus the consul, how considerate his colleague ^{h} also showed himself towards me ; and how, after declaring that our differences in political opinion had made him my enemy, his colleague said that he would sacrifice his resentment to the will of the House and to the interests of the State.

into another *gens*. Others adopt Mommsen's *Galatis*, thus hinting at Gallic descent in the intruder.

^{f} He entered in his account-books the bribe promised him by Clodius and then removed his name from the board on which the proposal for Cicero's recall, with the names of the proposers, was posted. There is a play on two senses of the word *tabula*.

^{g} The opening day of 57 B.C. when the new consuls entered upon their duties.

^{h} Q. Metellus Nepos, a cousin of P. Clodius. Soon after becoming tribune on 10 December 63 B.C., he began to attack Cicero for the execution of the Catilinarian conspirators. He prevented him from addressing the people on the last day of his consulship, and allowed him only to take the usual oath that he had faithfully discharged his duty. On 3 January 62 B.C. he attacked him in the Senate. But he did not oppose his recall. See § 130 and *De prov. cons.* 22.

73 XXXIV. Tum princeps rogatus sententiam L. Cotta
dixit id, quod dignissimum re publica fuit, nihil de me
actum esse iure, nihil more maiorum, nihil legibus ;
non posse quemquam de civitate tolli sine iudicio ;
de capite non modo ferri, sed ne iudicari quidem
posse nisi comitiis centuriatis ; vim fuisse illam, flam-
mam quassatae rei publicae perturbatorumque tem-
porum, iure iudiciisque sublatis ; magna rerum per-
mutatione impendente declinasse me paulum et spe
reliquae tranquillitatis praesentes fluctus tempesta-
temque fugisse. Quare, cum absens rem publicam
non minus magnis periculis quam quodam tempore
praesens liberassem, non restitui me solum, sed etiam
ornari a senatu decere. Disputavit etiam multa pru-
denter, ita de me illum amentissimum et profligatis-
simum hostem pudoris et pudicitiae scripsisse, quae
scripsisset, iis verbis, rebus, sententiis, ut, etiamsi
iure esset rogatum, tamen vim habere non posset.
Quare me, qui nulla lege abessem, non restitui
lege, sed revocari senatus auctoritate oportere. Hunc
74 nemo erat quin verissime sentire diceret. Sed post
eum rogatus Cn. Pompeius adprobata laudataque

---

a Consul in 65 B.C., an eminent jurist. When praetor in
70 B.C., he carried the *lex Aurelia,* by which the *iudices* in the
quaestiones perpetuae were chosen from the three classes of
senators, *equites,* and *tribuni aerarii.*
134

XXXIV. Then Lucius Cotta,[a] having been asked 73
to open the debate, delivered an opinion which
was most worthy of the State. He said that the
measures that had been taken against me were all
unconstitutional, all opposed to the custom of our
ancestors, and all illegal; that no one could be
deprived of his citizenship without a trial; that not
only could no motion be made concerning a man's
civil status, but not even could any judgment be pronounced against it, without reference to the *comitia
centuriata*; that all that business was brute force, a
blaze from the collapse of the State when the world
was in confusion, when right and justice were overthrown; that when a great political upheaval was
imminent, I had turned aside a little and, in the hope
of finding calm hereafter, had avoided the stormy
waves before me. Since by my absence I had saved
the State from dangers as threatening as those from
which I had once [b] delivered it by my presence, it
was therefore fitting that I should not only be reinstated, but also honoured by the Senate. He also argued at great length, and with common sense, that the
proposal drawn up by that demented and abandoned
enemy of modesty and decency had been so drawn
up in its words, facts, and intentions, that even if it
had been legally made, it could not be valid; and
therefore since I had been banished under no law,
I did not need to be rehabilitated by a law, but to be
recalled by a resolution of the Senate.[c] There was
no one who did not agree that this opinion was sound.
But after him Gnaeus Pompeius was called upon, and 74

[b] *i.e.* during the conspiracy of Catiline.
[c] *Lex*, a vote of the People, which was not necessary as the
rogatio of Clodius had been informal.

Cottae sententia dixit sese otii mei causa, ut omni
populari concitatione defungerer, censere, ut ad
senatus auctoritatem populi quoque Romani beneficium erga me adiungeretur. Cum omnes certatim
aliusque alio gravius atque ornatius de mea salute
dixisset fieretque sine ulla varietate discessio, sur-
rexit, ut scitis, Atilius hic Gavianus ; nec ausus est,
cum esset emptus, intercedere ; noctem sibi ad
deliberandum postulavit. Clamor senatus, querellae,
preces, socer ad pedes abiectus. Ille se adfirmare
postero die moram nullam esse facturum. Creditum
est ; discessum est. Illi interea deliberatori merces
longa interposita nocte duplicata est. Consecuti dies
pauci omnino Ianuario mense, per quos senatum
haberi liceret ; sed tamen actum nihil nisi de me.

75   XXXV. Cum omni mora, ludificatione, calumnia
senatus auctoritas impediretur, venit tandem in[1]
concilio de me agendi dies, viii Kal. Febr. Princeps
rogationis, vir mihi amicissimus, Q. Fabricius, templum aliquanto ante lucem occupavit. Quietus eo

---

[1] in *inserted by Madvig.*

---

[a] *Defungi* seems here to mean " to avoid, be rid of," as
in Cicero, *Epp. ad Fam.* viii. 1. 5, " hoc mendacio, si qua
pericula tibi impenderent ut (sc. iis periculis) defungeremur
optavi "—" and I prayed that at the cost of this lie we might
get rid of whatever dangers hung over you " (Tyrrell). It
is, however, possible that the phrase may mean, " in order
that I might have full experience (*defungerer*) of popular
encouragement (*concitatione*)," since *defungi* clearly bears
such a meaning in Q. Curtius, vi. 2. 3 (" solitos parco victu
ad implenda naturae desideria defungi "), and viii. 1. 18
(" prospero eventu defunctus erat Alexander ").

[b] A polite form of *intercessio*, when it was not found to be
possible to prevent a vote being taken by wasting a whole
day in speaking (" talking the House out ").

he praised and commended the opinion of Cotta. He then said, that to make my position secure, and to be rid of all popular excitement against me,[a] he thought it advisable that a resolution of the Senate should be accompanied by a favourable vote of the Roman People. Succeeding speakers all urged my recall, rivalling one another in the weight of their compliments, and a unanimous vote was on the point of being given, when up rose this Atilius Gavianus, as you know ; he did not dare to exercise his veto, although he had been bought, but he asked for a night to consider.[b] There was a great outcry in the Senate, reproaches, entreaties ; his father-in-law threw himself at his feet.[c] He declared that he would cause no delay at the next sitting. He was believed ; the meeting broke up. But in the meantime the intervention of a long night afforded that man of consideration time to get his price doubled. There were only a few days in all left in the month of January on which the Senate could hold sittings ; none the less no business was transacted except as to myself.

XXXV. While the resolution of the Senate was 75 being hindered by every kind of delay, farce, and chicanery, at length the day arrived for dealing with my case in the Assembly[d] on 23 January. Quintus Fabricius, the proposer of the bill, a very great friend of mine, occupied the Rostra[e] some time before daybreak. On that day Sestius, the man who is now

[c] See Cicero, *Epp. ad Atticum*, iv. 2. 4. The father-in-law was Gnaeus Oppius Cornicinus (or Cornicen).

[d] The *concilium plebis tributum*. See note on § 65.

[e] The *Rostra* were sometimes called *templum* : *cf.* Livy, viii. 14. 12 : "rostris earum (the ships captured from the Antiates, 338 B.C.) suggestum in foro exstructum adornari placuit, rostraque id templum appellatum."

die Sestius, is qui est de vi reus ; actor hic defensorque
causae meae nihil progreditur, consilia exspectat
inimicorum meorum. Quid ? illi, quorum consilio
P. Sestius in iudicium vocatur, quo se pacto gerunt ?
Cum forum, comitium, curiam multa de nocte armatis
hominibus ac servis plerisque occupavissent, impetum
faciunt in Fabricium, manus adferunt, occidunt non
76 nullos, vulnerant multos.   Venientem in forum
virum optimum et constantissimum, M. Cispium,
tribunum pl., vi depellunt, caedem in foro maximam
faciunt universique destrictis gladiis et cruentis in
omnibus fori partibus fratrem meum, virum optimum,
fortissimum meique amantissimum, oculis quaere-
bant, voce poscebant. Quorum ille telis libenter in
tanto luctu ac desiderio mei non repugnandi, sed
moriendi causa corpus obtulisset suum, nisi suam
vitam ad spem mei reditus reservasset.   Subiit tamen
vim illam nefariam consceleratorum latronum et,
cum ad fratris salutem a populo Romano deprecandam
venisset, pulsus e rostris in comitio iacuit[1] seque servorum et libertorum corporibus obtexit vitamque
tum suam noctis et fugae praesidio, non iuris iudi-
77 ciorumque defendit.   Meministis tum, iudices, corporibus civium Tiberim compleri, cloacas refarciri, e
foro spongiis effingi sanguinem, ut omnes tantam
illam copiam et tam magnificum apparatum non

[1] latuit *Reid*.

---

[a] An open space at the N.W. end of the Forum, the political

accused of violence, remained quiet ; this pleader and champion of my cause does not take the initiative ; he waits to see what my enemies intend to do. How then do those behave at whose instigation Publius Sestius has been put on trial ? Having occupied the Forum, the Comitium,*a* and the Senate House late at night with armed men, for the most part slaves, they attack Fabricius, lay hands upon him, kill some of his party, wound many. As that excellent and most sted- 76 fast man, Marcus Cispius, a tribune of the commons, was coming into the Forum, they drive him away by force, wreak great slaughter in the Forum, and then all together, their swords drawn and dripping with blood, it was my brother, my excellent, my most brave and devoted brother, that they began to search for, to clamour for, in every quarter of the Forum. Gladly, amid all his sorrow and yearning for me, would he have faced their weapons, not to offer resistance, but to meet death, had he not reserved his life for the hope of my restoration. Yet he could not escape the infamous violence of those villainous brigands, and having come to beseech the Roman People for his brother's recall, after being driven from the Rostra he lay down in the Comitium, sheltering himself behind the bodies of slaves and freedmen, and then defended his life by the protection of darkness and flight, not of law and justice. You remember, 77 gentlemen, how the Tiber was filled that day with the bodies of citizens, how the sewers were choked, how blood was mopped up from the Forum with sponges, enough to make everyone think that so great an array and so magnificent a show of gladiators was not pro-

centre of Rome until the second century B.C. See Platner and Ashby, *op. cit.* pp. 134-137.

CICERO

privatum aut plebeium, sed patricium et praetorium
esse arbitrarentur.

XXXVI. Nihil neque ante hoc tempus neque hoc
ipso turbulentissimo die criminamini Sestium. Atqui
vis in foro versata est. Certe ; quando enim maior ?
Lapidationes persaepe vidimus, non ita saepe, sed
nimium tamen saepe gladios, caedem vero tantam,
tantos acervos corporum exstructos nisi forte illo
Cinnano atque Octaviano die quis umquam in foro
vidit ? Qua ex concitatione animorum ? Nam ex
pertinacia aut constantia intercessoris oritur saepe
seditio, culpa atque improbitate latoris commodo
aliquo oblato[1] imperitis aut largitione, oritur ex con-
certatione magistratuum, oritur sensim ex clamore
primum, deinde aliqua discessione contionis, vix sero
et raro ad manus pervenitur ; nullo vero verbo facto,
nulla contione advocata, nulla recitata[2] lege concita-
78 tam nocturnam seditionem quis audivit ? An veri
simile est, ut civis Romanus aut homo liber quisquam
cum gladio in forum descenderit ante lucem, ne de
me ferri pateretur, praeter eos, qui ab illo pestifero
ac perdito civi iam pridem rei publicae sanguine
saginantur ? Hic iam de ipso accusatore quaero, qui
P. Sestium queritur cum multitudine in tribunatu

---

[1] *Others read* proposito : oblato *Halm. The participle
would seem to be better inserted after* largitione, *either* proposita *or* ostentata (*Reid*).
[2] recitata *two* MSS. : lata *Halm* : promulgata *Lambinus.*

---

[a] Appius Claudius Pulcher, who was both a patrician and
praetor (57 B.C.), seems to have lent his brother Publius
Clodius, who was out of office and, by transfer, a plebeian,
some gladiators he had assembled for the funeral games of
a kinsman. See Dio Cassius, xxxix. 7.
[b] Cn. Octavius (consul 87 B.C.) drove his colleague Cinna
from Rome with great carnage. (The " BellumOctavianum.")
140

vided by any private person, nor by any plebeian, but by a patrician and a praetor.[a]

XXXVI. Neither before this time, nor on this day of disorder, do you bring any charge against Sestius. —" And yet violence took place in the Forum."— Undoubtedly ; in fact, when greater ? Time and again have we seen stones thrown ; not so often, but still too often, swords drawn ; but who has ever seen such a massacre, such heaps of slain piled up in the Forum, except perhaps on that day when Cinna and Octavius fought ?[b] And what was the excitement that caused it ? A riot often arises from a veto by an obstinate or uncompromising tribune, or from a culpable and unscrupulous proposal meant to win over the ignorant by a promise of advantage ; or again from rivalry between magistrates. It begins imperceptibly ; first comes an uproar, and then a sort of taking of sides within a meeting. But it is only late in the day and seldom that men actually come to blows. But who has ever heard of a riot breaking out in the night, when no word has been said, no meeting summoned, no law publicly read out ?[c] Is it likely that any Roman citizen or free 78 man went down into the Forum before daybreak, sword in hand, to prevent my recall being proposed, unless it be those who have long battened on the life-blood of the State, by the agency of that pestilent and abandoned citizen ? I now ask the accuser himself, who complains that Publius Sestius was attended by a numerous escort and a large body-

[c] *recitata* (the reading of two mss.) seems better than Halm's alteration *lata* ; the disturbance would not arise after the law had been passed, but before, to prevent its being carried.

et cum praesidio magno fuisse, num illo die fuerit.
Certe non fuit. Victa igitur est causa rei publicae, et
victa non auspiciis, non intercessione, non suffragiis,
sed vi, manu, ferro. Nam si obnuntiasset Fabricio
is praetor, qui se servasse de caelo dixerat,[1] accepisset
res publica plagam, sed eam, quam acceptam gemere[2]
posset ; si intercessisset collega Fabricio, laesisset rem
publicam, sed rei publicae iure[3] laesisset. Gladiatores
tu novicios pro exspectata aedilitate suppositos cum
sicariis e carcere emissis ante lucem immittas, magistratus templo deicias, caedem maximam facias,
forum purges et, cum omnia vi et armis egeris,
accuses eum, qui se praesidio munierit, non ut te
oppugnaret, sed ut vitam suam posset defendere ?

79 XXXVII. Atqui ne ex eo quidem tempore id egit
Sestius, ut a suis munitus tuto in foro magistratum
gereret, rem publicam administraret. Itaque fretus
sanctitate tribunatus cum se non modo contra vim et
ferrum, sed etiam contra verba atque interfationem
legibus sacratis esse armatum putaret, venit in
templum Castoris, obnuntiavit consuli : cum subito

---

[1] *The* MS. *reading is preferred. Madvig (after Manutius)
proposes* : is, qui se servasse de caelo diceret.
[2] gemere MSS.: gemere non *Bake*: reddere *Koch*: sanare
Reid : qua accepta emergere *Dryander*.
[3] tribunicio iure *Peterson*.

---

[a] That the praetor must have been Appius Claudius
Pulcher is an argument for the retention of the MS. reading.
For the bearing of this on the problem of Clodius and the
lex Aelia Fufia see p. 318, note *d*.
[b] Since *obnuntiatio*, though regrettable, was constitutional and would not have been fatal to the State. This is
Halm's interpretation ; but *gemere* is strained. Other sug-

guard during his tribunate, whether he was so attended on that day. Certainly he was not. And that is why the cause of the State was defeated, and defeated not by the auspices, nor by a veto, nor by votes, but by violence, by force, and the sword. For if the praetor,[a] who said that he had watched for signs from the sky, had announced an evil omen to Fabricius, the State would have received a blow, but one which it could survive [b] ; if a colleague had put a veto on Fabricius, he would have injured the State, but would have done so by a constitutional procedure. Are you [c] to send into the Forum before daybreak your raw gladiators, provided for an expected aedileship,[d] with a pack of assassins discharged from prison ? are you to drive magistrates from the Rostra ? are you to wreak great slaughter ? are you to empty the Forum and, after you have done all this by force of arms, are you to accuse one who protected himself with a guard, not to attack you, but to defend his own life ?

XXXVII. And yet not even since that time has 79 Sestius taken any pains to be guarded by his friends, so as to act as a magistrate in the Forum, and perform his official duties in safety. Accordingly, relying upon the sanctity of his tribunate, and thinking that he was protected by the *leges sacratae*,[e] not only against violence and the sword, but also against words and interruptions, he went to the Temple of Castor and announced to the consul that there were unfavourable

gested readings are *sanare, redimere, qua accepta emergere, contemnere.* May *mederi* be suggested ?

[c] Addressed to Clodius as represented by the accuser of Sestius.

[d] The aediles exhibited games and Clodius was a candidate for an aedileship to which he was elected on 20 January 56 B.C.   [e] See p. 54, note e.

manus illa Clodiana in caede civium saepe iam victrix exclamat, incitatur, invadit ; inermem atque imparatum tribunum alii gladiis adoriuntur, alii fragmentis saeptorum et fustibus. A quibus hic multis vulneribus acceptis ac debilitato corpore et contrucidato se abiecit exanimatus neque ulla re ab se mortem nisi opinione mortis depulit. Quem cum iacentem et concisum plurimis vulneribus extremo spiritu exsanguem et confectum viderent, defatigatione magis et errore quam misericordia et modo aliquando caedere 80 destiterunt. Et causam dicit Sestius de vi ? quid ita ? Quia vivit. At id non sua culpa ; plaga una illa extrema defuit, quae si accessisset, reliquum spiritum exhausisset. Accusa Lentidium ; non percussit locum[1]; male dic Titio, Sabino homini Reatino, cur tam temere exclamarit occisum. Ipsum vero quid accusas ? num defuit gladiis, num repugnavit, num, ut gladiatoribus imperari solet, ferrum non recepit ?

XXXVIII. An haec ipsa vis est, non posse emori ? an illa, quod tribunus pl. templum cruentavit ? an, quod, cum esset ablatus primumque resipisset, non 81 se referri iussit ? Ubi est crimen ? quid reprehenditis ? Hic quaero, iudices : Si illo die gens ista Clodia, quod facere voluit, effecisset, si P. Sestius,

---

[1] totum *Eberhard*.

[a] The consul here was probably Q. Metellus Nepos. On Sestius' action see p. 319.

[b] Probably torn from voting-enclosures in the Forum.

[c] The people called out to a defeated gladiator to expose his breast to receive a final blow (*cf.* Cicero, *Pro Roscio Amerino*, 33).

[d] The brothers Appius and Publius, together with their

omens.[a] Then suddenly that gang of Clodius',
which often before has triumphantly murdered citizens, raises an outcry, rushes on him, attacks him.
The tribune is unarmed and off his guard ; some assail
him with swords, some with pieces of railing,[b] others
with clubs. Covered with wounds from these, wearied
out and mangled, he threw himself down exhausted,
and escaped with his life only because he was thought
to have lost it. When they saw him lying on the
ground, hacked with many wounds, collapsed from
exhaustion and almost at his last gasp, they at last
ceased to strike, more from fatigue and the mistake
of thinking him dead than from any feeling of pity
or restraint. And is Sestius on trial for violence ? 80
Why so ? Because he is alive. But that is not his
fault. The final blow was wanting ; had that been
added, he would have breathed his last. Blame Len-
tidius ! he missed his mark. Abuse Titius, a Sabine
from Reate, for crying out so indiscreetly that he
was dead ! But why accuse Sestius himself ? Did
he shrink from the sword ? Did he resist ? Did he
fail, as gladiators are ordered to do, to " accept the
stroke " ? [c]

XXXVIII. Or is it violence, simply to be unable
to die ? or that he, a tribune of the commons, stained
a temple with his blood ? or that, after he had been
carried off and had just recovered his senses, he did
not order that he should be carried back ? Where is 81
the ground for accusation ? What fault do you find
with him ? I now put this question, gentlemen. If
on that day this Clodian family [d] had done what it
wished, if P. Sestius, who had been left for dead, had

freedmen and slaves. For this murderous attack on Sestius
see Cicero, *Epp. ad Quintum fratrem*, ii. 3. 6.

qui pro occiso relictus est, occisus esset, fuistisne
ad arma ituri ? fuistisne vos ad patrium illum animum maiorumque virtutem excitaturi ? fuistisne
aliquando rem publicam a funesto latrone repetituri?
an etiam tum quiesceretis, cunctaremini, timeretis,
cum rem publicam a facinerosissimis sicariis et a
servis esse oppressam atque conculcatam videretis ?
Cuius igitur mortem ulcisceremini, siquidem liberi
esse et habere rem publicam cogitaretis, de eius
virtute vivi quid vos loqui, quid sentire, quid cogitare,
82 quid iudicare oporteat, dubitandum putatis ? At
vero ipsi illi parricidae, quorum effrenatus furor alitur
impunitate diuturna, adeo vim facinoris sui per-
horruerunt, ut, si paulo longior opinio mortis Sesti
fuisset, Gracchum illum suum transferendi in nos
criminis causa occidere cogitarint. Sensit rusticulus
non incautus (neque enim homines nequam tacere
potuerunt) suum sanguinem quaeri ad restinguendam
invidiam facinoris Clodiani ; mulioniam paenulam
arripuit, cum qua primum Romam ad comitia venerat ;
messoria se corbe contexit. Cum quaererent alii Numerium, alii Quintium, gemini nominis errore serva-
tus est. Atque hoc scitis omnes, usque adeo hominem
in periculo fuisse, quoad scitum est Sestium vivere.
Quod ni esset patefactum paulo citius, quam vellem,

ᵃ See p. 186, note *b*.   ᵇ See § 72.
ᶜ His name was Numerius Quintius Rufus. Some called
for Numerius, which was usually a gentile name, but also
a *praenomen*; others, who only knew his *nomen* Quintius
and his *cognomen* Rufus, asked, " Which Numerius ? We

been killed, would you have been ready to rush to arms ? would you have been ready to rouse yourselves to the patriotic spirit and courage of your ancestors ? would you at last have been ready to rescue the State from that pernicious brigand ? or would you even then have remained quiet, irresolute, and fearful, when you saw the State overthrown and trampled upon by the most execrable assassins and by slaves ? As then, if you had any thought of freedom or of upholding the State you would have avenged his death, do you think, since he is still alive, that you should hesitate as to what should be your language, your feelings, your thoughts, your judgment about his deserts ? But surely those traitors 82 themselves,[a] whose unbridled frenzy battens on long-continued impunity, were so horrified at the effect of their crime, that if their belief in the death of Sestius had lasted a little longer, they would have been ready to think of putting that Gracchus [b] of theirs to death and shifting the charge upon us. That bumpkin, who did not lack caution—for those villains could not hold their tongues—saw that his own blood was wanted to allay the indignation aroused by the crime of Clodius, picked up a mule-driver's cloak, in which he had originally come to Rome for the Assembly, and covered his head with a reaper's basket. While some were asking for Numerius, and others for Quintius, he was saved through a mistake due to his two names.[c] And you are all aware that he was in danger right up to the time when it became known that Sestius was alive. If this had not been disclosed a little sooner than I

want Quintius." Thus the confusion about his names saved him.

non illi quidem morte mercennarii sui transferre
potuissent invidiam, in quos putabant, sed acerbis-
simi sceleris infamiam grato quodam scelere minuis-
83 sent. Ac si tum P. Sestius, iudices, in templo Castoris animam, quam vix retinuit, edidisset, non dubito,
quin, si modo esset in re publica senatus, si maiestas
populi Romani revixisset, aliquando statua huic ob
rem publicam interfecto in foro statueretur. Nec
vero illorum quisquam, quos a maioribus nostris morte
obita positos in illo loco atque in rostris conlocatos
videtis, esset P. Sestio aut acerbitate mortis aut animo
in rem publicam praeponendus; qui cum causam
civis calamitosi, causam amici, causam bene de re
publica meriti, causam senatus, causam Italiae,
causam rei publicae suscepisset, cumque auspiciis
religionique parens obnuntiaret, quod senserat, luce
palam a nefariis pestibus in deorum hominumque
conspectu esset occisus sanctissimo in templo, sanc-
tissima in causa, sanctissimo in magistratu. Eius
igitur vitam quisquam spoliandam ornamentis esse
dicet, cuius mortem ornandam monumento sempi-
terno putaretis ?

84   XXXIX. " Homines," inquit, " emisti, coegisti,
parasti." Quid uti faceret ? senatum obsideret,

ᵃ *Mors acerba* is often " a premature death," but Cicero
seems to refer also to the cruel wound it would have caused.
   ᵇ *Calamitas* : often used for disfranchisement or loss of
civil rights.
   ᶜ As empowered by the *lex Aelia Fufia*. See p. 311.
   ᵈ An allusion to the story (Plutarch, *Cicero*, 31), wherein
Clodius is described as σιδηροφορούμενος περὶ τὸ βουλευτήριον
(" in arms around the Senate House ") when measures in
favour of Cicero were being proposed. For a further exam-

could wish, they certainly would not have been able, by killing their own hireling, to shift the odium upon those they thought they could, but they would have lessened the infamy of a heart-rending crime by one that would almost excite gratitude. And if, gentle- 83 men, Publius Sestius had then breathed his last in the Temple of Castor, for he was at the point of death, I have no doubt, if only there were a Senate in the State, if the majesty of the Roman People should come to life again, that a statue would one day be set up to him in the Forum as having been slain in defence of the State. And indeed, of those departed heroes whose statues you see, set up by our ancestors, in the Forum and on the Rostra, not one would be preferred to Publius Sestius, either because of the cruelty of his death [a] or of his devotion to his country : if he, having undertaken the defence of a citizen threatened with loss of civil rights,[b] of a friend, of one who had deserved well of his country, the defence of the Senate, of Italy, and of the State, if he then, obedient to the auspices and religious observance, having announced an evil omen,[c] had been slain openly in broad daylight, in the sight of gods and men, by those villainous pests, in a most sacred temple, in a most sacred cause, while holding a most sacred office. Will anyone, then, venture to say that in life a man ought to be robbed of his honours, whom in death you would think worthy to be honoured by an everlasting memorial ?

XXXIX. " You bought, you collected, you 84 equipped a force," says the accuser. For what purpose ? to besiege the Senate ?[d] to drive out citizens

ple of intimidation see Cicero, *Epp. ad Quintum fratrem,* ii. 1. 3.

cives indemnatos expelleret, bona diriperet, aedes
incenderet, tecta disturbaret, templa deorum immortalium inflammaret, tribunos pl. ferro e rostris
expelleret, provincias, quas vellet, quibus vellet,
venderet, reges appellaret, rerum capitalium con-
demnatos in liberas civitates per legatos nostros
reduceret, principem civitatis ferro obsessum teneret ?
Haec ut efficere posset, quae fieri nisi armis oppressa
re publica nullo modo poterant, idcirco, credo,
manum sibi P. Sestius et copias comparavit. " At
nondum erat maturum, nondum res ipsa ad eius
modi praesidia viros bonos compellebat." Pulsi nos
eramus non omnino ista manu sola, sed tamen non
85 sine ista ; vos taciti maerebatis. Captum erat
forum anno superiore, aede Castoris tamquam arce
aliqua a fugitivis occupata ; silebatur. Omnia
hominum cum egestate tum audacia perditorum
clamore, concursu, vi, manu gerebantur ; perfere-
batis. Magistratus templis pellebantur, alii omnino
aditu ac foro prohibebantur ; nemo resistebat.
Gladiatores ex praetoris comitatu comprensi, in
senatum introducti, confessi, in vincla coniecti a
Milone, emissi a Serrano ; mentio nulla. Forum
corporibus civium Romanorum constratum caede
nocturna ; non modo nulla nova quaestio, sed etiam

a See § 56.

b An allusion to Cato's commission to restore Byzantine
exiles.

c Pompey, who, after Clodius' attempt at his assassination
in August 58 B.C., remained in seclusion till the end of
Clodius' tribunate.   *d* 58 B.C.

uncondemned ? to pillage their property ? to fire
their houses ? to demolish their dwellings ? to set the
temples of the Immortal Gods in flames ? to drive
tribunes of the commons from the Rostra with the
sword ? to sell what provinces he pleased to whom he
pleased ? to style men kings ? [a] to send commissioners
of ours to bring back into independent states men
convicted of capital offences ? [b] to beleaguer the leading man of the State ? [c] To be able to do these things,
which was utterly impossible unless the State had
been crushed by force of arms—this was the reason, I
suppose, why Publius Sestius got together his band
and his forces ! " But," says my opponent, " the time
was not yet ripe; the situation itself was not yet
obliging good citizens to resort to such measures of
protection." I had been driven out, certainly not
altogether by your band alone, Clodius, but yet not
without its help ;—you all mourned without saying a
word. The Forum had been seized in the year before 85
last,[d] and the Temple of Castor garrisoned by runaway
slaves, as if it were a sort of fortress ;—not a word ! All
business was carried on amid the uproar, the disturbances, the violence, the attacks of men rendered
desperate by poverty and recklessness ;—you bore it
patiently. Magistrates were driven from temples ;
others were debarred from coming near, kept out of
the Forum ; no man resisted. Gladiators belonging
to a praetor's [e] retinue were arrested, brought into
the Senate, made to confess, put in chains by Milo,
set free by Serranus [f] ; it was never mentioned.
The Forum was strewn with the bodies of Roman
citizens murdered by night ; not only was no special

---

[e] Appius Claudius Pulcher. See § 78.
[f] As tribune, by his right of *intercessio*.

vetera iudicia sublata. Tribunum pl. plus viginti
vulneribus acceptis iacentem moribundumque vidistis;
alterius tribuni pl., divini hominis (dicam enim, quod
sentio, et quod mecum sentiunt omnes[1]) divini,
insigni quadam, inaudita, nova magnitudine animi,
gravitate, fide praediti, domus est oppugnata ferro,
facibus, exercitu Clodiano.

86   XL. Et tu hoc loco laudas Milonem et iure laudas.
Quem enim umquam virum tam immortali virtute
vidimus ? qui nullo praemio proposito praeter hoc,
quod iam contritum et contemptum putatur, iudicium
bonorum omnia pericula, summos labores, gravissimas
contentiones inimicitiasque suscepit, qui mihi unus
ex omnibus civibus videtur re docuisse, non verbis,
et quid oporteret a praestantibus viris in re publica
fieri et quid necesse esset, oportere hominum audacium eversorum rei publicae sceleri legibus et
iudiciis resistere ; si leges non valerent, iudicia non
essent, si res publica vi consensuque audacium armis
oppressa teneretur, praesidio et copiis defendi vitam
et libertatem necesse esse. Hoc sentire prudentiae
est, facere fortitudinis, et sentire vero et facere per-

---

[1] *Halm here inserts* boni viri, *Maehly* honesti viri.

---

[a] *Nova quaestio* as opposed to the *quaestiones perpetuae.*
Such *novae quaestiones* could be appointed for special cases
which did not fall within the scope of the *iudicia publica.*
The massacre is described in §§ 75-77.

[b] It is possible that the riot of 23 January 57 B.C. was
followed by the proclamation of a *iustitium,* a suspension of
public business. See §§ 89 and 95. Ed. Meyer, *Caesars
Monarchie und das Principat des Pompeius,* ed. 2, pp. 110-
112, discusses the problem.

[c] Titus Annius Milo. The context shows that this attack
by Clodius on Milo's house must have occurred soon after
the riot of 23 January and the wounding of Sestius, and is

commission [a] appointed, but even the existing courts were suppressed.[b] You saw a tribune of the commons lying on the ground, with more than twenty wounds, at the point of death ; the house of another tribune [c] of the commons—one noble beyond the measure of man—for I am going to say what I feel and what everyone feels with me—beyond the measure of man, one for greatness of spirit, for dignity, for loyalty, pre-eminent, paramount, unapproached, was attacked with fire and sword by the army of Clodius.

XL. Even you praise Milo's conduct in this con- 86 nexion, and rightly so.[d] For where have we ever seen a man of such immortal courage ? who without expectation of any reward, except that which is now considered stale and contemptible, the esteem of good citizens, took upon himself all dangers, grievous toils, most painful struggles and enmities ; who appears to me to be the only citizen who taught, by deed and not by words, both what should and must be done in the State by loyal men ; that it was their duty to resist the crimes of reckless men, men who would overthrow the State, by means of the laws and courts of law ; if the laws had no force and there were no courts of law, if the State were shackled by violence and crushed by a conspiracy of desperadoes, then life and liberty must be defended by a protecting force. To understand this is a sign of wisdom, to act accordingly, of courage : both to understand and to act, a sign of perfect and consummate merit.

not to be identified with a later attack on 12 November 57 B.C., described by Cicero in *Epp. ad Att.* iv. 3. 3.

[d] Cicero here addresses the prosecutor, P. Tullius Albinovanus, who had praised Milo's conduct when his house was attacked by Clodius.

87 fectae cumulataeque virtutis. Adiit ad rem publicam
tribunus pl. Milo—(de cuius laude plura dicam, non
quo aut ipse haec dici quam existimari malit aut ego
hunc laudis fructum praesenti libenter impertiam,
praesertim cum verbis consequi non possim, sed quod
existimo, si Milonis causam accusatoris voce conlau-
datam probaro, vos in hoc crimine parem Sesti causam
existimaturos) adiit igitur T. Annius ad causam rei
publicae sic, ut civem patriae recuperare vellet ereptum. Simplex causa, constans ratio, plena consen-
sionis omnium, plena concordiae. Collegas adiutores
habebat ; consulis alterius summum studium, alterius
animus paene placatus, de praetoribus unus alienus,
senatus incredibilis voluntas, equitum Romanorum
animi ad causam excitati, erecta Italia. Duo soli
erant empti ad impediendum ; qui si homines despecti
et contempti tantam rem sustinere non potuissent, se
causam, quam susceperat, nullo labore peracturum
videbat. Agebat auctoritate, agebat consilio, agebat
per summum ordinem, agebat exemplo bonorum ac
fortium civium ; quid re publica, quid se dignum esset,
quis ipse esset, quid sperare, quid maioribus suis
reddere deberet, diligentissime cogitabat.

88 XLI. Huic gravitati hominis videbat ille gladiator

---

^a Milo was present in court. For further compliments to
Milo see Cicero, *Epp. ad Att.* iv. 3. 5.

^b Because he had got a body of armed men together, only
to protect his life and property. " Cicero assumes that Milo
and Sestius had done the same thing, and if Milo deserves
the praise given him by the prosecutor, Sestius deserves it
equally " (Long).

^c P. Lentulus Spinther ; Q. Metellus Nepos.

^d Appius Claudius Pulcher.

^e Numerius Quintius Rufus and Sextus Atilius Serranus.

^f Clodius.

Milo, as a tribune of the commons, took up the 87
cause of the State. I propose to say more in his
praise, not because he would himself wish my words
to be spoken rather than to remain matters of
opinion, nor because I would gladly address these
compliments to him in person,[a] especially since I
cannot find words to express them ; but because I
think that if I have shown that Milo's case has been
commended by Sestius' prosecutor, you will consider that Sestius has an equally good case against
the charge [b] brought against him. Milo then took
up the cause of the State with the desire to restore
a citizen who had been violently taken from it. His
purpose was simple, his method was consistent, fully
supported by general agreement and complete
unanimity. He had his colleagues to help him ;
one consul showed the greatest cordiality on his
behalf, the other was almost reconciled to him [c] ; of
the praetors one was unfavourable to him [d] ; the
enthusiasm of the Senate was extraordinary, the spirit
of the Roman Knights was aroused in his cause,
Italy was on the tiptoe of expectation. Two men [e]
only had been bought to offer obstruction ; and if
those despicable and contemptible men should prove
unequal to so great a task, he saw that he would carry
through the cause which he had undertaken without
difficulty. He acted with energy, with judgment,
with the sanction of that exalted Order of the Senate,
with the example of loyal and brave citizens before
him ; he most carefully considered what was worthy
of the State, what was worthy of himself, who he
was, what he felt bound to hope for, what was due
to the traditions of his ancestors.

XLI. That swordster [f] felt that he could not be a 88

155

se, si moribus ageret, parem esse non posse; ad ferrum, faces, ad cotidianam caedem, incendia, rapinas se cum exercitu suo contulit; domum oppugnare, itineribus occurrere, vi lacessere et terrere coepit. Non movit hominem summa gravitate summaque constantia; sed quamquam dolor animi, innata libertas, prompta excellensque virtus fortissimum virum hortabatur, vi vim oblatam, praesertim saepius, ut frangeret et refutaret, tanta moderatio fuit hominis, tantum consilium, ut contineret dolorem neque eadem se re ulcisceretur, qua esset lacessitus, sed illum tot iam in funeribus rei publicae exsultantem ac tripudiantem

89 legum, si posset, laqueis constringeret. Descendit ad accusandum. Quis umquam tam proprie rei publicae causa, nullis inimicitiis, nullis praemiis, nulla hominum postulatione aut etiam opinione id eum umquam esse facturum? Fracti erant animi hominis; hoc enim accusante pristini illius sui iudicii turpitudinem desperabat. Ecce tibi consul, praetor, tribunus pl. nova novi generis edicta proponunt, ne reus adsit, ne citetur, ne quaeratur, ne mentionem omnino cuiquam iudicum aut iudiciorum facere liceat! Quid ageret vir ad virtutem, dignitatem, gloriam natus vi sceleratorum hominum conroborata, legibus

---

a When accused of violating the worship of the Bona Dea he was acquitted (before 15 May 61 B.C.), thanks to the nonchalance of Caesar and to Crassus' bribery of the *iudices*.

b In 57 B.C. Milo twice unsuccessfully attempted to prosecute Clodius for breach of the peace under the *lex Plautia de vi*. On the first occasion, probably sometime in February, the consul (Q. Metellus Nepos), with the support of a praetor (Appius Claudius) and a tribune (Sextus Atilius Serranus), refused to accept the charges. See §§ 85, 95. After Clodius had attacked his house on 12 November Milo renewed his attempt, but was foiled by constitutional

match for a man of such determination if he acted only according to established rules. He had recourse to arms, to firebrands, to daily assassination, incendiarism, and pillage with his army ; he proceeded to attack his house, to lie in wait for his passage, to assault and threaten him with violence. But that most firm and resolute man could not be disconcerted. Although his indignation, his natural spirit of liberty, his ready and surpassing courage urged that most gallant of men to meet force with force, to break down and repel the violence directed against him, and that repeatedly ; so great was his moderation, so great his wisdom, that he restrained his indignation, and did not avenge himself by the same means by which he had been provoked, but endeavoured, if he could, to bind tight in the meshes of the law the man who was dancing and leaping for joy at all the disasters of the State. He came down to court 89 to prosecute him. Who ever did this so specially for public reasons—without enmity, without reward, without solicitation, or even without any expectation that he would ever do so ? The fellow's courage was broken ; for with such an accuser he had no hope of a disgraceful farce like his former trial.[a] Then, lo and behold, a consul, a praetor, a tribune of the commons published new edicts of a new kind : " Let not the accused appear, let him not be summoned, let there be no inquiry, let no one be allowed ever to mention judges or judicial proceedings." [b] What was a man to do, who was born for courage, honour, and glory, when the violence of scoundrels was reinforced, laws and proceedings

obstructions created by Nepos and his friends. For the whole question see Ed. Meyer, *op. cit.* p. 109, n. 3.

iudiciisque sublatis ? Cervices tribunus pl. privato,
praestantissimus vir profligatissimo homini daret an
causam susceptam abiceret[1] an se domi contineret ?
Et vinci turpe putavit et deterreri et latere ; perfecit,
ut,[2] quoniam sibi in illum legibus uti non liceret,
illius vim neque in suo neque in rei publicae periculo
pertimesceret.

90   XLII. Quo modo igitur hoc in genere praesidii com-
parati accusas Sestium, cum idem laudes Milonem ?
An, qui sua tecta defendit, qui ab aris, focis ferrum
flammamque depellit, qui sibi licere vult tuto esse
in foro, in templo, in curia, iure praesidium comparat ;
qui vulneribus, quae cernit cotidie toto corpore,
monetur, ut aliquo praesidio caput et cervices et
iugulum ac latera tutetur, hunc de vi accusandum
91 putas ? Quis enim nostrum, iudices, ignorat ita
naturam rerum tulisse, ut quodam tempore homines
nondum neque naturali neque civili iure descripto
fusi per agros ac dispersi vagarentur tantumque
haberent, quantum manu ac viribus per caedem ac
vulnera aut eripere aut retinere potuissent ? Qui
igitur primi virtute et consilio praestanti exstiterunt,
ii perspecto genere humanae docilitatis atque ingenii

[1] adfligeret *MSS.* : abiceret *Mommsen.*

[2] *After* deterreri *MSS. variously give* etiam eripere eicit
(*or* elegit) ; etiam eripi reiecit ut ; et latere (*or* lamentari) ;
et deterreri et clam eripi ; id egit ut *Peterson* : perfecit ut
Madvig.

---

[a] He made up his mind to have an armed bodyguard.

[b] Sestius, who was in court.

[c] *Ius naturale = ius gentium,* " the law of the world," an
antithesis to *ius civile,* the law of independent communities.

abolished ?   Was a tribune of the commons to be at
the mercy of a private person, a man of high excellence
at the mercy of a complete scoundrel ?   Was he to
abandon the cause he had undertaken ?   Was he
to shut himself up in his house ?   He thought that to
accept defeat, to be frightened off, to take to hiding,
was dishonour; he so acted that, since he was not
allowed to invoke the law against Clodius, he need
not fear his violence, whether it was himself or the
State that was in danger.[a]

XLII. How then is it that, in this matter of 90
getting together a bodyguard, you make it a crime in
Sestius, while at the same time you make it a merit
in Milo ?   Or does the man who defends his home,
who repels sword and fire from altar and hearth, who
desires that he may be allowed to appear without
danger in the Forum, on the Rostra, in the Senate;—
does he get together an armed force lawfully ?   But
the man [b] who is warned by the wounds which he sees
daily all over his body, to protect his head and neck
and throat and sides by some defence—think you that
he should be accused of violence ?   For which of us, 91
gentlemen, does not know the natural course of human
history—how there was once a time, before either
natural or civil law [c] had been formulated, when men
roamed, scattered and dispersed over the country, and
had no other possessions than just so much as they had
been able either to seize by strength and violence, or
keep at the cost of slaughter and wounds ?   So then
those who at first showed themselves to be most eminent for merit and wisdom, having perceived the essen-
tial teachableness of human nature, gathered together

_Cf._ Cicero, _De officiis_, iii. 17. 69 : " maiores aliud ius gentium,
aliud ius civile esse voluerunt."

dissipatos unum in locum congregarunt eosque ex
feritate illa ad iustitiam atque ad mansuetudinem
transduxerunt. Tum res ad communem utilitatem,
quas publicas appellamus, tum conventicula hominum,
quae postea civitates nominatae sunt,[1] tum domicilia
coniuncta, quas urbes dicimus, invento et divino iure
92 et humano moenibus saepserunt. Atque inter hanc
vitam perpolitam humanitate et illam immanem nihil
tam interest quam ius atque vis. Horum utro uti
nolumus, altero est utendum. Vim volumus ex-
stingui ; ius valeat necesse est, id est iudicia, quibus
omne ius continetur. Iudicia displicent aut nulla
sunt ; vis dominetur necesse est. Hoc vident omnes ;
Milo et vidit et fecit, ut ius experiretur, vim de-
pelleret. Altero uti voluit, ut virtus audaciam vin-
ceret ; altero usus necessario est, ne virtus ab audacia
vinceretur. Eademque ratio fuit Sesti si minus in
accusando (neque enim per omnes fuit idem fieri
necesse), at certe in necessitate defendendae salutis
suae praesidioque contra vim et manum comparando.
93 XLIII. O di immortales ! quemnam ostenditis
exitum nobis, quam spem rei publicae datis ? quotus
quisque invenietur tanta virtute vir, qui optimam
quamque causam rei publicae amplectatur, qui bonis
viris deserviat, qui solidam laudem veramque quaerat ?
cum sciat duo illa rei publicae paene fata, Gabinium

---

[1] instituerunt *supplied by Madvig after* nominatae sunt.

[a] For *fata cf.* Ovid, *Fasti*, v. 389, where Hercules and
Achilles are described as *Troiae duo fata.*

into one place those who had been scattered abroad, and brought them from that state of savagery to one of justice and humanity. Then things serving for common use, which we call public, associations of men, which were afterwards called states, then continuous series of dwelling-places which we call cities, they enclosed with walls, after divine and human law had been introduced. Now, between life thus 92 refined and humanized, and that life of savagery, nothing marks the difference so clearly as law and violence. Whichever of the two we are unwilling to use, we must use the other. If we would have violence abolished, law must prevail, that is the administration of justice, on which law wholly depends ; if we dislike the administration of justice, or if there is none, force must rule. All are aware of this ; Milo both knew it and so acted as to make trial of law, but to repel force. He was desirous to make use of the first, that virtue might overcome audacity ; he was compelled to use the second, that virtue might not be overcome by audacity. And Sestius' method was the same, if not in regard to prosecution—for it was not necessary for every one to do the same—yet certainly in regard to the necessity of defending his life and assembling a bodyguard to protect himself against force and violence.

XLIII. Immortal Gods ! what is the issue that 93 you reserve for us ? What hope do you grant to the State ? how few men will be found so courageous as to undertake the defence of the State in every just cause, to devote themselves to the service of loyal citizens, to seek solid and true glory ? when they think upon Gabinius and Piso, those two men who brought [a] the State to the brink of ruin ! when

CICERO

et Pisonem, alterum haurire cotidie ex pacatissimae[1]
atque opulentissimae[1] Syriae gazis innumerabile
pondus auri, bellum inferre quiescentibus,[2] ut eorum
veteres inlibatasque divitias in profundissimum libi-
dinum suarum gurgitem profundat, villam aedificare
in oculis omnium tantam, tugurium ut iam videatur
esse illa villa, quam ipse tribunus pl. pictam olim in
contionibus explicabat, quo fortissimum ac summum
civem in invidiam homo castus ac non cupidus vocaret ;
94 alterum Thracibus ac Dardanis primum pacem maxima
pecunia vendidisse, deinde, ut illi pecuniam conficere
possent, vexandam iis Macedoniam et spoliandam
tradidisse, eundemque bona creditorum civium Romanorum cum debitoribus Graecis divisisse, cogere
pecunias maximas a Dyrrachinis, spoliare Thessalos,
certam Achaeis in annos singulos pecuniam impera-
visse neque tamen ullo in publico aut religioso loco
signum aut tabulam aut ornamentum reliquisse ;
illos sic inludere, quibus omne supplicium atque
omnis iure optimo poena debetur ; reos esse hos

---

[1] pacatissimis . . . opulentissimis *MSS.*: pacatissimae . . .
opulentissimae *Hirschfeld* : paratissimis *Koch* : beatissimis
Kiessling.   [2] quietis gentibus *Weidner.*

---

[a] Gabinius, proconsul of Syria (57–54 B.C.).

[b] Hirschfeld's conjecture is adopted.

[c] That of L. Lucullus near Tusculum, of which Gabinius,
when tribune in 67 B.C., showed the Romans a picture to
emphasize the extravagance of the man whom he wanted to
be superseded by Pompey. Or *explicabat* may mean " described in his speeches."

[d] Piso, proconsul of Macedonia (57–55 B.C.). For an
assessment of the conduct of Piso and Gabinius as provincial
governors see Butler and Cary, *Cicero, De provinciis consularibus*, Appendices I and II.

they know how the one [a] is daily draining from the
treasure-houses of Syria, that rich land now completely pacified,[b] an enormous mass of gold, waging
war upon quiet peoples, that he may pour into the
bottomless whirlpool of his lusts their ancient and
untouched wealth ; how he is building for all men
to see a mansion of such extent that that villa [c]
would seem to be a hut by comparison, which this
very man when he was tribune of the commons once
displayed in a picture before meetings, in the character of an honest and unselfish man, that he might
excite your indignation against one of the bravest
and best of citizens ;—and the other,[d] when they 94
know how he first sold peace to the Thracians and
Dardanians [e] for an immense sum, and next, that
they might be able to make up the money, handed
Macedonia over to them to harass and rob ; and
how he also divided the goods of creditors, citizens
of Rome, among Greeks who were their debtors ;
how he is extorting large sums from the people of
Dyrrhachium,[f] and robbing the Thessalians, how he
has imposed upon the people of Achaia [g] a fixed annual
tax, and has not left in any public or consecrated place
a single statue or picture or ornament,—when they
know, I say, that these two men, to whom every kind
of punishment and every penalty are most justly due,
are acting with such insolence, while these two [h]
whom you see before you are on their trial.   I say

[e] A warlike Illyrian tribe in the south of the later province
of Moesia Superior, which finally yielded to M. Licinius
Crassus (29 and 28 B.C.).
   [f] See *De prov. cons.* 5.
   [g] The inhabitants of the Peloponnese. See *De prov. cons.* 5.
   [h] Sestius and Milo. Milo was at the time being prosecuted
by Clodius for breach of the peace.

duos, quos videtis. Omitto iam Numerium, Ser-
ranum, Aelium, quisquilias seditionis Clodianae;
sed tamen hi quoque etiam nunc volitant, ut videtis,
nec, dum vos de vobis aliquid timebitis, illi umquam
de se pertimescent.

95 XLIV. Nam quid ego de aedile ipso loquar, qui
etiam diem dixit et accusavit de vi Milonem? Neque
hic tamen ulla umquam iniuria adducetur, ut eum
tali virtute tantaque firmitate animi se in rem publicam fuisse paeniteat; sed qui haec vident adulescentes, quonam suas mentes conferent? Ille, qui
monumenta publica, qui aedes sacras, qui domos inimicorum suorum oppugnavit, excidit, incendit, qui
stipatus semper sicariis, saeptus armatis, munitus
indicibus fuit, quorum hodie copia redundat, qui
et peregrinam manum facinerosorum concitavit et
servos ad caedem idoneos emit et in tribunatu carcerem totum in forum effudit, volitat aedilis, accusat
eum, qui aliqua ex parte eius furorem exsultantem
repressit; hic, qui se est tutatus sic, ut in privata re
deos penates suos, in re publica iura tribunatus atque
auspicia defenderet, accusare eum moderate, a quo

---

a Aelius Ligus. See § 69.

b *Quisquiliae* and *volitant* belong to the same metaphor,
as is suggested by a fanciful derivation of *quisquiliae* given
by Festus, p. 340, l. 12 (Lindsay). See also *Remains of Old
Latin* (L.C.L.), i, pp. 554-555, where *quisquiliae* appears in
Frag. No. 260 of Caecilius Statius and the passage from
Festus is quoted.

c Clodius was elected aedile on 20 January 56 B.C. On
2 February he began to impeach Milo " *de vi*," " *quod
gladiatores adhibuisset ut rogationem posset de Cicerone
perferre*," but was defeated by continual postponements and
finally dropped the case.

d He pulled down the Porticus Catuli, built on the Palatine by Catulus, the colleague of Marius in the victory at

nothing now of Numerius, Serranus, Aelius,[a] the drifting refuse [b] of the Clodian revolutionaries ; and yet these men even now are fluttering about, as you see ; nor, as long as you are afraid about yourselves, will these others have any fear about themselves.

XLIV. For what am I to say about the aedile 95 himself, who even gave notice that he would bring an action against Milo, and prosecuted him for violence ? [c] No doubt Milo will never be prevailed upon by any outrage to regret having shown such energy and resolution in state affairs. But the young men who see these things, whither will they turn their thoughts ? The man who attacked, destroyed, and burnt public monuments, sacred temples,[d] and the houses of his enemies ; the man who has always been closely fenced in by assassins, guarded by armed men, fortified by informers, of whom at the present day there is an abundant supply, who has incited to violence a band of foreign scoundrels, has bought slaves ready for murder, and during his tribunate has emptied the whole jail into the Forum, now flutters about as aedile, and prosecutes the man who to some extent checked his exultant fury ; while he who protected himself only so as to be able to defend, as a private individual, the gods of his home, and, in his public capacity as a magistrate, the rights of the tribunate and the auspices, has not been allowed by a resolution [e] of the Senate to prose-

Vercellae (101 B.C.), and set fire to the Nympharum Aedes, a temple in the Campus Martius containing the records of the censors. His henchman, Sextus Clodius, joined him in this violence (Cicero, *Pro Caelio*, 78). See p. 218, note *b*.

[e] Apparently the *edicta* mentioned in § 89 were sanctioned by the Senate. See Cicero's complaint to Lentulus in *Epp. ad Fam.* i. 9. 15.

ipse nefarie accusatur, per senatus auctoritatem non
96 est situs.   Nimirum hoc illud est, quod de me potissimum tu in accusatione quaesisti, quae esset nostra
" natio optimatium " ; sic enim dixisti.   Rem quaeris
praeclaram iuventuti ad discendum nec mihi difficilem
ad perdocendum ; de qua pauca, iudices, dicam, et,
ut arbitror, nec ab utilitate eorum, qui audient, nec
ab officio vestro nec ab ipsa causa P. Sesti abhorrebit
oratio mea.

XLV. Duo genera semper in hac civitate fuerunt
eorum, qui versari in re publica atque in ea se ex-
cellentius gerere studuerunt ; quibus ex generibus
alteri se populares, alteri optimates et haberi et esse
voluerunt.   Qui ea, quae faciebant quaeque dicebant,
multitudini iucunda volebant esse, populares, qui
autem ita se gerebant, ut sua consilia optimo cuique
97 probarent, optimates habebantur.   " Quis ergo iste
optimus quisque ? "   Numero, si quaeris, innumerabiles (neque enim aliter stare possemus) ; sunt
principes consilii publici, sunt, qui eorum sectam se-
quuntur, sunt maximorum[1] ordinum homines, qui-

---

[1] maxime eorum *Weidner.*

---

[a] An account of the Optimates follows (§§ 96-143).
[b] I am indebted to some renderings in *From Alexander to
Constantine* (*Passages and Documents illustrating the History of Social and Political Ideas, 336 B.C.–A.D. 337*), Ernest

cute dispassionately the man by whom he himself is prosecuted with such virulence. This is no doubt 96 the reason why,[a] in the body of the charge, you made a point of asking me especially what was the meaning of our " Breed of Aristocrats," to use your own term. You ask about a matter, which is most proper for the young to learn, while it is not difficult for me to offer some instruction ; and I will say a few words about it, gentlemen, nor, I think, will what I say be irrelevant, either to the advantage of those who hear me, or to the discharge of your duties, or to the case itself of Publius Sestius.

XLV. There have always been two classes of men in this State who have sought to engage in public affairs and to distinguish themselves in them.[b] Of these two classes, one aimed at being, by repute and in reality, " Friends of the People," the other " Aristocrats." Those who wished everything they did and said to be agreeable to the masses were reckoned as " Friends of the People," but those who acted so as to win by their policy the approval of all the best citizens were reckoned as " Aristocrats." " Who then are these 97 " Best Citizens " of yours ? " In number, if you ask me, they are infinite ; for otherwise we could not exist. They include those who direct the policy of the State,[c] with those who follow their lead. They include those very large classes to whom the Senate is open[d] ;

Barker (Oxford, 1956), pp. 202-204 ; and in *Christianity and Classical Culture*, C. N. Cochrane (Oxford, 1940), pp. 44-45.

[c] Or, " the Council of State " (*i.e.* the Senate).

[d] In theory every free-born citizen was eligible, through the quaestorship, for the Senate, but in practice equestrian wealth and standing were requisite. Cicero means the wealthy classes in Rome and the Italian towns.

bus patet curia, sunt municipales rusticique Romani,
sunt negotii gerentes, sunt etiam libertini optimates.
Numerus, ut dixi, huius generis late et varie diffusus
est ; sed genus universum, ut tollatur error, brevi
circumscribi et definiri potest. Omnes optimates
sunt, qui neque nocentes sunt nec natura improbi
nec furiosi nec malis domesticis impediti. Sequitur[1]
igitur, ut ii sint, quam tu " nationem " appellasti, qui
et integri sunt et sani et bene de rebus domesticis
constituti. Horum qui voluntati, commodis, opinionibus[2] in gubernanda re publica serviunt, defensores optimatium ipsique optimates gravissimi et clarissimi
98 cives numerantur et principes civitatis. Quid est
igitur propositum his rei publicae gubernatoribus,
quod intueri et quo cursum suum derigere debeant ?
Id quod est praestantissimum maximeque optabile
omnibus sanis et bonis et beatis, cum dignitate otium.
Hoc qui volunt, omnes optimates, qui efficiunt, summi
viri et conservatores civitatis putantur. Neque enim
rerum gerendarum dignitate homines efferri ita con-
venit, ut otio non prospiciant, neque ullum amplexari
otium, quod abhorreat a dignitate.

XLVI. Huius autem otiosae dignitatis haec fundamenta sunt, haec membra, quae tuenda principibus
et vel capitis periculo defendenda sunt, religiones,

---

[1] *MSS. give* esto *and* est: sequitur *Madvig is adopted and
translated.*
[2] opibus *Koch* : opinionibus *Halm.*

---

[a] This virtually means the citizen population of Italy
resident outside the *territorium* of the city of Rome itself.
See § 32. The citizenship of Rome had become, through the
franchise legislation of 90–89 B.C., the citizenship of Italy.
[b] See pp. 302–304. *otium*, " freedom from civil strife " ;
dignitas, " a man's honour, or position."

they include Romans living in municipal towns *a* and in country districts ; they include men of business ; freedmen also are among the " Aristocrats." In its numbers, I repeat, this class is spread far and wide and is variously composed. But, to prevent misunderstanding, the whole class can be summed-up and defined in a few words. All are " Aristocrats " who are neither criminal nor vicious in disposition, nor mad revolutionaries, nor embarrassed by home troubles. It follows, then, that those who are upright, sound in mind, and easy in circumstances are those whom you have called a " Breed." Those who serve the wishes, the interests and principles of these men in the government of the State are called the supporters of the " Aristocrats " and are themselves reckoned as the most influential of the " Aristocrats," the most eminent citizens, and the leaders of the State. What 98 then is the mark set before those who guide the helm of state, upon which they ought to keep their eyes and towards which they ought to direct their course ? It is that which is far the best and the most desirable for all who are sound and good and prosperous ; it is " Peace with Honour." *b* Those who desire this are all reckoned as " Aristocrats," those who achieve it as the foremost men and the saviours of the State. For just as it is unfitting for men to be so carried away by the honour of public office that they are indifferent to peace, so too it is unfitting for them to welcome a peace which is inconsistent with honour.

XLVI. Now this " Peace with Honour " has the following foundations, the following elements, which our leaders ought to protect and defend even at the risk of life itself : religious observances, the auspices,

auspicia, potestates magistratuum, senatus auctoritas, leges, mos maiorum, iudicia, iuris dictio, fides,
provinciae, socii, imperii laus, res militaris, aerarium.
99 Harum rerum tot atque tantarum esse defensorem
et patronum magni animi est, magni ingenii mag-
naeque constantiae. Etenim in tanto civium numero
magna multitudo est eorum, qui aut propter metum
poenae peccatorum suorum conscii novos motus con-
versionesque rei publicae quaerant, aut qui propter
insitum quendam animi furorem discordiis civium
ac seditione pascantur, aut qui propter implica-
tionem rei familiaris communi incendio malint quam
suo deflagrare. Qui cum auctores[1] sunt et duces
suorum studiorum vitiorumque nacti, in re publica
fluctus excitantur, ut vigilandum sit iis, qui sibi
gubernacula patriae depoposcerunt, enitendumque
omnia scientia ac diligentia, ut conservatis iis, quae
ego paulo ante fundamenta ac membra esse dixi,
tenere cursum possint et capere otii illum portum et
100 dignitatis. Hanc ego viam, iudices, si aut asperam
atque arduam et[2] plenam esse periculorum aut
insidiarum negem, mentiar, praesertim cum id non
modo intellexerim semper, sed etiam praeter ceteros
senserim.

XLVII. Maioribus praesidiis et copiis oppugnatur
res publica quam defenditur, propterea quod audaces
homines et perditi nutu impelluntur et ipsi etiam
sponte sua contra rem publicam incitantur ; boni

---

[1] tutores MSS.: auctores *Naugerius*.
[2] aut MSS.: et *Kayser*.

the powers of the magistrates, the authority of the Senate, the laws, ancestral custom, criminal and civil jurisdiction, credit,[a] our provinces, our allies, the prestige of our government, the army, the Treasury. To be a defender and an advocate of so many and so 99 important interests requires an exalted spirit, great ability, and great resolution. For, in so large a body of citizens, there are great numbers of men who, either from fear of punishment, being conscious of their crimes, seek to cause revolution and changes of government ; or who, owing to a sort of inborn revolutionary madness, batten on civil discord and sedition ; or who, on account of embarrassment in their finances, prefer a general conflagration to their own ruin. When such men as these have found advisers and leaders for their vicious aims, storms are aroused in the commonwealth, so that those who have hitherto claimed possession of the helm of state must watch and strive with all their skill and devotion that they may be able, without any damage to those foundations and elements of which I have just spoken, to keep on their course and to reach that haven of " Peace with Honour." If I were to deny, gentlemen, 100 that this course is stormy and difficult, perilous and treacherous, I should be telling a lie, the less excusable since not only have I always understood it to be so, but experience also has convinced me more than anyone else.

XLVII. There are greater forces and means for attacking than for defending the State. The reason is, that reckless and abandoned men need only a nod to set them moving, and their own natural disposition incites them against the State ; while honest

[a] Financial credit. See Cicero, *De officiis*, ii. 84.

nescio quo modo tardiores sunt et principiīs rerum
neglectis ad extremum ipsa denique necessitate excitantur, ita ut non numquam cunctatione ac tarditate,
dum otium volunt etiam sine dignitate retinere, ipsi
101 utrumque amittant. Propugnatores autem rei publicae qui esse voluerunt, si leviores sunt, desciscunt,
si timidiores, desunt ; permanent illi soli atque omnia
rei publicae causa perferunt, qui sunt tales, qualis
pater tuus, M. Scaure, fuit, qui a C. Graccho usque
ad Q. Varium seditiosis omnibus restitit, quem numquam ulla vis, ullae minae, ulla invidia labefecit, aut
qualis Q. Metellus, patruus matris tuae, qui cum
florentem hominem in populari ratione, L. Saturninum, censor notasset cumque insitivum Gracchum
contra vim multitudinis incitatae censu prohibuisset
cumque in eam legem, quam non iure rogatam iudi-
carat, iurare unus noluisset, de civitate maluit quam

---

a Cicero is obviously referring to events since 59 B.C.

b *i.e.* men of distinction who take part in public affairs,
as opposed to the mass of loyal citizens (*boni homines*) ;
cf. § 103.

c M. Aemilius Scaurus was probably the praetor presiding
at the trial of Sestius. Of his father, M. Aemilius Scaurus,
who was consul 115 B.C., censor 109 B.C., and *princeps
senatus* from 115 B.C., Cicero says, *Pro Fonteio*, 24, " cuius
nutu prope terrarum orbis regebatur." He was a leading
Optimate. See also § 39 and note.

d When the Social War had broken out at the end of
91 B.C. Q. Varius Hybrida (trib. 90 B.C.), of Spanish descent,
began under the *lex Varia* to impeach those alleged to have
contributed to the outbreak, Scaurus among them. By asking his hearers to decide between the word of the *princeps
senatus* and that of Q. Varius *Hispanus*, Scaurus foiled his
prosecutor.

172

folk somehow or other show less activity, neglect the
beginnings of movements, and are aroused to action
at the last moment only by simple necessity ; so
that sometimes, owing to their hesitation and indolence, while they wish still to enjoy peace even
with the loss of honour, through their own fault
they lose both.[a] But among those who have wished 101
to be defenders of the State,[b] the weaker desert,
the more timid are not to be found, those only remain
firm and endure everything for the sake of the State
who are like your father, Marcus Scaurus,[c] who resisted all revolutionaries from Gaius Gracchus to
Quintus Varius,[d] whom no violence, no threats, no
unpopularity ever caused to waver ; or like Q.
Metellus,[e] your mother's uncle, who, in his censorship, after he had placed his ban on L. Saturninus,
a notable leader of the popular persuasion,[f] and
after he had excluded from the list of citizens, in
spite of the violence of an excited mob, one who
claimed to be a Gracchus but was an impostor,[g]
and after he alone had refused to take an oath to
a law which he judged to have been illegally proposed, preferred to renounce his country rather

[e] Q. Metellus Numidicus (consul 109, censor 102 b.c.) set
on Saturninus and Glaucia his *nota censoria* which, with the
concurrence of his colleague, would remove them from the
Senate. A riot ensued. But his colleague and cousin, C.
Metellus Caprarius, refused to concur, and so preserved
them their status.

[f] The words *in populari ratione* recur in § 114 (of P. Vatinius) and in Cicero, *Brutus*, 103 (of C. Papirius Carbo,
tribune 131 b.c., consul 120 b.c.).

[g] L. Equitius, who claimed to be a son of Tiberius
Gracchus, was denounced as an impostor by Sempronia,
sister of the Gracchi. Elected tribune in 100 b.c. he was
killed on 10 December, the day he entered office.

de sententia demoveri, aut, ut vetera exempla, quorum est copia digna huius imperii gloria, relinquam neve eorum aliquem, qui vivunt, nominem, qualis nuper Q. Catulus fuit, quem neque periculi tempestas neque honoris aura potuit umquam de suo cursu aut spe aut metu demovere.

102   XLVIII. Haec imitamini, per deos immortalis, qui dignitatem, qui laudem, qui gloriam quaeritis ! Haec ampla sunt, haec divina, haec immortalia ; haec fama celebrantur, monumentis annalium mandantur, posteritati propagantur. Est labor, non nego ; pericula magna, fateor,

> multae insidiae sunt bonis

verissime dictum est ; sed te

> id, quod multi invideant multique expetant, inscitia est,

inquit,

> postulare, nisi laborem summa cum cura ecferas.

Nollem idem alio loco dixisset, quod exciperent improbi cives :

> oderint, dum metuant ;

103 praeclara enim illa praecepta dederat iuventuti. Sed tamen haec via ac ratio rei publicae capessendae olim erat magis pertimescenda, cum multis in rebus multitudinis studium ac populi commodum ab utilitate

---

    [a] See § 37.

    [b] Q. Lutatius Catulus, consul 78 B.C., censor 65 B.C., and *princeps senatus*, a resolute conservative and in the forefront of opposition to all popular movements. He died in 61 or early 60 B.C., to the grief of Cicero. See *Epp. ad Att.* i. 20. 3.

    [c] The quotations are the words of Atreus to his sons from

than his principles [a] ; or—not to recall so many
ancient examples, the number of which is worthy of
the glory of this Empire, and without mentioning by
name any of the great men still alive—such a man
as Quintus Catulus [b] lately was, whom neither danger's stormy wind nor honour's gentle air could ever
deflect from his course either by hope or by fear.

XLVIII. Imitate these examples, I beg you in 102
the name of the Immortal Gods, you who aspire
to honour, praise, and glory ! These examples are
glorious, they are superhuman, they are immortal ;
they are proclaimed in common talk, are committed
to the records of history, are handed down to posterity.
It is a difficult task ; I do not deny it. There are
great risks ; I confess it. Most truly has it been
said,

> Many the snares that for the good are set,

but the poet adds :

> What many envy, many strive to win,
> For you to claim is foolishness, unless
> You summon all your toil and all your care
> To win it. [c]

I could wish that the same poet had not elsewhere
used words for evil-minded men to lay hold of :

> Let them hate, so but they fear ;

for in those others he had given the young excellent advice. But formerly those who followed this 103
path and principle in affairs of state [d] had far more
to fear, for in many ways the desire of the masses
and the advantage of the People did not agree with

the *Atreus* of L. Accius, a Roman tragic poet (170–*c.* 86 B.C.).
See *Remains of Old Latin* (L.C.L.), ii, pp. 386-387.
   [d] *i.e.* pursued the policy of the Optimates.

rei publicae discrepabat. Tabellaria lex ab L. Cassio
ferebatur. Populus libertatem agi putabat suam.
Dissentiebant principes et in salute optimatium
temeritatem multitudinis et tabellae licentiam per-
timescebant. Agrariam Ti. Gracchus legem ferebat.
Grata erat populo ; fortunae constitui tenuiorum
videbantur. Nitebantur contra optimates, quod et
discordiam excitari videbant et, cum locupletes pos-
sessionibus diuturnis moverentur, spoliari rem publicam propugnatoribus arbitrabantur. Frumentariam
legem C. Gracchus ferebat. Iucunda res plebei ;
victus enim suppeditabatur large sine labore. Re-
pugnabant boni, quod et ab industria plebem ad
desidiam avocari putabant et aerarium exhauriri
videbant.

XLIX. Multa etiam nostra memoria, quae consulto
praetereo, fuerunt in ea contentione, ut popularis
104 cupiditas a consilio principum dissideret. Nunc iam
nihil est, quod populus a delectis principibusque dissentiat, nec flagitat rem ullam neque novarum rerum
est cupidus et otio suo et dignitate optimi cuiusque
et universae rei publicae gloria delectatur. Itaque

ᵃ The *lex Cassia tabellaria* of L. Cassius Longinus
(tribune 137 B.C.) extended to criminal trials before the
comitia centuriata (except in cases of *perduellio*) the principle
of the secret ballot introduced into elections by a *lex Gabinia*
(139 B.C.). The Optimates feared the secret ballot as a challenge to their control of the electorate.
ᵇ The *lex agraria* of Tiberius Gracchus (133 B.C.) provided that no tenant (*possessor*) of *ager publicus populi
Romani* should occupy more than 500 *iugera*, those with
one or two (not more) sons being allowed an extra 250 for
each ; and that the land resumed should be distributed to the
poor in small allotments (size depending on circumstances),

the public interest. A law to provide for voting by ballot was proposed by Lucius Cassius.[a] The people thought that their liberty was at stake. The leaders of the State held a different opinion ; in a matter that concerned the interests of the Optimates, they dreaded the impetuosity of the masses and the licence afforded by the ballot. Tiberius Gracchus proposed an agrarian law.[b] The law was acceptable to the People : the fortunes of the poorer classes seemed likely to be established. The Optimates opposed it, because they saw in it an incentive to dissension, and also thought that the State would be stripped of its champions by the eviction of the rich from their long-established tenancies. Gaius Gracchus brought forward a corn law.[c] It was agreeable to the masses, for it provided food in abundance without work. Loyal citizens were against it, because they thought that it was a call to the masses to desert industry for idleness, and saw that it was a drain upon the Treasury.

XLIX. Many matters also within my own recollection, which I purposely leave unnoticed, were subjects of dispute, for in them the desires of the People did not agree with the views of the leading men. But just at the present time there is no 104 reason for the People to disagree with their picked and chief men. They demand nothing, they do not desire revolution, they delight in their own peace, in the honour of the " Best Men," and in the glory of the whole State.[d] And so those who are for revolu-

not alienable, but capable of passing by inheritance, and subject to a small rent.   [c] See § 55.
  [d] For the bearing of this sentence on the interpretation of the phrase *cum dignitate otium* see p. 303.

homines seditiosi ac turbulenti, quia nulla iam largitione populum Romanum concitare possunt, quod plebes perfuncta gravissimis seditionibus ac discordiis otium amplexatur,[1] conductas habent contiones neque id agunt, ut ea dicant aut ferant, quae illi velint audire, qui in contione sunt, sed pretio ac mercede perficiunt, ut, quicquid dicant, id illi velle audire
105 videantur. Num vos existimatis Gracchos aut Saturninum aut quemquam illorum veterum, qui populares habebantur, ullum umquam in contione habuisse conductum ? Nemo habuit. Ipsa enim largitio et spes commodi propositi sine mercede ulla multitudinem concitabat. Itaque temporibus illis qui populares erant, offendebant illi quidem apud graves et honestos homines, sed populi iudiciis atque omni significatione florebant. His in theatro plaudebatur, hi suffragiis, quod contenderant, consequebantur, horum homines nomen, orationem, vultum, incessum amabant. Qui autem adversabantur ei generi, graves et magni homines habebantur ; sed valebant in senatu multum, apud bonos viros plurimum, multitudini iucundi non erant, suffragiis offendebatur saepe eorum voluntas ; plausum vero etiam si quis eorum aliquando acceperat, ne quid peccasset, pertimescebat. Ac tamen, si quae res erat maior, idem ille populus horum auctoritate maxime commovebatur.
106 L. Nunc, nisi me fallit, in eo statu civitas est, ut, si

---

[1] malexatur, male vexatur *mss.* : amplexatur *Madvig.*

---

[a] Of land and cheap corn.
[b] *Cf.* Plutarch, *Apophthegmata*, p. 180 A : " Once when he (Phocion) expressed an opinion before the people, he was well received, and seeing that all readily accepted what he

tion and riot, unable any longer to arouse the Roman
People by state-bounty, because the common folk,
after passing through so many serious insurrections
and disorders, welcome peace—they now hold meetings packed with hirelings, nor is it their aim to say
or propose what those present wish to hear, but they
use corruption and bribery to make it appear that
everything they say is listened to with pleasure. Do 105
you suppose that the Gracchi, or Saturninus, or any
of those men of former times who were regarded as
" Friends of the People," ever had any hired supporter at a meeting ? No one had ; for state-bounty [a]
itself and hope of some privilege offered to them
aroused the masses without any need of bribery. And
so, in those times, those who were " Friends of the
People " certainly gave offence to serious and honourable men but won regard from every demonstration
of popular approval. They were applauded in the
theatre ; they obtained by votes whatever they had
striven for ; their names, their words, their looks,
their bearing, were objects of popular affection. The
opponents of that class were considered estimable
and great men ; but, although they had much influence in the Senate, and were highly esteemed by
loyal citizens, they were not acceptable to the masses ;
their purpose was often thwarted by the voters, and
even if any of them was ever applauded, he was
afraid that he had done something wrong.[b] And yet
in any matter of high importance, it was by their authority that that same People was chiefly influenced.

L. At present, unless I am mistaken, such is the 106
political situation, that apart from bands of hirelings,

said, he turned to his friends and asked, ' Have I by mistake said something bad ? ' "

operas conductorum[1] removeris, omnes idem de re
publica sensuri esse videantur. Etenim tribus locis
significari maxime de re publica[2] populi Romani
iudicium ac voluntas potest, contione, comitiis,
ludorum gladiatorumque consessu. Quae contio fuit
per hos annos, quae quidem esset non conducta, sed
vera, in qua populi Romani consensus perspici non[3]
posset ? Habitae sunt multae de me a gladiatore
sceleratissimo, ad quas nemo adibat incorruptus,
nemo integer ; nemo illum foedum vultum aspicere,
nemo furialem vocem bonus audire poterat. Erant
illae contiones perditorum hominum necessario tur-
107 bulentae. Habuit de eodem me P. Lentulus consul
contionem ; concursus est populi Romani factus,
omnes ordines, tota in illa contione Italia constitit.
Egit causam summa cum gravitate copiaque dicendi
tanto silentio, tanta adprobatione omnium, nihil ut
umquam videretur tam populare ad populi Romani
aures accidisse. Productus est ab eo Cn. Pompeius,
qui se non solum auctorem meae salutis, sed etiam
supplicem praebuit[4] populo Romano. Huius oratio
ut semper gravis et grata in contionibus fuit, sic con-
tendo numquam neque sententiam eius auctoritate
108 neque eloquentiam iucunditate fuisse maiore. Quo
silentio sunt auditi de me ceteri principes civitatis !
quos idcirco non appello hoc loco, ne mea oratio, si

[1] conductas *is conjectured by Lambinus.*
[2] *Baiter's reading :* Mommsen omits *populi Romani.*
[3] *Omitted in most* MSS.
[4] *The gap in* P *is thus filled up by Madvig :* Reid
suggests praedicavit, *on the ground that a word of speaking
would be expected :* professus est *Koch.*

all citizens seem likely to hold the same opinion in regard to public affairs. For the opinion and feeling of the Roman People in public affairs can be most clearly expressed on three occasions, at a meeting, at an Assembly,[a] at a gathering for plays and gladiatorial shows. What meeting has been held within these years—I mean one that has not been packed with hirelings, but a real one worthy of the name—in which the unanimous agreement of the Roman People could not be clearly seen ? Many were summoned about myself by a most scoundrelly swordster,[b] which were attended by no one who was not bribed nor by any honest citizen ; no good man could look upon that repulsive face, nor listen to that raving voice. Those meetings of scoundrels could not be other than stormy. Publius Lentulus, when 107 consul, held a meeting, also about myself ; the Roman People came in crowds ; men of all ranks, all Italy, stood there. He pleaded his cause with the greatest weight and eloquence ; the silence and the approval of all present were so intense that it seemed as if nothing so popular had ever reached the ears of the Roman People. He brought forward Gnaeus Pompeius, who not only showed himself as a champion of my welfare, but also as a suppliant of the Roman People. A speech by him had always been impressive and listened to with pleasure at meetings ; yet I maintain that his opinion never had greater authority nor his eloquence greater charm. What a 108 silence there was, to hear the rest of the leading men of the State when they spoke of me ! I pass by their names in this place, for fear that my words might

---

[a] See note on § 33.
[b] P. Clodius.

minus de aliquo dixero, ingrata, si satis de omnibus,
infinita esse videatur. Cedo nunc eiusdem illius inimici mei de me eodem ad verum populum in campo
Martio contionem ! Quis non modo adprobavit, sed
non indignissimum facinus putavit illum non dicam
loqui, sed vivere ac spirare ? quis fuit, qui non eius
voce maculari rem publicam seque, si eum audiret,
scelere adstringi arbitraretur ?

109 LI. Venio ad comitia, sive magistratuum placet
sive legum. Leges videmus saepe ferri multas.
Omitto eas, quae feruntur ita, vix ut quini, et ii ex
aliena tribu, qui suffragium ferant, reperiantur. De
me, quem tyrannum atque ereptorem libertatis esse
dicebat illa ruina rei publicae, dicit se legem tulisse.
Quis est, qui se, cum contra me ferebatur, inisse
suffragium confiteatur ? cum autem de me eodem ex
senatus consulto comitiis centuriatis ferebatur, quis
est, qui non profiteatur se adfuisse et suffragium de
salute mea tulisse ? Utra igitur causa popularis debet
videri, in qua omnes honestates civitatis, omnes
aetates, omnes ordines una mente[1] consentiunt, an in
qua furiae concitatae tamquam ad funus rei publicae
110 convolant ? An, sicubi aderit Gellius, homo et fratre

[1] una *MSS.* : *Müller adds* mente.

---

[a] When Clodius spoke against a proposal for Cicero's
recall.

[b] This passage suggests that at ordinary times the majority
of the voters present at the *comitia* and the *concilium plebis*
came from Rome itself and the neighbourhood and that
unscrupulous tactics were often employed to secure a quorum.

[c] L. Gellius Poplicola, a witness at Sestius' trial, was a
half-brother of L. Marcius Philippus, consul 56 B.C. He is

seem ungrateful, if I were to speak inadequately of one or other of them, while, if I were to say all that I ought to say of them all, I should never finish. Now compare the speech of that same enemy of mine, also about myself, delivered in the Campus Martius before the real People![a] Who was there who did not disapprove of it—no, did not consider it utterly disgraceful—I will not say, that he should speak, but that he should live and breathe? Who was there who did not think that his voice polluted the State and that he himself, if he listened to him, would be an accomplice in his crime?

LI. I now come to the Assemblies, whatever their 109 purpose, whether for the election of magistrates or the passing of laws. We often see many laws passed. I say nothing about those which are passed under such conditions that scarcely five in each tribe, and those not from their own tribe, are found to vote.[b] That curse of the State says that he passed a law concerning myself, whom he used to call a tyrant and destroyer of liberty. Who is there who admits that he recorded his vote for the proposition against me? But when, in accordance with a decree of the Senate, a law was brought forward at the *comitia centuriata* also about myself, who was there who did not proclaim that he had been present and had voted for my recall? Which cause, then, of the two ought to be considered the popular one? that in which all the respectable men of the State, men of all ages, and all classes, are animated by the same spirit, or that in which frenzied furies flock together as it were to the funeral of the State? Or, if a Gellius[c] shows him- 110

called by Cicero (*In Vatinium*, 4) *nutricula seditiosorum omnium.*

183

indignus, viro clarissimo atque optimo consule, et ordine equestri, cuius ille ordinis nomen retinet, ornamenta confecit, id erit populare ?   " Est enim homo iste populo Romano deditus." Nihil vidi magis ; qui, cum eius adulescentia in amplissimis honoribus summi viri, L. Philippi vitrici, florere potuisset, usque eo non fuit popularis, ut bona solus comesset. Deinde ex impuro adulescente et petulante, posteaquam rem paternam ab idiotarum divitiis ad philosophorum reculam perduxit, Graeculum se atque otiosum putari voluit, studio litterarum se subito dedidit. Nihil suavitates iuvabant anagnostae,[1] libelli etiam saepe pro vino oppignerabantur ; manebat insaturabile abdomen, copiae deficiebant. Itaque semper versabatur in spe rerum novarum, otio et tranquillitate rei publicae consenescebat.

LII. Ecquae seditio umquam fuit, in qua non ille princeps ? ecqui seditiosus, cui ille non familiaris ? ecquae turbulenta contio, cuius ille non concitator ? cui bene dixit umquam bono ? bene dixit ? immo

---

[1] *The text is extremely corrupt here* : *P has* nihil saueate, *with* iuvabant anagnostae *over the line, hence various conjectures. Halm suggests* nihil satiabant eum libelli, pro vino saepe oppignerabantur ; *Reid suggests* nihil sani e libellis, " *he got no good from the books.*" *Müller's text is followed.*

---

[a] Of five *ornamenta* the chief were a tunic with a narrow purple stripe and a golden ring. A *census equester*, probably first fixed by C. Gracchus and possibly of 400,000 sesterces, existed in 76 B.C. Cicero, *Pro Roscio Comoedo*, 42.

[b] L. Marcius Philippus, consul 91 B.C., censor 86 B.C.

[c] *i.e.* the wealth without which the ignorant think life is

self anywhere, a man unworthy alike of his distinguished brother, that excellent consul, and of the Equestrian Order, of which rank he still keeps the name but has squandered the trappings,[a] will that be popular ? " Yes, for he is a man devoted to the Roman People." I have never seen anyone more so ! A man who in youth might have derived reflected glory from the distinguished career of that eminent man his stepfather, Lucius Philippus,[b] was so far not a " Friend of the People " that he consumed all his substance by himself. Then, after a youth of shameful viciousness, after he had reduced his paternal inheritance from vulgar wealth [c] to philosophic penury, he wanted to be thought a wit [d] and a man of leisure, and suddenly devoted himself to the study of literature. The delicacies of his reader gave him no pleasure ; his books were often actually pledged for wine ; his belly remained insatiable, supplies ran out. He was therefore always living in the hope of a revolution ; while the State was quiet and peaceful, he grew senile.

LII. Was there ever any riot in which he was not the leader ? any rioter with whom he was not intimate ? any disorderly meeting where he was not the ringleader ? has he ever said a good word of an honest man ?—said a good word ? rather,

not worth living. *Recula* (a diminutive of *res*) is a correction of the MSS. *regula*. If the latter be retained and *deliciis* (Pantagathus for *divitiis*) be read, we can get a satisfactory meaning : " after he had reduced his inheritance from the enjoyments in which the ignorant delight to tally with the discipline of the philosophers " ; *i.e.* when he became poor, he affected the philosopher.

[d] *Graeculus:* a contemptuous diminutive. The Romans pretended to despise literary pursuits.

quem fortem et bonum civem non petulantissime
est insectatus ? qui, ut credo, non libidinis causa,
sed ut plebicola videretur, libertinam duxit uxorem.
111 Is de me suffragium tulit, is adfuit, is interfuit
epulis et gratulationibus parricidarum ; in quo tamen est me ultus, cum illo ore inimicos est meos
saviatus. Qui quasi mea culpa bona perdiderit,
ita ob eam ipsam causam est mihi inimicus, quia
nihil habet. Utrum ego tibi patrimonium eripui,
Gelli, an tu comedisti ? Quid ? tu meo periculo,
gurges ac vorago patrimonii, helluabare, ut, si
ego consul rem publicam contra te et gregales tuos
defendissem, in civitate esse me nolles ? Te nemo
tuorum videre vult, omnes aditum, sermonem,
congressum tuum fugiunt ; te sororis filius Postumius, adulescens gravis, senili iudicio, notavit, cum
in magno numero tutorem liberis non instituit.
Sed elatus odio et meo et rei publicae nomine,
quorum ille utri sit inimicior, nescio, plura dixi, quam
dicendum fuit, in furiosissimum atque egentissimum
112 ganeonem. Illuc revertor : contra me cum sit actum,
capta urbe atque oppressa, Gellium, Firmidium,
Titium, eiusdem modi furias illis mercennariis gregibus duces et auctores fuisse, cum ipse lator nihil

---

^a A parody on his name Poplicola. Since Cicero implies
that unions between slave-born and *ingenui* were legal marriages, it is difficult to accept Mommsen's belief that Augustus
first legalized them. The *lex Papia Poppaea* (A.D. 9), which
completed the *lex Iulia de maritandis ordinibus* (18 B.C.),
recognized marriages between free-born and freed, but denied
them to senators and their descendants to the third generation in the male line. *C.A.H.* x, pp. 448-449.
^b For *parricida* " traitor " see How, *Cicero, Select Letters*,
ii, p. 540, and Nisbet, *op. cit.* p. 91.

what brave and loyal citizen has he not attacked most wantonly ? and has married a freedwoman, not, I suppose, to gratify his lust, but that he might appear to be " a friend of the commons."[a] He voted 111 about me ; he was present, he shared in, the banquets and jubilations of those traitors to their country [b] ; and yet there he avenged me, when with those lips he slobbered my enemies. Just as if it was my fault that he lost his property, he is my enemy just because he has nothing. Did I rob you of your inheritance, Gellius, or did you yourself devour it ? Again, was it at my risk, you spendthrift and waster of your inheritance, that you were to gormandize, so that, if I when consul defended the State against you and your cronies, you would be resolved that I should not remain in it ? [c] None of your relatives want to see you ; they all run when they see you coming, will not talk with you nor meet you. Your nephew Postumius, a serious youth with an old man's judgment, showed his disapproval of you by not appointing you as a guardian of his children amongst a large number of others. But I have let myself be carried away by my hatred of him, for my country's sake as well as my own—I do not know which of the two he hates the more—and I have said more than I ought to have said against a frenzied and penniless waster. I turn to what I was saying.[d] 112 When proceedings were taken against me, when the city was captured and crushed, Gellius, Firmidius, Titius, madmen of the same type, acted as leaders and directors of those bands of hirelings, while the

---

[c] *i.e.*, because you had been extravagant, is that a reason why I should suffer ?

[d] See § 109, where Cicero turned to *comitia*.

CICERO

ab horum turpitudine, audacia, sordibus abhorreret.
At cum de dignitate mea ferebatur, nemo sibi nec
valetudinis excusationem nec senectutis satis iustam
putavit ; nemo fuit, qui se non rem publicam mecum
simul revocare in suas sedes arbitraretur.

113 LIII. Videamus nunc comitia magistratuum. Fuit
collegium nuper tribunicium, in quo tres minime,
vehementer duo populares existimabantur. Ex iis,
qui populares non habebantur, quibus in illo genere
conductarum contionum consistendi potestas non
erat, duo a populo Romano praetores video esse
factos ; et, quantum sermonibus vulgi et suffragiis
intellegere potui, prae se populus Romanus ferebat
sibi illum in tribunatu Cn. Domiti animum constantem
et egregium et Q. Anchari fidem ac fortitudinem,
etiamsi nihil agere potuissent, tamen voluntate ipsa
gratum[1] fuisse. Iam de C. Fannio quae sit existi-
matio, videmus ; quod iudicium populi Romani in
honoribus eius futurum sit, nemini dubium esse
114 debet. Quid ? populares illi duo quid egerunt ?
Alter, qui tamen se continuerat, tulerat nihil, senserat tantum de re publica aliud atque homines
exspectabant, vir et bonus et innocens et bonis viris

---

[1] gratam *Manutius 1*, grata 2.

---

[a] In 59 b.c.   [b] Cn. Domitius, Q. Ancharius, C. Fannius.
[c] C. Alfius Flavus, P. Vatinius.
[d] Cn. Domitius Calvinus, tribune 59, praetor 56, consul
53 b.c., commanded under Caesar in the Civil War.
[e] C. Fannius, tribune 59 b.c., became a governor of Asia
in the Civil War. He was probably a praetor in 55 b.c.
[f] C. Alfius Flavus and P. Vatinius.
[g] C. Alfius Flavus, a supporter of Cicero in 63, joined
Caesar in 59 b.c. In 57 b.c. he failed to be elected praetor,
but held that magistracy in 54 b.c. See *In Vatinium*, 38
and *Epp. ad Quintum fratrem*, iii. 1. 24 ; 3. 3.

proposer of the law himself yielded to none of them in baseness, effrontery, and vileness. But when it was proposed that my honour should be restored, no one thought himself sufficiently excused by ill-health or old age from staying away ; there was no one who did not feel that in recalling me he was recalling the State to its own home.

LIII. Let us now consider Assemblies for the election of magistrates. Of late [a] there was a college of tribunes, three [b] of whom were considered by no means " Friends of the People," two [c] extremely so. Of these three who were not considered " Friends of the People," and who were not strong enough to maintain their ground in those meetings packed with hirelings I have mentioned, I see that two have been made praetors by the Roman People ; and, so far as I have been able to judge from the talk and votes of the commons, the Roman People openly declared that, although Gnaeus Domitius [d] and Quintus Ancharius had not been able to accomplish anything during their tribunate, the stedfast and excellent spirit of the former and the loyalty and courage of the latter were nevertheless welcome by the mere goodwill they showed. As for Gaius Fannius,[e] we are aware now what public opinion thinks of him. No one ought to have any doubt what the judgment of the Roman People will be in regard to his candidature for offices. Well, then, how did those two tribunes [f] fare who were " Friends of the People " ? One [g] of them, who, however, had kept himself within the bounds of moderation, had proposed no law, had merely held different political opinions from what people expected. He was a worthy man, of blameless life, and always esteemed

113

114

semper probatus, quod parum videlicet intellexit in
tribunatu, quid vero populo probaretur, et quod illum
esse populum Romanum, qui in contione erat, arbitrabatur, non tenuit eum locum, in quem, nisi popularis
esse voluisset, facillime pervenisset.   Alter, qui ita
se in populari ratione iactarat, ut auspicia, legem
Aeliam, senatus auctoritatem, consulem, collegas,
bonorum iudicium nihili putaret, aedilitatem petivit
cum bonis viris et hominibus primis sed non prae-
stantissimis opibus et gratia ; tribum suam non tulit,
Palatinam denique, per quam omnes illae pestes
vexare rem publicam dicebantur,[1] perdidit nec quicquam illis comitiis, quod boni viri vellent, nisi repulsam tulit.   Videtis igitur populum ipsum, ut ita
dicam, iam non esse popularem, qui ita vehementer
eos, qui populares habentur, respuat, eos autem, qui
ei generi adversantur, honore dignissimos iudicet.

115   LIV. Veniamus ad ludos.   Facit enim, iudices,
vester iste in me animorum oculorumque coniectus,

---

[1] ordiebantur *Eberhard* : moliebantur *Rossberg* : solebant
Koch.

---

[a] P. Vatinius.   [b] See pp. 313-315.
[c] Much of the legislation which Caesar initiated in 59 B.C.
was presented directly to the *concilium plebis* by a tribune,
P. Vatinius, his chief subordinate, *e.g.*, the *lex Vatinia de
Caesaris provincia* (Cisalpine Gaul and Illyricum).   From
the Senate, however, not from the People, Caesar got Transalpine Gaul.
[d] M. Calpurnius Bibulus, who after Caesar's first land law
had been passed by violence, shut himself up in his house
and issued notices (*obnuntiationes per edicta*) that he was
watching the heavens for unfavourable omens.   His seclusion
lasted till the end of the year 59 B.C.

by honest men ; but because during his tribunate he naturally failed to understand what the real People desired, and because he thought that an audience at a meeting was the Roman People, he did not reach that position which he might have easily attained, had he not desired to be a " Friend of the People." The other,[a] who had made such a parade of being a " Friend of the People " that he thought nothing of the auspices, the Aelian Law,[b] the will of the Senate,[c] a consul,[d] his colleagues, the esteem of honest men, became a candidate for the aedileship together with loyal citizens and men of the highest rank, but not remarkable either for wealth or for influence. He did not receive the votes of his own tribe [e] : he lost even the Palatine tribe,[f] which was said to help all these villains to trouble their country ; nor did he get anything at that Assembly which loyalists would like him to get, except rejection.[g] You see, then, that the People themselves are, if I may say so, by now no longer " all for the People," seeing that they so vigorously reject those who are considered " Friends of the People," but judge those who are opposed to that class to be most worthy of public office.

LIV. Let us now come to the shows [h] : for your attention, gentlemen, and the manner in which you direct your eyes to me, make me believe that I

115

[e] The *tribus Sergia*. See *In Vatinium*, 36. Vatinius was a candidate for an aedileship of 57 B.C.

[f] One of the four *tribus urbanae*, traditionally ascribed to Servius Tullius, of narrow political outlook.

[g] Cicero implies that they would have liked to see him roughly handled.

[h] For the chief uses of the word *ludi* see *Oxford Classical Dictionary*, p. 518.

ut mihi iam licere putem remissiore uti genere dicendi. Comitiorum et contionum significationes sunt interdum verae, sunt non numquam vitiatae atque corruptae ; theatrales gladiatoriique consessus dicuntur omnino solere levitate non nullorum emptos plausus exiles et raros excitare ; ac tamen facile est, cum id fit, quem ad modum et a quibus fiat, et quid integra multitudo faciat, videre. Quid ego nunc dicam, quibus viris aut cui generi civium maxime plaudatur ? Neminem vestrum fallit. Sit hoc sane leve, quod non ita est, quoniam optimo cuique impertitur, sed, si est leve, homini gravi leve est, ei vero, qui pendet rebus levissimis, qui rumore et, ut ipsi loquuntur, favore populi tenetur et ducitur, plausum immor-
116 talitatem, sibilum mortem videri necesse est. Ex te igitur, Scaure, potissimum quaero, qui ludos apparatissimos magnificentissimosque fecisti, ecquis istorum popularium tuos ludos aspexerit, ecquis se theatro populoque Romano commiserit. Ipse ille maxime ludius, non solum spectator, sed actor et acroama, qui omnia sororis embolia novit, qui in coetum mulierum pro psaltria adducitur, nec tuos ludos aspexit in illo ardenti tribunatu suo nec ullos alios nisi eos, a quibus vix vivus effugit. Semel, inquam,

---

^a See § 101.
^b Given by him as aedile in 58 B.C. (see Pliny, *Nat. Hist.* xxxvi. 113).
^c P. Clodius.
^d One who performs or entertains : an extension of the literal sense of this Greek word which, properly meaning " a thing heard," was specially applied to music, covers also a performance or entertainment of whatever kind.

may now speak in a lighter vein. Expressions of public opinion at Assemblies and at meetings are sometimes the voice of truth, but sometimes they are falsified and corrupt : at theatrical and gladiatorial shows it is said to be common for some feeble and scanty applause to be started by a hired and unprincipled claque, and yet, when that happens, it is easy to see how and by whom it is started and what the honest part of the audience does. Why should I tell you to-day what men or what class of citizens is chiefly applauded ? Not one of you fails to understand. Suppose applause to be a trivial matter, which it is not, since it is given to all the best citizens ; but if it is trivial, it is so only to a man of character, but to those who depend upon the merest trifles, who are controlled and governed by rumour and, as they themselves put it, by the favour of the People, applause must seem immortality, and hissing death. I therefore ask you particularly, Scaurus,[a] 116 you who gave most magnificently appointed shows,[b] did any one of those " Friends of the People " visit your shows, or venture to appear in the theatre before the Roman People ? That arch-comedian himself,[c] not merely a spectator, but an actor and virtuoso,[d] who knows all the pantomimic interludes [e] of his sister, who is admitted into a party of women in the guise of a harp-girl,[f] neither visited your shows during that fiery tribunate of his, nor any others except once when he scarcely escaped alive. Once

[e] This word properly means " things thrown in," or " interludes," items interposed between plays or acts of a play. A secondary meaning is " love-affairs."
[f] An allusion to Clodius' escapade at the rites of the Bona Dea.

se ludis homo popularis commisit omnino, cum in templo Virtutis honos habitus esset virtuti Gaique Mari, conservatoris huius imperii, monumentum municipi eius et rei publicae defensori sedem ad salutem praebuisset.

117 LV. Quo quidem tempore quid populus Romanus sentire se ostenderet, utroque in genere declaratum est, primum cum audito senatus consulto rei[1] ipsi atque absenti senatui plausus est ab universis datus, deinde cum senatoribus singulis spectatum e senatu redeuntibus ; cum vero ipse, qui ludos faciebat, consul assedit, stantes ei manibus passis gratias agentes et lacrimantes gaudio suam erga me benevolentiam ac misericordiam declararunt. At cum ille furibundus incitata illa sua vaecordi mente venisset, vix se populus Romanus tenuit, vix homines odium suum a corpore eius impuro atque infando represserunt ; voces quidem et palmarum intentus 118 et maledictorum clamorem omnes profuderunt. Sed quid ego populi Romani animum virtutemque commemoro, libertatem iam ex diuturna servitute dispicientis, in eo homine, cui tum petenti iam aedilitatem ne histriones quidem coram sedenti pepercerunt ? Nam cum ageretur togata " Simulans,"

---

[1] ore *MSS.* : rei *Garatoni.*

---

[a] The Ludi Apollinares held 6-13 July.

[b] In July 57 B.C., at the time of the Ludi Apollinares, the Senate, meeting in the Aedes Honoris et Virtutis, passed certain decrees complimentary to Cicero who was, like Marius, born at the *municipium* Arpinum. See § 50. The site of this temple is unknown, but is generally assumed to be on the Capitoline Hill ; the temple was built by Marius from spoil taken from the Cimbri and Teutones.

only, I say, did that man who was a " Friend of the People " venture to show himself at the games,[a] when in the Temple of Virtue honour was paid to merit, and the monument of Gaius Marius, saviour of our Empire, afforded his fellow-townsman and defender of the State a place for securing his own recall.[b]

LV. What feelings the Roman People showed that they entertained at that time, was made plain in both ways. First, when the decree of the Senate had been heard, unanimous applause was given to the measure itself, and to the Senate, before they came in ; next, to the senators, when they returned one by one from the Senate to see the shows. But when the consul [c] himself, who gave the entertainment, took his seat, people stood up with outstretched hands, giving thanks, and weeping for joy openly showed their goodwill and sympathy for myself. But when Clodius arrived, that raging fiend, at the height of his frenzy, the Roman People could scarcely restrain themselves, men could scarcely help wreaking their hatred upon his foul and abominable person ; cries, menacing gestures, loud curses came in a flood from all. But why do I speak of the spirit and courage of the Roman People, when at last after long servitude they had a glimpse of freedom, in their attitude towards a man whom even the actors did not spare to his face as he sat in the audience, though he was then a candidate for an aedileship ! For when a comedy,[d]

[c] P. Lentulus Spinther, consul 57 B.C.
[d] *Togata*, Roman comedy, in which the everyday life of Italy was dramatized and the actors wore a *toga*, as opposed to *palliata*, in which the scenes were Greek and the actors wore a *pallium* (Gr. ἱμάτιον).

ut opinor, caterva tota clarissima concentione in ore
impuri hominis imminens contionata est :

huic, Tite, tua post principia atque exitus vitiosae vitae— !¹

Sedebat exanimatus, et is, qui antea cantorum convicio contiones celebrare suas solebat, cantorum ipsorum vocibus eiciebatur. Et quoniam facta mentio
est ludorum, ne illud quidem praetermittam, in
magna varietate sententiarum numquam ullum fuisse
locum, in quo aliquid a poeta dictum cadere in tempus
nostrum videretur, quod aut populum universum
119 fugeret aut non exprimeret ipse actor. Et quaeso
hoc loco, iudices, ne qua levitate me ductum ad
insolitum genus dicendi labi putetis, si de poetis,
de histrionibus, de ludis in iudicio loquar.

LVI. Non sum tam ignarus, iudices, causarum, non
tam insolens in dicendo, ut omni ex genere orationem
aucuper et omnes undique flosculos carpam atque
delibem. Scio, quid gravitas vestra, quid haec advo-
catio, quid ille conventus, quid dignitas P. Sesti, quid
periculi magnitudo, quid aetas, quid honos meus
postulet. Sed mihi sumpsi hoc loco doctrinam quandam iuventuti, qui essent optimates. In ea expli-
canda demonstrandum est non esse populares omnes
eos, qui putentur. Id facillime consequar, si universi

---

¹ *The text is corrupt. Halm's version is followed.*

ª Simulans = Gk. Εἴρων. A comedy by L. Afranius
(born *c.* 150 B.C.), who in a period of literary reaction from
the *palliatae* of the age of Terence, wrote *togatae.*

ᵇ There is a double meaning of *cantores* in this passage,
i.e. the actors playing in *The Pretender* and Clodius' hired
brawlers.

ᶜ The behaviour of an audience at the Ludi Apollinares
in July 59 B.C. affords a parallel. See Cicero, *Epp. ad Att.*
ii. 19. 3.

The Pretender,[a] I fancy, was being performed, the whole company, speaking all together in loud tones, bent forward threateningly and looking straight at the foul wretch, loudly chanted the words,

> This, Titus, is the sequel, the end of your vicious life!

He sat utterly disconcerted, and the man who used to make his meetings resound with the hoots of a ribald claque was hooted away by the speech of genuine actors.[b] And since I have mentioned theatrical performances, I will not omit to say that, among many and varied reflections in the comedy, there was never a passage, seeming, from the poet's words, to have some bearing on our times, either where the whole People failed to grasp, or where the actor himself failed to give, the special point.[c] And here, 119 gentlemen, I beg you not to think that any spirit of levity has led me to fall into an unusual method of speaking, if I talk about poets, actors, and plays in the course of a trial.

LVI. I am not so ignorant of legal proceedings, gentlemen, not so unaccustomed to speaking, as to hunt for what I intend to say from every kind of subject, and to pluck and cull all kinds of flowers of speech from every source. I know what is due to your dignity, to this body of counsel, that gathering of citizens, what the high character of Publius Sestius, the greatness of his danger, my age, and my position demand. But on this occasion I have undertaken, if I may say so, to instruct our youth, as to who are the " Aristocrats." In making that clear, I must show that not all those are " Friends of the People " who are thought to be so. I shall most easily be able to do that, if I describe the true and uncorrupted

populi iudicium verum et incorruptum et si intimos
120 sensus civitatis expressero. Quid fuit illud, quod
recenti nuntio de illo senatus consulto, quod factum
est in templo Virtutis, ad ludos scaenamque perlato
consessu maximo summus artifex et mehercule
semper partium in re publica tam quam in scaena
optimarum flens et recenti laetitia et mixto dolore
ac desiderio mei egit apud populum Romanum multo
gravioribus verbis meam causam, quam egomet de
me agere potuissem ? Summi enim poetae ingenium
non solum arte sua, sed etiam dolore exprimebat.
Qua enim vi[1] :

> qui rem publicam certo animo adiuverit,
> statuerit, steterit cum Achivis—

vobiscum me stetisse dicebat, vestros ordines demonstrabat ! revocabatur[2] ab universis.

> re dubia
> haut dubitarit vitam offerre nec capiti pepercerit.

121 Haec quantis ab illo clamoribus agebantur ! Cum iam
omisso gestu verbis poetae et studio actoris et ex-
spectationi nostrae plauderetur :

> summum amicum summo in bello—

nam illud ipse actor adiungebat amico animo et
fortasse homines propter aliquod desiderium adpro-
babant :

> summo ingenio praeditum.

[1] *Added by Köchly.*
[2] quia enim . . . demonstrabat, revocabatur *Klotz* :
quom enim ita . . . demonstrabat, revocabatur *Reid.*

---

[a] Claudius Aesopus, the greatest tragic actor in Cicero's
time, as Roscius was the greatest comedian. *Cf.* Horace,
Epistles, ii. 1. 82 : " quae gravis Aesopus, quae doctus Roscius
egit."
[b] L. Accius (170–*c.* 86 B.C.), a Roman tragedian. The

judgment of the whole People, and the inmost feelings of the country. What, then, do you think of this? 120
When news had just been brought to the shows and
to the stage of that decree of the Senate which was
passed in the Temple of Virtue, before a vast audience
a great artist who,^a upon my soul, has always played
a most noble part in public life as well as on the stage,
weeping with joy still fresh, with mingled grief and
longing for me, pleaded my cause before the Roman
People in much weightier words than I could have
pleaded myself! For he expressed the genius of a
great poet ^b not only by the exercise of his art, but
also by his own grief. For while he uttered the
words :

> Who with firm spirit helped the public cause,
> Upheld it, ever stood with the Achivi—

with what force he made it clear that I had stood
on your side, as he pointed to your assembled Orders !
He was encored by all when he went on to say :

> In wavering affairs did never waver
> His life to offer, nor did spare his head.

What shouts of applause greeted his performance 121
of this passage, when they took no notice of the
acting, but applauded the words of the poet, the
earnestness of the actor and the hope of my recall !

> Our greatest friend, in this our greatest war.

The actor himself added the words

> Endowed with greatest genius

out of friendship for me, and perhaps the spectators
approved owing to some regret for my absence.

verses quoted are said to be from his *Eurysaces*. See
Remains of Old Latin (L.C.L.), ii, pp. 446-449.

CICERO

LVII. Iam illa quanto cum gemitu populi Romani ab eodem paulo post in eadem fabula sunt acta !

O pater—

Me, me ille absentem ut patrem deplorandum putabat, quem Q. Catulus, quem multi alii saepe in senatu patrem patriae nominarant. Quanto cum fletu de illis nostris incendiis ac ruinis, cum patrem pulsum, patriam adflictam deploraret, domum incensam eversamque, sic egit, ut, demonstrata pristina fortuna cum se convertisset :

> haec omnia vidi inflammari

122 fletum etiam inimicis atque invidis excitaret ! Pro di immortales ! quid ? illa quem ad modum dixit idem ! quae mihi quidem ita et acta et scripta videntur esse, ut vel a Q. Catulo, si revixisset, praeclare posse dici viderentur ; is enim libere reprehendere et accusare populi non numquam temeritatem solebat aut errorem senatus :

> O ingratifici Argivi, immunes Graii immemores benefici !

Non erat illud quidem verum ; non enim ingrati, sed miseri, quibus reddere salutem, a quo acceperant, non liceret, nec unus in quemquam umquam gratior quam in me universi ; sed tamen illud scripsit diser-

---

^a These words, as is shown by *haec omnia vidi inflammari* below, are really from the *Andromache* of Ennius (see the passage quoted in Cicero, *Tusc. Disp.* iii. 19, and *Remains of Old Latin* (L.C.L.), i, pp. 250-253). It is probable that Aesopus transferred them to the *Eurysaces* of Accius, just as he added *summo ingenio praeditum* above. *O pater*—is spoken by Andromache, whose father was Eetion, slain at the capture of his city.

^b A reminder of Cicero who had been saluted as *pater patriae* by Catulus after 6 December 63 B.C. See Cicero, *In Pisonem*, 5. Catulus was dead by 60 B.C.

^c See p. 174, note *b*.

LVII. A little later in the same play, how the
Roman People groaned when they heard these words
spoken by the same actor !

> O my father ! [a]

He thought that it was I, I in my absence, who
ought to be lamented as a father, whom Quintus
Catulus and many others in the Senate had often
called " Father of his Country.[b] " How he wept as
he spoke of the burning and destruction of my house,
when lamenting an exiled father, his afflicted fatherland, his house burnt and ruined, where his acting
was so pathetic, that after having described his
former prosperity, he turned to the audience with
the words

> All these things I have seen in flames,

and drew tears even from my enemies and from
my detractors ! And then again, by heaven, how 122
he declaimed these other words ! — words which
seemed to me to have been so delivered and
written that they might well have been uttered
even by Quintus Catulus,[c] had he come to life again ;
for he was sometimes in the habit of freely censuring
and blaming rashness by the People or error by the
Senate :

> O thankless Argives, disobliging Greeks,
> Forgetful of past kindness !

No, that was not true, for they were not ungrateful,
but unfortunate, because they were not permitted to
save him who had saved them, nor has anyone ever
found one person more grateful to anyone than they
have all been to me. But, be that as it may, a most
eloquent poet must have written the following words

tissimus poeta pro me,[1] egit fortissimus actor, non
solum optimus, de me, cum omnes ordines demon-
straret, senatum, equites Romanos, universum populum Romanum accusaret :

exsulare sinitis, sistis pelli, pulsum patimini !

Quae tum significatio fuerit omnium, quae declaratio
voluntatis ab universo populo Romano in causa
hominis non popularis, equidem audiebam, existi-
mare[2] facilius possunt, qui adfuerunt.

123 LVIII. Et quoniam huc me provexit oratio, histrio
casum meum totiens conlacrimavit, cum ita dolenter
ageret causam meam, ut vox eius illa praeclara
lacrimis impediretur ; neque poetae, quorum ego
semper ingenia dilexi, tempori meo defuerunt ; eaque
populus Romanus non solum plausu, sed etiam gemitu
suo comprobavit. Utrum igitur haec Aesopum potius
pro me aut Accium dicere oportuit, si populus
Romanus liber esset, an principes civitatis ? Nominatim sum appellatus in Bruto :

Tullius, qui libertatem civibus stabiliverat.

Miliens revocatum est. Parumne videbatur populus
Romanus iudicare id a me et a senatu esse constitutum, quod perditi cives sublatum per nos crimi-
124 nabantur ? Maximum vero populi Romani iudicium
universi consessu gladiatorio declaratum est. Erat

---

[1] pro re *Madvig.*
[2] aestimare *cod. Ursini.*

---

[a] *Non popularis* : ironical.
[b] A *fabula praetexta* of Accius. *Remains of Old Latin*
(L.C.L.), ii, pp. 560-565.

in my interest, and the actor, as remarkable for his
courage as for his acting, applied them to me, when
he pointed to all the Orders and accused the Senate,
the Roman Knights, and the entire Roman People :

> A banished man you leave him ; you consent,
> As you consented to his banishment !

How on that occasion the whole audience indicated
their feelings, how the whole Roman People declared
their goodwill for a man who was not a " Friend
of the People," [a] I heard by report ; those who were
present can more readily estimate.

LVIII. And since my speech has led me thus far, 123
the actor bewailed my lot so often, as he pleaded
my cause with such emotion, that that splendid
voice of his was choked with tears ; nor did the
poets, whose talents have always been my delight,
fail me in my trouble ; and the Roman People showed,
not only by applause but also by lamentation, how
much they approved of these allusions. Ought then
Aesopus or Accius to have pleaded thus for me, had
the Roman People been free, or ought the chief men
of the State ? In the *Brutus* [b] I was mentioned by
name :

> Tullius, [c] who stablished safe the people's freedom.

The line was encored a thousand times. Did the
Roman People fail to express their judgment, that
what scoundrels charged us with overthrowing had
in fact been established by myself and the Senate ?
But the strongest expression of the judgment of the 124
whole Roman People was plainly given by an audience
at gladiatorial games. They were a show given by

[c] The name of Tullius is meant for Servius Tullius, a king
of Rome during the sixth century B.C.

enim munus Scipionis dignum et eo ipso et illo Q. Metello, cui dabatur. Id autem spectaculi genus erat, quod omni frequentia atque omni genere hominum celebratur, quo multitudo maxime delectatur. In hunc consessum P. Sestius tribunus pl., cum ageret nihil aliud in eo magistratu nisi meam causam, venit et se populo dedit non plausus cupiditate, sed ut ipsi inimici nostri voluntatem universi populi viderent. Venit, ut scitis, a columna Maenia. Tantus est ex omnibus spectaculis usque a Capitolio, tantus ex fori cancellis plausus excitatus, ut numquam maior consensio aut apertior populi Romani universi fuisse ulla 125 in causa diceretur. Ubi erant tum illi contionum moderatores, legum domini, civium expulsores ? aliusne est aliquis improbis civibus peculiaris populus, cui nos offensi invisique fuerimus ?

LIX. Equidem existimo nullum tempus esse frequentioris populi quam illud gladiatorium neque contionis ullius neque vero ullorum comitiorum. Haec igitur innumerabilis hominum multitudo, haec populi Romani tanta significatio sine ulla varietate universi,

---

a P. Cornelius Scipio Nasica, adopted by Q. Metellus Pius, son of Q. Metellus Numidicus, became Q. Caecilius Metellus Pius Scipio. He was the father of Cornelia whom Pompey married after the death of Julia, and from August 52 b.c. was associated as consul with Pompey. He committed sui-

Scipio, one worthy both of the giver and of Quintus Metellus in whose honour it was given.[a] And it was that kind of show which is attended by crowds of all classes in great numbers, and which has a special charm for the masses. Into that crowd of spectators came Publius Sestius, then tribune of the commons, who was wholly devoted to my cause during his term of office ; he came and showed himself to the People, not that he was eager for applause, but he wished that our enemies themselves might recognize the goodwill of the whole Roman People. He came, as you know, from the Maenian Column.[b] At once from all the spectators' seats right down from the Capitol, and from all the barriers [c] of the Forum, there were heard such shouts of applause, that it was said that the whole Roman People had never shown greater nor more manifest unanimity in any cause. Where then were those who lord over meetings, who 125 tyrannize over laws, who drive citizens into exile ? Or have those traitors some other People of their own, to whom I have been odious and hateful ?

LIX. I for my part think that there has never been a greater crowd than at that gladiatorial show, neither at any meeting nor indeed at any Assembly. What then did this countless throng of men, this unanimous expression of the feeling of the entire Roman People, at the very time when it was

cide after his defeat at Thapsus. His gladiatorial show was given in 57 B.C. in honour of his adoptive father, Q. Metellus Pius, consul 80 B.C., and joint-commander with Pompey against Sertorius.

[b] Probably erected in the Forum in 338 B.C. in honour of C. Maenius (consul), victor over Antium. See p. 58, note a.

[c] Railings set up to mark out the place for the games, which were exhibited in the Forum.

CICERO

cum illis ipsis diebus de me actum iri putaretur, quid
declaravit nisi optimorum civium salutem et digni-
126 tatem populo Romano caram esse universo? At vero
ille praetor, qui de me non patris, avi, proavi, maiorum
denique suorum omnium, sed Graeculorum instituto
contionem interrogare solebat, velletne me redire,
et, cum erat reclamatum semivivis mercennariorum
vocibus, populum Romanum negare dicebat, is cum
cotidie gladiatores spectaret, numquam est conspectus, cum veniret. Emergebat subito, cum sub
tabulas subrepserat, ut

mater, te appello

dicturus videretur. Itaque illa via latebrosior, qua
spectatum ille veniebat, Appia iam vocabatur. Qui
tamen quoquo tempore conspectus erat, non modo
gladiatores, sed equi ipsi gladiatorum repentinis
127 sibilis extimescebant. Videtisne igitur, quantum
intersit[1] inter populum Romanum et contionem ;
dominos contionum omni odio populi notari ; quibus

----

[1] *Supplied by Wesenberg.*

----

[a] Appius Claudius, brother of Publius Clodius, praetor,
57 B.C. His great-grandfather was father-in-law of the tribune, Tiberius Gracchus.   [b] *Cf.* § 110.

[c] From the *Scholiasta Bobiensis* it would appear that
Appius made his way under the theatre and emerged through
a trap-door through which ghosts appeared on the stage.
It is, however, much more probable that Appius, who came
to *see* the show, not to appear on the stage, entered the
" theatre " under the floor of the " auditorium," not of the
stage, and slipped into his seat through a hole, as if he were
on the stage playing the part of the ghost of Deiphilus.

[d] The words are from the *Iliona* of M. Pacuvius (*c.* 220–*c.*
130 B.C.) and are spoken by the ghost of Deiphilus son of

thought that my recall was going to be dealt with—
what did it declare except that the welfare and
honour of the best citizens was dear to the whole
Roman People ? But that praetor,[a] who used to put 126
a question about me to a meeting, not like his
father, grandfather, great-grandfather, nor indeed
any of his ancestors, but after the fashion of mere
Greeklings,[b] " Did they want me to return ? ", and
when the half-dead voices of his hirelings had
shouted back " No ! ", used to say that the Roman
People were against my return—he, although he was
present every day at the gladiatorial games, was never
seen when he came. He used to creep up underneath
the flooring [c] and appear all of a sudden, as though
he were going to cry out,

Mother, to thee I cry ! [d]

And so that somewhat skulking path by which Appius
came to see the games began to be called " The
Appian Way." Yet, whenever he was seen, not only
the gladiators, but the very horses of the gladiators [e]
took fright at the sudden hissings. Do you see, 127
then, how great is the difference between the Roman
People and a meeting ? that those who tyrannize
over meetings are branded with every mark of hatred
by the People ? but that those who are not allowed

Iliona, daughter of Priam and Hecuba and wife of Polymestor. Deiphilus who, after the fall of Troy, had been
killed by his father Polymestor, returned from the lower
regions to greet his mother Iliona, and to entreat her to
bury his body. (*Remains of Old Latin* (L.C.L.), ii, pp. 238-
239.)

[e] The horses of the *andabatae* and the *essedarii*, of whom
the former fought (in helmets without eye-holes) on horseback
and the latter in Celtic two-wheeled war-chariots (*esseda*).

autem consistere in operarum contionibus non liceat, eos omni populi Romani significatione decorari ?

Tu mihi etiam M. Atilium Regulum commemoras, qui redire ipse Carthaginem sua voluntate ad supplicium quam sine iis captivis,[1] a quibus ad senatum missus erat, Romae manere maluerit, et mihi negas optandum reditum fuisse per familias comparatas et homines armatos ?

LX. Vim scilicet ego desideravi, qui, dum vis fuit, nihil egi, et quem, si vis non fuisset, nulla res 128 labefactare potuisset. Hunc ego reditum repudiarem, qui ita florens fuit, ut verear, ne quis me studio gloriae putet idcirco exisse, ut ita redirem ? Quem enim umquam senatus civem nisi me nationibus exteris commendavit, cuius umquam propter salutem nisi meam senatus publice sociis populi Romani gratias egit ? De me uno patres conscripti decreverunt, ut, qui provincias cum imperio obtinerent, qui quaestores legatique essent, salutem et vitam custodirent. In una mea causa post Romam conditam factum est, ut litteris consularibus ex senatus consulto cuncta ex Italia omnes, qui rem publicam salvam vellent, convocarentur. Quod numquam senatus in universae rei publicae periculo decrevit,

---

[1] quam eis invitis *Jeep* : quam salvis captivis *is suggested by Reid since, according to the story, the reason why Regulus did not remain in Rome was not the opinion of the prisoners left behind at Carthage, but his own determination that none of the prisoners should be ransomed.*

---

[a] The prosecutor had compared the conduct of Cicero to his disadvantage with that of Marcus Atilius Regulus (consul 256 B.C.). The latter, he urged, refused to stay in Rome

a place at meetings of hirelings, are adorned with every mark of goodwill by the Roman People ?

Do you also invite me to recall how Marcus Atilius Regulus [a] preferred to return to Carthage of his own free will, to meet his punishment, rather than to remain at Rome without those prisoners from among whom he had been sent to the Senate, and do you say that I ought not to have desired a return secured by armed men and by the enrolment of slaves ?

LX. Violence ! of course I desired violence, when I did nothing as long as violence ruled, and when nothing would have been able to overthrow me, if it had not been for violence ! Was I to reject a return, 128 which was so brilliant that I am afraid it may be thought that the desire of glory made me leave Rome just that I might have such a return ? What citizen, except myself, has ever been commended to foreign peoples by the Senate ? For whose welfare, except mine, has the Senate ever officially thanked the allies of the Roman People ? I am the only man for whom the members of the Senate have decreed that those who held provinces with military command, and those who were quaestors or legates, should be answerable for my welfare and life. On my behalf alone, since the foundation of Rome, has it happened that in accordance with a decree of the Senate all those who had the interests of the State at heart should be summoned from all Italy by letter from the consuls. What the Senate has never decreed when the

while his fellow-captives were in the enemy's hands, but Cicero preferred to secure his own return by violence and the help of armed men rather than remain in exile. For the peace-mission of Regulus see T. Frank in *Classical Philology*, 1926, pp. 311 ff.

id in unius mea salute conservanda decernendum putavit. Quem curia magis requisivit, quem forum luxit, quem aeque ipsa tribunalia desideraverunt? Omnia discessu meo deserta, horrida, muta, plena luctus et maeroris fuerunt. Quis est Italiae locus, in quo non fixum sit in publicis monumentis studium salutis meae, testimonium dignitatis?

129 LXI. Nam quid ego illa de me divina senatus consulta commemorem? vel quod in templo Iovis optimi maximi factum est, cum vir is, qui tripertitas orbis terrarum oras atque regiones tribus triumphis adiunctas huic imperio notavit, de scripto sententia dicta mihi uni testimonium patriae conservatae dedit; cuius sententiam ita frequentissimus senatus secutus est, ut unus dissentiret hostis idque ipsum tabulis publicis mandaretur ad memoriam posteri temporis sempiternam; vel quod est postridie decretum in curia populi ipsius Romani et eorum, qui ex municipiis convenerant, admonitu, ne quis de caelo servaret, ne quis moram ullam adferret; si quis aliter fecisset, eum plane eversorem rei publicae fore idque senatum gravissime laturum, et ut statim de eius facto referretur. Qua gravitate sua cum frequens senatus non nullorum scelus audaciamque tardasset, tamen illud

---

a *i.e.* Pompey's, over Africa (80 or 79 B.C.), over Spain (71 B.C.), over Asia (61 B.C.).

b Cicero, *Post reditum in senatu*, 26. The voting was 416 to 1, Clodius being the dissentient.

c Julius Caesar in 59 B.C. first arranged for the compilation and publication of the *acta diurna senatus et populi*. See Suetonius, *Div. Iul.* 20. 1.

d See § 33. A temporary suspension of the *lex Aelia*

whole State was in danger, it thought fit to decree for my salvation alone. Whom has the Senate House missed more ? whom has the Forum lamented more ? whose absence have the Courts themselves regretted as much ? When I withdrew, all was deserted, grim, silent, full of grief and mourning. What place in Italy is there, in which there is not engraved on public monuments zeal for my welfare and testimony to my worth ?

LXI. Why need I mention those decrees of the 129 Senate, full of more than human goodwill towards me ? or what took place in the Temple of Juppiter Best and Greatest, when that hero, who marked three separate regions and divisions of the world as having been added to our Empire by his three triumphs,[a] delivering his speech from writing, declared that I alone had saved the State ; his opinion was adopted by a crowded Senate, with my enemy as the sole dissentient,[b] and the fact was committed to the public records [c] for the eternal remembrance of future ages ; or what was decreed on the next day in the Senate House, at the suggestion of the Roman People itself and of those who had come together from the municipal towns,—that no one should watch for signs from the heavens,[d] nor attempt to stop proceedings ; and that anyone who did otherwise would clearly be a destroyer of the constitution, and that the Senate would take a most grave view of such an act ; and that the matter should at once be referred to it for consideration. And although a well-attended Senate had thus checked by its own solemn act the criminal audacity of a few, it further added,

Fufia for the special purpose of securing Cicero's recall. See p. 319.

addidit, ut, si diebus quinque, quibus agi de me potuisset, non esset actum, redirem in patriam dignitate omni recuperata.

LXII. Decrevit eodem tempore senatus, ut iis, qui ex tota Italia salutis meae causa convenerant, agerentur gratiae, atque ut idem, ad res redeuntes
130 ut venirent, rogarentur. Haec erat studiorum in mea salute contentio, ut ii, qui a senatu de me rogabantur, eidem senatui pro me supplicarent. Atque ita in his rebus unus est solus inventus, qui ab hac tam impensa voluntate bonorum palam dissideret, ut etiam Q. Metellus consul, qui mihi vel maxime ex magnis contentionibus rei publicae fuisset inimicus, de mea salute rettulerit. Qui excitatus cum summa auctoritate senatus, tum P. Servili incredibili[1] quadam gravitate dicendi, cum ille omnes prope ab inferis evocasset Metellos et ad illius generis, quod sibi cum eo commune esset, dignitatem propinqui sui mentem a Clodianis latrociniis reflexisset, cumque eum ad domestici exempli memoriam et ad Numidici illius[2] Metelli casum vel gloriosum vel gravem convertisset, conlacrimavit vir egregius ac

___

[1] MSS. *have* excitatus summa cum auctoritate p. servili quadam gravitate dicendi: senatus *added by Klotz*: tum incredibili *by Manutius.*

[2] ad unum dicitius, dicto citius, dictitius MSS.: ad Numidici illius *Manutius.*

___

[a] Under the *leges Caecilia Didia* (98 B.C.) and *Licinia Iunia* (62 B.C.) a minimum period of three *nundina* (eightday weeks) was required to elapse between the promulgation of a bill and the voting upon it. See p. 221, notes *i* and *j*.

[b] See § 72 and *De prov. cons.* 22.

[c] P. Servilius Vatia Isauricus, a grandson of Q. Metellus Macedonicus, consul 79 B.C. In 74 B.C. he triumphed for

that if a vote should be delayed for more than five
days on which a resolution about me might be made,
I might return to my country and recover all my
rights.

LXII. At the same time, the Senate decreed that
those who had assembled from all parts of Italy to
procure my recall should be thanked, and that they
should be asked to return when business was resumed.[a]
So great a rivalry was there in the endeavour to ensure 130
my welfare, that those whom the Senate solicited in my
cause themselves implored the Senate on my behalf.
And so, in these proceedings, only one man was
found to dissent openly from the goodwill of loyal
citizens so strongly expressed. Even Quintus
Metellus the consul, who in consequence of great
political controversies had been most unfriendly to
me,[b] introduced a motion for my recall. Moved both
by the great influence of the Senate, and by the
almost incredible power of the speech of Publius
Servilius[c] when he summoned nearly all the
Metelli from the lower world, and had turned
the thoughts of his relative away from the Clodian
acts of brigandage to the honour of that family
to which they both belonged; when he had recalled him to the recollection of an example from
that house, and of the fate (was it glorious or
regrettable?[d]) of the great Metellus Numidicus—
then that illustrious man, a true Metellus, burst

successful operations (78–75 B.C.) against pirates in Lycia,
Pamphylia, and Isauria. In 63 B.C. he was defeated by
Caesar at the election to the office of *pontifex maximus*.
[d] The reference is to the refusal in 100 B.C. of Q. Metellus
Numidicus to take an oath of obedience to Saturninus'
colonial law. See § 37 and notes.

vere Metellus totumque se P. Servilio dicenti etiam
tum tradidit, nec illam divinam gravitatem plenam
antiquitatis diutius homo eiusdem sanguinis potuit
sustinere et mecum absens beneficio suo rediit in
131 gratiam. Quod certe, si est aliqui sensus in morte
praeclarorum virorum, cum omnibus Metellis, tum
vero uni viro fortissimo et praestantissimo civi gratis-
simum, fratri suo, fecit, socio laborum, periculorum,
consiliorum meorum.

LXIII. Reditus vero meus qui fuerit, quis ignorat ?
quem ad modum mihi advenienti tamquam totius
Italiae atque ipsius patriae dextram porrexerint
Brundisini, cum ipsis Nonis Sextilibus idem dies
adventus mei fuisset reditusque natalis, idem caris-
simae filiae, quam ex gravissimo tum primum desiderio
luctuque conspexi, idem etiam ipsius coloniae Brun-
disinae, idem ut scitis, aedis Salutis, cumque me
domus eadem optimorum et doctissimorum virorum,
M. Laeni Flacci et patris et fratris eius, laetissima
accepisset, quae proximo anno maerens receperat et
suo praesidio periculoque defenderat. Cunctae itinere
toto urbes Italiae festos dies agere adventus mei
videbantur, viae multitudine legatorum undique mis-
sorum celebrabantur, ad urbem accessus incredibili

---

[a] Q. Metellus Celer, praetor 63 B.C., consul 60 B.C., who
strongly supported Cicero's measures against the Catilinarians. He died suddenly in 59 B.C. It was suspected
that he had been poisoned by his wife Clodia, sister of
P. Clodius. See *Pro Caelio*, 59.

[b] Described by Cicero in *Epp. ad Att.* iv. 1. 4-5.

[c] *i.e.* the first day.

[d] Founded on 5 August 244 (or 246) B.C. The best
harbour on the east coast of Italy, it was made a Latin
colony and became the terminal point of the extended Via
Appia.

into tears, and gave himself up wholly to Publius Servilius while he was still speaking ; nor could he, a man of the same blood, any longer resist that god-like impressiveness, so full of the spirit of days of old ; and, without waiting for my return, he became reconciled to me by his generous action. And 131 assuredly, if great men have any consciousness beyond the grave, then indeed his action was most welcome to all the Metelli, and above all to one, to that bravest of men and that most excellent of citizens, his brother,[a] who shared my labours, my dangers and my counsels.

LXIII. But who does not know what my return was like ?[b] how the people of Brundisium held out to me on my way home the right hand, as it were, of all Italy, and of my country herself. For that very fifth of August was the birthday[c] of my arrival and return. It was also the birthday of my beloved daughter, whom I then saw for the first time after cruel longing and sorrow, the birthday too of that colony of Brundisium itself,[d] and the birthday, as you know, of the Temple of Salus[e] ; and it was the day when the self-same house of those excellent and most learned men, Marcus Laenius Flaccus and his father and brother, gave me most joyful welcome, which the year before had offered me refuge in grief, and protected me at its own peril.[f] Everywhere, during my journey, all the cities of Italy seemed to be keeping the day of my arrival a holiday ; the roads were crowded with deputations sent from all parts to meet me ; my approach to the city was a triumphal pro-

[e] On the Quirinal, dedicated on 5 August 302 B.C.
[f] In spite of the penalties threatened by Clodius against those who received Cicero.

hominum multitudine et gratulatione florebat, iter
a porta, in Capitolium ascensus, domum reditus erat
eius modi, ut summa in laetitia illud dolerem, civitatem tam gratam tam miseram atque oppressam fuisse.

132 Habes igitur, quod ex me quaesisti, qui essent
optimates. Non est " natio," ut dixisti ; quod ego
verbum agnovi ; est enim illius, a quo uno maxime
P. Sestius se oppugnari videt, hominis eius, qui hanc
" nationem " deleri et concidi cupivit, qui C. Caesarem, mitem hominem et a caede abhorrentem,
saepe increpuit, saepe accusavit, cum adfirmaret
illum numquam, dum haec natio viveret, sine cura
futurum. Nihil profecit de universis ; de me agere
non destitit, me oppugnavit primum per indicem
Vettium, quem in contione de me et de clarissimis
viris interrogavit (in quo tamen eos cives coniunxit
eodem periculo et crimine, ut a me inierit gratiam,
quod me cum amplissimis et fortissimis viris con-
gregavit).

133 LXIV. Sed postea mihi nullo meo merito, nisi
quod bonis placere cupiebam, omnes est insidias
sceleratissime machinatus. Ille ad eos, a quibus
audiebatur, cotidie aliquid de me ficti[1] adferebat ;
ille hominem mihi amicissimum, Cn. Pompeium,

---

[1] defecti *MSS.* : de me ficti *Manutius, Halm.*

---

[a] The Porta Capena where the Via Appia passed through
the " Servian " Wall.
[b] His father's house on the Carinae occupied by his brother
Quintus. His own house on the Palatine had been destroyed
by Clodius.   [c] P. Vatinius.
[d] In 59 B.C. L. Vettius, a professional spy, informed the
Senate of a plot to murder Pompey and implicated many
eminent members of the aristocracy. He was sent to prison
by Vatinius, where he died. M. Cary in *Camb. Anc. Hist.* ix,
p. 521 concludes, " The origin of Vettius' romance and the

gress amid a vast cheering multitude ; the road from
the gate,[a] the way up to the Capitol, my return
home [b] were such that in the midst of my great joy
I could not help feeling sad when I remembered how
this so grateful city had been so unfortunate and so
crushed.

Here, then, is my answer to your question : who 132
are the " Aristocrats " ? They are not a " Breed,"
as you have called them ; I recognize the word, for
it is the invention of that man [c] by whom more than
anyone else Publius Sestius finds himself attacked,
that man who wanted this " Breed " to be destroyed
and cut to pieces ; who has often reproached, often
accused Gaius Caesar, a man who loves mercy and
abhors bloodshed, telling him that as long as this
" Breed " existed, he would never be free from
anxiety. Not having succeeded against the whole
body, he never ceased to deal with me. He attacked
me, first through an informer Vettius,[d] whom he
publicly questioned, concerning myself and some
distinguished citizens. Nevertheless, since he in-
volved those citizens in the same accusation and
risk with myself, he earned my gratitude for having
associated me with some most eminent and most
courageous men.

LXIV. But afterwards, without my having done 133
anything to deserve it, except that I desired to
please the loyal, he set on foot against me all kinds
of most wicked plots. Every day he carried some
fictitious tale about me to those who listened to him;
he warned Gnaeus Pompeius, a very great friend of

manner of his death are still unsolved problems." See also
In Vatinium, 24-26, and Pocock, *In Vatinium*, Appendix vi.

CICERO

monebat, ut meam domum metueret atque a me ipso
caveret ; ille se sic cum inimico meo copularat, ut
illius meae proscriptionis, quam adiuvabat, Sex.
Clodius, homo iis dignissimus, quibuscum vivit,
tabulam[1] Vatinium, sese scriptorem esse diceret ; ille
unus ordinis nostri discessu meo, luctu vestro palam
exsultavit. De quo ego, cum cotidie rueret, verbum
feci, iudices, numquam neque putavi, cum omnibus
machinis ac tormentis, vi, exercitu, copiis oppugnarer,
de uno sagittario me queri convenire. Acta mea sibi
ait displicere. Quis nescit ? qui legem meam con-
temnat, quae dilucide vetat gladiatores biennio, quo
134 quis petierit aut[2] petiturus sit, dare. In quo eius
temeritatem satis mirari, iudices, non queo. Facit
apertissime contra legem, facit is, qui neque elabi
ex iudicio iucunditate sua neque emitti gratia potest
neque opibus et potentia leges ac iudicia perfringere.
Quae res hominem impellit, ut sit tam intemperans ?
[Iste nimia gloriae cupiditate.][3] Familiam gladia-
toriam, credo, nactus est speciosam, nobilem, glori-
osam. Norat studia populi, videbat clamores et
concursus futuros. Hac exspectatione elatus homo
flagrans cupiditate gloriae tenere se non potuit, quin
eos gladiatores induceret, quorum esset ipse pul-
cherrimus. Si ob eam causam peccaret, pro recenti

[1] tubam *is conjectured by Müller* : ut illius proscriptionis . . . ambo una sese scriptores esse dicerent *Madvig*.
[2] petierit aut *is bracketed by Madvig*.
[3] *Halm, after Jeep, has* est enim nimia gloriae cupiditate.
Madvig and others bracket the words as above.

[a] P. Clodius.
[b] A dependant of Clodius, possibly descended from a freed-
man. Condemned in 52 B.C. for riots at Clodius' funeral, he
lived in exile till 44 B.C. See p. 502, note c.   [c] As consul.
218

mine, to fear my house and to beware of me. He had become so intimately associated with my enemy,[a] that Sextus Clodius,[b] a fellow most worthy of those with whom he lives, asserted that as regards my proscription, which he supported, Vatinius was the writing-tablet but that he was the writer ; he was the only man of our Order who openly rejoiced at my departure and at your sorrow. But although he acted like a madman every day, gentlemen, I never said a word about him ; nor, attacked as I was by all kinds of engines of war, by violence, by an army, by great forces, did I think it becoming to complain of a single archer. He says that he disapproves of my acts.[c] Everybody knows that, since he treats with disdain a law of mine,[d] which explicitly forbids any-one to give gladiatorial games within two years of his being a candidate for office either actually or pro-spectively. In this, gentlemen, I cannot sufficiently 134 admire his audacity. He acts most openly contrary to the law ; he does so, and yet he cannot slip out of a judgment by his pleasant manners, nor escape by favour, nor break through laws and courts by wealth and influence. What then makes him so uncontrolled ? He got together, I believe, a company of gladiators, impressive, grand, magnificent ; he knew what the people wanted, he foresaw their applause and their crowds. Inspired by this hope, burning with his greed for glory, the fellow could not refrain from exhibiting those gladiators in the arena, himself the handsomest of them all.[e] If that was why he did

---

[d] The *lex Tullia de ambitu* passed in 63 B.C. See *In Vatinium*, 37. Vatinius broke this law when canvassing for a praetorship of 55 B.C. to which he was elected by fraudulent means.   [e] A sarcastic reference to Vatinius' ugliness.

populi Romani in se beneficio populari studio elatus,
tamen ignosceret nemo ; cum vero ne de venalibus
quidem homines electos, sed ex ergastulis emptos
nominibus gladiatoriis ornarit et sortito alios Samnites, alios provocatores fecerit, tanta licentia, tanta
legum contemptio nonne quem habitura sit exitum
135 pertimescit ? Sed habet defensiones duas, primum
" Do," inquit, " bestiarios ; lex scripta de gladiatoribus." Festive ! Accipite aliquid etiam acutius.
Dicet se non gladiatores, sed unum gladiatorem dare
et totam aedilitatem in munus hoc transtulisse. Praeclara aedilitas ! unus leo, ducenti bestiarii. Verum
utatur hac defensione ; cupio eum suae causae
confidere. Solet enim tribunos pl. appellare et vi
iudicium disturbare, cum diffidit. Quem non tam
admiror, quod meam legem contemnit hominis
inimici, quam quod sic statuit, omnino consularem
legem nullam putare. Caeciliam Didiam, Liciniam
Iuniam contempsit. Etiamne eius, quem sua lege

---

^a He had been rejected for an aedileship of 57 B.C. ; see
§ 114.

^b Where slave-herdsmen were incarcerated ; perhaps the
pastorum stabula of § 12.

^c They wore the same arms as the Samnites.

^d Nothing is known of these gladiators.

^e The money which he would have expended on games,
if he had been elected aedile.

^f According to the Scholiast, one of his gladiators was
called Leo.

^g As he did in 58 B.C. when prosecuted under the *lex
Licinia Iunia*. See *In Vatinium*, 33-34.

^h The *lex Tullia de ambitu* (63 B.C.). See p. 219, note *d*.

wrong, carried away by a desire to please the Roman
People in return for their recent favour [a] towards
him, still no one would forgive him ; but when he did
not even choose picked men from the slave-market,
but bought men from the farm-prisons,[b] and provided
them with the names of gladiators, cast lots which
should be Samnites [c] and which Challengers,[d] does he
not fear the probable consequences of such licence
and defiance of the laws ? But he has two excuses. 135
" In the first place," he says, " I exhibit beast-fighters,
and the law refers to gladiators only." A humorous
distinction ! Now listen to something still cleverer.
He is going to say, " I have not shown gladiators, but
one gladiator only ; I have transferred all the cost of
my aedileship [e] to his exhibition." What a splendid
aedileship ! one Lion,[f] two hundred beast-fighters !
But let him make use of this excuse ; I wish him to
have confidence in his cause ; for, when he lacks confidence, he is in the habit of appealing to tribunes of
the commons and of breaking up a court by violence.[g]
I am not surprised so much at his defying my law,[h]
the law of an enemy, but at his having made it his
principle not to recognize any consular law as law.
He has defied the Caecilian and Didian Law [i] and the
Licinian and Junian Law.[j] Does he also refuse to

[i] The *lex Caecilia Didia* (98 B.C.) forbade " tacking "—
the inclusion of unconnected topics in one bill—and prescribed that after promulgation an interval of three *nundina*
(probably twenty-four days) should elapse before a measure
should be submitted to a vote. See p. 212, note *a*.
[j] The *lex Licinia Iunia* (62 B.C.) apparently confirmed
the *lex Caecilia Didia* (Cicero, *Phil.* v. 8) and (*Schol. Bob.*
310) enacted that copies of promulgated proposals should be
deposited, before voting, in the archives in the Temple of
Saturn. See p. 212, note *a*.

et suo beneficio ornatum, munitum, armatum solet
gloriari, C. Caesaris, legem de pecuniis repetundis[a]
non putat esse legem ? Et aiunt alios esse, qui acta
Caesaris rescindant, cum haec optima lex et ab illo
socero eius[b] et ab hoc adsecula[d] neglegatur ! LXV.
Et cohortari ausus est accusator in hac causa vos,
iudices, ut aliquando essetis severi, aliquando medi-
cinam adhiberetis rei publicae. Non ea est medicina,
cum sanae parti corporis scalpellum adhibetur atque
integrae ; carnificina est ista et crudelitas ; ei
medentur rei publicae, qui exsecant pestem aliquam
tamquam strumam civitatis.

136   Sed ut extremum habeat aliquid oratio mea, et ut
ego ante dicendi finem faciam quam vos mei tam
attente audiendi, concludam illud de optimatibus
eorumque principibus ac rei publicae defensoribus
vosque, adulescentes, et qui nobiles estis, ad maiorum
vestrorum imitationem excitabo, et qui ingenio
ac virtute nobilitatem potestis consequi, ad eam
rationem, in qua multi homines novi et honore
137 et gloria floruerunt, cohortabor. Haec est una via,
mihi credite, et laudis et dignitatis et honoris, a bonis
viris sapientibus et bene natura constitutis laudari
et diligi, nosse discriptionem civitatis a maioribus

---

[a] The *lex Iulia de pecuniis repetundis* passed by Caesar in
59 B.C.

[b] Vatinius when tribune in 59 B.C. carried the law which
gave Caesar the governorship of Cisalpine Gaul and Illyricum for five years from 1 March 59 B.C.

[c] By L. Calpurnius Piso as governor of Macedonia (57–
55 B.C.), father of Caesar's last wife.

[d] Vatinius had made money when tribune by illegal means.
See *In Vatinium*, 29. The *lex Iulia* applied not only to
provincial magistrates and their wives, but to all state
officials.

recognize as a law the law [a] of Gaius Caesar against extortion, the man who, he boastfully asserts, has been distinguished, set up in power and armed by a law of his [b] and by his favour ? And do they say that there are others who would annul the acts of Caesar, when this most excellent law is disregarded both by his father-in-law [c] and this satellite of his ? [d] LXV. And now, gentlemen, while bringing this accusation he has dared to exhort you in this case at last to show yourselves severe, and at last to administer some healing remedy to the State ! It is not a remedy to apply a lancet to a sound and healthy part of the body ; that is an act of butchery and cruelty. They heal the State who cut out a diseased portion, as some foul growth, from the body of the Commonwealth. [e]

But, that my speech may have some termination, 136 and that I may cease speaking before you cease to listen to me so attentively, I will finish my remarks about the " Aristocrats " and their leaders and about the defenders of the State. You, young Romans, who are nobles by birth, I will rouse to imitate the example of your ancestors ; and you who can win nobility by your talents and virtue, I will exhort to follow that career in which many " new men " [f] have covered themselves with honour and glory. Believe 137 me, the only way to esteem, to distinction, and to honour, is to deserve the praise and affection of patriots who are wise and of a good natural disposition and to understand the organization of the State

---

[e] An allusion to Vatinius' deformity, or " wen " (*struma*, Cic. *Epp. ad Att.* ii. 9. 2).

[f] In the Ciceronian Age *novi homines* were men born outside those families whose members or ancestors had reached the consulship. See Syme, *The Roman Revolution*, p. 10.

nostris sapientissime constitutam, qui cum regum
potestatem non tulissent, ita magistratus annuos
creaverunt, ut consilium senatus rei publicae prae-
ponerent sempiternum, deligerentur autem in id
consilium ab universo populo aditusque in illum
summum ordinem omnium civium industriae ac
virtuti pateret. Senatum rei publicae custodem,
praesidem, propugnatorem conlocaverunt ; huius
ordinis auctoritate uti magistratus et quasi ministros
gravissimi consilii esse voluerunt ; senatum autem
ipsum proximorum ordinum splendore confirmari,[1]
plebis libertatem et commoda tueri atque augere
voluerunt.

138   LXVI. Haec qui pro virili parte defendunt, optimates sunt, cuiuscumque sunt ordinis ; qui autem
praecipue suis cervicibus tanta munia atque rem
publicam sustinent, hi semper habiti sunt optimatium
principes, auctores et conservatores civitatis. Huic
hominum generi fateor, ut ante dixi, multos adver-
sarios, inimicos, invidos esse, multa proponi pericula,
multas inferri iniurias,[2] magnos esse experiundos et
subeundos labores ; sed mihi omnis oratio est cum
virtute, non cum desidia, cum dignitate, non cum

---

[1] splendore confirmari *MSS.*: splendorem confirmare *Bake.*
[2] iniurias, iniudias *MSS.*: insidias *Naugerius.*

---

[a] This is the principle of indirect popular election to the
Senate. In the fifth and fourth centuries B.C. the Senate was
enrolled by the consuls or military tribunes, probably from
ex-magistrates. But by the *plebiscitum Ovinium* (passed
probably between 318 and 312 B.C.) the right of enrolment
was transferred to the censors who were directed to enrol,
probably, ex-magistrates. See H. M. Last, " The Servian
Reforms," *J.R.S.* xxxv, p. 32.
[b] See Reid in Holden's *Pro Sestio*, p. 249.

so wisely established by our ancestors. When the rule of kings had become intolerable to them, they created magistracies to be held for a year only, with the restriction, that the Senate was set up as a Council over the State for ever, and they ordained that the members of that Council should be chosen by the whole people,[a] and that industry and merit should open the way for admission to that exalted Order for all citizens.[b] The Senate was set up as the guardian, the president, the defender of the State ; they willed that the magistrates should be guided by the authority of this Order, and should act as if they were the ministers of this great Council. Moreover, they wished that the Senate itself should be supported by the prestige of the Orders which came immediately next to it,[c] and should always be ready to protect and enlarge the liberty and interests of the commons.

LXVI. All those who defend these principles to the best of their power are " Aristocrats," to whatever Order they belong. But those who more than others carry upon their shoulders the burden of such duties and the public administration, are always considered as leaders of the " Aristocrats," as counsellors and saviours of the State. This class of men, I confess (as I have already said), has many opponents, many enemies, many who wish them ill ; many perils threaten them, many injustices are inflicted upon them, they have to undertake and to endure great labours. But my speech is wholly addressed to virtue, not to indolence ; to honour, not to sloth ; to those

[c] The Equestrian Order and the strata of population forming the " middle " class. See H. Hill, *The Roman Middle Class in the Republican Period* (Oxford, 1952).

voluptate, cum iis, qui se patriae, qui suis civibus, qui
laudi, qui gloriae, non qui somno et conviviis et
delectationi natos arbitrantur. Nam, si qui voluptatibus ducuntur et se vitiorum inlecebris et cupidi-
tatium lenociniis dediderunt, missos faciant honores,
ne attingant rem publicam, patiantur virorum for-
139 tium labore se otio suo perfrui. Qui autem bonam
famam bonorum, quae sola vere gloria nominari
potest, expetunt, aliis otium quaerere debent et
voluptates, non sibi. Sudandum est iis pro com-
munibus commodis, adeundae inimicitiae, subeun-
dae saepe pro re publica tempestates, cum multis
audacibus, improbis, non numquam etiam potenti-
bus dimicandum. Haec audivimus de clarissimorum
virorum consiliis et factis, haec accepimus, haec
legimus. Neque eos in laude positos videmus, qui
incitarunt aliquando populi animos ad seditionem,
aut qui largitione caecarunt mentes imperitorum,
aut qui fortes et claros viros et bene de re publica
meritos in invidiam aliquam vocaverunt. Leves hos
semper nostri homines et audaces et malos et perni-
ciosos cives putaverunt. At vero qui horum impetus
et conatus represserunt, qui auctoritate, qui fide, qui
constantia, qui magnitudine animi consiliis audacium
restiterunt, hi graves, hi principes, hi duces, hi
auctores huius dignitatis atque imperii semper habiti
sunt.

140   LXVII. Ac ne quis ex nostro aut aliquorum praeter-

---

a Cicero may be hinting at Pompey, Caesar, and Crassus.

who think they are born for their country, for their
fellow-citizens, for esteem, for glory, not for sleep,
for feasting, for enjoyment. For if they are led
astray by pleasures, and have given themselves up to
the seductions of vice and the allurements of desire,
let them renounce public office, let them not touch
political life, let them be content to enjoy their ease
and to owe it to the labour of brave men. But those 139
who seek the reputation of loyal citizens, which alone
can be called true glory, ought to seek security and
pleasures for others, not for themselves. They
must sweat for the common interests ; they must
expose themselves to enmity ; they must often face
storms for the sake of the State ; they must be
ready to fight with many audacious, wicked, and
sometimes even powerful men.[a] That is what we
have heard, what tradition tells us, what we have
read as to how our most famous men have thought
and acted. Nor do we ever see as objects of praise
those men who have at any time roused the temper
of the commons to sedition, or who have blinded the
minds of the inexperienced by bribery, or who have
brought odium upon brave and illustrious men that
have deserved well of the State. Our people have
always considered such men to be untrustworthy, and
to be reckless, wicked, and pernicious citizens. But,
on the other hand, those who have checked their
attacks and efforts, those who by their influence,
their loyalty, their stedfastness, their greatness of
soul, have resisted the schemes of adventurers, have
always been regarded as men of solid worth, as
chiefs and leaders, and as those to whom we owe our
present eminence and Empire.

LXVII. And that no one may dread to follow this 140

ea casu hanc vitae viam pertimescat, unus in hac civitate, quem quidem ego possum dicere, praeclare vir de re publica meritus, L. Opimius, indignissime concidit ; cuius monumentum celeberrimum in foro, sepulchrum desertissimum in litore Dyrrachino relictum est. Atque hunc tamen flagrantem invidia propter interitum C. Gracchi [semper][1] ipse populus Romanus periculo liberavit ; alia quaedam civem egregium iniqui iudicii procella pervertit. Ceteri vero aut repentina vi perculsi ac tempestate populari per populum tamen ipsum recreati sunt atque revocati aut omnino invulnerati inviolatique vixerunt. At vero ii, qui senatus consilium, qui auctoritatem bonorum, qui instituta maiorum neglexerunt et imperitae aut concitatae multitudini iucundi esse voluerunt, omnes fere rei publicae poenas aut praesenti morte aut turpi exsilio dependerunt. Quodsi apud Athenienses, homines Graecos longe a nostrorum hominum gravitate diiunctos, non deerant, qui rem publicam contra populi temeritatem defenderent, cum omnes, qui ita fecerant, e civitate eicerentur, si Themistoclem illum, conservatorem patriae, non deterruit a re publica defendenda nec Miltiadi calamitas, qui illam civitatem paulo ante

141

---

[1] *Bracketed by C. F. Hermann on the ground that it is due to* Sempr. *added in the margin of the* MS.

---

[a] Consul 121 B.C., whose operations, under the *senatus consultum de re publica defendenda*, the Senate's " Last Decree," were responsible for the deaths of C. Gracchus and some three thousand victims.

[b] In 121 B.C. Opimius restored the Temple of Concord and erected near by the Basilica Opimia, to commemorate the restoration of senatorial authority.

[c] In 120 B.C. he was prosecuted for his action in 121 B.C. and, defended by the consul, C. Papirius Carbo, was

path of life owing to my misfortune or that of any others, one person only in this State, as far as my recollection serves me, that illustrious public servant, Lucius Opimius,[a] did meet with most undeserved disaster; and his monument in the Forum[b] is visited by crowds, even if his tomb on the shore at Dyrrhachium is left deserted. And even he, although he was violently hated for the death of Gaius Gracchus, was set free from his danger by the Roman People itself. It was a storm from another quarter, and an unjust prosecution, that ruined that distinguished citizen.[c] The others, however, even if overthrown by sudden violence and an outbreak of popular fury, have yet been recalled and reinstated by that same People, or have lived their lives wholly uninjured and unattacked. But, on the other hand, those who disregarded the counsel of the Senate, the authority of loyal citizens, or the institutions of our ancestors, and endeavoured to make themselves agreeable to the ignorant or excited masses, nearly all paid a penalty to the State, either by instant death or ignominious exile. But if 141 among the Athenians, who were Greeks, differing greatly from our people in strength of character, there has never been a lack of defenders of the State against the foolhardiness of the populace, although all those who did so defend it were usually banished from the State; if the great Themistocles, the saviour of his country, was not deterred from defending the State either by the calamity of Miltiades, who a little before had saved it, or by the

acquitted. But in 110 B.C. he was, among other senatorial leaders, condemned by the *Quaestio Mamilia* for compromising the interests of Rome by intrigues with Jugurtha. He died in exile at Dyrrhachium.

CICERO

servarat, nec Aristidi fuga, qui unus omnium iustis-
simus fuisse traditur, si postea summi eiusdem civitatis viri, quos nominatim appellari non est necesse,
propositis tot exemplis iracundiae levitatisque popularis tamen suam rem publicam illam defenderunt,
quid nos tandem facere debemus primum in ea
civitate nati, unde orta mihi gravitas et magnitudo
animi videtur, tum in tanta gloria insistentes, ut
omnia humana leviora videri debeant, deinde ad eam
rem publicam tuendam adgressi, quae tanta dignitate
est, ut eam defendentem occidere optabilius[1] sit
quam oppugnantem rerum potiri ?

142 LXVIII. Homines Graeci, quos antea nominavi,
inique a suis civibus damnati atque expulsi tamen,
quia bene sunt de suis civitatibus meriti, tanta hodie
gloria sunt non in Graecia solum, sed etiam apud nos
atque in ceteris terris, ut eos, a quibus illi oppressi
sint, nemo nominet, horum calamitatem dominationi
illorum omnes anteponant. Quis Carthaginiensium
pluris fuit Hannibale consilio, virtute, rebus gestis,
qui unus cum tot imperatoribus nostris per tot annos
de imperio et de gloria decertavit ? Hunc sui cives e civitate eiecerunt ; nos etiam hostem litteris
143 nostris et memoria videmus esse celebratum. Quare

---

[1] non aliud sit MSS. : optabilius Schütz-Dobree : lauda-
bilius Müller : nobilius Reid : optatius Peterson.

---

[a] Optabilius is translated. There may be a reference here
to Caesar, a contrast between his exploits in Gaul and his
proceedings as consul. A parallel sentiment is to be found
in Cicero, Epp. ad Fam. i. 9. 7 : " dixi me M. Bibuli fortunam
. . . omnibus triumphis victoriisque anteferre."
[b] Hannibal, strictly speaking, was not exiled. In view of
the constitutional and economic reforms which he carried out

230

exile of Aristides, who is said to have been the most just of all men ; if, later, distinguished men of the same state, whom it is unnecessary to mention by name, although having before their eyes so many instances of hasty temper and fickleness shown by the people, still stood up for that State of theirs : what, I ask, ought we to do, who in the first place have been born in a state, which is the very birthplace, it seems to me, of strong and lofty character ; who in the next place are raised to such a height of glory, that all human records must seem trivial in comparison ; who, lastly, have undertaken the defence of that State, whose worth is so great that to die in its defence is more to be desired than by fighting against it to attain supreme power ? [a]

LXVIII. Those men of Greece whom I mentioned 142 before, who have been unjustly condemned and banished by their fellow-citizens, nevertheless, because they deserved well of their cities, are at the present day in such repute not only in Greece but also among ourselves and in all other countries, that no one mentions the names of their oppressors, and all men rank their fall above the supremacy of the others. Who of the Carthaginians was valued more highly for wisdom, for valour, for achievements, than Hannibal, who alone for so many years contended for rule and glory with so many of our generals ? He was driven out by his fellow-citizens [b] ; but, although he was our enemy, we find him celebrated in our literature and in our memory. Accordingly let us imitate 143

as suffete (196 B.C.), his enemies informed Rome that he was intriguing with Antiochus of Syria. On the arrival of a Roman commission Hannibal fled (195 B.C.), ultimately to Antiochus.

imitemur nostros Brutos, Camillos, Ahalas, Decios, Curios, Fabricios, Maximos, Scipiones, Lentulos, Aemilios, innumerabiles alios, qui hanc rem publicam stabiliverunt ; quos equidem in deorum immortalium coetu ac numero repono. Amemus patriam, pareamus senatui, consulamus bonis ; praesentes fructus neglegamus, posteritatis gloriae serviamus, id esse optimum putemus, quod erit rectissimum, speremus, quae volumus, sed, quod acciderit, feramus, cogitemus denique corpus virorum fortium magnorumque hominum esse mortale, animi vero motus et virtutis gloriam sempiternam, neque, hanc opinionem si in illo sanctissimo Hercule consecratam videmus, cuius corpore ambusto vitam eius et virtutem immortalitas excepisse dicatur, minus existimemus eos, qui hanc tantam rem publicam suis consiliis aut laboribus aut auxerint aut defenderint aut servarint, esse immortalem gloriam consecutos.

144 LXIX. Sed me repente, iudices, de fortissimorum et clarissimorum civium dignitate et gloria dicentem et plura etiam dicere parantem horum aspectus in ipso cursu orationis repressit. Video P. Sestium, meae salutis, vestrae auctoritatis, publicae causae defensorem, propugnatorem, actorem, reum ; video hunc praetextatum eius filium oculis lacrimantibus me intuentem ; video T. Milonem, vindicem vestrae

---

a Similar lists of the " grand old men " of Roman history are frequent in Cicero and are part of the " stock-in-trade " of later rhetorical writers.

b This is important evidence for religious development at the end of the Republic. Under Stoic influence the idea that worthy individuals might become divine after death appeared in Cicero, *Somnium Scipionis*.

c Cicero's *miseratio* (" appeal to pity ") now begins, a form of oratory in which he excelled.

men like our Bruti, Camilli, Ahalae, Decii, Curii,
Fabricii, Maximi, Scipiones, Lentuli, Aemilii, and
countless others,[a] who firmly established this State,
whom, indeed, I reckon among the company and
number of the Immortal Gods.[b] Let us love our
country ; let us obey the Senate, let us serve the
interests of loyal citizens ; let us disregard present
advantages, let us work for glory in years to come ;
let us regard that as best which is most truly good; let
us hope for our wishes, but let us bear what comes.
Lastly, let us remember, that if the body of a brave
and great man is mortal, yet the impulses of the
mind and the glory of virtue are eternal ; and, when
we see this belief consecrated in the person of
Hercules, that most venerable of heroes, whose courageous life is said to have passed into immortality
after his body had been reduced to ashes, let us none
the less believe that those who have enlarged, defended, or preserved this mighty State by their
counsels or labours have obtained immortal glory.

LXIX. But, gentlemen, while speaking of the 144
honour and glory of our bravest and most illustrious
citizens, and preparing to say even more, I am suddenly checked in the very course of my speech by the
sight of these my friends.[c] I see Publius Sestius,
defender of my life, champion of your authority, advocate of the cause of the State, on the bench of the
accused ; I see his son still in his childhood [d] turning
towards me with his eyes full of tears ; I see Titus

---

[d] The *toga praetexta*, of fine white wool, was marked by
a purple border for curule magistrates and the higher orders
of priests and for youths till at seventeen or earlier they
assumed the *toga virilis*. See vol. ii, p. 706, note *c*. For
Sestius' son see pp. 326-327.

libertatis, custodem salutis meae, subsidium adflictae
rei publicae, exstinctorem domestici latrocinii, re-
pressorem caedis cotidianae, defensorem templorum
atque tectorum, praesidium curiae, sordidatum et
reum ; video P. Lentulum, cuius ego patrem deum
ac parentem statuo fortunae ac nominis mei et fratris
liberorumque nostrorum, in hoc misero squalore et
sordibus ; cui superior annus idem et virilem patris et
praetextam populi iudicio togam dederit, hunc hoc
anno in hac toga rogationis iniustissimae subitam acer-
bitatem pro patre fortissimo et clarissimo cive depre-
145 cantem. Atque hic tot et talium civium squalor, hic
luctus, hae sordes susceptae sunt propter unum me,
quia me defenderunt, quia meum casum luctumque
doluerunt, quia me lugenti patriae, flagitanti senatui,
poscenti Italiae, vobis omnibus orantibus reddiderunt.
Quod tantum est in me scelus ? quid tanto opere
deliqui illo die, cum ad vos indicia, litteras, confes-

---

^a Clodius' prosecution of Milo (see p. 31) was still in
progress.

^b Reid rejects *deum fortunae* as not Ciceronian and sug-
gests *patrem eundem parentem* for *patrem deum ac parentem*.
P. Lentulus Spinther, as consul-elect in 58 B.C., and as consul
in 57 B.C., had been most active in the movement for Cicero's
recall. See §§ 72, 107.

^c Since the *toga praetexta* (see p. 233, note *d*) was worn
not only by youths and curule magistrates, but also by the
higher orders of priests, the young Lentulus was entitled to
wear it after his admission to the College of Augurs, who
were elected by an Assembly composed of 17 out of the 35
tribes, under the *lex Domitia* (104 B.C.), repealed by Sulla,
but re-enacted by T. Labienus, tribune 63 B.C.

^d P. Lentulus Spinther, who was due as proconsul to
govern Cilicia in 56 B.C., had been commissioned by the
Senate to restore Ptolemy Auletes, the exiled king of Egypt.
Early in 56 B.C. a proposal was made by a tribune, C. Cato,

Milo, restorer of your liberty, protector of my life, mainstay of our afflicted State, who has put an end to brigandage in our midst, and checked daily bloodshed, defender of your temples and homes, guardian of the Senate House, sitting in mourning and under accusation.[a] I see Publius Lentulus, whose father I consider the god and father of my fortune,[b] of my name, of my brother and my children, in these squalid mourning garments ; I see the man who in the past year received his toga of manhood from the hand of his father, and his purple-bordered toga [c] by the will of the People, and now in the present year, in this toga, he begs you to spare his father, one of our bravest and most illustrious citizens, the bitterness of a proposal as unjust as it was unexpected.[d] And this 145 mean apparel worn by so many distinguished citizens, these marks of sorrow, these melancholy rags, have been assumed for my sake alone, because they defended me, because they grieved for my misfortune and sorrow, because they restored me to my mourning country, to the demands of the Senate, to the request of Italy, to your unanimous entreaties. What great wickedness is in me ? what great crime did I commit on that day,[e] when I brought before you information,

that Lentulus be deprived of his *imperium*, and consequently of this commission. See Cicero, *Epp. ad Quintum fratrem*, ii. 3. 1. The charge was foiled by the consul Lentulus Marcellinus. Finally, on the plea that the Sibylline Books forbade the restoration of a king of Egypt by armed force, the Senate shelved the matter. Ptolemy was restored by A. Gabinius, governor of Syria, before April 55 B.C. ; see Cicero, *Epp. ad Att.* iv. 10. 1. See p. 28.

[e] 3 December 63 B.C., when Cicero reported to the Senate his capture of the envoys of the Allobroges at the Mulvian Bridge and disclosed the plans of Catiline's accomplices in Rome.

siones communis exitii detuli, cum parui vobis ? Ac
si scelestum est amare patriam, pertuli poenarum
satis ; eversa domus est, fortunae vexatae, dissipati
liberi, raptata coniunx, frater optimus, incredibili
pietate, amore inaudito maximo in squalore volutatus
est ad pedes inimicissimorum ; ego pulsus aris, focis,
deis penatibus, distractus a meis carui patria, quam,
ut levissime dicam, certe dilexeram[1] ; pertuli crudelitatem inimicorum, scelus infidelium, fraudem in-
146 vidorum. Si hoc non est satis, quod haec omnia
deleta videntur reditu meo, multo mihi, multo,
inquam, iudices, praestat in eandem illam recidere
fortunam quam tantam importare meis defensoribus
et conservatoribus calamitatem. An ego in hac urbe
esse possim his pulsis, qui me huius urbis compotem
fecerunt ? Non ero, non potero esse, iudices ; neque
hic umquam puer, qui his lacrimis, qua sit pietate,
declarat, amisso patre suo propter me me ipsum incolumem videbit nec, quotienscumque me viderit,
ingemescet ac pestem suam ac patris sui se dicet
videre. Ego vero hos in omni fortuna, quaecumque
erit oblata, complectar, nec me ab iis, quos meo
nomine sordidatos videtis, umquam ulla fortuna
divellet, neque eae nationes, quibus me senatus

---

[1] *Madvig's reading* : certe texeram *mss.* : corpore texeram
Koch : certe protexeram *Peterson* : corpore defenderam
Klotz : certe a caede texeram *Halm*.

---

[a] Those of the Senate for the keeping in custody of
Catiline's accomplices. Cicero here addresses those senators
who were amongst the *iudices*.

letters, confessions of those who had planned our
general destruction, when I obeyed your orders ? [a]
And yet, if it is a crime to love one's country, I have
been punished enough for it.   My house has been
pulled down, my property ravaged, my children separated,[b] my wife dragged through the city,[c] my excellent
brother, a man whose love and affection are beyond belief, has rolled prostrate in filthy rags at the feet of my
implacable enemies ; while I, driven from hearth and
home,[d] torn away from my friends, have been parted
from my country, which, to say the very least, I
had certainly loved.   I have borne the cruelty of
enemies, the crime of traitors, the perfidy of those
who wish me ill.   If this is not enough, because all 146
seems to be wiped out by my return, I would much
rather, much rather, I repeat, gentlemen, fall back
into the same ill-fortune, than bring so disastrous a
calamity upon my defenders and saviours.   Can I
remain in this city if those [e] who have given me my
share in it have been driven out ?   I will not, I cannot,
gentlemen, nor shall this youth, whose tears attest his
filial affection, if he loses his father through me, ever
see me myself safe amongst you, nor shall he lament
whenever he sees me, and say that he sees the man
who caused his own ruin and that of his father.   Indeed
I will cling to these, in every state of life, whatever be
their plight ; nor shall my lot ever tear me away from
those whom you see dressed in mourning on my
account ; nor shall those peoples, to whom the Senate

[b] His son Marcus from his daughter Tullia.
[c] See § 54.
[d] See R. G. Nisbet's note on the words *arae, foci, di
penates* in Cicero, *De domo sua*, 1 ; *op. cit.* p. 67.
[e] Sestius and Milo.

commendavit, quibus de me gratias egit, hunc
exsulem propter me sine me videbunt.

147 Sed haec di immortales, qui me suis templis ad-
venientem receperunt stipatum ab his viris et P.
Lentulo consule, atque ipsa res publica, qua nihil est
sanctius, vestrae potestati, iudices, commiserunt.
Vos hoc iudicio omnium bonorum mentes confirmare,
improborum reprimere potestis, vos his civibus uti
optimis, vos me reficere et renovare rem publicam.
Quare vos obtestor atque obsecro, ut, si me salvum
esse voluistis, eos conservetis, per quos me recupera-
vistis.

commended me, whom it thanked for me, ever see this man an exile on my account without me as his companion.

But the Immortal Gods, who received me in their temples on the day of my arrival, with these same men [a] and Publius Lentulus the consul in close attendance, and the State itself, most venerable of all things, have entrusted your authority, gentlemen, with the decision of these matters. By your verdict you can sustain the resolution of all loyal citizens and weaken that of the disloyal; you can enjoy the services of these best citizens, you can renew my courage, and you can give new life to the State. Wherefore I beg and beseech you, if you willed my salvation, to preserve those by whose efforts I have been restored to you. 147

[a] Sestius and Milo.

III. M. TULLI CICERONIS
IN P. VATINIUM TESTEM
INTERROGATIO

1 I. Si tua tantummodo, Vatini, quid indignitas po-
stularet, spectare voluissem, fecissem id, quod his
vehementer placebat, ut te, cuius testimonium propter turpitudinem vitae sordesque domesticas nullius
momenti putaretur, tacitus dimitterem. Nemo enim
horum aut ita te refutandum ut gravem adversarium
aut ita rogandum ut religiosum testem arbitrabatur.
Sed fui paulo ante intemperantior fortasse, quam
debui. Odio enim tui, in quo etsi omnes propter
tuum in me scelus superare debeo, tamen ab omnibus
paene vincor, sic sum incitatus, ut, cum te non minus
contemnerem quam odissem, tamen vexatum potius
2 quam despectum vellem dimittere. Quare ne tibi
hunc honorem a me haberi forte mirere, quod inter-
rogem, quem nemo congressu, nemo aditu, nemo suf-

---

a His: the advocates of Sestius; others, with less probability, refer the word to the jurymen.
b A reference to Vatinius' humble origin rather than an
attack on his morals.

III. A CROSS-EXAMINATION BY MARCUS TULLIUS CICERO OF THE WITNESS PUBLIUS VATINIUS

I. If I had merely wished, Vatinius, to consider **1** what your complete unimportance required, I should have done what my friends *a* here earnestly desired, and, regarding you as a man whose disgraceful life and domestic disrepute *b* would make his evidence to be accounted of no weight, I should dismiss you in silence. For none of them thought that you were either an adversary sufficiently important to be worth refutation, or a witness sufficiently conscientious to be questioned. But perhaps a little while ago I was somewhat more intemperate than I ought to have been.*c* For because of my hatred of you—which ought to have been greater than that of all others, owing to your crime against me,*d* but almost seems to be less —I was so carried away that, although I despised you no less than I hated you, yet I preferred to let you go in confusion rather than in contempt. Accordingly, **2** in case you should perhaps be surprised that I do you the honour of questioning you, when no one deems you worthy of his converse or his acquaintance, no one

---

c Probably on the previous day of the trial.
d In 59 B.C. he attacked Cicero through Vettius and in 58 B.C. he helped Clodius to exile him.

fragio, nemo civitate, nemo luce dignum putet, nulla
me causa impulisset, nisi ut ferocitatem istam tuam
comprimerem et audaciam frangerem et loquacitatem
paucis meis interrogationibus inretitam retardarem.
Etenim debuisti, Vatini, etiamsi falso venisses in suspicionem P. Sestio, tamen mihi ignoscere, si in tanto
hominis de me optime meriti periculo et tempori eius
3 et voluntati parere voluissem. Sed te die[1] hesterno
pro testimonio esse mentitum, cum adfirmares nullum
tibi omnino cum Albinovano sermonem non modo de
Sestio accusando, sed nulla umquam de re fuisse, paulo
ante imprudens indicasti, qui cum et T. Claudium
tecum communicasse et a te consilium P. Sesti
accusandi petisse et Albinovanum, quem antea vix
tibi notum esse dixisses, domum tuam venisse, multa
tecum locutum dixeris, denique contiones P. Sesti
scriptas, quas neque nosset neque reperire posset, te
Albinovano dedisse easque in hoc iudicio esse reci-
tatas. In quo alterum es confessus, a te accusatores
esse instructos et subornatos, in altero inconstantiam
tuam cum levitate, tum etiam periurio implicatam
refellisti,[2] cum, quem a te alienissimum esse dixisses,
eum domi tuae fuisse, quem praevaricatorem esse ab

---

[1] te *added by Lambinus*, die *by Schütz*.
[2] *Busche conjectures* praetulisti.

---

[a] Since in 57 B.C. Vatinius when a candidate for the
aedileship failed to secure the vote of his own tribe (*tribus
Sergia*), " to receive a vote " may be preferable to the
alternative rendering, " to cast a vote."

[b] Of joining in the prosecution of Sestius.

[c] Apparently a *subscriptor* (a subordinate accuser) of
P. Tullius Albinovanus, the prosecutor of Sestius.

deems you worthy of a vote,[a] of citizenship, or even
of the light of day, I declare that nothing would have
induced me to do so, except my desire to curb your
violence, to crush your effrontery, and to put a check
on your loquacity, by embarrassing you with a few
questions. For granting that Publius Sestius had
wrongly suspected you,[b] yet you ought to have
pardoned me if, when a man who had rendered me
such great services was in danger, I showed myself
ready to consider his difficulties and to comply with
his wishes. But yesterday you bore false witness 3
when you declared that, far from having discussed
with Albinovanus the question of accusing Sestius,
you had never spoken about anything at all with
him ; you lied, and, a little before without thinking,
revealed it, when you said that Titus Claudius [c]
had communicated with you, and had sought your
advice in the prosecution of Publius Sestius, and
that Albinovanus, whom you had previously said
you hardly knew, came to your house and had a long
conversation with you ; and lastly, that you sent
him copies of the speeches of Publius Sestius,[d] of
which he had no knowledge, nor could he have pro-
cured them, and that they were read at the trial.
Whereby on the one hand you admitted that the
accusers had been instructed and suborned by you,
and on the other hand you showed up [e] your own inconsistency, in its combination of folly and perjury
besides, when you said that the same man whom you
had declared to be an utter stranger to you had
visited you at your house, and that you had given
the man, whom you had at the outset considered to

---

[d] Made while he was tribune (57 B.C.).
[e] See Cicero, *Pro Ligario*, 16 for a similar use of *refellere*.

initio iudicasse, ei te, quos rogasset ad accusandum libros, dixeris dedisse.

4 II. Nimium es vehemens feroxque natura ; non putas fas esse verbum ex ore exire cuiusquam, quod non iucundum et honorificum ad aures tuas accidat. Venisti iratus omnibus, quod ego, simulac te aspexi, priusquam loqui coepisti, cum ante Gellius, nutricula[a] seditiosorum omnium, testimonium diceret, sensi atque providi. Repente enim te tamquam serpens e latibulis oculis eminentibus, inflato collo, tumidis cervicibus intulisti, ut mihi renovatus ille tuus in to . . .[d]

5 . . . veterem meum amicum, sed tamen tuum familiarem, defenderim, cum in hac civitate op- pugnatio soleat, qua tu nunc uteris, non numquam, defensio numquam vituperari. Sed quaero a te, cur C. Cornelium non defenderem ; num legem aliquam Cornelius contra auspicia tulerit, num Aeliam, num Fufiam legem neglexerit, num consuli vim attule-

---

[a] L. Gellius Poplicola. See *Pro Sestio*, 110.
[b] *Nutricula* is clearly used offensively.
[c] An allusion to the disfigurements of Vatinius.
[d] Lambinus' conjectural insertion is translated : *ut mihi renovatus tuus ille tribunatus videretur*. There is a large gap in *P*, in which about forty lines are omitted. Pocock suggests that the missing passage describes how Vatinius obtained leave to address the court, accused Albinovanus of collusion with the defence (*tergiversatio*) and attacked Cicero's whole career.
[e] [*Ac mihi primum obiecisti, quod Cornelium*] suggested by Lambinus.
[f] C. Cornelius, tribune 67 B.C., challenged the right usurped by the Senate of passing acts (*privilegia*) for or against an individual without reference to the People. He proposed that the People alone should grant *privilegia* and defied the veto of a fellow-tribune, P. Servilius Globulus, employed by

be in collusion with the accused, the copies of the speeches of Sestius which he had asked for to support his accusation.

II. In disposition you are too violent and arrogant; 4 you do not think that it is right for anyone to utter a word which does not fall on your ears as agreeable and flattering. You came here in a rage with everybody ; the moment I saw you, before you opened your mouth, while Gellius,[a] indulgent nanny [b] of all seditious men, was giving evidence earlier, I felt it and foresaw it. For all of a sudden, like a serpent from its hiding-place, with protruding eyes, with bulging neck and swollen throat,[c] in you came, so that I thought that I was back again [in the days of your tribunate.[d]

And you first reproached me with defending Cor- 5 nelius,][e] an old friend of mine, yet an intimate acquaintance of your own, although in Rome one is sometimes blamed for bringing such an accusation as you are now doing, but for defending, never. But I ask you, why was I not to defend Cornelius ? [f] Did he carry any law in defiance of the auspices ? [g] Did he ignore the Aelian Law or the Fufian Law ? [h] Did he lay violent hands on a consul ? Did he pack

the Optimates. But he agreed to a compromise that the Senate should continue to grant *privilegia*, with the safeguard that a quorum of two hundred members should be required for the vote. See H. M. Last in *C.A.H.* ix, p. 344 and W. F. McDonald, " The Tribunate of Cornelius " in *C.Q.* xxiii, p. 201. Subsequently he was prosecuted under the *lex Cornelia de maiestate* for refusing to yield to the *intercessio* of a colleague and in his trial concluded in 65 B.C. he was successfully defended by Cicero, fragments of whose speech survive with commentary by Q. Asconius Pedianus.

[g] The legislation of Caesar and Vatinius in 59 B.C. was so carried. [h] See *Pro Sestio*, 33, 34.

rit, **num** armatis hominibus templum tenuerit, num
intercessorem vi deiecerit, num religiones polluerit,
aerarium exhauserit, rem publicam compilarit. Tua
sunt, tua sunt haec omnia ; Cornelio eius modi nihil
obiectum est. Codicem legisse dicebatur ; defende-
bat testibus conlegis suis non se recitandi causa
legisse, sed recognoscendi. Constabat tamen Cornelium concilium illo die dimisisse, intercessioni
paruisse. Tu vero, cui Corneli defensio displicet,
quam causam ad patronos tuos aut quod os afferes ?
quibus iam praescribis, quanto illis probro futurum
sit, si te defenderint, cum tu mihi Corneli defen-
6 sionem in maledictis obiciendam putaris. Ac tamen
hoc, Vatini, memento, paulo post istam defensionem
meam, quam tu bonis viris displicuisse dicis, me
cum universi populi Romani summa voluntate, tum
optimi cuiusque singulari studio magnificentissime
post hominum memoriam consulem factum, omniaque
ea me pudenter vivendo consecutum esse, quae tu
impudenter vaticinando sperare te saepe dixisti.

---

^a Vatinius occupied the Temple of Castor (Dio Cassius,
xxxviii. 6. 2-3), the scene also of a disturbance in 62 B.C.
(*Pro Sestio*, 62).

^b When Bibulus, accompanied by tribunes, made his way
to the Temple of Castor and endeavoured to prevent Caesar
from carrying his first agrarian law.

^c The auspices and the *leges Aelia et Fufia*.

^d Cicero must refer to expenditure under the *lex Vatinia
de Caesaris provincia* and to the financial loss sustained
through the remission, by a *lex Vatinia*, to the *publicani* of
one-third the contract price for the collection of tithes from
the Province of Asia.

^e *Concilium plebis tributum.* For the distinction between
comitia, concilium, and *contio* see *C.A.H.* vii, pp. 444 and
451.

^f Cicero here takes advantage of ambiguity in the phrases

a temple [a] with armed men ? Did he throw a man
who vetoed violently down the steps ? [b] Did he
profane religious observances ? [c] Did he empty the
Treasury ? Did he plunder the State ? [d] These
crimes are yours, all yours ; no one has reproached
Cornelius with any such act. He was said to have
read out the text of his bill. His defence, attested by
his colleagues, was that he had done so, not for the
sake of reading it out publicly, but for the purpose of
revising it. Yet it is at least certain that he dismissed
the Meeting [e] on that day, and respected the veto
of a tribune. But you, who disapprove of my defence of Cornelius—what case, or rather what face,
will you present to your own advocates, when you
already give them definite warning how disgraceful it
will be for them if they undertake your defence, since
you think that my undertaking that of Cornelius is a
matter for accusation and abuse ? However, Vatinius, 6
remember this, that a little while after my defence,
which you say displeased "Good Men," I was elected
consul with the complete approval of the whole
Roman People, with remarkable enthusiasm of all the
best men,[f] an election more glorious than any within
the memory of man ; and finally, that I by living
modestly have secured all that you in your immodest
vaticinations often said that you hoped for.[g]

---

boni viri and *optimi cuiusque*. Asconius says that the
leading Optimates gave evidence against Cornelius at his
trial. Vatinius was right there, but Cicero conveniently
takes the phrase *boni viri* in its moral sense, " men of high
principles," not in its political sense, " Aristocrats " or
" Conservatives."

  [g] See § 11 where Vatinius when a candidate in 64 B.C. for the
quaestorship had spoken *de altero consulatu gerendo*. There
is a play here on *Vatinius* and *vaticinando*.

III. Nam quod mihi discessum obiecisti meum, et quod horum, quibus ille dies acerbissimus fuit, qui idem tibi laetissimus, luctum et gemitum renovare voluisti, tantum tibi respondeo, me, cum tu ceteraeque rei publicae pestes armorum causam quaereretis, et cum per meum nomen fortunas locupletium diripere, sanguinem principum civitatis exsorbere, crudelitatem vestram odiumque diuturnum, quod in bonos iam inveteratum habebatis, saturare cuperetis, scelus et furorem vestrum cedendo maluisse frangere quam 7 resistendo. Quare peto a te, ut mihi ignoscas, Vatini, ei cum patriae pepercerim,[1] quam servaram, et, si ego te perditorem[2] et vexatorem rei publicae fero, tu me conservatorem et custodem feras. Deinde eius viri discessum increpas, quem vides omnium civium desiderio, ipsius denique rei publicae luctu esse revocatum. At enim dixisti non mea, sed rei publicae causa homines de meo reditu laborasse. Quasi vero quisquam vir excellenti animo in rem publicam ingressus optabilius quicquam arbitretur quam se a 8 suis civibus rei publicae causa diligi. Scilicet aspera mea natura, difficilis aditus, gravis voltus, superba responsa, insolens vita ; nemo consuetudinem meam, nemo humanitatem, nemo consilium, nemo auxilium requirebat ; cuius desiderio, ut haec minima dicam, forum maestum, muta curia, omnia denique bonarum

---

[1] *Peterson's reading is adopted.*
[2] *Reid suggests* proditorem.

---

[a] *Rei publicae causa* : Vatinius uses this as meaning " for political reasons," but Cicero gives it the sense of " for the welfare of the State."

III. In answer to your taunt that I left the city, and your desire to renew the grief and sorrow of those to whom that day was the most grievous, as it was to you the gladdest of days, my only answer is this : when you and the other curses of the country were seeking an excuse to take up arms, and when you were eager, under the shelter of my name, to plunder the fortunes of the wealthy, to drain the blood of the leaders of the State, and to glut at once your cruelty and that lasting and now inveterate hatred which you cherish against honest men—then I preferred to overcome your criminal madness by giving way, rather than by resistance.   And so I beg you to pardon me, Vatinius, 7 for having spared that country which I had preserved, and if I bear with you, who wanted to ruin and disturb the State, to bear with me, its preserver and its guardian.   In the next place, you censure the departure of the man, who, you see, was recalled by the longing of all citizens, indeed by the mourning of the State herself.   Oh, but you said that it was not for my sake that men made these efforts for my recall, but for " reasons of State." [a]   As if indeed any man who has entered public life with a high purpose could think anything more desirable than that he should be loved by his fellow-citizens " for the sake of the State "!   No doubt my character is 8 harsh, I am difficult to approach, my looks are stern, my answers are haughty, my conduct is arrogant, no one missed my society, my human feelings, my counsel, my support [b] ; and yet, if I may mention things so unimportant, in sorrow for my absence, the Forum was in mourning, the Senate was dumb, all care for the

[b] Ironically : and yet true in comparison with what he is going to relate.

artium studia siluerunt. Sed nihil sit factum mea
causa ; omnia illa senatus consulta, populi iussa,
Italiae totius, cunctarum societatum, collegiorum
omnium decreta de me rei publicae causa esse facta
fateamur. Quid ergo, homo imperitissime solidae
laudis ac verae dignitatis, praestantius mihi potuit
accidere, quid optabilius ad immortalitatem gloriae
atque ad memoriam mei nominis sempiternam, quam
omnes hoc cives meos iudicare, civitatis salutem
9 cum unius mea salute esse coniunctam ? Quod
quidem ego tibi reddo tuum.[1] Nam ut tu me carum
esse dixisti senatui populoque Romano non tam mea
causa quam rei publicae, sic ego te, quamquam es
omni diritate atque immanitate taeterrimus, tamen
dico esse odio civitati non tam tuo quam rei publicae
nomine.

IV. Atque ut aliquando ad te veniam, de me hoc sit
extremum. Quid quisque nostrum de se ipse loquatur,
non est sane requirendum ; boni viri quid iudicent,[2]
10 id est maximi momenti et ponderis. Duo sunt tem-
pora, quibus nostrorum civium spectentur iudicia de
nobis, unum honoris, alterum salutis. Honos tali
populi Romani voluntate paucis est delatus ac mihi,
salus tanto studio civitatis nemini reddita. De te
autem homines quid sentiant, in honore experti sumus,

---

[1] mutuum *Pluygers*.
[2] *MSS.* iudicent : *Peterson conjectures* quid dicant, *Jordan*
quid iudicent.

---

[a] See *Pro Sestio*, 32, 129, and elsewhere.
[b] In his rejection when a candidate in 57 B.C. for the
aedileship. See note on § 2.

liberal arts was stilled. But suppose that nothing was done for my sake ; let us admit that all those resolutions of the Senate, those orders of the People, those decrees of the whole of Italy, of every society, every association, concerning myself were made " for the sake of the State." [a] What then, O utterly incapable as you are of judging genuine merit and true worth ! what then more honourable could have happened to me, what more desirable for an immortality of glory and everlasting perpetuation of my name, than that all my fellow-citizens should think that the welfare of the State was bound up with the welfare of my single self ? I give you tit for tat. For 9 as you said that I was dear to the Senate and the Roman People, not so much for my own sake as for the sake of the State, so in return I say that you, foulest of men though you are, in all your horror and monstrosity, are yet an object of hatred to the State, not so much on your own account as on that of the State.

IV. And in order that I may come at last to you, let this be the last word about myself. What each of us says about himself is not really the question. Let good men form their judgment ! that is of the greatest importance and weight. There are two 10 occasions suitable for testing the opinions of our fellow-citizens about us—the one has to do with public office, the other with personal position. Upon few men has office been conferred with such approval of the whole State as upon myself ; no one has been restored to his position with such great public enthusiasm. But what your fellow-citizens think of you, we have seen when you sought office [b] ; what they will do when your position is at stake—we still

in salute exspectamus. Sed tamen ne me cum his principibus civitatis, qui adsunt P. Sestio, sed ut tecum, cum homine uno non solum impudentissimo . . .[1] atque infimo, conferam, de te ipso, homine et adrogantissimo et mihi inimicissimo, quaero, Vatini, utrum tandem putes huic civitati, huic rei publicae, huic urbi, his templis, aerario, curiae, viris his, quos vides, horum bonis, fortunis, liberis, civibus ceteris, denique deorum immortalium delubris, auspiciis, religionibus melius fuisse et praestabilius me civem in hac civitate nasci an te. Cum mihi hoc responderis aut ita impudenter, ut manus a te homines vix abstinere possint, aut ita dolenter, ut aliquando ista, quae sunt inflata, rumpantur, tum memoriter respondeto ad ea, quae te de 11 te ipso rogaro. V. Atque illud tenebricosissimum tempus ineuntis aetatis tuae patiar latere. Licet impune per me parietes in adulescentia perfoderis, vicinos compilaris, matrem verberaris; habeat hoc praemii tua indignitas, ut adulescentiae turpitudo obscuritate et sordibus tuis obtegatur.

Quaesturam petisti cum P. Sestio, cum hic nihil loqueretur, nisi quod agebat, tu de altero consulatu gerendo te diceres cogitare. Quaero abs te, teneasne

---

[1] sed contemptissimo *is added by Madvig*: sed etiam sordidissimo *Peterson*.

---

[a] C. Licinius Calvus was preparing to prosecute Vatinius, who, however, was not tried till 54 B.C.

[b] Madvig inserts *sed contemptissimo*, because of *non solum* preceding.

wait to see.[a] However, not to compare myself with these chief men of the State who are supporting Publius Sestius by their presence, but with you, not only the most shameless [b] [but the most contemptible] and the basest of men, I ask you yourself, however great your arrogance and however great your hatred for me, Vatinius, which of us do you think it would have been better and preferable for this State, this commonwealth, this city, these temples, the Treasury, the Senate House, these men whom you see here, their goods, fortunes, children, the rest of the citizens, and lastly the shrines of the Immortal Gods, the auspices and religious observances, that he should have been born in it— you or I ? When you have answered this, either so impudently that people can hardly keep their hands off you, or so painfully that all these swellings of yours at last burst,[c] then answer, sir, with careful recollection, the questions I shall put to you concerning yourself. V. And I will not lift the veil of utter darkness in which your early years are wrapped. For all I care you may have broken into houses in your youth with impunity, robbed your neighbours, and beaten your mother. Let the meanness of your condition have so much profit, that the baseness of your youth be hidden by your obscurity and vileness.

You were a candidate for the quaestorship[d] with Publius Sestius, when he, in all he said, kept strictly to the business in hand, while you said that you were thinking about holding a second consulship. I ask you whether you remember that when Publius Sestius

[c] The words refer both to his conduct which was "swollen" and "puffed up" and also to his personal disfigurement.

[d] In 64 b.c. See p. 247, note g.

memoria, cum P. Sestius quaestor sit cunctis suffragiis factus, tunc te vix invitis omnibus non populi
12 beneficio, sed consulis extremum adhaesisse ; in eo
magistratu cum tibi magno clamore aquaria provincia
sorte obtigisset, missusne sis a me consule Puteolos,
ut inde aurum exportari argentumque prohiberes ;
in eo negotio cum te non custodem ad continendas,
sed portitorem ad partiendas merces missum putares
cumque omnium domos, apothecas, naves furacissime scrutarere hominesque negotii gerentes iudiciis
iniquissimis inretires, mercatores e navi egredientes
terreres, conscendentes morarere, teneasne memoria
tibi in conventu Puteolis manus esse adlatas, ad me
consulem querellas Puteolanorum esse delatas ; post
quaesturam exierisne legatus in ulteriorem Hispaniam
C. Cosconio pro consule ; cum illud iter Hispaniense
pedibus fere confici soleat aut, si qui navigare velit,
certa sit ratio navigandi, venerisne in Sardiniam atque
inde in Africam, fuerisne, quod sine senatus consulto

---

^a Cicero suggests that one of the consuls of 64 B.C.,
probably L. Iulius Caesar, son of a consul of 90 B.C. and so
a relative of Vatinius by marriage, manipulated the return.

^b It is best to take *aquaria* as equivalent to *maritima* and
to suppose that Vatinius was commissioned for service on the
Italian coast and was posted by Cicero, as consul, to Puteoli.
We know that a quaestor superintended the importation of
corn at Puteoli and we hear of one at the port of Antium
(Cicero, *Epp. ad Att.* ii. 9. 1).

was unanimously elected quaestor, then you, with difficulty, against everybody's wishes, not by the favour
of the Roman People, but of a consul,[a] just stuck on
to the end. When in your quaestorship you had 12
drawn by lot, amid an uproar, the department of
coastal duties,[b] were you not sent by me when I was
consul to Puteoli, that you might prevent the expor-
tation of gold and silver ? [c] While thus employed,
thinking that you had been sent, not as a guard to
keep, but as a customs-house officer, to share out the
merchandise,[d] when you searched every house, ware-
house, and ship like a thief indeed, entangled men
while carrying on their business in iniquitous legal
proceedings, frightened merchants when they dis-
embarked and hindered them when they went on
board,—do you remember that in a court[e] at Puteoli
violent hands were laid upon you ? do you remember
that complaints from the inhabitants were brought
before me as consul ? After your quaestorship did
you not leave for Further Spain on the staff of the
governor, C. Cosconius ? Although the journey to
Spain is usually made by land, or, if a sea voyage
is preferred, a certain route is prescribed, did you
not first visit Sardinia, and then Africa ? Did you

[c] Cicero, *Pro Flacco*, 67, says that restrictions were frequently placed by the Senate upon the export of bullion
from Italy, notably in 63 B.C.

[d] The exactions of customs-house officers were notorious.
Cicero (*Epp. ad Quintum fratrem*, i. 1. 33) says that the
abolition of customs- and harbour-dues by Q. Metellus
Nepos in 60 B.C. was due less to the incidence of the dues
themselves than to the exactions of the *portitores*.

[e] Although there is no evidence that *iudicia* in a *praefectura* (Puteoli was one) were called *conventus*, it is reasonable
to suppose that *conventus* here means an assembly where
judicial business could be dealt with.

tibi facere non licuit, in regno Hiempsalis, fuerisne in
regno Mastanesosi, venerisne ad fretum per Maure-
taniam ; quem scias umquam legatum Hispaniensem
istis itineribus in illam provinciam pervenisse ?

13 Factus es tribunus pl. (quid enim te de Hispa-
niensibus flagitiis tuis sordidissimisque furtis inter-
rogem ?) Quaero abs te primum universe, quod genus
improbitatis et sceleris in eo magistratu praeter-
miseris ? Ac tibi iam inde praescribo ne tuas sordes
cum clarissimorum virorum splendore permisceas.
Ego te quaecumque rogabo, de te ipso rogabo neque
te ex amplissimi viri dignitate, sed ex tuis tenebris
extraham, omniaque mea tela sic in te conicientur, ut
nemo per tuum latus, quod soles dicere, saucietur ;
in tuis pulmonibus ac visceribus haerebunt.

14 VI. Et quoniam omnium rerum magnarum ab dis
immortalibus principia ducuntur, volo, ut mihi respondeas tu, qui te Pythagoreum soles dicere et
hominis doctissimi nomen tuis immanibus et bar-

---

[a] Hiempsal, son of Gauda, was restored by Pompey to
the Numidian throne in 81 B.C. Numidia, which was not
under Roman jurisdiction, could not be visited by a Roman
magistrate without an order of the Senate. C. Cosconius
was a praetor in 63 B.C.

[b] It is probable that this name, otherwise unknown, is to
be equated with that of Masintha, a Numidian chieftain
defended by Julius Caesar in Rome in 62 B.C. against
Hiempsal. Possibly Masintha was a son of Iarbas, deposed
by Pompey in favour of Hiempsal, and had attempted to set
himself up as an independent prince. Vatinius clearly visited
Numidia on a secret mission from Julius Caesar. See
Suetonius, *Div. Iul.* 71.

[c] *i.e.* that of Gibraltar.

not stop in the kingdom of Hiempsal, which you were not allowed to do without a decree of the Senate ? [a] Then in that of Mastanesosus ? [b] Did you cross Mauretania on your way to the Strait ? [c] What legate have you ever known who reached that province in Spain after a route of that sort ?

You became tribune of the commons [d]—for why 13 question you about your misdeeds and shameful robberies in Spain ? I ask you first in general terms what kind of iniquity and crime did you not commit during your tribunate ? And I warn you from the beginning not to mix up your dirty tricks with the glorious reputation of our most distinguished men. Whatever I ask you will be something about yourself. I shall drag you from your own proper obscurity, not from the dignified company of a great man. [e] And all my shafts will be so aimed against you that no one else will be wounded, as you are in the habit of saying, through your body [f]; they will remain fixed in your lungs and your vitals.

VI. And, since all important things have their 14 beginning with the Immortal Gods, I wish you to answer a few questions. You are in the habit of calling yourself a Pythagorean, and of hiding your ferocious and barbarous manners behind the name

[d] Cicero (*Epp. ad Fam.* i. 9. 7) says " My whole cross-examination (of Vatinius) was nothing but a denunciation of his tribunate " (59 B.C.).

[e] The phrases *cum clarissimorum virorum splendore* and *ex amplissimi viri dignitate*, referring to Caesar, betray the caution with which Cicero begins to deal with the political associations between Caesar and Vatinius.

[f] Although Cicero here asserts that he will not wound Caesar through Vatinius, it cannot be denied that the language of § 15 is a reflection on Caesar. See p. 308.

baris moribus praetendere, quae te tanta pravitas
mentis tenuerit, qui tantus furor, ut, cum inaudita
ac nefaria sacra susceperis, cum inferorum animas
elicere, cum puerorum extis deos manes mactare
soleas, auspicia, quibus haec urbs condita est,
quibus omnis res publica atque imperium tenetur,
contempseris initioque tribunatus tui senatui de-
nuntiaris tuis actionibus augurum responsa atque
eius collegii adrogantiam impedimento non futura.
15 Secundum ea quaero, servarisne in eo fidem ; num
quando tibi moram attulerit, quo minus concilium
advocares legemque ferres, quod eo die scires de caelo
esse servatum. Et quoniam hic locus est unus, quem
tibi cum Caesare communem esse dicas, seiungam te
ab illo non solum rei publicae causa, verum etiam
Caesaris, ne qua ex tua summa indignitate labes illius
dignitati aspersa videatur. Primum quaero, num tu

---

a Possibly P. Nigidius Figulus, praetor in 59 B.C. and a
senator, mentioned by the Scholiast. Or the scholar might
be Pythagoras himself, Cicero meaning that Vatinius calls
himself a Pythagorean, but does worse things than the
Pythagoreans ever did.

b Such charges, with little probability, were made against
Pythagorean society. Vatinius, says Cicero, might indulge
in such practices, but contempt for the auspices was a graver
matter.

c The members of the College of Augurs possessed almost
unlimited powers of political obstruction since they pronounced judgment upon the validity of the auspices taken
before the transaction of every piece of public business. See
Cicero, *De haruspicum responsis*, 48. Although there is no

258

of a profound scholar [a] : pray tell me, however much
you have engaged in unknown and mysterious rites,
however accustomed you may be to evoke spirits from
the underworld, and to appease the infernal deities
with the entrails of boys,[b] what monstrous perversity,
what madness led you to show contempt for the
auspices under which this city has been founded, upon
which the whole State and its authority depend, and
to declare to the Senate, in the first days of your
tribunate, that the pronouncements of the augurs and
the pretensions of their college would be no obstacle
to your undertakings? [c] Next I ask you, whether 15
you kept your promise in this. Were you ever prevented from summoning a Meeting and passing a
law, because you knew that announcement had been
made that the heavens had been observed on that
day? [d] And since this is the only point in which you
claim to have something in common with Caesar, I
will separate your case from his,[e] not only for the sake
of the State,[f] but for Caesar also, lest a stain from
your gross unworthiness should seem to tarnish his
worthy name. I ask you first whether you entrust

evidence that Caesar formally endorsed this declaration by
Vatinius, which was without precedent, and was apparently
made on his own initiative, the legislation of 59 B.C. was, in
effect, carried through by such means.

[d] Under the *leges Aelia et Fufia* a statement by a magistrate that he intended to watch the skies for omens (*spectio*
or *servare de caelo*) was sufficient to suspend public business.
Nisbet, *Cicero, De domo*, p. 203. See pp. 311 ff. The Meeting
was *concilium plebis tributum*.

[e] Yet Cicero is reflecting on Caesar as much as on Vatinius.

[f] Since it would create disturbance if the laws of Caesar
were declared to be irregular and therefore illegal. Or perhaps *rei publicae causa* may mean (as in § 7) " for reasons of
state," on the ground of expediency.

senatui causam tuam permittas, quod facit Caesar;
deinde, quae sit auctoritas eius, qui se alterius facto,
non suo defendat; deinde (erumpet enim aliquando
ex me vera vox, et dicam sine cunctatione, quod
sentio), si iam violentior aliqua in re C. Caesar fuisset,
si eum magnitudo contentionis, studium gloriae, praestans animus, excellens nobilitas aliquo impulisset,
quod in illo viro et tum ferendum esset et maximis
rebus, quas postea gessit, oblitterandum : id tu tibi,
furcifer, sumes, et Vatini latronis ac sacrilegi vox
audietur hoc postulantis, ut idem sibi concedatur quod
Caesari?

16 VII. Sic enim ex te quaero. Tribunus pl. fuisti;
seiunge te a consule; collegas habuisti viros fortes
novem. Ex iis tres erant, quos tu cotidie sciebas
servare de caelo, quos irridebas, quos privatos esse
dicebas; de quibus duos praetextatos sedentes vides,
te aediliciam praetextam togam, quam frustra con-
feceras, vendidisse, tertium scis ex illo obsesso atque
adflicto tribunatu consularem auctoritatem hominem
esse adulescentem consecutum. Reliqui sex fuerunt,
e quibus partim plane tecum sentiebant, partim
medium quendam cursum tenebant; omnes habue-

---

[a] The present tense (*facit*) suggests an improvement at the
moment in the relations between Caesar and the Senate.
But, although Caesar had approved the restoration of Cicero
and had received from the Senate, on the proposal of Cicero,
the unprecedented honour of a *supplicatio* of fifteen days for
his Gallic victories in 58 and 57 B.C., it is difficult to accept
a reconciliation between Caesar and the Senate as anything
more than a pious hope.

[b] The Gallic campaigns of 58 and 57 B.C.

[c] Who had not the power of watching the heavens.

[d] Cn. Domitius Calvinus and Q. Ancharius : they were
praetors of the year 56 B.C. See *Pro Sestio*, 113.

your cause to the Senate, as Caesar does [a]; in the second place, what is the authority of a man who defends himself by the act of another, not by his own. Next, for the truth shall at length force utterance, and I shall not hesitate to say what I think. Suppose for a moment that Caesar did break out into some excesses; that the strain of conflict, his passion for glory, his outstanding genius, his exalted birth, did drive him into some acts which at that moment and in such a man might be tolerable, but should be wiped out of memory by his subsequent mighty achievements [b]; will you, you rascal, claim the same forbearance; and shall we give ear to the voice of Vatinius, brigand and temple-robber, demanding for himself the same privileges as Caesar?

VII. Now I ask you this. You were tribune of the 16 commons—separate yourself from the consul—your colleagues were nine courageous men. Of these there were three whom you knew to be watching the heavens every day, whom you ridiculed, whom you declared to be private persons [c]; two of whom you can see sitting in Court, wearing their *toga praetexta*,[d] —while you have sold the one you had had made in vain for your aedileship [e]; the third,[f] you know, after the troubles that beset his tribunate, enjoyed, while still young, as much authority as if he had been a consul. The six others were either entirely on your side, or kept a sort of middle course; laws were pro-

---

[e] *Te . . . vendidisse*: generally taken as accusative and infinitive after *vides*. Bake suggests the insertion of *meministi,* and the Oxford text (Peterson) makes it an exclamation. It is probable that is was as a candidate for an aedileship of 57 B.C. that Vatinius was defeated.

[f] C. Fannius; see *Pro Sestio,* 113.

runt leges promulgatas, in eis multas meus necessarius,
etiam de mea sententia, C. Cosconius, iudex noster,
17 quem tu dirumperis cum aedilicium vides. Volo, uti
mihi respondeas, num quis ex toto collegio legem sit
ausus ferre praeter unum te ; quae tanta in te fuerit
audacia, quae tanta vis, ut, quod novem tui collegae
sibi timendum esse duxerint, id unus tu emersus e
caeno, omnium facile omnibus rebus infimus contem-
nendum, despiciendum, irridendum putares ; num
quem post urbem conditam scias tribunum pl. egisse
cum plebe, cum constaret servatum esse de caelo.
18 Simul etiam illud volo uti respondeas, cum te tribuno
pl. esset etiam tum in re publica lex Aelia et Fufia,
quae leges saepe numero tribunicios furores debili-
tarunt et represserunt, quas contra praeter te nemo
umquam est facere conatus (quae quidem leges anno
post sedentibus in templo duobus non consulibus, sed
proditoribus huius civitatis ac pestibus una cum
auspiciis, cum intercessionibus, cum omni iure publico
conflagraverunt), ecquando dubitaris contra eas leges
cum plebe agere et concilium convocare ; num quem
ex omnibus tribunis pl., quicumque seditiosi fuerunt,
tam audacem audieris fuisse, ut umquam contra
legem Aeliam aut Fufiam concilium advocaret.

---

^a *Promulgatas* is used because these laws were not yet
proposed, but only announced.
^b In 58 B.C. for 57. Were the reference to the election of
aediles on 20 January 56 B.C. (Cicero, *Epp. ad Quintum
fratrem*, ii. 2. 2), Cosconius would have been called *aedilem* ;
he was a tribune of 59 B.C., not a praetor of 63 B.C. (§ 12).
^c See p. 315.
^d A. Gabinius and L. Calpurnius Piso: see *Pro Sestio*, 33.

mulgated [a] by all, many of them, with my approval also, by my friend Gaius Cosconius, a member of this jury, successful in the aediles' election,[b] whom you cannot see without bursting with envy. I wish you would tell me whether any one of the whole college ventured to propose a law except yourself. What audacity was yours, what violence ! what your nine colleagues held should be regarded with awe, you alone, one sprung from the mud, the lowest of the land in every way, regarded as contemptible, trivial, ridiculous ! Do you know of any tribune of the commons since the foundation of Rome who transacted business with the commons, when it was well known that an announcement had been made that the heavens had been watched ? I should also like you to answer this. During your tribunate of the commons, the Aelian and Fufian Laws [c] still existed in the State, those laws which often checked and crippled the revolutionary tribunes, those laws which no one except yourself has ever ventured to resist ; laws, I may say, which the year after, while two men [d] were seated on the Rostra [e]—I will not say consuls, but two betrayers and plagues of our country,—were destroyed in the same conflagration as the auspices, as vetoes, and as all public law : I ask you, did you ever hesitate, contrary to those laws, to transact business with the commons and summon a Meeting ? [f] Have you ever heard that any of the most seditious tribunes of the commons was so audacious as to summon a Meeting in defiance of the Aelian or the Fufian Law ?

[e] *Templum*, " a consecrated place," is here applied to the Rostra. See § 5 and *Pro Sestio*, 75.

[f] *Concilium plebis tributum.* See p. 246, note *e*.

19 VIII. Quaero illud etiam ex te, conatusne sis, voluerisne, denique cogitaris (est enim res eius modi, ut, si tibi in mentem modo venit, nemo sit, qui te ullo cruciatu esse indignum putet) cogitarisne in illo tuo intolerabili non regno (nam cupis id audire), sed latrocinio augur fieri in Q. Metelli locum, ut, quicumque te aspexisset, duplicem dolorem gemitumque susciperet et ex desiderio clarissimi et fortissimi civis et ex honore turpissimi atque improbissimi; adeone non labefactatam rem publicam te tribuno neque conquassatam civitatem, sed captam hanc urbem atque perversam putaris, ut augurem Vatinium ferre possemus.

20 Hoc loco quaero, si, id quod concupieras, augur factus esses (in qua tua cogitatione nos, qui te oderamus, vix dolorem ferebamus, illi autem, quibus eras in deliciis, vix risum tenebant); sed quaero, si ad cetera vulnera, quibus rem publicam putasti deleri, hanc quoque mortiferam plagam inflixisses auguratus tui, utrum decreturus fueris, id quod augures omnes usque ab Romulo decreverunt, Iove fulgente cum populo agi nefas esse, an, quia tu semper sic egisses, auspicia fueris augur dissoluturus.

21 IX. Ac ne diutius loquar de auguratu tuo (quod

---

a Cicero alludes to his conduct in 59 B.C.

b Q. Caecilius Metellus Celer, elder brother of Q. Metellus Nepos (consul 57 B.C.) and an augur, was praetor 63 B.C. and consul 60 B.C. He was governor-elect of Transalpine Gaul, but died suddenly in 59 B.C. in or before April, when the

VIII. I also ask you, whether you have tried, have 19
ever had the wish or even the idea—for the crime is
of such a kind that, if it only entered your mind, no
one would fail to think you worthy of the extremest
punishment—whether you ever had the idea, during
your intolerable—I will not say reign as king (for that
is what you like to hear) but your career as brigand,[a]
of being elected augur in place of Quintus Metellus,[b]
so that whoever saw you might be twice pierced
and twice anguished, both by the loss of a brave and
illustrious man, and by the elevation of an infamous
scoundrel? Did you indeed think that the State had
been so undermined and the constitution so shaken
under your tribunate—no, that Rome had fallen into
captivity and ruin, so that we could endure Vatinius
as augur? At this point I ask, if you had been 20
elected augur as you had desired—and what an
idea it was! we who hated you could scarcely control
our indignation, while those[c] whose darling you were
could hardly restrain their laughter!—but I ask you,
after all those other wounds, by which you thought
the State was being destroyed, if you had inflicted
this mortal blow also by your augurate, did you propose to decree, as all augurs since Romulus have decreed, that when Juppiter lightens it is sacrilege to
transact business with the People, or, because you
had always so transacted it, did you propose as augur
to make a complete end of the auspices?

IX. And now, not to speak at greater length about 21

question of his successor in the augurate was discussed (Cic.
Epp. ad Att. ii. 5. 2). See *Pro Caelio*, 59.
[c] Pompey, Caesar, and Crassus. Cicero, however (*Epp.
ad Att.* ii. 9. 2), says that they were thinking of making
Vatinius an augur.

CICERO

invitus facio, ut recorder ruinas rei publicae ; neque
enim tu umquam stante non modo maiestate horum,
sed etiam urbe te augurem fore putasti) ; verum
tamen ut somnia tua relinquam, ad scelera veniam,
volo, uti mihi respondeas, cum M. Bibulum consulem
non dicam bene de re publica sentientem, ne tu mihi
homo potens irascare, qui ab eo dissensisti, sed hominem certe nusquam progredientem, nihil in re publica
molientem, tantum animo ab actionibus tuis dissenti-
entem, cum eum tu consulem in vincula duceres et a
tabula Valeria collegae tui mitti iuberent, fecerisne
ante rostra pontem continuatis tribunalibus, per quem
consul populi Romani moderatissimus et constantis-
simus sublato auxilio, exclusis amicis, vi perditorum
hominum incitata turpissimo miserrimoque spectaculo
non in carcerem, sed ad supplicium et ad necem duce-
22 retur. Quaero, num quis ante te tam fuerit nefarius,
qui id fecerit, ut sciamus, utrum veterum facinorum
sis imitator an inventor novorum ; idemque tu cum
his atque huius modi consiliis ac facinoribus nomine
C. Caesaris, clementissimi atque optimi viri, scelere

---

a The audacity of Vatinius showed how the State was
ruined.   *b* *Horum* : the jurymen.
    c He was content with passive resistance to Caesar and
his partners.
    d Neither a bank (Tyrrell on Cicero, *Epp. ad Fam.* xiv. 2. 2)
nor a tablet bearing the text of the Valerio-Horatian Laws,
but a painting on the wall of the Curia Hostilia representing
the diplomatic victory of M'. Valerius Messalla over Hiero and
Carthage in 263 B.C. (Pliny, *Nat. Hist.* xxxv. 22) and mark-
ing the site of an office or headquarters used by the tribunes
in the Forum near the Basilica Porcia (Plutarch, *Cato Minor*,
5) which adjoined the Curia Hostilia. See Platner and Ashby,
op. cit. pp. 505, 506 and 608, and Pocock, *op. cit.* Appendix v.

your augurate (which I speak of reluctantly, only to
recall the ruin of the State,[a] for even you never
thought that you would become augur while the city
of Rome stood, not to mention the dignity of this
Court[b])—but nevertheless to dismiss your dreams and
come to your crimes, I wish you to answer me this:
When Marcus Bibulus was consul—I do not say that
he had sound views on constitutional matters, for fear
I may offend a powerful person like yourself, who disagreed with him, but he was certainly a man who took
no forward steps,[c] nor planned any political enterprise, who only disagreed inwardly with what you did,
—when Marcus Bibulus was consul, and you cast the
consul into prison, and your colleagues [from their
place] by Valerius' picture[d] ordered his release, did you
not make a gangway in front of the Rostra by joining
together the seats, through which a consul of the
Roman People, a man of the greatest restraint and
stedfastness, deprived of the protection of the tribunes, shut off from his friends by the excited violence
of a band of scoundrels, a most disgraceful and deplorable sight, was led to prison, if not to punishment
and even to death?[e] I ask whether anyone before 22
you has been so wicked as to act in such a manner,[f]
that we may know whether you are an imitator of
old crimes, or an inventor of new. Further, when
by these and the like designs and atrocities, committed in the name of that most merciful and excellent man, Gaius Caesar, but really by your own

[e] Probably a rhetorical flourish.
[f] A consul is known to have been arrested and imprisoned
by a tribune (*e.g.* Q. Metellus Celer by L. Flavius in 60 B.C.,
Dio Cassius, xxxvii. 50. 1-3), but a tribune had never ventured
to arrest a consul in face of the opposition of his colleagues.

CICERO

vero atque audacia tua M. Bibulum foro, curia, templis, locis publicis omnibus expulisses, inclusum domi contineres, cumque non maiestate imperii, non iure legum, sed ianuae praesidio et parietum custodiis consulis vita tegeretur, miserisne viatorem, qui M. Bibulum domo vi extraheret, ut, quod in privatis semper est servatum, id te tribuno pl. consuli domus exsilium esse 23 non posset. Simulque mihi respondeto tu, qui nos, qui de communi salute consentimus, tyrannos vocas, fuerisne non tribunus pl., sed intolerandus ex caeno nescio qui atque ex tenebris tyrannus, qui primum eam rem publicam, quae auspiciis inventis constituta est, isdem auspiciis sublatis conarere pervertere, deinde sanctissimas leges, Aeliam et Fufiam dico, quae in Gracchorum ferocitate et in audacia Saturnini et in colluvione Drusi et in contentione Sulpici et in cruore Cinnano, etiam inter Sullana arma vixerunt, solus conculcaris ac pro nihilo putaris, qui consulem morti obieceris, inclusum obsederis, extrahere ex suis tectis conatus sis, qui in eo magistratu non modo[1] emerseris

[1] *Angelius adds* modo.

---

[a] Vatinius, however, relented before the opposition of his colleagues.

[b] The Optimates who empowered Cicero to execute the Catilinarian conspirators in 63 B.C.

[c] See pp. 313-315.

[d] Tiberius, tribune in 133, Gaius, tribune in 123-122 B.C., inaugurated the revolutionary period that ended the Republic.

[e] L. Appuleius Saturninus, tribune 103 and 100 B.C., a violent opponent of the Senate.

[f] The schemes of reform of the younger M. Livius Drusus (tribune 91 B.C.) were complicated by his pledges to the Italian allies.

[g] P. Sulpicius Rufus (tribune 88 B.C.) carried, after violence in the Forum and the expulsion from Rome of the consuls

criminal audacity, you had driven Marcus Bibulus
from the Forum, the Senate House, the temples and
all public places, kept him shut up in his house, and
when the life of a consul was no longer protected by
the prestige of his power nor by the authority of the
laws, but by such defence as a door, such security as
the walls of a house afforded, did you not send an
usher to drag Bibulus from his house,[a] so that a man's
house, which has always been a sanctuary for a private
person, might be no refuge for a consul while you
were tribune of the commons? At the same time 23
answer me this, you who call us tyrants,[b] who are
of one heart about the welfare of all, were you a
tribune of the commons, or were you not yourself
an insufferable tyrant, a nobody sprung from mud
and obscurity? You who first, by abolishing the
auspices, attempted to destroy this State founded
upon these same auspices ; who next alone trampled
under foot and reckoned as nought those most holy
laws, I mean the Aelian and Fufian,[c] which endured
amid the vehemence of the Gracchi,[d] the daring of
Saturninus,[e] the turmoil under Drusus,[f] the fervour of
Sulpicius,[g] the carnage under Cinna,[h] and even the
warfare under Sulla[i]; you who exposed a consul to
death, imprisoned and beleaguered him in his own
house, and endeavoured to drag him from under his
own roof ; who not only rose from poverty in the

Sulla and Q. Pompeius Rufus, two highly controversial
measures, the transfer of the command in the Mithridatic
War from Sulla to Marius, and the distribution of freedmen
and the new citizens over all the thirty-five tribes.

[h] The capture of Rome in 87 B.C. by Marius and Cinna
and the massacres which followed.

[i] Sulla's conquest of Italy (83-82 B.C.) and military
dictatorship.

CICERO

ex mendicitate, sed etiam divitiis nos iam tuis terreas.

24   X. Fuerisne tanta crudelitate, ut delectos viros et principes civitatis tollere et delere tua rogatione conarere, cum L. Vettium, qui in senatu confessus esset se cum telo fuisse, mortem Cn. Pompeio, summo et clarissimo civi, suis manibus offerre voluisse, in contionem produxeris, indicem in rostris, in illo, inquam, augurato templo ac loco conlocaris, quo auctoritatis exquirendae causa ceteri tribuni pl. principes civitatis producere consuerunt, ibi tu indicem Vettium linguam et vocem suam sceleri et menti[1] tuae praebere voluisti—dixeritne L. Vettius in contione tua rogatus a te sese auctores et impulsores et socios habuisse sceleris illius eos viros, quibus e civitate sublatis, quod tu eo tempore moliebare, civitas stare non posset. M. Bibulum, cuius inclusione contentus non eras, interficere volueras, spoliaras consulatu, patria privare cupiebas. L. Lucullum, cuius tu rebus gestis, quod ipse ad imperatorias laudes a puero videlicet spectaras, vehementius invidebas, C. Curionem, perpetuum hostem improborum omnium, auctorem publici consilii libertate communi tuenda maxime

---

[1] menti *MSS.* : dementiae *Gulielmus.*

---

[a] On the plot of Vettius see *Pro Sestio*, 132.

[b] See §§ 5 and 18.

[c] *e.g.* Cicero, *Epp. ad Att.* i. 14. 1, where Pompey was invited to speak (in the Circus Flaminius) by Q. Fufius Calenus, tribune 61 B.C.

[d] L. Lucullus, who commanded in the Near East from 74–66 B.C., was the real conqueror of Mithridates. Vatinius distinguished himself in the Civil War, especially in Illyria, and triumphed over the Dalmatians in 42 B.C. See pp. 332-334.

[e] C. Scribonius Curio, consul 76 B.C., was in general on the

course of your office, but even now terrify us by your wealth ?

X. Were you so cruel, as to attempt to put out of 24 the way and destroy some distinguished persons and foremost men of the State, by a proposal of yours ? When you brought up before a meeting Lucius Vettius,[a] who had confessed before the Senate that he had armed himself with the intention of murdering with his own hand Gnaeus Pompeius, our greatest and most illustrious citizen; when you placed an informer on the Rostra, on that sacred spot[b] and place, I say, consecrated by the augurs, where other tribunes of the commons were accustomed to bring forward leading men of the State in order to ask their advice,[c] in that same place did you not desire that Vettius an informer should lend his tongue and voice for your crime and purpose ?—and did not Lucius Vettius declare, when questioned by you at the meeting you had summoned, that the prime movers, instigators, and associates in that crime had been men on whose removal from the State, which you were then compassing, the State could not exist ? Not content with having imprisoned Marcus Bibulus, with having wished to kill him, with having robbed him of his consulship, you desired to deprive him of his country. Lucius Lucullus, of whose achievements you were bitterly jealous, no doubt because you yourself from boyhood had aspired to the honours of a general,[d] Gaius Curio,[e] an irreconcilable enemy of all the disloyal, a director of public policy, most outspoken in defending the common liberty, together

Optimate side. But in 61 B.C. he supported Clodius, possibly through enmity to Caesar, and was attacked by Cicero in his *Oratio in Clodium et Curionem* (fragmentary).

liberum, cum filio principe iuventutis cum re publica
coniunctiore etiam, quam ab illa aetate postulandum
25 fuit, delere voluisti. L. Domitium, cuius dignitas et
splendor praestringebat, credo, oculos tuos, Vatini,[1]
quem tu propter commune odium in bonos oderas, in
posterum autem propter omnium spem, quae de illo
est atque erat, ante aliquanto timebas, L. Lentulum,
hunc iudicem nostrum, flaminem Martialem, quod
erat eo tempore Gabini tui competitor, eiusdem Vetti
indicio opprimere voluisti ; qui si tum illam labem
pestemque vicisset, quod ei tuo scelere non licuit, res
publica victa non esset. Huius etiam filium eodem
indicio et crimine ad patris interitum adgregare
voluisti. L. Paullum, qui tum quaestor Macedoniam
obtinebat, quem civem, quem virum ! qui duo nefarios
patriae proditores domesticos hostes legibus exter-
minarat, hominem ad conservandam rem publicam
natum, in idem Vetti indicium atque in eundem hunc

---

[1] *Halm proposes* Vettii. *Madvig says that* Vatinii *has been
inserted by a copyist to explain the meaning* : oculos tuos,
Vatini *Jordan.*

---

[a] C. Scribonius Curio, tribune 50 B.C., defeated and killed
by Juba in Africa, 49 B.C. *Princeps iuventutis* is probably
used in a complimentary sense, but, if technical, it means
that his name headed the *album equitum equo publico.*

[b] L. Domitius Ahenobarbus, a bitter antagonist of Caesar,
praetor 58 B.C., consul 54 B.C. Defeated at Corfinium and
Massilia (49 B.C.), he fell at Pharsalus (48 B.C.).

[c] A bold thrust, for Domitius when praetor in 58 B.C. had
invited the Senate to declare Caesar's legislation invalid, and
as a candidate for the consulship of 55 B.C. was declaring that
if elected he would deprive Caesar of his provinces.

[d] L. Cornelius Lentulus Niger, who assisted in the prosecu-

with his son, a leader among our young men,[a] more intimate with state affairs than might have been expected in one so young,—these men you wanted to destroy. Lucius Domitius,[b] whose rank and glamour dazzled your eyes, I imagine, Vatinius, whom you hated because of your general hatred of loyalists, but whom for the future you had already for some considerable time been fearing on account of the universal hopes which were and still are entertained about him[c]; Lucius Lentulus, one of our judges to-day, priest of Mars, you were also anxious to ruin by the information of this same Vettius because at the time he was a candidate for the consulship against your dear friend Gabinius[d]; and if he had won the day against that plague and scourge, a victory which your wickedness denied to him, the State would not have been overthrown. His son,[e] too, you desired by the same information and charges to involve in his father's ruin. Lucius Paullus,[f] who was then as quaestor in charge of the province of Macedonia— what a citizen, what a man !—who had banished by the authority of the laws two infamous traitors against their country, two enemies of their own household[g] : this man also, born to be a saviour of Rome, you crowded into this same catalogue of

25

tion of Clodius in 61 B.C., was prevented from standing for the consulship in 59 B.C. because he was included in the *quaestio* of Vatinius mentioned in § 26 below.

[e] He prosecuted A. Gabinius in 54 B.C. See Cicero, *Epp. ad Quintum fratrem*, iii. 4. 1.

[f] L. Aemilius Paullus, consul 50 B.C. As quaestor he was probably acting for the governor of Macedonia. As aedile (55 B.C.) he began to rebuild the Basilica Aemilia.

[g] According to the Scholiast, L. Sergius Catilina and C. Cethegus.

26 numerum congregasti. Quid ergo de me querar ? qui
etiam gratias tibi agere debeo, quod me ex fortissimorum civium numero seiungendum non putasti.

XI. Sed qui fuit tuus ille tantus furor, ut, cum iam
Vettius ad arbitrium tuum perorasset et civitatis
lumina notasset descendissetque de rostris, eum
repente revocares, conloquerere populo Romano
vidente, deinde interrogares, ecquosnam alios posset
nominare ? Inculcarisne, ut C. Pisonem, generum
meum, nominaret, qui in summa copia optimorum
adulescentium pari continentia, virtute, pietate re-
liquit neminem, itemque M. Laterensem, hominem
dies atque noctes de laude et de re publica cogi-
tantem ; promulgarisne, impurissime et perditissime
hostis, quaestionem de tot amplissimis et talibus viris,
indicium Vettio, praemia amplissima ; quibus rebus
omnium mortalium non voluntate, sed convicio repudiatis fregerisne in carcere cervices ipsi illi Vettio,
ne quod indicium corrupti indicii exstaret eiusque
sceleris in te ipsum quaestio flagitaretur ?

---

^a By implication Cicero was added to the list of con-
spirators. Cicero, *Epp. ad Att.* ii. 24. 3.

^b Cicero, *Epp. ad Att.* ii. 24. 3.

^c C. Calpurnius Piso Frugi, who married Tullia in 63 B.C.
and died during Cicero's exile. See *Pro Sestio*, 54.

^d In 59 B.C. M. Iuventius Laterensis threw up his candi-
dature for the tribunate rather than swear allegiance to
Caesar's *lex Iulia de agro Campano*. See Cicero, *Epp. ad
Att.* ii. 18. 2.

Vettius' information. Why, then, should I complain 26
about myself ? [a] I ought rather to thank you because
you did not think that I ought to be separated from
the ranks of our bravest citizens.

XI. But how mad you must have been, after
Vettius had finished speaking as you desired and had
calumniated the most illustrious men in Rome, and
had come down from the Rostra, to call him back
suddenly, converse with him in the sight of the
Roman People, and then ask him if he could name any
others ! [b] Did you not press him to name Gaius Piso,
my son-in-law,[c] who, rich though we are in an abundance of excellent young men, left none behind him
equal in restraint, virtue, and filial affection ; and
Marcus Laterensis also, a man whose thoughts night
and day were fixed on renown and on the State ? [d]
Did you not, you most infamous and abandoned of
the enemies of the State, announce that you would
propose that there should be a commission of inquiry [e] about all these men of such high distinction,
that Vettius should be allowed to lay information
and be amply rewarded ? And when these proceedings had been repudiated by the whole world,
not merely in thought but in open reproaches, did
you not cause this same Vettius to be strangled in
prison, that there might remain no trace of his false
information and that no commission to investigate
that crime might be demanded against yourself ? [f]

---

[e] A commission on the lines of the *Quaestio Mamilia*
(110 B.C.) before which Vettius could lay information with
impunity.
[f] There is no evidence that Vatinius' bill was rejected by the
concilium plebis. The death of Vettius, an unsolved mystery,
closed the whole matter.

27 Et quoniam crebro usurpas legem te de alternis
consiliis reiciendis tulisse, ut omnes intellegant te ne
recte quidem facere sine scelere potuisse, quaero, cum
lex esset aequa promulgata initio magistratus, multas
iam alias tulisses, exspectarisne, dum C. Antonius reus
fieret apud Cn. Lentulum Clodianum, et, posteaquam
ille est reus factus, statim tuleris " quicumque tuam
post legem reus factus esset," ut homo consularis
exclusus miser puncto temporis spoliaretur beneficio
28 et aequitate legis tuae. Dices familiaritatem tibi
fuisse cum Q. Maximo. Praeclara defensio facinoris
tui ! Nam Maximi quidem summa laus est sumptis
inimicitiis, suscepta causa, quaesitore consilioque
delecto commodiorem inimico suo condicionem re-
iectionis dare noluisse. Nihil Maximus fecit alienum
aut sua virtute aut illis viris clarissimis, Paullis, Maxi-

---

^a A *consilium* was a body of *iudices* assigned by a praetor
for a criminal trial. Even before this reform of Vatinius,
defence and prosecution had a limited right of challenging
individual jurors. Although the scope of this measure can
only be conjectured (Greenidge, *The Legal Procedure of
Cicero's Time*, pp. 451-452, and Pocock, *op. cit.* p. 111), it is
clear that it was equitable and favourable to the accused,
and it is possible that it empowered parties to challenge in
turn not individual jurors, but any of the groups of jurors
(*decuriae*) assigned by a praetor for a trial.

^b C. Antonius Hybrida, consul 63 B.C. and subsequently
governor of Macedonia, was in March or April 59 B.C.
prosecuted, probably on a charge of *maiestas* covering treasonable conduct in his province and collusion with Catiline
(see p. 11), and was condemned. Cn. Lentulus Clodianus,
president of the court, praetor 59 B.C., and consul 56 B.C., is
elsewhere described as Cn. Cornelius Lentulus Marcellinus.

^c The law had so far only been " promulgated."

^d According to the Scholiast, C. Antonius was prosecuted by

You frequently claim that you have carried a law 27
about allowing the two parties in a suit to challenge
jurymen alternately.[a] Now then, to make every one
understand that you could not even do right without
being guilty of wrong, I ask you this : after you had,
early in your tribunate, promulgated a just law, and
already passed many others, did you not wait till Gaius
Antonius [b] was prosecuted before Gnaeus Lentulus
Clodianus, and as soon as he was accused, did you
not immediately add to your law " that it should
only apply to those who were accused after your law
was passed,"[c] in order that a man of consular rank
might thus, poor man, be excluded by a moment of
time, and robbed of the benefit and justice of your
law ? You will say that you were intimate with 28
Quintus Maximus.[d] An admirable excuse for your
misdeed ! For Maximus indeed deserves the highest
praise because, after his enmity had been declared,[e]
the case undertaken and the president and jurymen chosen, he refused to allow his opponent a
method of challenging the jury which would have
been more to his advantage. Maximus did nothing
that was unworthy[f] either of his own virtue or of those
most distinguished men, the Paulli, the Maximi and

Q. Fabius Maximus and M. Caelius Rufus. Cicero suggests
that Vatinius added the supplementary clause to his proposal
to oblige Fabius. Fabius was *consul suffectus* in 45 B.C.
   [e] That is, after Fabius had decided to prosecute Antonius.
   [f] Unless the text is corrupt the meaning seems to be that
Fabius Maximus could not be accused of unchivalrous or
ungentlemanly conduct, in keeping to the letter of the law
by conforming to the existing statute dealing with the challenging of juries, and by refusing to allow Antonius the
benefit of a reform, favourable to a defendant, promulgated
by Vatinius, but specifically denied to Antonius by the malice
of the proposer.

mis, Africanis, quorum gloriam huius virtute renovatam non modo speramus, verum etiam iam videmus ;
tua fraus, tuum maleficium, tuum scelus illud est,
te id, quod promulgasses misericordiae nomine, ad
crudelitatis tempus distulisse. Ac nunc quidem C.
Antonius hac una re miseriam suam consolatur, quod
imagines patris et fratris sui fratrisque filiam non in
familia, sed in carcere collocatam audire maluit
quam videre.

29   XII. Et quoniam pecunias aliorum despicis, de tuis
divitiis intolerantissime gloriaris, volo, uti mihi respondeas, fecerisne foedera tribunus pl. cum civitatibus, cum regibus, cum tetrarchis, erogarisne pecunias
ex aerario tuis legibus, eripuerisne partes illo tempore
carissimas partim a Caesare, partim a publicanis.
Quae cum ita sint, quaero ex te, sisne ex pauperrimo
dives factus illo ipso anno, quo lex lata est de pecuniis
repetundis acerrima, ut omnes intellegere possent a

---

  ^a His exile.
  ^b M. Antonius, who as praetor (102 B.C.) made Rome's first
drive against piracy in the Levant. He was murdered in the
Marian massacres (87 B.C.).
  ^c M. Antonius (Creticus), a praetor, who in 74 B.C. received a special command for three years against the Medi-
terranean pirates, and died in 71 B.C. after a disaster in Crete.
  ^d Antonia, married to Vatinius, was a daughter of M. Antonius (Creticus), and sister of M. Antonius, the Triumvir.
  ^e The portrait-busts, taken away no doubt at the condemnation of Antonius, would be transferred by Vatinius to
his own house along with his bride. Pocock (*op. cit.* p. 114)
read a double meaning in *familia* and an allusion to Vatinius'
troupe of gladiators.
  ^f This refers to the ratification *en bloc* by a *lex Vatinia* in
59 B.C. of Pompey's settlement of the Near East.

the Africani, whose glory we not only hope for—nay, rather, we already see, revived in their illustrious descendant. Yours is the treachery, yours the crime, yours the guilt of having made a proposal on the pretence of pity, and then of delaying it so as to be an opportunity for cruelty. And at the present time, Antonius has at least one consolation in his misfortune [a]—that he has preferred to hear, rather than to see, how the portrait-busts of his father [b] and brother [c] were taken along with his niece [d] and set up, not in a household, but in a gaol.[e]

XII. And since you despise the wealth of others, 29 while you boast immoderately of your own, I wish you to answer me this question. During your tribunate of the commons, did you not make treaties with states, with kings, with tetrarchs?[f] Did you disburse sums from the Treasury by your laws?[g] Did you not at the same time filch shares when they were at their highest, in part from Caesar, in part from the tax-farmers themselves?[h] This being so, I ask you whether, after being so poor, you became rich in that very same year in which a most severe law was passed against extortion,[i] that all may understand that you treated with contempt not only the

[g] Pocock (*op. cit.* Appendix iv. B) connects this with the agrarian legislation of 59 B.C. Heavy expenditure, however, was incurred also by the *lex Vatinia de Caesaris provincia* and by the concession to the *publicani*.

[h] *Partes* = shares in the capital of a tax-farming company. Vatinius secured a remission to the *publicani* of one-third of the original purchase price of the Asian tax-contract. His commission for this service was paid in gifts of shares in the favoured company, greatly appreciated in value, from Caesar and the company. See Pocock (*op. cit.* Appendix iv. C).

[i] Caesar's *lex Iulia de pecuniis repetundis*.

te non modo nostra acta, quos tyrannos vocas, sed etiam amicissimi tui legem esse contemptam ; apud quem tu etiam nos criminari soles, qui illi sumus amicissimi, cum tu ei contumeliosissime totiens male dicas, quotiens te illi adfinem esse dicis.

30 Atque etiam illud scire ex te cupio, quo consilio aut qua mente feceris, ut in epulo Q. Arri, familiaris mei, cum toga pulla accumberes ; quem umquam videris, quem audieris ; quo exemplo, quo more feceris. Dices supplicationes te illas non probasse. Optime ; nullae fuerint supplicationes. Videsne me nihil de anni illius causa, nihil de eo, quod tibi commune cum summis viris esse videatur, sed de tuis propriis sceleribus ex te quaerere ? Nulla supplicatio fuerit. Cedo, quis umquam cenarit atratus. Ita enim illud epulum est funebre, ut munus sit funeris, epulae quidem ipsae dignitatis.

31 XIII. Sed omitto epulum populi Romani, festum diem argento, veste, omni apparatu ornatuque

---

ᵃ The measures against Catiline and the *lex Tullia de ambitu* (63 B.C.).

ᵇ Vatinius' mother-in-law was a daughter of L. Iulius Caesar (consul 90 B.C.), whose precise relationship to the Dictator cannot be ascertained.

ᶜ In 59 B.C. Q. Arrius celebrated in the Temple of Castor, with proverbial magnificence (Horace, *Sat.* ii. 3. 85-86), either the actual funeral or a funeral festival in memory of his father Q. Arrius, possibly a praetor of 72 B.C. The son, an unsuccessful candidate in 59 B.C. for the consulship, may have been the " Harrius " of Catullus, 84.

ᵈ According to the Scholiast, who quotes no authority, these *supplicationes* (59 B.C.) were in honour of C. Pomptinus, who as governor of Gallia Narbonensis crushed a revolt of the Allobroges in 61 B.C. Although these *supplicationes* were opposed by Vatinius and his friends, acting in Caesar's interests, Pomptinus was ultimately awarded a triumph, but

acts *a* of us whom you call tyrants, but also the law of your best friend, to whom you are in the habit of slandering even us, who are his greatest friends, and whom you grievously insult whenever you boast of being connected with him.*b*

Another thing also I should like to learn from you : 30 what was your design, what was your intention, in being present in a dark dress at the funeral celebration given by my friend Quintus Arrius ? *c* Had you ever seen, ever heard of anyone presenting himself on such an occasion in such a costume ? What example, what custom authorized you to do so ? You will say that you disapproved of the public thanksgivings that were then being held.*d* Very well, I grant you that those thanksgivings were nothing. Do you see that I am not questioning you on the subject of that year, nor about the interests you seem to share with very high personages,*e* but about your own misdeeds ? Let us dismiss the thanksgiving from consideration. Tell me, whoever took his place at table in mourning ? A funeral celebration, certainly, is so far funereal that gladiatorial games are part of the funeral, but the banquet itself is in honour of the celebrant.*f*

XIII. But I say nothing of the public funeral cele- 31 bration, of the festal day with its silver, dresses, all kinds of magnificence, and decorations worth seeing.

not till 54 B.C. (*C.I.L.* i². 2, p. 50). But the connexion, if any, between the festival of Arrius and the *supplicationes* of Pomptinus is not revealed.

e In the phrase *cum summis viris* Cicero refers either to Pompey and Caesar, or to Caesar alone.

f Mourning might be worn at the gladiatorial games, which were part of a funeral celebration, but at the banquet a light dress was *de rigueur.*

visendo ; quis umquam in luctu domestico, quis in
funere familiari cenavit cum toga pulla, cui de balineis
exeunti praeter te toga pulla umquam data est ?
Cum tot hominum milia accumberent, cum ipse epuli
dominus, Q. Arrius, albatus esset, tu in templum
Castoris te cum C. Fibulo atrato ceterisque tuis furiis
funestum intulisti. Quis tum non ingemuit, quis non
doluit rei publicae casum ? qui sermo alius in illo epulo
fuit nisi hanc tantam et tam gravem civitatem sub-
iectam esse non modo furori, verum etiam inrisioni
32 tuae ? Hunc tu morem ignorabas ? numquam epulum
videras, numquam puer aut adulescens inter cocos
fueras ? Fausti, adulescentis nobilissimi, paulo ante
ex epulo magnificentissimo famem illam veterem tuam
non expleras ? Quem accumbere atratum videras ?
dominum cum toga pulla et eius amicos ante con-
vivium ? Quae tanta te[1] tenuit amentia, ut, nisi id
fecisses, quod fas non fuit, nisi violasses templum
Castoris, nomen epuli, oculos civium, morem veterem,
eius, qui te invitarat, auctoritatem, parum putares
testificatum esse supplicationes te illas non putare ?
33 XIV. Quaero etiam illud ex te, quod privatus
admisisti, in quo certe iam tibi dicere non licebit cum
clarissimis viris causam[2] tuam esse coniunctam, postu-

---

[1] te *inserted by Baiter.*
[2] cum clarissimi viri causa *Madvig.*

---

[a] A bath was a ceremony of purification after a funeral.
A dress for dinner was given to a person after he left the bath.
[b] In 60 B.C. Faustus Sulla, son of the Dictator, gave on a
lavish scale a funeral festival in memory of his father. Such
commemorations were not infrequently held years after the
event commemorated.

Whoever took his seat at dinner in a dark dress, when there was death in the family or domestic sorrow? To whom except yourself on leaving the bath has a dark dress ever been handed? [a] Although so many thousands were at table, and the celebrant of the festival himself, Quintus Arrius, all in white, you betook yourself into the Temple of Castor in funeral garb, with Gaius Fibulus and your other evil spirits in black. Who then did not lament? Who did not deplore the misfortunes of the State? What else was the subject of conversation at that funeral celebration, except that this State, so great and so respected, was the victim not only of your madness, but also the butt of your ridicule? Were you ignorant 32 of this custom? Had you never seen a funeral celebration? Had you never, boy or young man, been among the cooks? Had you not satisfied that inveterate hunger of yours a little while before at a magnificent festival celebrated by a brilliant young noble, Faustus? [b] Whom had you ever seen take his seat at a banquet in black? The master of the feast or his friends in mourning in the presence of their guests? What folly so possessed you that, unless you had done what was wrong, unless you had profaned the Temple of Castor and the name of a public festival, offended the eyes of citizens, violated old customs, and the dignity of your host, you thought that you would have given insufficient evidence that you did not regard that occasion as one of thanksgiving?

XIV. I ask you also about what you did when out 33 of office,[c] and here at any rate you will no longer be able to say that your case is linked with that of the most illustrious men. Were you not arraigned

---

[c] In 58 B.C.

latusne sis lege Licinia et Iunia; edixeritne C. Memmius praetor ex ea lege, ut adesses die tricensimo; cum is dies venisset, fecerisne, quod in hac re publica non modo factum antea numquam est, sed in omni memoria est omnino inauditum, appellarisne tribunos pl., ne causam diceres—levius dixi; quamquam id ipsum esset et novum et non ferendum—sed appellarisne nominatim pestem illius anni, furiam patriae, tempestatem rei publicae, Clodium. Qui tamen cum iure, cum more, cum potestate iudicium impedire non posset, rediit ad illam vim et furorem suum ducemque se militibus tuis praebuit. In quo ne quid a me dictum in te potius putes quam abs te esse quaesitum, nullum onus imponam mihi testimonii; quae mihi brevi tempore ex eodem isto loco video esse dicenda, servabo teque non arguam, sed, ut in ceteris 34 rebus feci, rogabo. Quaero ex te, Vatini, num quis in hac civitate post urbem conditam tribunos pl. appellarit, ne causam diceret, num quis reus in

---

a For the *lex Licinia Iunia* see notes on pp. 212 and 221; also p. 317. It is possible that his ratification of Pompey's settlement of the Near East broke this statute.

b C. Memmius, to whom Lucretius dedicated his poem, was praetor in 58 b.c. and early in his office joined L. Domitius Ahenobarbus in an attack on Caesar's legislation. Suetonius, *Div. Iul.* 23. 1.

c The phrasing suggests that appearance in court on the
284

under the Licinian and Junian Law ? [a] Did not Gaius Memmius, a praetor,[b] summon you, in virtue of that law, to appear at the end of thirty days ? [c] When that day came, did you not do what had not only never been done before in this State, but had never been heard of within the memory of man ? Did you not appeal to the tribunes of the commons to save you from answering the charge [d]—I have spoken too lightly, although by itself this would be strange and intolerable—but did you not appeal by name to the curse of that year, to the evil spirit of his country, to the storm that burst over the State, to Clodius who, although he could not, either by law, by custom, or by authority, obstruct your trial, had recourse to that mad violence of his,[e] and put himself at the head of your armed bands. And as to this matter, that you may not think that I am declaiming against you instead of asking you questions, I will not burden myself with bringing evidence against you ; I will reserve what I think I ought to say very soon from this same place, and instead of accusing you I will ask you questions, as I have hitherto done. I ask 34 you, Vatinius, whether anyone in this State, since the foundation of Rome, has ever appealed to the tribunes of the commons to be saved from pleading. Has any

thirtieth day after the *nominis receptio* was prescribed by the *lex Licinia Iunia* ; otherwise the words " edixeritne . . . ex ea lege, ut adesses " must be taken together, and must mean that Vatinius was to be prosecuted for an offence against the *lex Licinia Iunia*.

[d] Cicero denounces as unprecedented and illegal Vatinius' appeal to the tribunes' *ius auxilii* to quash his trial. Greenidge, however (*op. cit.* p. 517), makes out a case for Vatinius' action.

[e] Of the years 58 and 57 B.C.

tribunal sui quaesitoris escenderit eumque vi detur-
barit, subsellia dissiparit, urnas deiecerit, eas denique
omnes res in iudicio disturbando commiserit, quarum
rerum causa iudicia sunt constituta ; sciasne tum
fugisse Memmium, accusatores esse tuos de tuis tuo-
rumque manibus ereptos, iudices quaestionum de
proximis tribunalibus esse depulsos, in foro, luce, in-
spectante populo Romano quaestionem, magistratus,
morem maiorum, leges, iudices, reum, poenam esse
sublatam ; haec omnia sciasne diligentia C. Memmi
publicis tabulis esse notata atque testata ? Atque
illud etiam quaero, cum, posteaquam es postulatus,
ex legatione redieris, ne quis te iudicia defugere
arbitraretur, teque, cum tibi, utrum velles, liceret,
dictitaris causam dicere maluisse, qui consentaneum
fuerit, cum legationis perfugio uti noluisses, appel-
latione improbissima te ad auxilium nefarium confugisse.

35   XV. Et quoniam legationis tuae facta mentio est,
volo audire de te, quo tandem senatus consulto legatus
sis. De gestu intellego, quid respondeas ; tua lege,

---

   a According to the Scholiast, Memmius wished to appoint
the *quaesitor*, president of the court, by lot, but Vatinius
demanded that he should be chosen by a process of elimina-
tion, in accordance with his own *lex de alternis consiliis
reiciendis* ; and upon that point the law was obscure.
Pocock, however (*op. cit.* Appendix vii), defends this explana-
tion and considers that the violence of Vatinius and Clodius
was intended to demonstrate the complete illegality of the
prosecution.

   b The prosecutor was probably C. Licinius Calvus Macer,
the poet and friend of Catullus: the names of the *subscriptores*
(subordinates) are unknown.

accused person mounted the tribunal of his judge[a]
and violently thrust him down from it, scattered the
benches, thrown down the urns, and, in short, in order
to upset a trial, committed all those excesses, which
were the very reason why trials were established ?
Do you not know that Memmius then took to flight ?
That your accusers[b] had to be rescued from your
hands and from those of your accomplices ?   That the
presidents of the neighbouring courts were turned
out of their seats ?   That in the Forum, in broad
daylight, in view of the Roman People, a court of
law, magistrates, old customs, laws, judges, a defendant, a penalty, were set at nought ?   Do you
not know that all this, thanks to the diligence of
Gaius Memmius, has been set down in the public
records and duly attested ?   And I ask you this also.
On being summoned, you returned from your staff-
appointment (for no one must think that you wanted
to shirk a trial),[c] and repeatedly declared that, although you could have your choice, you preferred
to plead your cause.   How then, after refusing to
use the means of escape offered by a staff-appointment, was it consistent to have sought a guilty
refuge in a most dishonest appeal ?[d]

XV. And since I have mentioned your staff- 35
appointment, I should like you to tell me by what
decree of the Senate[e] you were appointed a staff-
officer.   Your gesture gives me your answer : you

[c] Caesar had appointed Vatinius to his staff in Gaul.   His
return to Rome was a voluntary act, as one absent on public
service was immune from prosecution.
[d] To the tribunes of 58 B.C.
[e] Cf. Pro Sestio, 33.   It was customary for the Senate to
sanction the appointment of legati.

dicis. Esne igitur patriae certissimus parricida ?
spectarasne id, ut patres conscripti ex re publica
funditus tollerentur ? ne hoc quidem senatui relinque-
bas, quod nemo umquam ademit, ut legati ex eius
ordinis auctoritate legarentur ? Adeone tibi sordidum
consilium publicum visum est, adeo adflictus senatus, adeo misera et prostrata res publica, ut non
nuntios pacis ac belli, non oratores, non interpretes,
non bellici consilii auctores, non ministros muneris
provincialis senatus more maiorum deligere posset ?
36 Eripueras senatui provinciae decernendae potestatem,
imperatoris deligendi iudicium, aerarii dispensatio-
nem, quae numquam sibi populus Romanus appeti-
vit, qui numquam ad se summi consilii gubernationem transferre[1] conatus est. Age, factum est
horum aliquid in aliis ; raro, sed tamen factum
est, at populus deligeret imperatorem ; quis legatos
umquam audivit sine senatus consulto ? Ante te
nemo, post continuo fecit idem in duobus prodigiis
rei publicae Clodius ; quo etiam maiore es malo

---

[1] auferre *MSS.* : transferre *Müller* : qui numquam senatui
summi consili gubernationem auferre conatus est *Peterson.*

---

[a] The *lex Vatinia de Caesaris provincia* empowered Caesar
to appoint his staff of *legati* without consulting the Senate.
[b] See p. 186, note *b.*
[c] The operation of the *lex Sempronia de provinciis consularibus* was suspended by the *lex Vatinia.*
[d] *Cf.* § 29.
[e] This, as Cicero admits in the next sentence, is an over-
statement. At times of crisis, especially after the middle of
the second century B.C., the *populus Romanus* occasionally
overrode the Senate. Under Ti. and Gaius Gracchus, for
example, the People attacked the Senate's control of finance

say, in virtue of your own law.[a] Are you then beyond all doubt a traitor to your fatherland?[b] Was
it your object that not a trace of the Senate should
be left in the state? Did you wish to rob the Senate
even of that prerogative which no one had ever
denied to it, the right of appointing staff-officers by a
resolution of the House? Did this Council of State
appear so mean to you, the Senate so degraded, the
State so wretched and prostrate, that envoys of
peace and war, that ambassadors, that representa-
tives, that directors of policy in war, that assistants
in the administration of a province, should no longer,
according to the custom of our ancestors, be chosen
by the Senate? You had deprived the Senate of 36
the right of assigning provinces,[c] of sanctioning the
appointment of commanders, of administering the
Treasury.[d] These prerogatives the Roman People
has never desired for itself, nor has it ever attempted
to transfer to itself the control of high policy of
state.[e] Granted that something of this kind has
been done in other cases : rarely, but sometimes, the
People has appointed a general[f] ; but whoever heard
of the appointment of staff-officers save by decree of
the Senate? Before you, no one. Immediately after
you, Clodius did the same thing in the matter of two
public monsters,[g] so that still heavier curses should

and of provincial and foreign policy. The text has given
rise to many conjectures. Pocock suggests " aut a summi
consili gubernatione auferre conatus est," and translates
" or has ever attempted to remove from the control of the
Senate."

   [f] e.g., the elections to the consulship of Scipio Aemilianus
in 148 and 135 B.C., and of Marius in 108 B.C., the extraordinary commands conferred on Pompey in 67 and 66 B.C.

   [g] Piso and Gabinius, see *Pro Sestio*, 33.

mactandus, quod non solum facto tuo, sed etiam
exemplo rem publicam vulnerasti neque tantum ipse
es improbus, sed etiam alios docere voluisti. Ob
hasce omnes res sciasne te severissimorum hominum
Sabinorum, fortissimorum virorum Marsorum et Pae-
lignorum, tribulium tuorum, iudicio notatum, nec
post Romam conditam praeter te tribulem quemquam tribum Sergiam perdidisse.

37 Atque illud etiam audire de te cupio, quare, cum
ego legem de ambitu tulerim ex senatus consulto,
tulerim sine vi, tulerim salvis auspiciis, tulerim salva
lege Aelia et Fufia, tu eam esse legem non putes,
praesertim cum ego legibus tuis, quoquo modo latae
sunt, paream ; cum mea lex dilucide vetet BIENNIO,
QUO QUIS PETAT PETITURUSVE SIT, GLADIATORES DARE
NISI EX TESTAMENTO PRAESTITUTA DIE, quae tanta in te
sit amentia, ut in ipsa petitione gladiatores audeas
dare ; num quem putes illius tui certissimi gladiatoris
similem tribunum pl. posse reperiri, qui se interponat,
quo minus reus mea lege fias.

38 XVI. Ac si haec omnia contemnis ac despicis, quod
ita tibi persuaseris, ut palam dictitas, te dis homini-

---

[a] The fact that the Sabine town of Amiternum was in the
tribus Quirina casts doubt upon the statement of the Scholiast
that the *tribus Sergia* consisted of the Sabines, Marsi, and
Paeligni.

[b] At the election of aediles in 58 B.C.

[c] The *lex Tullia de ambitu*, passed during Cicero's consulship (63 B.C.), was a more severe measure than the *lex Cal-
purnia* of 67 B.C. and prescribed banishment from Rome and
probably from Italy also, for ten years. L. Licinius Murena,
consul-elect for 62 B.C., was in Nov. 63 B.C. prosecuted under
this law and successfully defended by Cicero.

[d] *Cf. Pro Sestio*, 61. Since Cicero in 59 B.C. persuaded
Cato to take an oath of obedience to Caesar's *lex Iulia de*

be invoked upon you, seeing that you have dealt a cutting blow against the State, not only by your acts but also by your example ; that not content with being a scoundrel yourself you have also desired to teach others to become the same. For all these offences do you know that the Sabines, most austere of people, the Marsians and Paelignians, most heroic of men, your fellow-tribesmen,[a] branded you as dishonoured, and that, since the foundation of Rome, you are the first member of the Sergian tribe [b] who has lost his tribal vote ?

And I should also like to hear from you for what 37 reason this law against bribery,[c] which I passed by the authority of the Senate, which I passed without violence, without neglecting the auspices, without infringing the Aelian and Fufian Laws, is not considered by you to be a law, especially when I obey your laws, however they have been passed.[d] My law clearly forbids " giving gladiatorial shows during the two years that one is a candidate for office actually or prospectively, except on a day fixed beforehand by a will " [e] ; notwithstanding, you are mad enough to venture to give one, even during your candidature.[f] Do you think that a tribune of the commons can be found sufficiently like that most loyal swordster of yours,[g] to offer an obstruction and prevent you from being accused under my law ?

XVI. And if you despise and regard all this as 38 nothing, because, as you openly boast, you are convinced that, in spite of gods and men, you will obtain

agro Campano, it is possible that the agrarian legislation is referred to in the words *tuis legibus*.

[e] See *Pro Sestio*, 133-135.

[f] For a praetorship of 55 B.C.   [g] P. Clodius, see § 33.

busque invitis amore in te incredibili quodam C.
Caesaris omnia, quae velis, consecuturum, ecquid
audieris, ecquisnam tibi dixerit C. Caesarem nuper
Aquileiae,[a] cum de quibusdam esset mentio facta,
dixisse se[1] C. Alfium[b] praeteritum permoleste tulisse,
quod in homine summam fidem probitatemque cog-
nosset, graviterque etiam se ferre praetorem aliquem
esse factum, qui a suis rationibus dissensisset ; tum
quaesisse quendam,[c] de Vatinio quem ad modum
ferret ; illum respondisse Vatinium in tribunatu gratis
nihil fecisse ; qui omnia in pecunia posuisset, honore
39 animo aequo carere debere. Quodsi ipse, qui te suae
dignitatis augendae causa, periculo tuo, nullo suo
delicto, ferri praecipitem est facile passus, tamen te
omni honore indignissimum iudicat, si te vicini, si
adfines, si tribules ita oderunt, ut repulsam[d] tuam
triumphum suum duxerint, si nemo aspicit, quin
ingemescat, nemo mentionem facit, quin exsecretur,
si vitant, fugiunt, audire de te nolunt, cum viderunt,
tamquam auspicium malum detestantur, si cognati
respuunt, tribules exsecrantur, vicini metuunt, adfines
erubescunt, strumae denique ab ore improbo demi-
grarunt et aliis iam se locis conlocarunt, si es odium
publicum populi, senatus, universorum hominum rusti-
canorum : quid est, quam ob rem praeturam potius

---

[1] se *added by* Baiter.

---

[a] A former Latin colony (181–89 B.C.) in Cisalpine Gaul,
seven miles from the head of the Adriatic (Livy, xl. 34. 2-4 ;
xliii. 17. 1) ; Caesar was there in the winter of 57–56 B.C.

[b] C. Alfius Flavus, tribune 59 B.C. In 57 B.C. he failed to
be elected praetor. See *Pro Sestio*, 114. He was praetor
in 54 B.C.

[c] Cn. Domitius Calvinus. See § 16 and *Pro Sestio*, 113.

[d] Vatinius' defeat for an aedileship of 57 B.C.

everything you desire through Gaius Caesar's almost
incredible affection for you, have you never heard,
has no one ever told you, what Caesar said about
you recently when he was at Aquileia?[a] When
certain citizens were being discussed, Caesar said
that he had been greatly annoyed that Gaius
Alfius had been passed over,[b] because he knew
him to be a man of the highest integrity and
honesty, and that he was also much vexed that a
certain person[c] who had expressed disagreement
with his views had been made praetor. When some
one then asked him what he thought of Vatinius,
he answered that Vatinius had done nothing during
his tribunate without being paid for it; that a man
who thought that money was everything ought to
bear the loss of office[d] with equanimity. But if the 39
very man, who, for the sake of increasing his own
prestige, at your risk and by no betrayal of his own
duty, readily allowed you to follow your headlong
course, yet thinks you utterly unworthy of any
office; if your neighbours and relatives, if the
members of your tribe so hate you, that they
looked upon your rejection as their own triumph;
if no one sees you without a groan; if no one
mentions your name without a curse; if every one
avoids you, shuns you, does not want to hear you
talked of, and when they see you show their detesta-
tion of you as a bird of ill-omen; if your kinsmen
loathe you, your fellow-tribesmen curse you, your
neighbours fear you, and your relatives blush for you;
lastly, if boils have left your nasty face and now take
up their quarters in other parts of your body, if you
are publicly hated by People, Senate, and country
folk to a man;—what is the reason why you prefer

exoptes quam mortem, praesertim cum popularem
te velis esse neque ulla re populo gratius facere
possis ?

40 Sed ut aliquando audiamus, quam copiose mihi ad
rogata respondeas, concludam iam interrogationem
meam teque in extremo pauca de ipsa causa rogabo.

XVII. Quaero, quae tanta in te vanitas, tanta
levitas fuerit, ut in hoc iudicio T. Annium isdem
verbis laudares, quibus eum verbis laudare et boni
viri et boni cives consuerunt, cum in eundem nuper
ab eadem illa taeterrima furia productus ad populum cupidissime falsum testimonium dixeris.   An
erit haec optio et potestas tua, ut, cum Clodianas
operas et facinerosorum hominum et perditorum
manum videris, Milonem dicas, id quod in contione
dixisti, gladiatoribus et bestiariis obsedisse rem publicam : cum autem ad tales viros veneris, non audeas
civem singulari virtute, fide, constantia vituperare ?

41 Sed, cum T. Annium tanto opere laudes et clarissimo
viro non nullam laudatione tua labeculam adspergas
(in illorum enim numero mavult T. Annius esse, qui
a te vituperantur), verum tamen quaero, cum in re
publica administranda T. Annio cum P. Sestio consiliorum omnium societas fuerit (id quod non solum
bonorum, verum etiam improborum iudicio declaratum
est ; est enim reus uterque ob eandem causam et
eodem crimine, alter die dicta ab eo, quem tu unum

---

    [a] T. Annius Milo had been accused by Clodius (*illa
taeterrima furia*) *de vi*. The case began on 2 February,
56 B.C., and after several adjournments was finally dropped.
Vatinius' evidence against Milo was given at one of the
preliminary *contiones*. See p. 31.
    [b] Of the Optimate persuasion.

the praetorship to death, especially since you wish
to be a " Friend of the People," and by no other
means can please the people more ?

But in order that we may at last hear how fully 40
you intend to answer my questions, I will conclude
my examination and will end by asking you a few
questions on the case itself.

XVII. Tell me, why were you so untruthful, so
inconsistent that, in this trial, you praised Titus
Annius in exactly the same words as good men and
good citizens have been accustomed to praise him,
although recently, when brought before the People
by that same loathsome fiend, you were eager to give
false evidence against him ? [a]   Or shall you have the
liberty to choose, the power to say what you please ?
So that, when you see Clodius' hirelings and his band
of criminals and scoundrels, you will say (as you
have said in a meeting) that Milo besieged the State
with gladiators and wild-beast fighters ; but, when
you appear before judges such as these,[b] you will
not dare to abuse a citizen distinguished for valour,
honour, and stedfastness.[c] But, since you praise Titus 41
Annius so generously, and by your praise do not leave
this illustrious man [d] altogether unsullied, for Titus
Annius prefers to be in the ranks of those whom you
abuse, nevertheless, I ask you this : in their public
life, Titus Annius and Publius Sestius have always
acted together and shared each other's counsels ;
this union is attested, not only by the opinion of
loyal, but also by that of disloyal citizens, for both
are accused for the same reason and on the same
charge—the one being prosecuted by him whom

[c] See Cicero, *Epp. ad Att.* iv. 3. 5.
[d] P. Sestius.

improbiorem esse quam te numquam soles[1] confiteri,
alter tuis consiliis, illo tamen adiuvante)—quaero,
qui possis eos, quos crimine coniungis, testimonio
diiungere.

Extremum illud est, quod mihi abs te responderi
velim, cum multa in Albinovanum de praevaricatione
diceres, dixerisne nec tibi placuisse nec oportuisse
Sestium de vi reum fieri ; quavis lege, quovis crimine
accusandum potius fuisse ; etiam illud dixeris, causam
Milonis, fortissimi viri, coniunctam cum hoc existimari ; quae pro me a Sestio facta sint, bonis esse
grata. Non coarguo inconstantiam orationis ac testimonii tui (quas enim huius actiones probatas bonis
esse dicis, in eas plurimis verbis testimonium dixisti ;
quicum autem eius causam periculumque coniungis,
eum summis laudibus extulisti) ; sed hoc quaero,
num P. Sestium, qua lege accusandum omnino fuisse
negas, ea lege condemnari putes oportere, aut, si te
in testimonio consuli noles, ne quid tibi auctoritatis
a me tributum esse videatur, dixerisne in eum testimonium de vi, quem negaris reum omnino de vi fieri
debuisse.

---

[1] nunquam soles *mss.* : *except Ed. Hervagiana (1534)* non
nunquam soles.

---

[a] In his speech before Cicero's cross-examination. See
p. 34.
[b] Because Vatinius did not think the charge likely to
succeed. In the autumn of 57 B.C. and winter of 57–56 B.C.
there was a reaction against the *populares*.
[c] Vatinius meant the Optimates ; Cicero uses the word in
the moral sense.
[d] In the speech possibly mentioned in the missing passage
in § 4, p. 245.

you are never in the habit of admitting to be a
greater scoundrel than yourself, the other at your
instigation, but with his assistance,—none the less I
ask you, then, how can you separate in your evidence two men whom you confound in the same
accusation ?

The last question to which I want an answer is this.
When you asserted at length *a* that Albinovanus was
acting collusively, did you not say that you had not
approved of Sestius being accused of violence, and
that he ought not to have been so accused *b* ; that he
should rather have been accused under any law, on
any charge ; did you not also say that the cause of
Milo, that heroic man, was thought to be bound up
with that of Sestius ; that all that had been done by
Sestius on my behalf was approved by good citizens ? *c*
I do not reproach you for the inconsistency between
your speech *d* and your evidence ; for you have given
evidence at length against those measures of Sestius
which you declare were approved by good citizens,
and you associate with the cause and accusation of
Sestius the man *e* whom you praised so highly. But
this I do ask, whether you think that Publius Sestius
ought to be condemned by virtue of that law, under
which you assert that he ought on no account to
have been accused ; or, if you object while giving
evidence to be asked your opinion, for fear that I
might seem to attach any weight to it, tell me—
whether you gave evidence on a charge of violence
against a man who, you said, ought never to have
been tried on a charge of violence.

e Milo.

297

IV. The Purpose of the *Pro Sestio* [a]

" One of Cicero's greatest speeches " [b]; " An admirable specimen of forensic oratory applied to a state trial . . . with every grace of language and every force of argument " [c]; " A trumpet-call to all loyal citizens to rally in defence of the republican constitution " [d]; " Cicero proclaimed the ideal of a conservative union of all classes bound in loyalty to the Senate and guided by modest and patriotic *principes*." [e]

In the above words the quality and the purpose of the *Pro Sestio* have received due appreciation. There can be no doubt of the merit of the speech as an example of Cicero's mature style ; nor of its political purpose. Two matters of controversy may be mentioned. First, it has been claimed that the speech in its present form has nothing in common with the one delivered in court, but is the result

[a] The following works have been found of great value : Ch. Wirszubski, *Libertas as a Political Idea at Rome during the Late Republic and Early Principate* (Cambridge, 1950), pp. 31-96, and his article, " Cicero's *Cum Dignitate Otium* : a Reconsideration," *J.R.S.* xliv, pp. 1-13. W. W. How, " Cicero's Ideal in his *De Republica*," *J.R.S.* xx, pp. 24-42.

[b] Heitland, *The Roman Republic*, iii, p. 80.

[c] Strachan-Davidson, *Cicero*, p. 256.

[d] How, *Cicero, Select Letters*, ii, p. 149.

[e] Syme, *The Roman Revolution*, p. 37.

of Cicero's elaboration of his spoken speech into a political manifesto.[a] Without going so far as this, it is immaterial for our purpose whether or not Cicero delivered in court in their present form the well-known sections (96-101 ; 136-139) which are his fullest extant declaration that the political programme of the Optimates was the establishment in the State of *cum dignitate otium*. Secondly, a suggestion has been made that it is not impossible that the prosecution of Sestius was a collusive prosecution [b] and that Cicero was a party to it. But the evidence for this suggestion hardly permits a decision to be reached.

A summary of the speech, found on pp. 336-346, shows that Cicero devoted over half of it (§§ 15-95) to a full narrative of the events which led to his banishment, and to the early and unsuccessful stage of the movement for his restoration. The failure of this having led the prosecution to compare the weakness of Cicero's friends with the success of his enemies, the orator passes to his main subject (§§ 96-143), an elaborate account of the Optimates, whose policy he defends as true patriotism. Having interwoven with this an account of the later and successful stage of the movement for his recall, Cicero concludes by an exhortation to the rising generation to be faithful to the political principles of the Optimates as expressed in government by the Senate and in their aim of *cum dignitate otium*.

Cicero's political experiences since his consulship had schooled him to make such an appeal. The hopes born in his consulship had been shattered by the formation of the Triumvirate and by the humilia-

---

[a] Meyer, *Caesars Monarchie*, p. 135.
[b] Pocock, *In Vatinium*, Appendix i, p. 145.

tion of exile. Though elated by his recall which he hailed as a triumph for constitutional government, Cicero at first remained in acquiescence and refrained from any marked political enterprise. But early in 56 B.C. he was tempted to an indiscretion which was to lose him his political independence. In 59 B.C. he had confessed to Atticus that hope for better things alone depended on dissension within the Triumvirate.[a] Amid feud and riot in February 56 B.C. he observed grave dissension between Pompey and Crassus, and he was suspicious of a rift between Pompey and Caesar. He was thus encouraged to the high hopes which first found expression in the theme of the *Pro Sestio* : a plea for his ideal constitution of an Optimate government, centred on a preeminent Senate and hostile to absolutism and democracy alike.

In sections 96-101 and 136-139 Cicero defines the class of citizens whom he regards as Optimates and expounds their political programme. His lengthy exposition is idealistic and is a homily specially addressed to the rising generation,[b] not only to young men who are *nobiles* by birth but also to those who can win *nobilitas* by *ingenium* and *virtus* (§ 136). Cicero's class of Optimates is not limited to those " who ruled Rome after Sulla, owing their primacy to birth and wealth and linked by bonds of kinship and reciprocal interest." [c] His class is far wider. In his consulship Cicero claimed to have made an alliance, *concordia ordinum*, between the Senate and

---

[a] *Epp. ad Att.* ii. 7. 3 : " una spes est salutis istorum inter ipsos dissensio."

[b] *Pro Sestio*, 51, 96, 103, 119, 136-137.

[c] Syme, *The Roman Revolution*, p. 22.

the *equites*,[a] and to have advocated as an addition to
this *coniunctio bonorum omnium* [b] and *consensus Italiae*,[c]
thereby forming a union of all law-abiding citizens
and of all the most respectable elements in Italy in
the defence of the established order against unconstitutional designs. This alliance of loyalists is revived
and enlarged in the *Pro Sestio* and defined (§ 97) as in-
cluding not only the senatorial class and potential
members of it, but other classes also, the enfranchised
Italians, townsmen and countryfolk, men of business,
and even freedmen ; in short, no narrow oligarchy,
but a union representative of all that was best in
Italy, materially and morally (*integri, sani, bene de
rebus domesticis constituti*, § 97). The political aim of
the leaders of these Optimates (*defensores optimatium,
principes civitatis*, § 97) is defined as *cum dignitate
otium* [d] (§ 98) or *otiosa dignitas* (§ 98).

The assertion of the prosecution that the Optimates
were a " Breed " (*natio*, § 96), a term of abuse origi-
nating from P. Vatinius (§ 132), is parried by Cicero
by a tendentious interpretation of the word Optimates. Making dexterous play with the flexibility of
the term *optimus quisque*, which may be rendered as
" every good citizen," he identifies Optimates with
optimi quique, and claims that the Optimates, so far
from being a " Breed of Aristocrats," are in fact the
whole *populus Romanus*, less, of course, the wicked
populares. The identity of the Optimates with all good
citizens thus established, Cicero goes on to say that
unlike the *populares*, whose aim is to ingratiate themselves with the masses, the Optimates are those public

[a] Cicero, *In Catilinam*, IV. 15, 22.
[b] *Epp. ad Att*. i. 16. 6.   [c] *Epp. ad Att*. i. 14. 4.
[d] The phrase recurs in *Epp. ad Fam*. i. 9. 21 (54 B.C.).

men who strive to govern in accordance with the wishes and interests of all good citizens. He then states the purpose of the Optimates : the establishment of that political condition which all the soundest elements in Italy regarded as indispensable, *cum dignitate otium* (§ 98).

The expression *cum dignitate otium*, found not only in the *Pro Sestio* but also in Cicero's political *apologia* to P. Lentulus Spinther of 54 B.C. (*Epp. ad Fam.* i. 9. 21), and its variant *otiosa dignitas* (§ 98), are political catchphrases expressing Cicero's political ideal. As the components of the phrase, *dignitas* and *otium*, admit of various meanings, it is not surprising that scholars differ in their interpretations. But, most recently, Ch. Wirszubski's [a] careful study of the phrase *cum dignitate otium* has illuminated obscurities and provided a cogent interpretation, which is here followed.

Cicero's extant works from 63 to 43 B.C. provide abundant evidence for the use of *otium* and *dignitas* as political terms. *Otium*, used in a collective sense, invariably means public tranquillity, in Roman party politics, not in the wider Roman world : peace and quietness in the City ; the traditional Republican government unchallenged ; the masses at one with their rulers. *Dignitas*, though capable of a collective

---

[a] Ch. Wirszubski, " Cicero's *Cum Dignitate Otium:* a Reconsideration," *J.R.S.* xliv (1954), pp. 1-13. The leading earlier discussions of the problem are : E. Remy, " *Dignitas cum otio*," *Musée Belge*, xxxii (1928), pp. 113-127 ; H. Wegehaupt, *Die Bedeutung und Anwendung von dignitas*, Breslau Dissertation, 1932 ; P. Boyancé, " *Cum dignitate otium*," *REA*, xliii (1941), pp. 172-191 ; Ch. Wirszubski, *Libertas as a Political Idea at Rome during the Late Republic and Early Principate* (Cambridge, 1950), pp. 36-39 ; 93-94.

meaning (*e.g. dignitas rei publicae*), means rather in the context under review the rank, prestige and honour of a Roman public man, what its possessor claims as his due. It was, for example, for the preservation of his *dignitas* that Julius Caesar went to war with Pompey.[a] Cicero conceived his own *dignitas* in terms of political standing, and in a letter [b] of early 45 B.C. provides us with some illuminating observations on the meaning of the word. Congratulated by his friend Cn. Plancius on maintaining his former political position (*pristina dignitas*) under Caesar's dictatorship, he replied : " If *dignitas* means the holding of sound political views and winning their approval by loyal citizens (*boni viri*), I do maintain my *dignitas.*; but, if *dignitas* means the power to give effect to your views, or even to defend them in free speech, there is not even a trace of *dignitas* left to me."

A sentence in the *Pro Sestio* which is cardinal for the meaning of *cum dignitate otium* occurs in section 104 : " Nunc iam nihil est, quod populus a delectis principibusque dissentiat, nec flagitat rem ullam neque novarum rerum est cupidus et *otio suo* et *dignitate optimi cuiusque* et universae rei publicae gloria delectatur " ; " But just at the present time there is no reason for the People to disagree with their picked and chief men. They demand nothing, they do not desire revolution, they delight in their own peace, in the honour of the ' Best Men,' and in the glory of the whole State." Cicero thus proclaims *cum dignitate otium* as a salutary condition enjoyed by the whole State : peace and quietness for the masses, political

---

[a] Cicero, *Epp. ad Att.* vii. 11. 1. R. E. Smith, *The Failure of the Roman Republic*, pp. 129-130.

[b] Cicero, *Epp. ad Fam.* iv. 14. 1.

prestige, influence and worthiness for the "Best Men."
Judging that the coalition of Pompey, Caesar and
Crassus, the source of the evils that had harassed the
State since 60 B.C., was in imminent danger of dissolution, Cicero in the *Pro Sestio* sounded a rally for the
restoration of his ideal Republic, the masses in quiet
contentment, the Optimates in full control of the
government, undisturbed by demagogy no less than
by absolutism.

There is, however, no obscurity about the part
cast for the Senate by Cicero at the conclusion of his
homily on Rome's ideal constitution. In section 137,
when describing "the organization of the State so
wisely established by our ancestors," he represents
the Senate as always having been the keystone of
the constitution.[a] His words contrast the transient
magistrate and the permanent Senate ; they insist
that the Senate is to be composed of ex-magistrates
who have been chosen by the whole electorate for
merit (*industria et virtus*) ; and they imply a belief
that the Senate was open to plebeians from the
beginning of the Republic.[b] Thus the Senate was
to be no narrow oligarchy, but representative of all
that was best in the citizen-body, merit and not
birth being the qualification for it. It is noteworthy
that such a Senate bears a striking resemblance to
the Senate which Sulla planned to set up in supreme
control of the State and to which he proposed to
give representative character by popular election.[c]

[a] As also in *De rep.* ii. 56 ; *De leg.* iii. 10 and 28.
[b] J. S. Reid, in Holden, *Pro Sestio*, p. 249 ; H. M. Last,
" The Servian Reforms," *J.R.S.* xxxv, p. 32.
[c] The *lex Cornelia de XX quaestoribus* is meant. See also
Cicero, *De leg.* iii. 27.

PRO SESTIO and IN VATINIUM

Cicero and the ruling nobility agreed that the constitution of the State should centre on the authority of the Senate. But they differed, not unnaturally, about the Senate's composition. The nobles regarded the Senate as their stronghold in a struggle to retain their power. Cicero, as a *novus homo*, held that the ruling class represented in the Senate should be drawn from those who possessed the qualification of *industria ac virtus* (§ 137). Such a Senate would be hostile to autocrats and *populares* alike. The bearing of this theory of government on the times when Cicero delivered the *Pro Sestio* needs no stressing.

V. Cicero and Caesar in the *In Vatinium*

The question of the responsibility of Caesar as consul for the irregularities committed by Vatinius during his tribunate calls for some consideration of Cicero's feelings towards Caesar as expressed in the speeches delivered after his return from exile.

Cicero's opening speeches, the two *Orationes post reditum* and *De domo sua*, are profuse in their thanks to Pompey and his other friends and helpers. References to Caesar are few, but are reserved and dignified. Caesar's association with Clodius was the trouble, for there can be no doubt that Caesar till he left the gates of Rome in March 58 b.c. knew and approved of everything that Clodius did. In the *De domo* Cicero refrained from mentioning Caesar by name as the recipient of the news of Cicero's criticism of the Triumvirate made at the trial of C. Antonius,[a] and as the commander of the army outside Rome when

[a] *De domo*, 41.

305

Clodius was preparing to banish Cicero.[a] Cicero disclaimed any intention of invalidating Caesar's *acta* as consul; although he had suffered from Caesar's responsibility for the adoption of Clodius, he was prepared to let bygones be bygones, and be guided by patriotism, not personal resentment.[b] Caesar, however, is expressly mentioned as the author of a letter of congratulation which Clodius said that he had received on his commissioning of Cato to Cyprus.[c]

Much the same tone of dignity and reserve is apparent in the *Pro Sestio* some five months later. Pompey is belauded as a world-conqueror; his efforts for Cicero's recall are gratefully described; his desertion of Cicero in 58 B.C. and his withdrawal from public life before the belligerent Clodius are glossed over. Clodius' claim to enjoy the support of Caesar is emphasized,[d] but Caesar's identity as the consul who presided over the transfer of Clodius is not revealed.[e] Little immediate success seems to have attended Sestius' visit to Caesar to intercede for Cicero, who, however, realized that Caesar gave permission for his recall.[f] Caesar is complimented on the excellence of his law *de pecuniis repetundis*,[g] and is himself described as *mitis homo et a caede abhorrens*.[h] Several passages [i] in which Cicero refutes, or tries to refute, assertions of unfriendly relations between Caesar and himself, lead to the conclusion that Caesar had been incensed by Cicero's obstinacy in refusing honourable employment under him which

    [a] *Post reditum in senatu*, 32.   [b] *De domo*, 39.
    [c] *De domo*, 22.   [d] *Pro Sestio*, 39-41.
        [e] *Pro Sestio*, 16.   [f] *Pro Sestio*, 71.
        [g] *Pro Sestio*, 135.   [h] *Pro Sestio*, 132.
    [i] *Post reditum in senatu*, 32 ; *Pro Sestio*, 16, 39, 41, 71.

would serve the double purpose of rendering Clodius harmless and of safeguarding the legislation of
59 B.C.

But when we come to the *In Vatinium* there is a
different story to tell. For the vehemence of Cicero's
attack on Vatinius himself and his tribunate there is
confirmatory evidence in two of Cicero's letters. In
Epp. ad Quintum fratrem, ii. 4. 1 (March 56 B.C.) we
read : " In conducting the defence (of Sestius) . . .
I cut up Vatinius, by whom he was being openly
attacked, just as I pleased, with applause from gods
and men." Cicero's letter to Lentulus of 54 B.C.
(*Epp. ad Fam.* i. 9. 7) tells us : " My whole cross-
examination [of Vatinius] was nothing but a denunciation of his tribunate." [a] Cicero's attack, however,
was not directed against Vatinius alone. In the on-
slaught which he launched, with Pompey and Crassus
present in court, he could not, though he claimed to
do so, dissociate Caesar from his subordinate and
acquit him of responsibility for the irregularities of
which Vatinius as tribune had been guilty. In his

---

[a] This passage also tells us that Vatinius, when giving
evidence against Sestius, taunted Cicero with having, in
admiration for Caesar's victories in Gaul, sought to be reconciled with him ; and that Cicero replied that he regarded
Bibulus' devotion to duty as more glorious than any triumph
or victory, and that he had been driven into exile by the
very men who had, in the troubles of 59 B.C., virtually imprisoned Bibulus in his house. No such remark is to be
found in the extant speeches, *Pro Sestio* and *In Vatinium*.
Two explanations have been offered : either, that the remark
may have been deleted from the published version as highly
offensive to Caesar ; or, that it may have appeared in a
lacuna of about forty lines occurring in the text of the MS.
of the *In Vatinium* known as P between the present sections
4 and 5. (Pocock, *In Vatinium*, pp. 47 and 80.)

two speeches *Post reditum*, in *De domo sua*, and in *Pro Sestio* itself, Cicero abstained from language which might offend Caesar. In the *In Vatinium*, however, Cicero used a bludgeon for Vatinius and a rapier for Caesar.[a] When beginning to cross-examine Vatinius on the misdeeds of his tribunate, Cicero insinuates that Vatinius had been in partnership with Caesar, but announces that Vatinius alone is to be his victim : " I warn you . . . not to mix up your dirty tricks with the glorious reputation of our most distinguished men . . . I shall drag you from your own proper obscurity, not from the dignified company of a great man. And all my shafts will be so aimed against you that no one else will be wounded " (§ 13). But a subtle attack on Caesar is made in the most entertaining paragraph of the speech (§ 15). In accusing Vatinius of disregarding an announcement that the heavens had been watched, Cicero says : " And since this is the only point in which you claim to have something in common with Caesar, I will separate your case from his . . . lest a stain from your gross unworthiness should seem to tarnish his worthy name. . . . Next, for the truth shall at length force utterance, and I shall not hesitate to say what I think. Suppose for a moment that Caesar did break out into some excesses ; that the strain of conflict, his passion for glory, his outstanding genius, his exalted birth, did drive him into some acts which at that moment and in such a man might be tolerable, but should be wiped out of memory by his subsequent achievements ; will you, you rascal, claim the same forbearance ; and shall we give ear to the voice of Vatinius . . . demanding

[a] The relevant sections are *In Vatinium*, 13, 15 and 39 (the opening words).

for himself the same privileges as Caesar ? " And, later in the speech,[a] a further dissociation of Caesar from Vatinius implies a criticism of Caesar : " the very man [Caesar], who, for the sake of increasing his own prestige, at your risk and by no betrayal of his own duty, readily allowed you to follow your headlong course. . . ." Where, then, is Cicero's claim to attack Vatinius alone ? Although this pretence is maintained by his compliments to Caesar, his language, with flattery and insinuation deftly interwoven, seems purposely chosen to reflect on Caesar no less than on Vatinius.

From the unanimous acquittal of Sestius, from Pompey's apparent indifference to Cicero's oblique attack on Caesar in the *In Vatinium*, and from his own belief that the coalition was already weakened by internal differences which might have fatal consequences, Cicero was encouraged to plan an attack on Caesar's Campanian Land Law.[b] This helped to induce a crisis in the coalition which was promptly and effectively met by the agreement reached by Pompey, Caesar and Crassus at the Conference of Luca.

VI. The *Lex Aelia Fufia* in the
Late Republic [c]

Of the five speeches of Cicero comprised in these volumes, three, *Pro Sestio*, *In Vatinium*, and *De Pro-*

[a] *In Vatinium*, 39.
[b] Cicero, *Epp. ad Fam.* 1. 9. 7 ; *Epp. ad Quintum fratrem*, ii. 5. 1.
[c] The present writer acknowledges the indispensable help which he has received from the writings of the scholars who have most recently investigated this topic : J. D. Denniston,

vinciis consularibus, contain important references [a] to the political exploitation of the *auspicia* at the end of the Republic. Since Cicero repeatedly accuses Clodius of having repealed, by a law passed during his tribunate, the *lex Aelia Fufia*, the earliest known statute regulating the observance of auspices (*auspicatio*), some account may be attempted of the theory and practice of the auspices in the Ciceronian Age, as a preliminary to a statement of the difficulty presented by the law of Clodius.

The use of *auspicia*, which was possibly in part of oriental origin, was, as evidence shows, widely practised from early times in Italy, among Etruscans, Umbrians and Romans. The Romans divided *auspicia* into two classes, *impetrativa* and *oblativa*.[b] *Auspicia impetrativa* were omens which were definitely sought; *auspicia oblativa* came unsought. In theory these two classes comprised several varieties : signs from the flight of birds, from the movement or sounds of animals, from thunder or lightning, or from the behaviour of special chickens. But in practice, during the Ciceronian Age, only *auspicia de caelo*, " omens from the sky," were used for political purposes ; these were specifically understood as thunder

Orationes Philippicae Prima et Secunda (Oxford, 1926), Appendix iii, pp. 180-186 ; A. H. J. Greenidge, " The Repeal of the *Lex Aelia Fufia*," *Classical Review*, vii, pp. 158-161 ; *Roman Public Life*, pp. 162-167 ; W. F. McDonald, " Clodius and the *Lex Aelia Fufia*," *J.R.S.* xix, pp. 164-179 ; S. Weinstock, " Clodius and the *Lex Aelia Fufia*," *J.R.S.* xxvii, pp. 215-222. Full references to earlier authorities are given by the above writers.

[a] *Pro Sestio*, 33, 56, 78, 79, 114, 129 ; *In Vatinium*, 5, 15, 18, 23 ; *De prov. cons.* 46.

[b] Servius, *ad Aen.* vi. 190.

and lightning, which, though propitious for private undertakings, were always regarded as unfavourable for the holding of Assemblies.

The right of looking for *auspicia impetrativa* was known as *spectio* ; and the exercise of that right as *servare de caelo*, " to look for something coming down from the sky." Mommsen assumed that this right [a] was confined to magistrates. According to strict practice, a magistrate, or otherwise qualified person, who had observed an unfavourable omen was bound to announce it to the magistrate who was about to preside over an Assembly. This announcement was called *obnuntiatio*. But such *obnuntiatio* would only be served when a magistrate persisted in his intention to hold an Assembly.[b] In general, an announcement by a magistrate or tribune that he had " watched the sky," or merely that he intended to do so, was in itself enough to deter a magistrate from holding an Assembly. Such an announcement implied that the watcher proposed, in any case, to observe an unfavourable omen and to report it. The

---

[a] *Staatsrecht*, i³, pp. 110 ff. This assumption is not adequately supported in the recorded evidence.

[b] Cicero, *Epp. ad Att.* iv. 3. 3-5, provides an instructive and amusing example. In Nov. 57 B.C. Clodius, to avoid being brought to trial *de vi* by Milo, was trying to save himself by being elected aedile. Milo, then tribune, in order to prevent the holding of elective *comitia*, gave notice that on every day when *comitia* might be held, he would exercise his right of *servare de caelo*. Q. Metellus Nepos, as presiding consul, showed that he intended to disregard Milo's announcement and attempted a ruse. But this was defeated by Milo who, after coming into the Comitium after midnight on 19-20 November, encountered the consul at dawn, and having exercised the right of *servare de caelo* served his *obnuntiatio*.

word *obnuntiatio*, properly denoting the formal completion of an act of obstruction, was commonly used to include the preliminary act *servare de caelo*.

The act *servare de caelo* had to take place before the holding of the proposed Assembly, as is clear from the passage of Cicero quoted on page 311, note *b*.[a] In the Ciceronian Age *servare de caelo* cannot have been anything more than a fiction, and an unfavourable omen anything more than a fabrication. The Roman religious conscience acquiesced in the manufacture of *auspicia impetrativa*, but required that *auspicia oblativa* should be genuine. This process of " make-believe " was perhaps originally helped [b] by the fact that a Roman Assembly met early in the day, and that *servare de caelo* would be carried out during the night or the small hours of the morning. If lightning, frequent during summer nights in southern Europe, had taken place during the night, few would be in a position to deny the occurrence of this unfavourable omen.

The right, however, to announce unfavourable *auspicia oblativa* was not restricted to magistrates or those otherwise qualified, but was open to all citizens. Augurs naturally had special competence in this matter. These omens might take the form, for example, of a flash of lightning, of an epileptic seizure (*morbus comitialis*) or even of a sudden noise.[c] A presiding magistrate could respect or ignore at will such an announcement by a private individual,

[a] See also Cicero, *Phil.* ii. 81.

[b] Valeton, *Mnemosyne*, xviii, p. 253.

[c] Valerius Maximus, i. 1. 5, says that the squeak of a mouse caused a flaw in the appointment of Q. Fabius Maximus to a dictatorship (his first, probably within 221–219 B.C.).

but an announcement by an augur,[a] coupled with his words, " *alio die*," [b] automatically disbanded an Assembly. Augurs, then, and private citizens had the right of *obnuntiatio* of *auspicia oblativa*. That such an announcement could be made only during an Assembly is a reasonable assumption which is confirmed by the recorded instances.

It may be safely assumed that originally the College of Augurs was in sole control of all *auspicatio*, that is, the observation and interpretation of *auspicia*. But we can only conjecture at what date magistrates acquired the right to take observations themselves, and when the earliest legal regulations were made. We cannot recover the date of the *vetus formula perpetua* [c] in the consular edict forbidding the minor magistrates (aediles, quaestors and other juniors) to exercise the right of *servare de caelo* against an Assembly of the *comitia centuriata*. But it is tempting to put at some date later than the *lex Ogulnia* (300 B.C.) which admitted plebeians to the Colleges of Augurs and Pontiffs, a regulation giving tribunes the right of *auspicatio*, and of *obnuntiatio*.[d]

The earliest known statute, which recognized the already existing rules of *obnuntiatio*, was called the *lex Aelia Fufia*.[e] A sentence from Cicero shows that

---

[a] It was in his capacity as augur, not as consul, that Pompey in 55 B.C. caused by his announcement of fictitious thunder the disbanding of *comitia praetoria*, to prevent Cato's election as praetor. Plutarch, *Cato Minor*, 42.

[b] Cicero, *Phil.* ii. 83.

[c] Gellius, xiii. 15. 1.

[d] Dio Cassius, v. 9 (=Zonaras, vii. 19. 2) connects this with the *leges Valeriae Horatiae* of 449 B.C., which are much too early.

[e] Several passages in Cicero, *e.g. De prov. cons.* 46 ; *De*

it was passed about the middle of the second century
B.C.,[a] shortly before senatorial supremacy was challenged by the Gracchi.

Our knowledge of the *lex Aelia Fufia* is defective,
for it is not possible to state the purpose of more than
two of its sections. One section regulated the use of
the *auspicia* with reference both to the *comitia populi*
(*centuriata*, *tributa*) and the *concilium plebis*, and
allowed not only curule magistrates to practise
obnuntiatio [b] at Meetings of the *concilium plebis* but
tribunes also at Assemblies of the *comitia populi*.
Another section forbade, by a regulation *de iure et de
tempore legum rogandarum*,[c] the holding of legislative
Assemblies on certain *dies fasti*, among which was the
period of three *nundina* [d] (probably twenty-four days)
between the announcement of elections and the
holding of the elections themselves.

For over eighty years from the date of its passing
the *lex Aelia Fufia* had no recorded history. Cicero
says that it was unviolated during the years of fre-

haruspicum responsis, 58, make it clear that there were two
laws, the *lex Aelia* and the *lex Fufia*, but the relation between
them is unknown.

[a] *In Pisonem*, 10 ; speaking in 55 B.C. of the *lex Aelia*
and the *lex Fufia* (which he holds to have been repealed by
Clodius in 58 B.C.), Cicero says : " centum prope annos
legem Aeliam et Fufiam tenueramus." Their passing may
perhaps be associated with an administrative reform under
which in 153 B.C. the consuls first entered office on 1 January.
Cicero speaks of them as : " certissima subsidia rei publicae
contra tribunicios furores " (*Post reditum in senatu*, 11) ;
" propugnacula murique tranquillitatis atque otii " (*In
Pisonem*, 9).

[b] Asconius, p. 8 (Clark).

[c] *Pro Sestio*, 56.

[d] Mommsen, *Staatsrecht*, iii, p. 375. *Schol. Bob.* on
Cicero, *In Vat.* 23, p. 148 (Stangl).

quent revolution between the Gracchi and Sulla.[a]
We hear that it was respected by C. Cornelius, a
vigorous and efficient *popularis* who was tribune in
67 B.C.,[b] and, less surprisingly, by Cicero, in securing
the passage during his consulship of his *lex Tullia de
ambitu*.[c] On two occasions, however, and under ex-
ceptional circumstances, in 67[d] and 61 B.C.,[e] the
Senate, for the purpose of passing a *lex de ambitu*,
voted the proposers of the law a dispensation from
that section of the *lex Aelia Fufia* which prohibited
the holding of a legislative assembly between the
announcement and the holding of the elections. So
far as our sources reveal, P. Vatinius[f] in 59 B.C. was
the first to defy the law, P. Clodius in 58 B.C. was the
first to attack it.

In 59 B.C. Bibulus, when attempting to obstruct
by *obnuntiatio* the holding of an Assembly at which
Caesar proposed to pass his first agrarian law, was
with his supporters driven from the Forum. Having
failed, when he summoned the senators to meet in
his house, to rouse them to resistance, he shut himself up there for the remainder of his consulship and
issued daily notices (*edicta*), which served as *obnuntiationes* and had the effect of declaring null and void,
as having been passed in unconstitutional fashion,
any laws which might subsequently be passed by the
Assembly.[g] These *obnuntiationes per edicta* were, of

---

[a] *In Vatinium*, 23.   [b] *In Vatinium*, 5.
[c] *In Vatinium*, 37.   [d] Dio Cassius, xxxvi. 39. 1.
[e] Cicero, *Epp. ad Att*. i. 16. 13.
[f] *In Vatinium*, 18. There is some suggestion but no
certainty that in 88 B.C. the revolutionary tribune P. Sulpicius Rufus ignored the *lex Aelia Fufia*. See *C.A.H*. ix,
p. 205 ; McDonald, *op. cit*. pp. 166 and 174.
[g] Suetonius, *Div. Iul*. 20.

course, ignored by Caesar and his tribune Vatinius, so that Caesar's first agrarian law, the transfer of Clodius into a plebeian family [a] by a *lex curiata*, and all the remaining legislation of the year 59 B.C., were by strict law invalid. Bibulus, however, did not extend his obstruction to the elections for 58 B.C., since we learn from Cicero that they were postponed by him from their normal date (at the end of July) to 18 October.[b]

Clodius opened the year of his tribunate (58 B.C.) by passing into law four bills.[c] One, which provided for the supply of free corn to citizens applying for it, was amended by Julius Caesar as dictator, who reduced from some 320,000 to 150,000 the number of the recipients of free corn.[d] A second, which restored the *collegia* or political clubs banned by the Senate in 64 B.C., and legalized the formation of new *collegia*, was repealed by Julius Caesar ; he banned all *collegia*, but made an exception in favour of the Jewish synagogues.[e] A third, which limited the power of the censors in compiling the roll of the Senate, was repealed by Q. Metellus Scipio,[f] Pompey's father-in-law, whom in August 52 B.C. Pompey co-opted as his colleague in the consulship.

These three measures were intended to win popular support for Clodius' later actions against Cicero.

---

[a] Cicero, *De domo sua*, 39 ; *De prov. cons.* 45.

[b] Cicero, *Epp. ad Att.* ii. 20. 6.

[c] Cicero, *Post reditum in senatu*, 11 ; *Pro Sestio*, 33 and 56 ; *De haruspicum responsis*, 58 ; *De prov. cons.* 46 ; *In Pisonem*, 9 ; Asconius, p. 8 (Clark) ; Dio Cassius, xxxviii. 13. 5-6 ; 14. 1.

[d] Suetonius, *Div. Iul.* 41.

[e] Suetonius, *Div. Iul.* 42 ; Josephus, *Ant.* xiv (10. 8). 216.

[f] Dio Cassius, xl. 57.

The purpose of his fourth measure was to surmount legal obstacles. From the language of Cicero it would appear that Clodius not only repealed the *lex Aelia Fufia* as a whole, by ordering disregard of the *auspicia*, by prohibiting *obnuntiatio* and *servare de caelo* and by making legislation possible on all *dies fasti*, but also went so far as to suspend the tribunician *ius intercessionis* and to repeal all the laws *de iure ac tempore legum ferendarum*.

In all probability, however, the *ius intercessionis* was not suspended but its use as a substitute for *obnuntiatio* was prohibited.[a] Of the laws *iure ac tempore legum ferendarum* [b] which Cicero alleges that Clodius repealed we have knowledge of two only : the *lex Caecilia Didia* and the *lex Licinia Iunia*. The *lex Caecilia Didia* (98 B.C.) prohibited the inclusion of miscellaneous measures in the same bill and ordered that, after the *promulgatio* of a bill, an interval of three *nundina* (probably twenty-four days) should elapse before it was submitted to the voters. The *lex Licinia Iunia* (62 B.C.) confirmed the *lex Caecilia Didia* and prescribed that legislative proposals should be published in advance by being deposited at the Aerarium (the Temple of Saturn).[c]

Certain incidents of the years 57 and 54 B.C. make it difficult, if not impossible, to believe that Clodius' repeal of the *lex Aelia Fufia* and perhaps, also, of the *leges Caecilia Didia* and *Licinia Iunia*, was anything more than an *ad hoc* suspension, without permanent validity. Yet, fourteen years later, in 44 B.C., M.

---

[a] Weinstock, *op. cit.* p. 217, refers to Mommsen, *Staatsrecht*, ii, pp. 3, 308, n. 3. McDonald interprets *intercessio* here as equivalent to *obnuntiando intercedere*, *op. cit.* p. 178.
[b] *Pro Sestio*, 56. [c] See p. 221, note *j*.

CICERO

Antonius as consul seems to have acknowledged the validity of Clodius' law. The two scholars who have most recently investigated this problem, W. F. McDonald and S. Weinstock, differ in their conclusions. McDonald [a] held that Clodius amended but did not wholly repeal the *lex Aelia Fufia* : in his view, tribunes and augurs were left with their general right of *obnuntiatio* ; curule magistrates were allowed to retain their right of *obnuntiatio* at elective, but to lose it at legislative, Assemblies ; and the Assemblies could meet for the transaction of business on all *dies fasti*. Weinstock,[b] however, concluded that there is evidence for the full observance of the *lex Aelia Fufia* immediately after Clodius' tribunate and that Dio Cassius' [c] statement that the purpose of Clodius' law was to facilitate proceedings against Cicero is wholly acceptable. In his view, Clodius repealed the whole of the *lex Aelia Fufia*, but the Senate, on an augural decision, pronounced his adoption illegal, and his legislation invalid (p. 13).

The relevant incidents of the years 57 and 54 B.C. which suggest that the *lex Aelia Fufia* was then in full operation may now be mentioned.

1. Cicero (*Pro Sestio*, 78) says that *obnuntiatio* could have been used to oppose the *rogatio* for Cicero's restoration which on 23 January 57 B.C. a tribune, Q. Fabricius, was proposing to submit to an Assembly. The Assembly, however, was broken up by Clodius' rioters reinforced by gladiators supplied by Clodius' brother, Appius Claudius, a praetor of the year.[d]

---

[a] *Op. cit.* p. 179.   [b] *Op. cit.* p. 220.   [c] xxxviii. 13. 6.
[d] McDonald, *op. cit.* pp. 174-175, who reads " p.r." not " praetor " in the text of this passage, refuses to accept it as evidence that a curule magistrate could, despite Clodius' law,

2. Cicero (*Pro Sestio*, 79) records that soon after the above incident one of the consuls of the year, without doubt Q. Metellus Nepos, suggested some proposal prejudicial to Cicero's interests, which was countered by an *obnuntiatio* served by the tribune P. Sestius.[a]

3. In July 57 the consul P. Lentulus Spinther submitted to the Senate a proposal for the restoration of Cicero which was passed by 415 votes to Clodius' solitary dissent.[b] Cicero (*Pro Sestio*, 129 ; *Post reditum in senatu*, 27) says that on the next day the Senate passed the following decree : " that no one should watch for signs from the heavens, nor attempt to stop proceedings ; and that anyone who did otherwise should be deemed a destroyer of the constitution." Such a *senatus consultum*, the wording of which corresponds with the wording used in Clodius' law, could have been passed only if the *lex Aelia Fufia* was still being fully observed. Thus the repeal for a specific purpose of the *lex Aelia Fufia* secured not only Cicero's exile but also his return.[c] The repeal was temporary only, for, as we shall see, the *lex Aelia Fufia* was in force in 54 B.C.

4. In November 57 B.C. Milo, when tribune, employed *obnuntiatio* in his attempts to bring Clodius

still use *obnuntiatio* against a legislative proposal. Weinstock (*op. cit.* p. 219) is more convincing when he accepts the emendation *praetor* as certain and connects the word with Appius Claudius, Clodius' brother, the praetor who led the opposition to Fabricius' bill.

[a] *Pro Sestio*, 79.

[b] *Pro Sestio*, 129 ; *Post reditum in senatu*, 26.

[c] Weinstock, *op. cit.* pp. 218–220, accepts as accurate the statement of Dio Cassius, xxxviii. 13. 6 that Clodius' law was expressly intended to facilitate proceedings against Cicero.

to trial before he could be saved from prosecution by being elected aedile.[a]

5. In the summer of 54 B.C. Cicero informed Atticus (*Epp. ad Att.* iv. 16. 5) that C. Cato, a tribune of 56 B.C., had been acquitted when prosecuted for a breach of the *lex Licinia Iunia*, and that he would be acquitted on a charge under the *lex Fufia*. Thus the *lex (Aelia) Fufia* and the *lex Licinia Iunia* (which, as has been suggested, may have come under Clodius' ban in 58 B.C.) were still in force in 54 B.C.[b]

6. Cicero (*Epp. ad Att.* iv. 17. 4 ; *Epp. ad Quintum fratrem*, iii. 3. 2) twice refers to the activity of tribunes in the late summer of 54 B.C. in obstructing the elections for 53 B.C. by the daily service of *obnuntiationes*.

It would seem, therefore, possible to conclude that Clodius' repeal of the *lex Aelia Fufia* was, after it had served its immediate purpose by removing legal obstacles to measures for the banishment of Cicero, disregarded, both for elections and for legislation.

In Weinstock's view, the Senate instituted an inquiry during Cicero's exile. The College of Augurs, after considering the evidence of Bibulus, given at a *contio* convened by Clodius, expressed the opinion that, since Clodius' adoption into a plebeian family by P. Fonteius through a *lex curiata* had been made invalid by Bibulus' *obnuntiatio*,[c] he was in law no tri-

[a] Cicero, *Epp. ad Att.* iv. 3. 3-5. See page 311, note *b*, above.
[b] McDonald, *op. cit.* p. 179, n. 3, identifies the *lex Fufia* with a *lex Fufia iudiciaria*. Weinstock, *op. cit.* p. 220, n. 30, disproves this by an apt reference to a collocation of the *lex Licinia Iunia* and the *lex Aelia* (*Fufia*) in 59 B.C., in Cicero, *Epp. ad Att.* ii. 9. 1.
[c] Cicero, *De domo*, 40-41 ; *De haruspicum responsis*, 48.

bune and his legislation was therefore invalid. But, on this hypothesis, it is difficult to see why Clodius' three other laws apparently remained in force until his law restricting the powers of the censors was repealed in 52 B.C. by Q. Metellus Scipio, and until his laws for the revival and increase of the *collegia* and for the provision of free corn were, in the former case, repealed and, in the latter, amended by Julius Caesar as dictator.

In conclusion, brief reference should be made to an incident in 44 B.C. which may suggest that M. Antonius as consul recognized the validity of Clodius' repeal of the *lex Aelia Fufia*. In that year Caesar, in view of his proposed absence in Parthia, planned to resign his consulship in favour of Dolabella who was to be elected *consul suffectus* as colleague of Antonius. Antonius, privately at feud with Dolabella, made it known that he would oppose the election. One interpretation of the relevant passage from Cicero,[a] which has been variously explained,[b] is that Antonius, reproached by Cicero for obstructing Dolabella's election not in his capacity as a consul but in that of an augur, chose to act as an augur because action as a consul (by *servare de caelo* and *obnuntiatio*) was forbidden " *per leges.*" Weinstock (*loc. cit.*), following Mommsen, sees no alternative but to suppose that by " *leges* " Clodius' law of 58 B.C. is meant, and assumes, though he admits that supporting evidence does not exist, that Julius Caesar brought Clodius' law again into force. Yet, in the same year, Antonius refused

---

[a] *Phil.* ii. 79-84.
[b] Weinstock, *op. cit.* pp. 221-222 ; McDonald, *op. cit.* pp. 168-171 ; Greenidge, *Classical Review*, vii, p. 160 ; Denniston, *Cicero, Phil. i and ii*, pp. 184-186.

to hold elections for the censorship on the ground,
Cicero asserts, that he feared a tribunician *obnuntiatio* ! [a]

The general conclusion suggested by these examples of the exploitation of the *auspicia* must be
that at the close of the Republic Roman politicians
showed themselves as adept as they were unscrupulous in the use and abuse of religious ritual, putting
on it whatever interpretation seemed to meet the demands of any particular situation.[b]

VII. P. Sestius

Our knowledge of the career and personality of
P. Sestius is derived mainly from Cicero's speech in
his defence and from over twenty references to him
in Cicero's *Letters*. His father's progress in the *cursus
honorum* did not go beyond the tribunate. His tenure
of a quaestorship in 63 B.C. suggests for the date of
his birth some year in the mid-90's. He married
twice. His first wife, daughter of an otherwise unknown C. Albinus, bore him a son and a daughter.
On her death he married Cornelia, a daughter of
L. Cornelius Scipio Asiaticus, a Marian who, when
consul in 83 B.C., was defeated by Sulla in Campania
and withdrew to Massilia, where he died in exile.

After his military tribunate Sestius was a quaestor
in 63 B.C. Reference has already been made to his
assignment to C. Antonius, his commander as consul,
and to the services which he rendered to Cicero ;
also to his quaestorship under Antonius as proconsul
of Macedonia. To the end of Sestius' first year in

[a] *Phil.* ii. 98-99.
[b] R. E. Smith, *The Failure of the Roman Republic*, p. 134.

Macedonia (62 B.C.) belongs Cicero's only surviving letter to him (*Epp. ad Fam.* v. 6.). Its topics are Cicero's promise to plead for an extension of his quaestorship in Macedonia ; an admission that Cicero's recent purchase from Crassus of a mansion on the Palatine had plunged him heavily into debt ; and a statement that he had defended Antonius in the Senate on some charge of which we know nothing.

In the summer of 58 B.C. Sestius was elected tribune and was soon busily helping in Pompey's campaign for the restoration of Cicero. Cicero's letter from Thessalonica early in August 58 B.C. to his brother Quintus (*Epp. ad Quintum fratrem,* i. 4) praises Sestius as *officiosissimus* and *amicissimus*, but on 4 October Cicero wrote to Atticus (*Epp. ad Att.* iii. 20. 3) criticizing a bill which Sestius had prepared for his restoration as " lacking in sufficient regard for my position and in sufficient care." Later in the year and before he entered upon his tribunate (10 December), Sestius visited Caesar in Cisalpine Gaul to intercede for Cicero, but with results which were not, apparently, immediately encouraging.[a]

The great services rendered in 57 B.C. by Sestius and his fellow-tribune Milo in crushing Clodius' opposition to measures for Cicero's recall have already been described (pp. 18-21). After his acquittal in 56 B.C. we next hear of him in 52 B.C. The fact that Sestius was in 49 B.C. invested with *imperium* as governor of Cilicia suggests that he was an ex-praetor. If so, we are compelled to conjecture the year of his praetorship, for our sources are silent. 55 B.C., which has been tentatively suggested, seems too near the

[a] *Pro Sestio*, 71.

year of his tribunate. 53 B.C. is more likely, but
meagre evidence makes certainty unattainable.[a]

In the autumn of 50 B.C. Sestius, in some semi-
official capacity, was on a visit to the province of
Cilicia,[b] of which Cicero had just relinquished the
government. As he seems to have taken over a
sum of money which Cicero had saved from his
allowance as governor, and had deposited with L.
Mescinius Rufus, one of his quaestors, it is probable
that Sestius had been marked out to succeed Cicero
as governor. Sestius had, of course, no *imperium*
during this visit to Cilicia, for in the political *impasse*
of 50 B.C. no provincial appointments were made. In
January 49 B.C. Sestius was back again in Italy, but

[a] Cicero defended Sestius (*Epp. ad Att.* xiii. 49. 1) on some
charge under the special laws (*de vi* and *de ambitu*) passed
by Pompey at the beginning of his sole consulship in 52 B.C.
If Sestius was prosecuted *de vi* in connexion with the rioting
which followed the murder of Clodius (and one would
naturally expect to find him in trouble again with Milo),
such a prosecution provides no evidence of date for his
praetorship. If, however, we may assume that he was in-
dicted *de ambitu* (as Appian states in *Bell. Civ.* ii. 2. 24,
although the possibility should not be excluded that he is
confusing this trial of Sestius with that of 56 B.C.), his praetorship may perhaps be dated to 53 B.C. If so, Sestius may have
been charged with corruption in an election to a praetorship
for the remainder of 53 B.C. at the elections held as late as
July in that year (Dio Cassius, xl. 45). A. C. Clark (Cicero,
Pro Milone, p. xii), has shown that it is exceedingly doubtful
that Pompey's law *de ambitu* embraced any offence committed earlier than 53 B.C. This would exclude a candidature
by Sestius for a praetorship of an earlier year. Broughton,
The Magistrates of the Roman Republic, ii, p. 621, says
" Praetor by 54 ? *or* 50 ? " We must assume that Cicero's
defence of Sestius was again successful.

[b] Cicero, *Epp. ad Fam.* v. 20. 5; Tyrrell and Purser, *The
Correspondence of Cicero*, vol. iv, pp. 11-12.

since Cicero says in a letter of 3 March 49 [a] that Sestius then had the *imperium*, it is probable that he and other governors obtained their *imperium* through the Pompeian Senate sometime between 7 January, when the *senatus consultum de re publica defendenda* was passed, and the end of February. Plutarch [b] says that Sestius was appointed governor of Cilicia and that M. Brutus sailed out with him as a legate.

As has been said, Sestius was back in Italy from Cilicia in January 49 B.C. He was one of Pompey's associates in the early days of the Civil War. On 23 January L. Julius Caesar, a son of one of Caesar's legates, arrived at Teanum from Ariminum with an offer from Caesar which he presented to the Pompeians : that Caesar would disarm if Pompey would dismiss his Italian levies and withdraw to Spain. Pompey and the others accepted Caesar's terms in principle, but, as a preliminary, required him to withdraw his garrisons and retire to Gaul. To Cicero's surprise, Sestius was commissioned by Pompey to compose and send this important communication. His comment was [c] " I blamed Pompey for having entrusted our friend Sestius with the writing of a despatch so important and certain to come into everybody's hands, though he has an admirable style of his own. And, true enough, I never read anything more ' Sestian.' " Further testimony to Sestius' failings as a literary man [d] is provided by the celebrated remark of Catullus,[e] who said that he caught such a cold and cough from

---

[a] *Epp. ad Att.* viii. 15. 3. See also xi. 7. 1, with Tyrrell and Purser's note, *op. cit.* vol. iv, pp. 293-294.

[b] *Brutus,* 4. [c] *Epp. ad Att.* vii. 17. 2.

[d] *Epp. ad Att.* vii. 32. 1. [e] Catullus, 44.

hearing Sestius read a speech of his own composition at a dinner-party, that he was obliged to retire to his place at Tibur for a change of air.

Sestius remained a Pompeian till Pharsalus, but he then joined Caesar and served under Caesar's legate Cn. Domitius Calvinus in his unsuccessful campaign in Asia Minor against Pharnaces of Pontus.[a]

The picture of Sestius that can be drawn from Cicero's letters is little more than a sketch in outline. But the lines are firmly drawn. He had his failings. He was obtuse,[b] of difficult temper [c] (*morosus*), a maker of frigid jests [d] ; and he may possibly have had a reputation for liking to entertain notabilities.[e] Yet he possessed qualities that made for a steady friendship between Cicero and himself. The tie that was first formed between the two men in the year of Cicero's consulship and Sestius' quaestorship was never broken. In 58 B.C., as we have seen (p. 323), Cicero called him *officiosissimus* and *amicissimus*, and fourteen years later, in October 44 B.C., Cicero wrote of him as *Sestium nostrum, optimum quidem illum virum nostrique amantissimum*.

In *dignitas*, at any rate, his son, L. Sestius, who appeared in court at the trial in 56 B.C., outstripped his father. Though a staunch Republican, who served with Horace under M. Brutus in the campaign of

---

[a] *Bellum Alexandrinum*, 34.
[b] *Epp. ad Brutum*, ii. 5. 4 (v. 4 L.C.L.).
[c] *Epp. ad Quintum fratrem*, ii. 4. 1.
[d] *Epp. ad Fam.* vii. 32. 1.
[e] *Epp. ad Att.* xiii. 2. 2. Cicero jocularly calls him a *parochus publicus* (" State Receptionist ") who entertained Ariarathes, brother of Ariobarzanes III of Cappadocia, when on a visit to Rome in 45 B.C.

Philippi, he later became an adherent of the new regime. Horace dedicated to him *Odes*, i. 4. As a significant gesture to Republicanism, L. Sestius was appointed *consul suffectus* in succession to Augustus when he resigned on 1 July 23 B.C. the consulship which he had held since 31 B.C.

VIII. P. VATINIUS

P. VATINIUS was of Sabine descent. There is mentioned in an incident of the year 168 B.C. a certain P. Vatinius of Reate who may have been an ancestor.[a] Beginning his political career as a *novus homo* and a *popularis*, he was a friend of C. Cornelius, a tribune of 67 B.C., an energetic and successful reformer, whom in 65 B.C. Cicero defended against Optimate attacks. In 64 B.C. he was last on the list of those elected quaestors for 63. Cicero, as consul, posted him for duty at Puteoli, where his behaviour, if we believe Cicero, was so irregular and violent that he was assaulted by the inhabitants. In 62 B.C. he was on the staff of C. Cosconius, governor of Further Spain. Possibly, even then, his association with Caesar had begun, for he travelled to his province by a circuitous route and spent some time in the kingdom of Hiempsal, client-king of Numidia, in whose affairs Caesar was interested.[b] Moreover, he became connected with Caesar by marriage, for he took the hand of Antonia, a daughter of M. Antonius (Creticus), who when praetor in 74 B.C. began unsuccessful operations against piracy, and of Julia, a daughter of L. Julius Caesar, consul in 90 B.C. His tribunate in

[a] Cicero, *De natura deorum*, ii. 6.
[b] Suetonius, *Div. Iul.* 71.

CICERO

59 B.C. was notorious for its complete defiance of the
authority of the Senate and of the practice of the
constitution : he at once declared that he would disregard the pronouncements of the augurs and the
laws regulating religious obstruction and legislative
procedure.[a] At the beginning of his consulship
Caesar attempted to win over the Senate to his
agrarian proposal for pensioning Pompey's veterans,
but, on meeting determined opposition, he allowed
Vatinius' methods, reinforced by some violence, to dis-
pose of Bibulus' *obnuntiationes* and other opposition,
so that Caesar's first agrarian law, the *lex Iulia de
agro Campano*, and the rest of the *acta* of the year,
whether in the name of Caesar or of Vatinius, were
passed in defiance of what Cicero called the " safe-
guards of the constitution." [b]

Vatinius' most important service to Caesar was
the *lex Vatinia de Caesaris provincia* which conferred
on him his governorship, with special privileges, of
Cisalpine Gaul and Illyricum. He also passed a *lex
de alternis consiliis reiciendis*, which may have allowed
defence and prosecution to challenge alternately not
individual jurors but the *decuriae*, or groups of jurors
(*senatores, equites, tribuni aerarii*) assigned by a praetor
for a trial.[c] Among *multas alias leges*,[d] which Cicero
ascribes to Vatinius, were probably, for Pompey, the
ratification of his settlement of the Near East, and,
for the *publicani* and their patron Crassus, the remis-

---

[a] The *leges Aelia Fufia, Licinia Iunia, Caecilia Didia*,
Cicero, *Epp. ad Att.* ii. 9. 1.
[b] Cicero, *Epp. ad Att.* ii. 9. 1 : " omnia remedia reipublicae."
[c] *In Vatinium*, 27.
[d] *In Vatinium*, 27.

sion of one-third of the purchase-price of their Asiatic tax-contract.[a]

Vatinius was associated also with two episodes in the year of his tribunate which are not easily to be explained. One was a plot for the assassination of Pompey, the authors of which were alleged by a professional spy called L. Vettius to be leading members of the aristocracy. If we may believe Cicero, Vatinius ordered Vettius, after he had given contradictory evidence before the Senate and at a *contio*, to be imprisoned and strangled. On its easiest interpretation this plot was probably invented by Vettius as a private speculation, in the hope of receiving from the Triumvirate a reward for the disclosure of a conspiracy.[b] The second was the appearance of Vatinius in a dark toga at a funeral feast given by Q. Arrius, apparently a deplorable breach of etiquette. This may perhaps be explained as a protest by Vatinius on behalf of Caesar against a *supplicatio*, or public thanksgiving for the quelling in 61 B.C. of a revolt of the Allobroges by C. Pomptinus, when propraetor of Gallia Narbonensis.[c]

For the considerable services which he rendered to Caesar in his tribunate Vatinius did not go unrewarded. In the winter of 57–56 B.C. Caesar is said to have declared at Aquileia that " Vatinius had done nothing in his tribunate without being paid for it." [d] There was some talk of electing him to the

---

[a] Pocock, *In Vatinium*, pp. 161-179.

[b] Cicero, *Epp. ad Att.* ii. 24 ; *In Vatinium*, 24-26 ; *C.A.H.* ix, pp. 520-521 ; Pocock, *op. cit.* pp. 183-185.

[c] Pomptinus, however, triumphed *De Allobrogibus* on 2 November 54 B.C. *C.I.L.* i². 2, p. 50.

[d] *In Vatinium*, 38.

College of Augurs,[a] an honour which he actually received eleven years later, in 48 B.C.

Early in 58 B.C. Vatinius was in Rome and was associated with Clodius in the manœuvres that led to Cicero's banishment. He then left Rome for service as a legate under Caesar in Gaul, but returned voluntarily to face a prosecution under the *lex Licinia Iunia*, which he had possibly contravened in his tribunate by his ratification of Pompey's settlement of the Near East. The actual charge was, presumably, one of *maiestas*, and the prosecutor seems to have been C. Licinius Calvus Macer, poet and orator, a friend of Catullus. An appeal by Vatinius to tribunes to help him to deny the validity of the prosecution was answered so effectively by Clodius that the court was broken up and the prosecution was not renewed. As a candidate for an aedileship, probably of 57 B.C., Vatinius was defeated.[b] We hear nothing of him in 57 B.C. He may have returned to his post under Caesar in Gaul, but in February 56 B.C. he helped Clodius in his prosecution of Milo for breach of the peace. On the acquittal of Sestius, Vatinius was threatened with a new prosecution, again by Licinius Calvus, but nothing was done, since Vatinius, if he had been formally charged, could not have stood for a praetorship of 55 B.C. The

---

'Cicero, *Epp. ad Att.* ii. 9. 2 ; *In Vatinium*, 19, 20.

Presumably at elections held in 58 B.C. although our sources are silent. The elections for the aedileships of 56 B.C. were not held till 20 January 56 B.C., when Clodius was elected an aedile. Cicero, *Epp. ad Quintum fratrem*, ii. 2. 2. Caesar's observation, made at Aquileia in the winter 57–56 B.C. on Vatinius' loss of office, must refer to his defeat for an aedileship of 57 B.C. See *Pro Sestio*, 114 ; *In Vatinium*, 16, 38.

year 56 B.C. having closed without elections, through the veto of a tribune C. Cato employed by Pompey and Crassus, 55 B.C. began with an *interregnum*. Either in January or early in February Pompey and Crassus secured by violence election to their second consulships ; they were in office by 11 February.[a] At the elections to praetorships, adjourned by unscrupulous methods, bribery and violence won for Vatinius a praetorship over the head of Cato.[b]

In 54 B.C., after his praetorship, Vatinius was prosecuted by Licinius Calvus and successfully defended by Cicero, probably in August. This was in token of Cicero's submission to the Triumvirate.[c] Caesar pressed Cicero to undertake the defence of Vatinius. Cicero says that Pompey had reconciled Vatinius to him immediately after his election to the praetorship, although Cicero had violently attacked his candidature in the Senate, not so much, he claims, out of animosity to Vatinius, as from devotion to Cato, his defeated rival. Cicero also mentions a further motive : the favour shown by the Optimates towards Clodius rankled with him and induced him to play off his own new client Vatinius against their protégé Clodius.

The defence of Vatinius, Cicero says, was easy.[d] The charge was probably one of *ambitus*, to which Vatinius was clearly liable as a result of a gladiatorial show which he gave as a candidate for the

---

[a] Cicero, *Epp. ad Quintum fratrem*, ii. 7. 3.
[b] Plutarch, *Cato Minor*, 42. The scandal of their election became proverbial. Seneca, *Epist.* 118. 4.
[c] Cicero, *Epp. ad Fam.* i. 9. 19. Asconius, p. 18 (Clark).
[d] Cicero, *Epp. ad Quintum fratrem*, ii. 16. 3. See also *Epp. ad Fam.* v. 9. 1.

CICERO

praetorship,[a] and of the corruption accompanying his election as praetor in 55 B.C. In the days of Tacitus [b] there existed at least three speeches of Calvus against Vatinius. Of these the second was probably delivered at the trial in 54 B.C., for the fragments surviving in the form of quotations seem mostly to refer to that year.

Our knowledge of Vatinius' later career, mainly military, begins in 51 B.C., when as a legate of Caesar in Gaul he shared with M. Antonius and C. Trebonius the command of four legions posted in Belgic Gaul.[c] His name does not recur till early in 48 B.C., when the troops of Caesar and Pompey were fraternizing on the banks of the river Apsus south of Dyrrhachium. He tried the effect of his vigorous oratory on Pompey's men, till Labienus intervened.[d] Soon afterwards he appears as in command at Brundisium, which he ably defended against the attacks of the Pompeian, D. Laelius,[e] and where, after Pharsalus, he showed much kindness to Cicero,[f] then a fugitive Pompeian. In the same year he was elected to fill a vacancy in the College of Augurs caused by the death of Appius Claudius Pulcher (consul 54 B.C.), the brother of Clodius.[g]

Five chapters in the *Bellum Alexandrinum* (43-47) show the energy and resource of Vatinius when in command at Brundisium early in 47 B.C. After the defeats and death of Gabinius in Illyria late in

[a] *Pro Sestio*, 134-135.
[b] Tacitus, *Dialogus*, 21.
[c] Caesar, *De bello gallico*, viii. 46.
[d] Caesar, *De bello civili*, iii. 19.
[e] Caesar, *De bello civili*, iii. 100.
[f] Cicero, *Epp. ad Att.* xi. 5. 4 ; 9. 2.
[g] Cicero, *Epp. ad Fam.* v. 10. 2.

48 B.C., M. Octavius, a Pompeian admiral, appeared to have Caesar's forces, then under Q. Cornificius, at his mercy. But Vatinius at Brundisium improvised a fleet, manned by veterans who had been left there sick, and answered Cornificius' urgent call for help by setting out to challenge M. Octavius, who was blockading Epidaurum, off the coast of Illyria. Octavius then sailed northwards and at the island of Tauris (Torcoli) was defeated by Vatinius' bold tactics. Cornificius was thus free to return to his task of pacifying Illyria. Vatinius returned to Italy in triumph and, as a reward, was made by Caesar *consul suffectus* for the last few days of the year 47 B.C.[a]

In 46 or 45 B.C. Caesar sent him with three legions to a command in Illyria, during which he made some successful expeditions against the Dalmatians. Vatinius has given us some account of these in his two and a half letters to Cicero which have come down to us. Blunt and amusing, they are an admirable pointer to his character.[b] He was then on the best of terms with Cicero. For his successes he was saluted *imperator* by his soldiers, and in 45 B.C. a *supplicatio* was decreed in his honour. In 43 B.C. he was again on the east coast of the Adriatic and held out for some time against the Republicans at Dyrrhachium, but finally surrendered to M. Brutus. Nevertheless, on his return to Rome the Triumvirs allowed him to triumph for his exploits in Dalmatia.

---

[a] Cicero's comment on the brevity of Vatinius' consulship has been preserved in Macrobius (ii. 3. 5). Asked by Vatinius why he did not call on him, Cicero replied: " I meant to call on you when you were consul, but I was overtaken by night."   [b] Cicero, *Epp. ad Fam.* v. 9, 10a, 10.

CICERO

On 31 July 42 B.C.[a] he entered Rome as *imperator* and celebrated his triumph. His name then disappears from our sources.

The personality of Vatinius has received from scholars an assessment which has gained in balance and judgment with the passing of time.[b] Virtually the last of the line of tribunes founded by the Gracchi, Vatinius has left a record which within its limits is not to be despised. A *novus homo*, he possessed qualities which soon recommended him to Julius Caesar : ability, determination, loyalty, and a measure of unscrupulousness. He is known to us chiefly for his services to Caesar during his tribunate and for Cicero's abuse in the *In Vatinium*. The law bearing his name, which was the basis of Caesar's Gallic command, is one of the landmarks in the transition at Rome from a republican to an imperial system of government. Cicero's comprehensive denunciations of him in the *In Vatinium* are a notable example of the length to which abuse, conventional and rarely taken at face value, could go in ancient oratory. Vatinius was certainly intensely disliked for his peculiarities by young Romans like Calvus and Catullus.[c] But there is no evidence that Cicero hated him as he hated Piso and Gabinius who had sold him to Clodius ; nor that he feared him in any way. In later years the two men were on most friendly terms. In 48 B.C. Cicero, in misery at Brun-

[a] *C.I.L.* i². p. 50.

[b] Tyrrell and Purser, *The Correspondence of Cicero*, vol. v (2nd Edition, 1915), pp. xciv-cii ; Pocock, *In Vatinium* (1926), pp. 29-45 ; Syme, *The Roman Revolution* (1939), pp. 66, 149, 150, 152.

[c] Catullus, 14 : " odio Vatiniano."

disium, could write [a] : " Vatinius would do anything if he could only find out in what way he could assist me " ; and, some three years later, Vatinius in Illyria, feigning horror and amazement at a seemingly preposterous request made to him by Cicero, yet expressed his willingness to help : " But, though you ask me, my dear Cicero, what can I do ? Upon my word, I do wish to carry out any command you lay upon me." [b]

With the exception of Gabinius and Labienus, Vatinius had the best military record, when in high command, of the tribunes of the late Republic : resource and energy shown, despite infirmity and disabilities, in naval warfare against the Pompeians in the Adriatic ; successes in Illyria ; resistance to M. Brutus at Dyrrhachium. The rewards of a consulship, a *supplicatio*, and a triumph were not ill-deserved.

A notable feature in his character was his robust and irrepressible good humour : he could joke about his feet and the glands of his neck [c] ; he could refuse to allow Clodius to rank above him as the biggest rascal in Rome [d] ; he could interrupt his prosecutor Licinius Calvus with a cry of praise : " I ask you, gentlemen, is it right that because this man is eloquent, I should be condemned ? " [e] Convention and political passion can explain much of the evidence on which Vatinius' reputation as one of the best hated men of his day was based. If he made money out of political life, so did his Optimate enemies, and

[a] *Epp. ad Att.* xi. 5. 4.
[b] *Epp. ad Fam.* v. 10.
[c] Seneca, *de Const. Sap.* 17 ; Quintilian, vi. 3. 77
[d] Cicero, *In Vatinium*, 41.
[e] Seneca, *Contr.* vii. 4 (19). 6.

to a greater degree. He was no political weather-vane, for he remained consistently loyal to Caesar. Nothing is known to his personal discredit, if we discount the mystery of the *affaire* Vettius. May not the verdict that he was " a vulgar agitator " [a] be now replaced by a more charitable interpretation ?

IX. Summary of the *Pro Sestio*

§§ 1-5. Since loyal citizens are now being attacked by disloyal in the courts of justice, it is my duty to defend them, and especially P. Sestius, a most active helper in my restoration from exile. As Q. Hortensius has dealt so fully with the charge itself, I will undertake a general defence of my client and begin with his career before his tribunate.

§§ 6-14. My client's family life reveals his domestic virtues. He displayed exemplary conduct as a military tribune. When quaestor (63 B.C.), though assigned to my colleague C. Antonius, he rendered me valuable aid against the Catilinarians not only by securing Capua but also by service in Rome. He then served under Antonius in the campaign when Catiline was defeated, and in his governorship of Macedonia (62–60 B.C.). Although Hortensius has spoken so admirably of Sestius' tribunate (57 B.C.), I also must give an account of it. If I attack some persons with asperity, I will be guided by my client's interests rather than my own indignation.

§§ 15-24. The troubles of the year (58 B.C.) before Sestius' tribunate arose from the transfer by a *lex curiata*, for which a consul (Caesar, 59 B.C.) was responsible, of P. Clodius into a plebeian family so as to

[a] Tyrrell and Purser, *op. cit.* p. cii.

qualify him for a tribunate. Clodius, breaking his word to Pompey, won over the consuls Gabinius and Piso to support his outrageous designs against me by a compact to procure them special provinces. Gabinius and Piso were a disgrace to the consulship : the former a penniless rake bent on public plunder ; the latter a disgusting voluptuary masquerading as a philosopher.

§§ 25-35. Clodius then brought forward bills to ruin me and to assign a province to each consul. The consuls derided all appeals and prohibited the wearing of mourning which senators had assumed in sympathy with me. An *eques*, L. Aelius Lamia, one of my loyal supporters, was arbitrarily banished by Gabinius. This preliminary narrative, even if tedious, is not irrelevant. With the support of the consuls, won over by the bargain about their provinces, Clodius then repealed the *lex Aelia Fufia* and other legal means of obstructing legislation, enrolled slaves and roughs, and converted the Temple of Castor into a stronghold. Though violence reigned I refrained, for certain reasons, from resistance.

§§ 36-52. My motives for leaving Rome justify me against a charge of cowardice. As I was in a far stronger position than Q. Metellus Numidicus who, having to face the power of Marius and Saturninus, preferred exile to civil war (100 B.C.), I could have overcome Gabinius, Piso and Clodius. But I was deterred by Clodius' boast that he was supported by Pompey, Crassus and Caesar who, in fear for their measures of the previous year (59 B.C.), did not wish to estrange him. Crassus and Pompey advised me to appeal to the consuls ; Caesar and his army were outside the gates of Rome. If, therefore, I

had crushed Clodius like a second Catiline, civil war
would have broken out. Rather than endanger the
State by my presence, I chose to yield. I should
have failed in my public duty if I had wantonly
sacrificed my life. Just as my death would have
been a triumph for the enemies of disorder, so my
restoration meant victory for the cause of order,
peace and the prestige of the State.

§§ 53-67. To turn to my subject. On the day of
my departure laws were passed to banish me and
to assign provinces to the consuls. My family were
persecuted ; my property was looted by the exultant
consuls ; my house was burnt. The consuls acquiesced
in the passing of other monstrous laws under which
the censors lost power, political clubs were sanctioned,
corn was issued free, Syria instead of Cilicia was
assigned to Gabinius as his province, all laws and
rules relating to ritual observances and legislative
procedure were repealed. Abroad, Brogitarus of
Galatia was made priest of Cybele at Pessinus ;
condemned exiles were restored to Byzantium ; an
inoffensive ruler and ally, King Ptolemy of Cyprus,
was to be dethroned, scandalous treatment compared
with our past generosity to enemies like Antiochus
the Great and Tigranes of Armenia. The appointment of Cato to annex Ptolemy's kingdom was a
means of banishing an outspoken antagonist and a
vain attempt to tarnish his integrity. The consuls'
irresponsibility in failing to protest against these
measures is in keeping with their neglect to save
from illegal banishment such a servant of the State
as myself. And far worse would have followed, had
not Pompey returned to public life after an absence
and at length declared himself against Clodius.

§§ 68-71. A movement for my restoration then began. A proposal to recall me, made by L. Ninnius (on 1 June 58 B.C.), was unanimously accepted by the Senate, but vetoed by Aelius Ligus. The Senate refused to transact any business till the consuls had proposed my recall, but Piso and Gabinius pretended that Clodius' law prevented them from doing so. An attempt by Clodius to assassinate Pompey forced him to withdraw from public life. The elections (for 57 B.C.) were in my favour. On 29 October eight of the tribunes announced a proposal for my recall which was welcomed by P. Lentulus, consul-elect, but vetoed by Aelius Ligus. P. Sestius, tribune-elect, visited Gaul to intercede with Caesar on my behalf.

§§ 71-85. Sestius entered on his tribunate (57 B.C.) after the consuls had left for their disasters in Macedonia and Syria. In the Senate on 1 January, with the consul Lentulus as my supporter and his colleague, Metellus Nepos, at least no longer as my enemy, L. Aurelius Cotta (consul 65 B.C.) expressed the opinion that a resolution of the Senate would be sufficient to secure my recall, but Pompey advised that the Assembly should confirm such a resolution. This resolution would have been passed unanimously but for the opposition at that and later meetings of the tribune Serranus. On 23 January a force of armed slaves and gladiators also, in the employment of Sestius' accusers, broke up an Assembly to which Q. Fabricius was preparing to submit a proposal for my recall. My brother all but lost his life in that murderous riot. Sestius was not then attended by a bodyguard. Since Fabricius' bill could have been opposed by constitutional means, this use of gladiators and assassins was criminal. Later, in the Temple of Castor, Sestius was grievously wounded when serving on the consul (Metellus Nepos) a notice of *obnuntiatio*. Is Sestius who, had he then been killed, would have fallen in the defence of the State, now on trial for breach of the peace because he is alive ? Sestius, accused of raising a bodyguard, did so only when it was necessary. Compare with Sestius' action the violence of Clodius and Sestius' other accusers since my banishment : the freeing by Serranus after their arrest by Milo of the gladiators from the escort of a praetor (Appius Claudius), who had confessed to the Senate their deed (of 23 January) ; the wounding of Sestius ; Clodius' attack on the house of Milo.

§§ 86-95. If Milo, who gallantly took up the cause of the State in working for my recall, has actually been commended by Sestius' prosecutor for his conduct when Clodius attacked his house, has not Sestius an equally good case against his charge ? Milo did not at first retaliate against Clodius' violent attacks but endeavoured to prosecute him ; in vain, for certain magistrates refused a trial. Milo, therefore, denied a legal remedy, enrolled a bodyguard. Why is Milo commended but Sestius condemned for such an action ? Why is self-defence by Milo construed as violence by Sestius ? The evolution of society shows that if law does not prevail violence must rule. Milo, unprotected by the law, raised a bodyguard in self-defence. Reflect on the excesses which Gabinius and Piso are now committing in their provinces, while men like Milo and Sestius are on trial here. Clodius, now an aedile, is prosecuting for violence the man who curbed his own violence. Milo, who retaliated only in self-defence, has been denied by the Senate an opportunity of prosecuting Clodius. With the Senate seemingly deserting its own party and my own defenders in jeopardy as compared with my enemies, it is not surprising that the prosecutor has inquired where our " Breed of Aristocrats " was to be found. I propose to answer that question, for the benefit alike of the rising generation and of my client's case.

§§ 96-105. Two classes of citizens have always played a part in our public life : *populares* (" Friends of the People "), who sought to win the favour of the masses by all that they said or did ; *optimates* (" Aristocrats "), who aimed for the approval of the " Best Men." The " Best Men," who are many in number, include the leaders of public policy, their supporters, and those qualified for the Senate ; town and country Italians ; men of business ; even freedmen. They are untainted by crime, debt, revolution or vice. Their interests are served by the " Aristocrats " whose aim is *cum dignitate otium* (" Peace with honour "). " Peace with honour " is founded on the time-honoured institutions of our rule at home and abroad, religious, political, judicial, military, financial. To uphold these, the Optimates must contend with criminals and revolutionaries, always ready for a change of government or even anarchy. My own experience shows what skill and vigilance are needed for so difficult a task. M. Aemilius Scaurus, Q. Metellus Numidicus and Q. Lutatius Catulus, worthy examples for us, were great Optimates and defenders of the State in difficult times when the work of the *populares*, such as the ballot-law of L. Cassius (137 B.C.), the land-law of Ti. Gracchus (133 B.C.) and the corn-law of C. Gracchus (123 B.C.), was often

341

opposed to the public interest. But now, since we enjoy " Peace with honour," there is no reason for any clash of interest between the masses and their chosen leaders. Whereas the Gracchi, Saturninus or other *populares* enjoyed a position based on genuine support or even affection, revolutionaries can now raise a following only by bribery. The opponents of those earlier popular leaders, highly esteemed by the Senate and all good citizens, were able, despite their unpopularity with the masses, to exert decisive influence.

§§ 106-108. Meetings, Assemblies, plays and gladiatorial shows make it clear that all of us, save hirelings, are at one in our political views. Clodius' meetings, packed with his hired rabble, cannot be compared with a meeting held for me by Lentulus as consul, and addressed by Pompey and himself.

§§ 109-112. Assemblies for the passing of laws tell the same tale. Although laws are often passed when scarcely five voters are present for each tribe, did one single citizen vote for Clodius' law against me ? But when the *comitia centuriata* sanctioned my recall, did anyone declare that he had not been present and voting ? Which of the two, then, was the " popular " cause ? Can the word " popular " be applied to L. Gellius Poplicola (a witness against Sestius), a disgrace to his half-brother the consul Philippus (56 B.C.) and a contemptible person who led a gang of hirelings when Clodius banished me ?

§§ 113-114. Of late, elections also reveal the feelings of the Roman People towards certain *populares*. Among the tribunes of a recent year (59 B.C.) three were by no means *populares*, Cn. Domitius, Q. Ancharius, C. Fannius. Of these, Domitius and

Ancharius are now praetors (56 B.C.), and Fannius is confidently expected to be elected to that magistracy. Two of the tribunes of that year were *populares*, C. Alfius and P. Vatinius, of whom Alfius failed to be elected praetor, and Vatinius was ignominiously defeated for an aedileship (for 57 B.C.).

§§ 115-127. At plays and gladiatorial games a hired claque sometimes starts a feeble demonstration, but it is easy to see what the honest part of the audience does, and what kind of citizen receives genuine applause. Clodius never attended the magnificent games given by M. Aemilius Scaurus when aedile (58 B.C.). Last year (57 B.C.) he appeared once only at shows in the theatre (probably at the Ludi Apollinares, 6-13 July), just when the Senate in the Temple of Honos and Virtus was passing decrees most complimentary to me. Although he was then a candidate for the aedileship he received a most hostile reception, but the whole Senate, and the consul Lentulus especially, were loudly applauded when they came in. Lines from *The Pretender*, of L. Afranius, which was being played, were taken as bearing on Clodius and our times.

As I have undertaken to teach our youth who are the " Best Men," I must show them what is the genuine feeling of the People. When news of the decrees about me passed by the Senate in the Temple of Honos and Virtus reached the theatre, the tragic actor Aesopus was playing in the *Eurysaces* of Accius. Many lines, which seemed to bear on my services to the State and my banishment, drew great emotion from the actor and his audience. Also a line in the *Brutus*, where the name Tullius occurred, was enthusiastically encored. But the Roman People best

343

expressed their feelings by their wonderful reception of Sestius when, in his tribunate, he appeared at the gladiatorial games celebrated by P. Cornelius Scipio in memory of Q. Metellus Pius. Contrast the behaviour of the praetor Appius Claudius who used to skulk under the flooring into his seat! When his hirelings at his meetings said that they were against my return, he used to say that that was the opinion of the Roman People!

§§ 127-131. The prosecutor contrasts me with M. Regulus (consul 256 B.C.) who preferred to return to captivity at Carthage, and says that I ought not to have desired a return which was secured by violence. Violence? Far from it. Could I refuse a return which was commended to the care of magistrates in the provinces and to foreign peoples? All loyal Italians were summoned to attend the Assembly which was to vote for my recall. In the Capitol a statement made by Pompey that I had saved the State was approved by a crowded Senate, Clodius alone dissenting. On the next day in the House the Senate resolved that any attempt to obstruct the holding of an Assembly to order my recall should be regarded as treasonable; and that, if such obstruction took place on five days when the Assembly could meet, I might return with full rights as a citizen; and that those who had assembled from Italy to support my recall should be thanked and asked to return to vote. Clodius alone dissented. Q. Metellus Nepos, my former enemy, in response to a moving appeal from P. Servilius Isauricus, declared himself reconciled to me. I arrived at Brundisium on 5 August (57 B.C.), where I was met by my daughter Tullia. I enjoyed a triumphal progress to Rome.

§§ 132-135. That is my answer to the prosecutor's question, who are the Optimates. They are not a " Breed," a disparaging term invented by P. Vatinius, Sestius' chief enemy. He has tried to incense Caesar against this " Breed." He attacked me through Vettius, an informer ; warned Pompey against me ; helped towards my banishment ; disregarded my law forbidding the giving of gladiatorial games within two years of a candidature for office. He has defied other laws also : the *lex Caecilia Didia*, the *lex Licinia Iunia*, the *lex Iulia de pecuniis repetundis*. He is at the back of this prosecution of Sestius.

§§ 136-143. I appeal to the younger generation, whether noble in family or not, to win distinction by following the example of the Optimates and by understanding the principles of senatorial government so wisely established by our ancestors on the fall of the Monarchy. The leaders of the Optimates bear the most grave and arduous responsibilities. Whereas unprincipled popular leaders have never won true renown, the Optimates who have opposed them have always been greatly honoured. One Optimate alone, L. Opimius, met with disaster, but it was undeserved. We Romans should not be deterred from the defence of our State by the exiling of Athenians like Miltiades, Themistocles and Aristides, who opposed the follies of popular leaders, but are still honoured while their adversaries are forgotten. Hannibal, our great antagonist, who was driven from Carthage, has won honour with us. Let us imitate our great and immortal statesmen of old.

§§ 144-147. I entreat your compassion for my client, P. Sestius, for his son, for the son of P. Lentulus, and for Milo, himself facing a charge. If,

when consul, I committed any crime in disclosing the
plans of Catiline's accomplices and in carrying out
the Senate's orders for their custody, I have been
punished enough. If my defenders should be condemned I would rather be exiled with them than
remain in Rome without them. Their acquittal will
promote the cause of law and order, and condemn
disloyalty.

X. SUMMARY OF THE *IN VATINIUM*

The four opening (1-4) and the two closing sections
(40-41) are alone relevant to the trial of Sestius or the
evidence given against him by Vatinius.

§§ 1-4. If, Vatinius, I had taken the advice of
my fellow-counsel, I would have disregarded your
evidence as valueless. But I allowed my feelings to
run away with me and, instead of leaving you alone,
I reduced you to confusion. I now want to embarrass
you with a few questions. Even if Sestius were
wrong in suspecting you of participation in his prosecution, you should have pardoned me for helping
my client (when I gave notice of my intention to
cross-examine you). But Sestius' suspicions were
justified, because your evidence contradicted itself.
Your statement of yesterday denying that you had
ever discussed the question of prosecuting Sestius
with Albinovanus (the prosecutor), whom you had
accused of collusion, is refuted by your remark that
Claudius (the junior prosecutor) had consulted you,
and that Albinovanus had visited your house and got
from you the copies of Sestius' speeches which have
been read in court. So you have given yourself away :
you are behind the prosecution ; and you are guilty

of inconsistency and perjury. Our suspicions about you were justified when, while Gellius was giving evidence, you came into court in such a rage that I thought I was back (in the days of your tribunate).

§§ 5-10. You first reproached me for defending C. Cornelius (tribune 67 B.C.). But he was neither guilty of your violence nor did he shatter the constitution, as you have done. Has not your behaviour been a warning to any advocate not to defend you ? You say that my defence of Cornelius displeased " Good Men." But recollect that soon afterwards I was raised to the consulship by the united approval of the Roman People.

You taunt me with exile, but by withdrawing I saved the State from the criminal designs of you and your fellows. You say that men worked for my recall not for my own sake but for that of the State. But that surely was the highest of compliments. I may well be an unpleasant character, but what was Rome like in my absence ? Was that universal enthusiasm for my return no more than feeling for the State ? But you are loathed not so much for your own as for the State's sake. Let us compare the way our fellow-citizens have treated us. I have been honoured by high office and restoration to my position ; you have recently been defeated (for the aedileship), and a prosecution awaits you. Who, then, is the better citizen ?

§§ 11-12. Thanks to a consul you were elected quaestor (in 64 B.C.), but were the last on the list. I posted you to Puteoli, where your rapacity led to your being assaulted. What was the meaning of your circuitous journey to Further Spain, where you

347

served under C. Cosconius ? What were you doing
in the country of Hiempsal and Mastanesosus ?

§§ 13-15. What crimes did you not commit during
your tribunate ? Do not seek shelter behind our
most distinguished men. My fire is directed at you
alone. What mad folly urged you to defy at once
the auspices, the findings of the augurs, and announcements that the sky had been watched ? You claim
that therein you were associated with Caesar. But
I must draw a distinction between an honourable
man like Caesar and a knave like you. Do you, as
Caesar does, respect the Senate ? Would Caesar
take cover behind another man ? Some of Caesar's
actions, pardonable enough in the man and the
occasion, have been far more than pardoned by the
greatness of his later illustrious deeds. How can a
man like you claim the same concessions as Caesar ?

§§ 16-18. Of your nine fellow-tribunes three, who
watched the skies in that year, have subsequently
won honour. You have had to sell the toga you
bought for your expected aedileship. Did any of
your fellow-tribunes dare, as you alone of all tribunes
have done, to defy the Aelian and Fufian laws which
next year, with two traitorous consuls consenting,
were swept away ?

§§ 19-20. Did you ever have the idea of becoming
an augur on the death of Q. Metellus Celer (59 B.C.) ?
Had the State suffered that mortal blow, would you
have declared, as augurs have done from time im-
memorial, that it is sacrilege " to deal with the
People " when Juppiter lightens, or would you as
augur have abolished the auspices ?

§§ 21-23. Has anyone ever been guilty of such
villainy as you in arresting Bibulus, a consul, in hurry-

ing him away to prison, if not to execution ; in not merely driving him out of public life, but even in planning to drag him from his own house ? And yet you claim that these and other atrocities were committed in the name of C. Caesar, that most merciful and excellent man. You call the Optimates tyrants. But are not you, rather, a tyrant, by your ruin of the auspices and of the hitherto inviolate Aelian and Fufian Laws, your criminal treatment of a consul, your ill-gotten gains of office ?

§§ 24-26. Did you not suborn for your criminal designs Vettius, who had confessed to the Senate his intention of murdering Pompey ? Did you not, through his false evidence, plan to ruin men like Bibulus, Lucullus, Curio, Domitius (whom you had good reason to fear), Lentulus, Paullus and myself ? Did you not call him back and compel him to add Piso, my son-in-law, and Laterensis to his list ? Did you not propose a commission of enquiry and a reward to Vettius for his information ? And when that was rejected, did you not murder Vettius in prison, for fear the truth might be disclosed ?

§§ 27-28. You carried a good law about the challenging of juries. But, after you had promulgated it, did you not delay its validity until it had been passed, so that C. Antonius was not helped by it at his trial (59 B.C.) ? You are to blame for that, not the prosecutor, Q. Fabius Maximus.

§ 29. You boast immoderately of your wealth. How did you acquire it ? When tribune, you made treaties with peoples and powers of the Near East, you passed laws ordering payments from the Treasury, you filched shares, when they were at their highest, from Caesar and from the *publicani*. That you rose from poverty to wealth in a year when a stringent law was passed (by Caesar), *de pecuniis repetundis*, shows your contemptible treatment of your so-called best friend.

§§ 30-32. What did you mean by appearing in a dark dress at the funeral banquet given by my friend Q. Arrius in the Temple of Castor, when everyone knows that at such a banquet a light dress is worn ? You will say that you disapproved of the public thanksgiving (for C. Pomptinus) which was then being held. Could you not express your disapproval otherwise than by such highly disrespectful behaviour ?

§§ 33-34. When you were out of office (58 B.C.), were you not summoned under the *lex Licinia Iunia* ? Was not your behaviour quite without precedent ? You returned from your staff-duties (with Caesar in Gaul) to face your charge and actually appealed to tribunes, and to Clodius by name, to stop the case. Though Clodius could not lawfully oppose your trial, he put himself at the head of your men, broke up the court, put Memmius the praetor to flight, and even evicted the presidents of the neighbouring courts. While you could have avoided a trial by remaining at your post, why did you behave in that dishonest fashion ?

§§ 35-36. Tell me what decree of the Senate conferred a staff-appointment upon you ? Your answer is your own law, the *lex Vatinia*. Did you plan to sweep the Senate from the constitution ? Not content with depriving the Senate of the right of assigning provinces, of appointing to military commands, of administering the Treasury, you commit the unexampled outrage of removing its ancient prerogative of appointing staff-officers. Clodius quickly followed your example. Your fellow-tribesmen have therefore dishonoured you and you are the first member of your tribe, the Sergia, to lose the tribal vote.

§ 37. You have also, by giving a gladiatorial show during your candidature (for the praetorship), broken a law of mine, carried in due constitutional fashion, even though I obey your laws, however they were carried. Are you looking for a second Clodius to save you from prosecution?

§§ 38-39. If you disregard all this in your reliance on Caesar's great affection for you, let me tell you what Caesar recently said at Aquileia. He expressed great annoyance at the defeat of C. Alfius (at the praetorian elections in 57 B.C.) and at the election (as praetor) of Cn. Domitius Calvinus. As for you, he said that Vatinius had done nothing during his tribunate without being paid for it, and that as he cared so much for money, he ought to put up with his defeat (for the aedileship). If Caesar, who allowed you to run amuck at your own risk, thinks that of you, and if your friends, relatives and fellow-tribesmen detest you, why not do the most popular thing you could ever do and seek death?

In the closing paragraphs (40-41) Cicero cross-examines Vatinius on some points arising from the trial of Sestius.

§§ 40-41. Finally, I will ask you a few questions on the case itself. Why are you so inconsistent as to praise Milo before a jury such as this, and, when you were recently brought up by Clodius before a meeting packed with his rabble, to say that Milo attacked the State with his gladiators? As all admit, Milo and Sestius have always been in close political partnership. Since Clodius and yourself are associated in prosecuting Milo and Sestius, how can you differentiate between the two in your evidence ?

Moreover, in your recent speech in court, when you were accusing Albinovanus of collusion, did you not say that Sestius should on no account have been charged with breach of the peace, since his case and Milo's were so similar, and that Sestius' work in my cause was approved by the best people in the State ? I pass over the inconsistency between your speech and your evidence. But tell me whether you think that Sestius should be condemned on a charge which you say should never have been brought against him ; and whether you gave evidence on a charge of breach of the peace against a man who, you say, should on no account have been so charged.

BIBLIOGRAPHY

I. Texts and Commentaries

Austin, R. G. *M. T. Ciceronis pro M. Caelio oratio.* Oxford (1933, 2nd edition, 1952).

Butler, H. E., and Cary, M. *M. T. Ciceronis de provinciis consularibus oratio ad senatum.* Oxford, 1924.

Clark, A. C. *M. T. Ciceronis orationes pro Sex. Roscio, etc.* Oxford (1905, new impr. 1908).

Holden, H. A. *M. T. Ciceronis pro P. Sestio oratio.* London (1883, 9th impr. 1933).

Klotz, A., und Schöll, F. *M. T. Ciceronis scripta*, vol. vii. Leipzig (Teubner), 1919.

Long, G. *Ciceronis orationes*, vols. iii, 1856, and iv, 1858. London.

Müller, C. F. W. *Ciceronis scripta*, ii. 3. Leipzig (Teubner), 1904.

Peterson, W. *M. T. Ciceronis orationes cum senatui gratias egit, etc.* Oxford, 1910.

Pocock, L. G. *A Commentary on Cicero in Vatinium.* London, 1926.

Reid, J. S. *M. T. Ciceronis pro L. Cornelio Balbo oratio.* Cambridge (1878, new impr. 1908).[a]

II. Principal Works consulted or referred to

Altheim, F. *Lex Sacrata: Die Anfänge der plebeischen Organisation.* Amsterdam, 1939.

Asconius Pedianus Q., *Orationum Ciceronis quinque enarratio.* A. C. Clark, Oxford, 1907.

[a] Professor J. S. Reid's widow presented to the Cambridge University Library an interleaved copy of this edition with full manuscript notes by the editor (Adv. d. 93. 3).

CICERO

Badian, E. " *Lex Servilia.*" *Classical Review*, New Series, vol. iv. 2 (1954), pp. 101-102.

Balsdon, J. P. V. D. " The History of the Extortion Court at Rome, 123–70 B.C." *Papers of the British School at Rome*, xiv (1938), pp. 98-114.

" Consular Provinces under the Late Republic." *Journal of Roman Studies*, xxix (1939), pp. 57-73 ; 167-183.

" Roman History, 58–56 B.C. Three Ciceronian Problems." *Journal of Roman Studies*, xlvii (1957), pp. 15-16.

Barker, Ernest. *From Alexander to Constantine* (*Passages and Documents illustrating the History of Social and Political Ideas, 336 B.C.–A.D. 337*). Oxford, 1956.

Boyancé, P. " *Cum dignitate otium.*" *Revue des Études anciennes*, xliii (1941), pp. 172-191.

Broughton, T. R. S. *The Magistrates of the Roman Republic*, vol. ii (99–31 B.C.). New York, 1952.

Cambridge Ancient History (edited by S. A. Cook, F. E. Adcock, M. P. Charlesworth). Vol. ix, chapter xii. Cambridge, 1932.

Cary, M. *A History of Rome.* London (2nd ed. 1954).

" Asinus germanus." *Classical Quarterly*, xvii (1923), pp. 103-107.

Ciaceri, E. *Cicerone e i suoi tempi*, vol. ii. Rome, 2nd edition, 1941.

Cichorius, C. *Das Offiziercorps eines römischen Heeres aus dem Bundesgenossenkriege. Römische Studien*, pp. 130-185. Berlin, 1922.

Clark, A. C. *Cicero, Pro T. Annio Milone.* Oxford, 1895.

Cochrane, C. N. *Christianity and Classical Culture*, pp. 44-45. Oxford, 1940.

Cousin, J. " *Lex Lutatia de Vi.*" *Revue historique de Droit français et étranger*, 1943, pp. 88-94.

Denniston, J. D. *M. T. Ciceronis in M. Antonium Orationes Philippicae, Prima et Secunda.* Oxford, 1926. (Appendix iii, pp. 180-186.)

Dessau, H. *Inscriptiones Latinae Selectae.* Berlin, 1892, etc. Nos. 8888, 9461 (vol. iii. 2, 1916).

Drexler, H. " Zu Ciceros Rede *pro Caelio.*" *Nachrichten*

BIBLIOGRAPHY

von der Akademie der Wissenschaften in Göttingen, Phil.-Hist. Kl., 1944, pp. 1-32.

Frank, Tenney. *Catullus and Horace*. Oxford (Blackwell), 1928.

Gelzer, M. *Die Nobilität der römischen Republic*. Leipzig-Berlin, 1912.

Grant, M. *From Imperium to Auctoritas*, pp. 5-6. Cambridge, 1946.

Greenidge, A. H. J. *The Legal Procedure of Cicero's Time*. Oxford, 1901.

Roman Public Life. London, 1901.

" The Repeal of the *Lex Aelia Fufia*." *Classical Review*, vii (1893), pp. 158-161.

Hardy, E. G. " The Transpadane Question and the Alien Act of 65 or 64 B.C." *Journal of Roman Studies*, vi (1916), pp. 77-82.

Cicero's Argument in Pro Balbo, 19-22, in *Some Problems in Roman History*. Oxford, 1924, pp. 326-330.

Haskell, H. J. *This was Cicero : Modern Politics in a Roman Toga*. New York, 1942 ; London, [1943].

Heinze, R. " Cicero's Rede *pro Caelio*." *Hermes*, lx (1925), pp. 193-258.

Heitland, W. E. *The Roman Republic*, vol. iii. Cambridge (1909, new impr. 1923).

Hill, H. *The Roman Middle Class in the Republican Period*. Oxford (Blackwell), 1952.

Holmes, T. Rice. *The Roman Republic and the Founder of the Empire*, vols. i and ii. Oxford, 1923.

Hough, J. N. " The *Lex Lutatia* and the *Lex Plautia de Vi*." *American Journal of Philology*, li (1930), pp. 135-147.

How, W. W. *Cicero, Select Letters*, vol. ii (notes). Oxford, 1926.

" Cicero's Ideal in his *De Republica*." *Journal of Roman Studies*, xx (1930), pp. 24-42.

Kroll, W. *Die Kultur der ciceronischen Zeit*, vols. i and ii. Leipzig, 1933.

Last, H. M. " The Servian Reforms." *Journal of Roman Studies*, xxxv (1945), esp. p. 32.

Marsh, F. B. *A History of the Roman World from 146 to 30 B.C.* 2nd ed. revised by H. H. Scullard. London, 1952.
The Founding of the Roman Empire. Oxford (2nd ed. 1927).
" The Policy of Clodius from 58 to 56 B.C." *Classical Quarterly*, xxi (1927), pp. 30-35.
McDonald, W. F. " Clodius and the *Lex Aelia Fufia*." *Journal of Roman Studies*, xix (1929), pp. 164-179.
Meyer, E. *Caesars Monarchie und das Principat des Pompeius.* Stuttgart (3rd ed. 1922).
Münzer, F. *Römische Adelsparteien und Adelsfamilien.* Stuttgart, 1920.
Nisbet, R. G. *M. T. Ciceronis de domo sua oratio.* Oxford, 1939.
Oxford Classical Dictionary. Oxford, 1949.
Pauly-Wissowa-Kroll. *Real-Encyclopädie der classischen Altertumswissenschaft.* Stuttgart, 1894–
    Gelzer, M. *s.v.* " M. Tullius Cicero," No. 29. Vol. viiA, cols. 935-947.
    Gundel, H. *s.v.* " P. Vatinius," No. 9. Second Series. Vol. viiiA 1, cols. 495-520.
    Laqueur, R. *s.v.* " Theophanes," No. 1. Second Series. Vol. v, cols. 2090-2127.
    Münzer, F. *s.v.* " Caelius," No. 35. Vol. iii, cols. 1266-1272.
        s.v. " L. Cornelius Balbus," No. 69. Vol. iv, cols. 1260-1268.
        s.v. " P. Sestius," No. 6. Second Series. Vol. ii, cols. 1886-1890.
    Strasburger, H. *s.v.* " Optimates." Vol. xviii. 1, cols. 773-798.
    Weinstock, St. *s.v.* " Obnuntiatio." Vol. xvii, cols. 1726-1735.
    Wissowa, G. *s.v.* " Auspicium." Vol. ii, cols. 2580-2587.
Peterson, W. " Cicero's *Post Reditum* and other Speeches." *Classical Quarterly*, iv (1910), pp. 166-177.
Platner, S. B., and Ashby, T. *A Topographical Dictionary of Ancient Rome.* Oxford, 1929.

BIBLIOGRAPHY

Pocock, L. G. " Publius Clodius and the Acts of Caesar." *Classical Quarterly*, xviii (1924), pp. 59-64.
" A Note on the Policy of Clodius." *Classical Quarterly*, xix (1925), pp. 182-184.
Reid, J. S. " The so-called ' *Lex Iulia Municipalis.*' " *Journal of Roman Studies*, v (1915), p. 239, n. 4.
Remy, E. " *Dignitas cum otio.*" *Musée Belge*, xxxii (1928), pp. 113-127.
Richards, G. C. *Cicero, a Study.* London, 1935.
Scullard, H. H. *Roman Politics 220–150 B.C.* Oxford, 1951, pp. 27-28 and Appendix iv, pp. 290-303.
Sherwin-White, A. N. *The Roman Citizenship.* Oxford, 1939.
Shuckburgh, E. S. *The Letters of Cicero*, vols. i and ii. London, 1899.
Sihler, E. G. *Cicero of Arpinum.* Yale Univ. Press, 1914.
Skutsch, O. " Cicero, *Pro Sestio, 72.*" *Classical Review*, lvi (1942), pp. 116-117, and *ibid.* lvii (1943), p. 67.
Smith, R. E. *The Failure of the Roman Republic.* Cambridge, 1955.
Stevenson, G. H. " Cn. Pompeius Strabo and the Franchise Question." *Journal of Roman Studies*, ix (1919), pp. 95-101.
Strachan-Davidson, J. L. *Cicero and the Fall of the Roman Republic.* London (1894, 2nd ed. 1925).
Problems of the Roman Criminal Law, vols. i and ii. Oxford, 1912.
Suetonius Tranquillus, C. *Divus Iulius.* Butler, H. E., and Cary, M. Oxford, 1927.
Syme, R. *The Roman Revolution.* Oxford, 1939.
Taylor, L. R. *Party Politics in the Age of Caesar.* Berkeley, 1949.
Tucker, G. M. " Cicero, *Pro Sestio,* 72." *Classical Review*, lvi (1942), p. 68.
Tyrrell, R. Y., and Purser, L. C. *The Correspondence of Cicero*, Dublin, vols. ii (2nd ed. 1906), iii (2nd ed. 1914), iv (2nd ed. 1918), v (2nd ed. 1915).
Valeton, I. M. J. " De modis auspicandi Romanorum." *Mnemosyne*, vols. xvii and xviii, 1889–1890.

Warde Fowler, W. *Social Life at Rome in the Age of Cicero*. London, 1909.

Warmington, E. H. *Remains of Old Latin*. Loeb Classical Library. London. Vols. i (1935), ii (1936), iii (1938), iv (1940).

Webster, T. B. L. *Cicero, Pro L. Flacco*. Oxford, 1931.

Wegehaupt, H. *Die Bedeutung und Anwendung von dignitas*. Diss. Breslau, 1932.

Weinstock, S. " Clodius and the *Lex Aelia Fufia*." *Journal of Roman Studies*, xxvii (1937), pp. 215-222.

Wilkinson, L. P. *Letters of Cicero : a New Selection in Translation*. London (Bles), 1949.

Willems, P. *Le Sénat de la République romaine*, vols. i and ii. Paris, 1878.

Williams, W. Glynn. *Cicero, The Letters to his Friends*. Loeb Classical Library, vols. i-iii. London, 1927–1929.

Winstedt, E. O. *Cicero, The Letters to Atticus*. Loeb Classical Library, vols. i-iii. London, 1913–1919.

Wirszubski, Ch. *Libertas as a Political Idea at Rome during the Late Republic and Early Principate*. Cambridge, 1950.

" Cicero's *Cum Dignitate Otium* : a Reconsideration." *Journal of Roman Studies*, xliv (1954), pp. 1-13.

III. Translations

A free translation in French of these five speeches is to be found in *Collection des auteurs latins avec la traduction en français publiés sous la direction de M. Nisard : Œuvres complètes de Cicéron*, vol. iii, Paris, 1852, pp. 54-170.

Bohn's Classical Library contains a translation of these speeches.

No translation has yet appeared in the series published by *L'Association Guillaume Budé* (Paris, Société d'Édition " Les Belles Lettres ").

Additions to the Bibliography

Austin, R. G. *M. T. Ciceronis pro M. Caelio oratio.* Oxford (1933, 3rd edition, 1960).

Balsdon, J. P. V. D. *Auctoritas, Dignitas, Otium. Classical Quarterly,* N.S. Vol. x. No. 1, 1960, pp. 43-50.

Cousin, J. Cicéron, Discours, Tome xiv, *Pour Sestius, Contre Vatinius.* Texte établi et traduit (Budé), Paris, 1965.

Dorey, T. A. (*ed.*). *Cicero.* London, 1965.

Lacey, W. K. Cicero, *Pro Sestio,* 96-143. *Classical Quarterly,* N.S. Vol. xii. No. 1, 1962, pp. 67-71.

Nisbet, R. G. M. *M. Tulli Ciceronis in L. Calpurnium Pisonem oratio.* Text, introduction, and commentary. Oxford, 1961.

Shackleton Bailey, D. R. *Cicero's Letters to Atticus.* Vols. i and ii (Books i-iv). Cambridge, 1965.

Shackleton Bailey, D. R. "*Sex. Clodius—Sex. Cloelius.*" *Classical Quarterly,* N.S. Vol. x. No. 1, 1960, pp. 41-42.

INDEX

Fairly full references to persons, places and certain topics are given, the footnotes being covered as well as the text. Persons are entered under their gentile names (*e.g.* for Bibulus, *see under* Calpurnius Bibulus), and the years of their most important tenures of office are supplied. References to the Table of Events in Roman Politics from 60 B.C. to 56 B.C. (pp. xi-xx), and to the Summaries of the *Pro Sestio* and the *In Vatinium* (pp. 336-352) have been excluded from the Index. The numbers refer to pages.

363

INDEX

INDEX

365

INDEX

Cornelius Sulla, Faustus, son of the Dictator, 282

Cornelius Sulla, L., Dictator (cos. 88, 80), 27, 33, 43 n., 108 n., 234 n., 268, 269 n., 282 n., 300, 315, 322

Cornelius Tacitus, historian, 332

Cornificius, Q. (quaest. 48), 333

Corycus, battle at, 112 n.

Cosconius, C. (praet. 63), 254, 327

Cosconius, C. (trib. 59), 262

Crassus, *see under* Licinius

Crete, 15

cum dignitate otium, otiosa dignitas, 168-172, 176, 299, 301-304

cura annonae, 26

Curia, Curia Hostilia, 21, 104, 138, 266 n., 268 ; *see also under* Senate

Curii, 232

Curio, *see under* Scribonius

Cybele, 110 n.

Cyprus, 15, 16, 110 n., 116 n., 118 n., 306

Cyrene, 15

Dalmatians, 270 n., 333

Dardani, 162

Decii, 232 ; Decius Mus, P. (cos. 340), 98; Decius Mus, P. (cos. 295), 98 n.; Decius Mus, P. (cos. 279), 98 n.

Deiotarus, king of Galatia (c. 52-40), 110 n.

Deiphilus, grandson of Priam, 206 n.

Domitius Ahenobarbus, Cn., son-in-law of Cinna, 124 n.

Domitius Ahenobarbus, L. (cos. 54), 32, 87 n., 272, 284 n.

Domitius Calvinus, Cn. (trib. 59, praet. 56, cos. 53), 33, 188, 260 n., 292 n., 326

Dyrrhachium, 19, 162, 228, 332-333, 335

Eetion, father of Andromache, 200 n.

Ennius, 200 n.

Epicureans, 62 n.

Epidaurum, 333

equester ordo, equites, 3, 4, 56, 58, 66-72, 78-82, 104, 126, 154, 184, 202, 225 n., 301

Equitius, L., " false Gracchus " (elected trib. 100), 172, 173 n.

Erechtheus, 96

Etruscans, 310

Eurysaces, a tragedy of L. Accius, 200 n.

Fabia, a Vestal, sister of Terentia wife of Cicero, 106 n.

Fabius Maximus, Q. (cos. 233, 228, 215, 214, 209 ; dict. 221 ?, 217), 312 n.

Fabius Maximus, Q. (*cos. suffect.* 45), 276

Fabius Quintilianus, M., 35

Fabricii, 232

Fabricius, Q. (trib. 57), 19, 136, 138, 142, 318

Fannius, C. (trib. 59), 188, 261 n.

Fibulus, C., associate of Vatinius, 282

367

INDEX

INDEX

INDEX

INDEX